THE
ETHICAL
SOCIETY

A Framework for a Peaceful, Sustainable World

William T. Carruthers Ph.D.

◆ FriesenPress

Suite 300 - 990 Fort St
Victoria, BC, V8V 3K2
Canada

www.friesenpress.com

ISBN
978-1-5255-2616-9 (Hardcover)
978-1-5255-2617-6 (Paperback)
978-1-5255-2618-3 (eBook)

1. PHILOSOPHY, ETHICS & MORAL PHILOSOPHY

Distributed to the trade by The Ingram Book Company

TABLE OF CONTENTS

TABLE SUMMARY

FIGURE SUMMARY

DEDICATION

This work is dedicated to the millions of Cultural and Smart Creatives who are actively looking for ways to build a world that works for everyone.

PREFACE

The world and humanity are in trouble. We seem to be heading toward ecological, political, and economic disaster; perhaps even extinction. It is as though we are moving ever closer to a precipice, never quite sure where the edge of the cliff is or how far away it might be, but we know it's out there and not too distant. It is not clear what event might trigger a major catastrophe, or that there will be such an event to plunge us over the edge. Our path is roughly parallel to and at the same time gradually converging with the cliff edge; there might also be a cleft in the edge that we are heading straight toward. It is also clear we are moving much too fast, and there is little chance of stopping or reversing course.

Humanity does not appear to have a viable, sustainable future. This leaves only one possible route. We must begin to turn away from the edge. We must deflect our course toward a more viable and sustainable way of living, which raises several questions. What can we do to deflect ourselves from our current course? What would the new path look like? How can we overcome centuries of traditions and ways of living to arrive at a truly global way of behaving? Are there simple things we can do to start the process?

"How is it that we know we are headed for destruction as a species, and yet are unable to effect the changes necessary for our survival?"

The short answer is, we do not think in species, global terms. There are two root causes of this problem. First, our thinking is entangled in power structure thinking, which teaches us to treat our cultural differences as sources of antagonism and aggression rather than as a basis for global sustainability. Second, our thinking is entangled in a religiocentric approach to civilization. The core values that ground our societies come from our various spiritual and political traditions, which are competitive rather than cooperative. Historically, understanding and meaning were intimately connected in religion as two sides of the same coin. Science has broken this connection. How we understand the world no longer connects with how we find meaning in our lives. Yet we have not developed an alternative value system. We are trying to cope with the systemic impacts of 21st-century science and technology with 19th-century (and some medieval) values.

To improve something, you must measure it. Ecologists define viability and sustainability in terms of the richness of an ecosystem's biodiversity. This book proposes a similar approach—we measure the richness of cultural diversity. But we currently use this diversity as a source of aggression and conflict. Our thinking must shift. This book is about identifying the values we need to promote a viable future for all humanity.

If we want to have a peaceful and sustainable future, we need to understand the kind of thinking that promotes and sustains such a world. *The Ethical Society* explores the structure of our thinking (called Frameworks) that characterizes how we think. It treats ethics as criteria for quality thinking, then marries this with cultural diversity and with four foundational ethical values (life, liberty, equality, and tolerance). This forms an Ethical way of thinking to realize sustainable behaviors. The work explores the rules for ethical reasoning and proposes rules for ethical thinking. These are then aligned with economic and political systems to indicate how we might shift to a more viable model. The idea is that with an example of how thinking in this new way works, we can comprehend how to make the changes necessary for survival. Finally, this book identifies four stakeholder interests, and provides a strategy map, which is converted into a series of eleven initiatives that could be undertaken to reach viable strategic objectives. The book argues that if we base our societies on ethical rather than traditional religious values, this solves our power structure thinking problems and reconnects understanding with meaning. In short, by addressing the root cause of our problems, we can solve many of the issues that are preventing us from changing toward viable and sustainable behaviors.

With a clear idea of the underlying values and principles needed to live in a peaceful, sustainable world, we have a vision of what we are trying to achieve. This then becomes the objective. We can then measure our progress towards that objective (or not), and evaluate the many ideas people have for achieving this result to determine which ideas best promote progress towards our goal.

CHAPTER 1
The Illusion of Civilization

With a rather loud bang on August 6, 1945, Christian civilization came to an end. We can be precise because that bang was the sound of the first nuclear devastation of an entire population, marking the start of the Nuclear Age.

Since that time, we have seen many instances of human destructiveness, and we are learning more about the destruction we cause every day, yet we seem helpless to do anything about it. The more science discovers the dangers we are creating for our planet and ourselves, the less control we have over our future. We appear to be out of control and moving headlong toward a global disaster.

The question to ask is, "Why does civilized humanity bring so much pain and suffering, not only to humans, but to the whole world?" Between the threats posed by nuclear devastation, biological terrors, environmental disasters, overpopulation, and dwindling resources, it appears that humanity's chances of long-term survival seem remote at best. And the list of ills to befall us grows almost daily. We are confronted with irrefutable evidence of global warming, which threatens to produce catastrophic outcomes. We hear that we will likely run out of oil by the year 2050. By that time, we will have suffered the collapse of a major ecosystem. And we have been assured from many sources that the Western world is likely to experience a terrorist attack with a weapon of mass destruction. The list goes on.

More alarming still is the timeframe for these events. Just a decade ago, we believed we were squandering resources at the expense of future generations. The impacts of our actions, we believed, would not be felt until long into the future. But, now we see the ramifications of our destructiveness hitting much closer to home. For most of us, the year 2050 is not so distant, and these impacts will happen to people we know and love. There is a growing urgency to do something.

Given that we know we are headed for destruction as a species, why aren't we making the changes necessary for our very survival? We seem unable to direct our considerable energies toward peace and world stability. Rather, we seem to persist in our destructive tendencies.

There are many barriers to a united world, especially when we consider that we seem unable to establish a common set of values to serve as the basis for a united worldview. We each are so intent on our own particular point of view that finding common ground to proceed toward a global community appears a very distant dream. Yet time is running out.

We need to achieve a better understanding of the values that define our times, to search behind the current disputes and competing religions and cultures for the real underlying principles that are the foundations of a modern global civilization. We need a values-based approach for a viable and sustainable global community. We need to reevaluate what we mean by *civilization*.

*

The British historian Arnold J. Toynbee, in his *A Study of History*,[1] provides an example of how we think of civilization. He describes a civilization as a universal society that encompasses a great state with great power and a great religion. These two assets—great power and great religion—form the linguistic, religious, and cultural infrastructure for a universal society. Could these elements in a global form be what we should look for toward a global society?

According to Toynbee, each civilization goes through several stages to reach its highest level of culture and values. The first stage, in which the new civilization is founded, is a *period of growth*. This period marks the response of a group to internal and external pressures to remain a cohesive

---

1   Toynbee outlines his model in the first five volumes (or Volume I in the abridged edition) under headings referring to the Genesis, Growths, and Breakdowns of Civilizations.

society. If the group overcomes all obstacles and progresses beyond simple survival to develop a viable culture, the seeds of a civilization are born.

After its period of growth, the society invariably encounters one or more challenges that it fails to overcome. This brings about a *time of troubles*, which is usually marked by violence and anarchy until a new direction is established. The new direction leads to a larger, all-encompassing solution, constituting what Toynbee calls a *universal state*. In the universal state, the society becomes a civilization by developing various comprehensive institutions and social structures. The value system, as instituted in a *universal church*, marks the rise of a great civilization. The political and social aspects of the universal state seldom last very long, and the civilization falls; what remains is the culture as instituted by the universal church. An *interruption* occurs, and a new civilization develops from the old.

Toynbee takes great care to hold up cultural values as the mark of a great civilization. In particular, the *spirit* of the civilization is embodied in the universal church, which lasts even beyond the fall of the universal state. Each of the great civilizations he identifies—the Sinic, the Hellenic, the Syriatic, the Indic—is associated with a great religion that is the focus of the culture. Buddhism, Islam, and Hinduism are the modern remnants of past civilizations. In fact, Toynbee sees all religions as remnants of universal states—all religions that is, except Christianity. Here, he claims that contemporary Europeans and their satellite cultures are living in the time of troubles stage and are still awaiting the universal state.

Toynbee's view is challenged by Paul Kennedy in *The Rise and Fall of the Great Powers*. Kennedy, like Toynbee, makes a distinction between the "Christian" civilization and the others, but on different grounds. He argues that all other civilizations achieved *universal states* through the institution of a homogeneous culture with a singular state, controlled through a central bureaucracy. Only in the West did this homogeneity fail to materialize. Europe remained a heterogeneous, pluralistic society despite the many attempts to impose homogeneity. The conquests of Charlemagne, the Hapsburg, Napoleon, and Hitler all failed to homogenize Europe into a common society.

Kennedy grants that this pluralistic society did go through all the stages that Toynbee identifies. The Christian faith instilled common values and culture in the very manner described for all civilizations. Politically, however, the universal homogeneous state failed to develop. Instead, universal empires of pluralistic and global proportions emerged, and the age of the Great Powers, with its attending global imperialism, produced the *Universal Christian State*. If this view is correct, then it is clear that the end of World War II marks the end of the Universal Christian State, as understood in its pluralistic form.

What is remarkable about these considerations is the implication that for the first time in human history, there are no great civilizations anywhere on the planet. At all other times, we can find some overlap between the fall of one civilization and the rise of another. Yet, if Kennedy is correct—and I think he is—all the old civilizations based on a universal church have passed, and no new universal religion is ascending. More than this, though, the Universal Christian State, because of its pluralism, has sown the seeds for a new kind of civilization that is different from the previous models founded on a central religion. It is this development that this book will explore.

*

World War II and the Holocaust represent the climax not just of the Universal Christian State but of all religiocentric civilizations. That is, while humans continue to wage conflicts in the name of religion, the kind of civilization based on a universal church (which defines its culture and values) is no longer viable, so these conflicts cannot be resolved using traditional methods. One does not have to be a Jew or a Christian to be horrified at the atrocities committed in the name of a homogeneous European community. An event so despicable as the Holocaust goes beyond any one civilization, and arouses a global awakening to the realization that ideologies such as Hitler's "Final Solution" can no longer be tolerated. The equally vile atrocity brought upon the city of Hiroshima in the dawn of the Nuclear Age only emphasizes the point: we must find a new way of generating values and cultures on which to base our civilizations.

Historically, religion has contributed to both understanding and meaning in the world. Religion originally sought to provide humans with ways to understand how the world works. In time, it also provided the source of meaning in people's lives. Understanding and meaning were connected in the metaphysics of the various religious frameworks through belief, faith, revelation, and enlightenment, and these connections were maintained through ritual. When we position religion at the center of our value system, we can see why Toynbee thought that a universal church presented the core of any great civilization.

In a well-ordered religion, understanding and meaning are two sides of the same coin. In modern times, however, science has broken this connection. Science disconnects understanding from meaning and reconnects it with observation. In this approach, science has increasingly discovered that religious understandings of how the world works are wrong. In fact, science has been so successful at improving our understanding of how the world actually works that it has largely discredited traditional religious understandings and approaches to understanding, in effect secularizing understanding and separating it from meaning. Without a doubt, science is very good at improving understanding of the world; however, unless you are a scientist, it is not designed to generate meaning, particularly any sense of personal meaning.

Science has two impacts on civilization in its historical form. First, by casting doubt on the traditional understanding of how the world works—an understanding that religions have been preaching for centuries—it has raised questions about whether metaphysical intuitions and beliefs can contribute to any understanding of the world, consequently marginalizing religious tools and methods. Second, by pushing religions to a smaller role associated with spiritual meaning and values, it has left civilizations without any alternative approach to generating meaning.

A further consequence of this separation is that ethical values have been secularized to the point that ethical and religious criteria can be at odds with one another. Below, we will see that actions based on a strong faith are not automatically ethical, even though religious authorities proclaim themselves to be the moral authorities of their communities. Ethical evaluations derive from ethical criteria, not religious or theological criteria. Whereas religion and ethics may align, this does not always happen, for morality and theology are, after all, not the same things. For example, the principles of liberty and equality are not core values of any of the world's major religions. Even tolerance is unnecessary to many religious value systems. From a modern perspective, the question to ask is, which one should be given priority when morality and theology collide?

Science alone is not to blame for failing to provide any alternatives for lost values or meaning. The world's major religions have remained distinct and have not provided common underlying values and meanings relevant to a global sphere. Many modern religions have failed to embrace even the basic ethical principles that have emerged over the past few hundred years. Religions still seek global reach in a competitive rather than a common or cooperative way. The result is that while the world gets smaller, with a greater need for common global ethical values and sources of meaning, religions remain largely regional and confined to their individual rituals, beliefs, and practices.

The result is what historians call *culture lag*. Modern understanding of how the world works is advancing by leaps and bounds, but our social and cultural institutions and beliefs are stagnating in outmoded religious frameworks. The American historian H.E. Barnes[2] estimates that current social and cultural institutions are circa 19th century in form and substance, and many of our fundamentalist beliefs are literally medieval.

Recent debates contrast scientific understanding with older religious understandings in what is often cast as a choice between faith and reason. The prevailing view seems to be that we must choose between rational scientific ways of understanding the world, or a simple reliance on faith that older religious understandings must still be correct. From a religious perspective, this view makes sense: because understanding and meaning are connected in and through the metaphysics of the religious doctrine, there is naturally a reluctance to abandon religious understanding. Religious doctrines would be hard-pressed to deliver meaning to people's lives if

---

2   In Volume 2, *Intellectual and Cultural History of the Western World*, page 1104, he argues, "Fundamentalists today, among whom are numbered the majority of religious communicants, live under the domination of the same intellectual patterns that prevailed in primitive times. ...It is probably no exaggeration to hold that not 10 per cent of Modernist theologians are really adjusted to contemporary knowledge and ways of thinking. The great majority of them are merely attempting to express archaic views in contemporaneous phraseology. Religion is slower in readjusting itself to new ways of living and thinking than any other phase of human culture."

there were absolutely no connection with any modern form of understanding. At the same time, traditional doctrines are not easily aligned with scientific perspectives. The choice seems to demand an act of faith, even at the expense of reason. My position is that this argument has been miscast. The root cause of the issue is the gap between understanding and meaning, not a failure of faith or reason. If we can reconnect understanding with meaning in a way that is neutral to the world's religions, and that also accommodates science, we should be able to align religious meaning with science. Of course, this means that a particular religious metaphysics will no longer be the central core of a global civilization.

*

To restate the problem, we are now painfully aware that our traditional ways of behaving are not sustainable or viable. The survival of the human race appears to be at stake. The way to avert disaster lies in completing the transition to a new kind of civilization—assuming we want to do this and can get everyone on the same page. This means that we must find the means to close the gap between scientific understanding and spiritual and personal meaning. It means that we need to get clear about the underlying values and culture that contribute to survivability and sustainability before we lose the chance to do so.[3]

In a scientific society, it is increasingly difficult to believe in an all-pervasive deity that would care about the trivial affairs of a single species on a remote planet in a rather insignificant solar system at the edge of a rather ordinary galaxy in a field of millions or perhaps billions of galaxies. Again, Barnes points out that most of the knowledge protected by the Catholic Church in the Middle Ages is now known to be wrong. He characterizes the Western church in the Dark and Middle Ages as a spiritual despotism enforced with psychic terrorism. Keep the masses ignorant and poor, fill their heads with superstitious nonsense, and then enforce, on pain of death, a static view of the world. Burning heretics at the stake

---

3   Of course, we have to want to do this. We argue that many are trapped in a mental/cultural Framework called Father Culture, which will try to sustain its current monopoly. Part of the solution will include the means to overcome this reticence. We will do this in Chapter 9 when we have all the pieces to address this problem.

for moving understanding forward from the accepted norm is today perceived as little more than a euphemism for murdering political opponents. History, armed with scientific advances in knowledge and modern ethical principles, can be a harsh judge of past doctrines and beliefs.

This brings us to the issue of culture lag. Culture lag is what happens when knowledge and understanding move forward at a pace that overtakes cultural and social institutions. There is a fine contemporary example of this in the current situation regarding world terrorism. In *The Lessons of Terror: A History of Warfare Against Civilians*, Caleb Carr likens global terrorism in the 21st century to 19th-century piracy. Piracy, he explains, was a problem tackled by the British and American navies, which went after the states that sponsored piracy and shut them down. It is evident that in contemporary times, the British and American militaries are leading the pursuit against states that sponsor terrorism. This is clearly a 19th-century solution to a 21st-century problem. Culture lag is alive and well in contemporary times.

Consider another example. By the mid-19th century, the world was well populated and divided into many nations. By this point in human history, there was really no new territory to be captured or exploited without encountering another nation ready to defend its soil. The world settled into a state of trying to balance the various power centers through diplomacy, politics, and economics. I call this *19th-century balance-of-power politics*. In a world where we cannot turn around without bumping into another society or culture, we continue to play 19th-century balance-of-power politics. It is as though we are doomed to suffer shifting centers of power across all future centuries. To make matters worse, these endless balance-of-power political games are largely responsible for the lack of sustainability we need to survive. How, then, do we get beyond these primitive games?

In essence, if we are to move forward, we need to connect understanding with meaning. In other words, if religion cannot fill the meaning gap, we need an alternative worldview. Such a worldview constitutes a philosophy—in this case Ethics.

A benefit of philosophy is that it can connect understanding with meaning, but without religious constraints on understanding. Philosophy can and does examine all aspects of reasoning and emotion in the context of values and culture, in addition to science. To understand who we are and where we are going as a species, therefore, requires a philosophy as its core presentation—in this case, an Ethics that supports a peaceful, viable, sustainable world.

The history of philosophy tells us that understanding and meaning play off each other, and that the connection between them is found in our mental structures. Religious metaphysical thinking was rather vague, and much of it was tied to various religious views and beliefs. In short, logical or rational thought was not clearly differentiated from the religion and cultures of our societies. I will argue there are clear principles that can connect understanding with meaning, and which also accord with science, and which can be brought into alignment with many religious beliefs. It is these principles that we need to harvest to move forward. I call these Ethics.

The approach would have to be *comprehensive* and avoid the error of not connecting understanding with meaning. It would have to have the appropriate global scope, and it would have to have sufficient depth to provide a sense of both understanding and meaning. Let me provide an example, using ethics, of how this works.

When we look back on the Greek conception of man, the Greeks thought of man as different from animals in three main ways: we express intelligence, spirituality, and we are the only animal who values things. This latter view introduces the concept of *thymos*. Thymos is derived from the Greek conception of the mental faculty of the living body, by means of which thinking, willing, and feeling are conducted. It refers to "what everyone learns from intercourse with his fellows. It is what a man knows about the way in which people value different conditions about their wishes, desires, and their plans to realize their wishes and desires."[4] In short, it refers to "man, the valuing animal." It is valuing that is the source of action and morality in the sense of how we realize our desires in the context of a social condition. For my purposes, *thymotic values* are the foundations of a modern ethics.

---

4   Von Mises, p. 25.

For example, the first thing an individual values is their self—the individual's own life and existence. From this self-worth come self-esteem and dignity. This is also the source of human interaction. Because we each value our self, we seek in relationships to find this value recognized by others. This recognition traditionally referred to what we will call an *authentic self*, who we are in our inner most core. This is the main source of the values that govern relationships and ultimately ground any culture.

Historically, there are four thymotic values: life, liberty, equality, and tolerance.[5] These fundamental values are the foundations of all our rights, duties, and moral obligations. An ethics would require that we promote all foundational values in a positively balanced way. We do not always do this.

Consider that any morality must support and uphold all four fundamental values, not just those that are convenient to a particular, say political, or economic, point of view. Thus, any moral theory or appeal to morality must tie back to all four foundational values. Any theory or appeal to morality that fails to support one or more foundational values would literally devalue ethics if it gained widespread acceptance in practice.

There are two ways that a morality can be devalued:

1. The moral theory or appeal could simply forget about one of the foundational values. That is, there could be a genuine mistake or overlooking of a needed value; and

2. The moral theory or appeal could deliberately ignore or subvert those values that are inconvenient to the theory or appeal being made.

Of the two, the first is fairly innocuous. We are not infallible. A thinker could mistake or simply fail to account for a moral value in their presentation. The second view is more sinister and suggests that the thinker has an agenda or a program that takes precedence over the foundational values. The inconvenient values are sacrificed to the agenda.

Many anti-abortionists in current debates present an example of the first kind of thinking. These individuals focus on the value of Life (of the

---

5   I explore the discovery and nature of these values and identify the modern sense of authentic self in later chapters.

fetus) and largely ignore the value of Liberty (of the mother). They suggest that abortion is wrong, and the very wrongness of abortion justifies the use of force (e.g., of law) to prevent abortions. But, the purpose of liberty is to protect the community from the arbitrary use of force, including the force of law (after all, there is such a thing as an unjust law). Society should not use force to persuade individuals to do as they are told. In the abortion debates, liberty has not been balanced with life in the anti-abortion moral view. These are not sinister people seeking to force their views on others. Indeed, they have a strong sense of morality, and this is what incites their anguish over the plight of a fetus. They have a genuine concern but have not balanced the two contending values in a proper moral view. The consequences of such a failure are to overlook or abandon a perfectly good value (liberty) with the result that they unintentionally devalue morality overall.[6]

Communism presents an example of the second kind of thinking. Communism is an economic/political theory that focuses on a social re-engineering program, and which seeks legitimacy for its program in the value of Equality. The slogan is "From each according to their ability, to each according to their need." In practice, life and liberty are ignored or even subjugated in the name of the communist agenda. What counts is the agenda, not the moral values that are supposed to legitimize it. Of course, once this move is accepted, then subverting all moral values becomes easier, and more likely. This leads directly to the actions of Stalin and Mao Tse Tung in the treatment of their people. Life and liberty are sacrificed to the communist program. As revealed by Stalin in his many purges or in Beijing in 1989, the only true crime against communism is that you are not with the program.

I call any moral theory or appeal to morality that is based on, uses, and supports all foundational values in a balanced way, an Ethics. I refer to any view that fails in the use and support of all foundational values, which are any views that have the effect of devaluing morality, a *mere ideology*. Finally, I call any view that actively suppresses one or more foundational values in the interests of an agenda or program a *vicious ideology*.

---

6   More on this in Chapter 4.

There is a spectrum of ideological types from a mere ideology to a vicious ideology. I need only add that a truly vicious ideology implies intent to do harm, either out of loyalty to the ideology (promote the agenda without regard to cost or suffering), or by those who would use the ideology to serve their own ends at the expense of others.

This leads to the view that the nature of ideology should be considered in and of itself, in the context of the history of ideas. I will confront this task later on. At present, I propose that mere ideologies will not do as a surrogate for religion, and that vicious ideologies will certainly not do to provide the kind of values we need for the future. This helps to define the nature of the task I am undertaking.

The point is that we need all the values in a balanced way to form an ethics. The same point holds true for principles more generally. Like fundamental values, founding principles of understanding and meaning do not magically disappear whenever they are inconvenient to a particular ideology—such as when we decide to table scientific principles when these are inconvenient to a particular political program. Part of my task is to determine what values are needed for a peaceful, sustainable future.

In this context, the task before us is to comprehend what it means to live in the 21st century. By "comprehend," I refer to both the scope and depth of understanding and meaning. We have reached a crossroads as a species. We have become conscious that the whole world is in trouble, and that we are the cause. Between nuclear war, terrorism, and ecological damage, we might be doomed to extinction. This self-consciousness shows itself in two senses of the word. We are aware of the damage we are doing, and we are uncomfortable about our situation. However, we do not seem to know what to do. There doesn't seem to be any leadership or direction to correct these problems or to give people any sense that they can effect real change. As a species, we appear to be out of control.

The first step, then, is to determine where we are going—or could be going, if we could get our act together. Once we have defined the destination, we can then compare that with our current location and develop a roadmap to get us to our destination. The idea is that by having a clear idea of what a viable world looks like, we can plan a set of measures or initiatives to get to that desirable state.

In any improvement project, there is a simple starting rule: "You cannot improve something if you do not measure it." I need, then, to establish a measure for viability and sustainability for human culture. In this book, I propose the following: System science tells us that the way to improve the adaptability and robustness of a system is to increase diversity within the system. For example, Ecologists measure the viability and sustainability of an ecosystem by measuring the richness of the biodiversity present in the ecosystem. I propose that we use a similar measure for global viability and sustainability. In this case, we would measure the richness of the cultural and individual diversity present across the planet.

This is a good news/bad news scenario. The good news is that there is already a very rich diversity of cultural and individual options. The bad news is that we treat diversity as a source of our various and sundry disagreements and conflicts. We tend to institute policies and systems that do not support or encourage cultural diversity, but which are rather designed to contain or control it.

We are locked into political, social, and economic systems that are based on *power structures*. Power structures are based on a single rule: divide and conquer. Quite simply, it is not in the best interests of our power elites that we should all get along. Imagine what would happen to the US military-industrial complex if there were no wars anywhere on earth. What would happen to all the wealth that is generated by these political and economic models? Such a scenario could not be allowed to happen. If there were no inherent basis for fomenting disagreements, the power elites would have to manufacture one. We are being kept revved up to support the various conflicts that make power structures necessary. We are taught from a very early age to treat our differences as sources of antagonism and, if needed, aggression. This is how we are taught to think. This is the root cause of our inability to bring about effective change. The power elites don't want real change, and they continue to both block new ways of thinking and promote old ways of thinking to sustain their positions as power elites.

*

However, the news is not all bad. If we define unity as, "many things taken together as one,"[7] rather than defined as, "a single homogeneous entity," then it is clear that we already have a united world. The problem is not how to unite the planet under a single homogeneous culture, but how to recognize the unity that is present and to use the inherent diversity as a strength toward a viable and sustainable future instead of as a weakness.

In moral terms, the question is, "Who are we as a species?" That is, "What kind of creatures (people) are we?" Partly, the question is about the ethics of who we are. It is about the way that we are in the world as a species. To answer these questions, we need to explore the underlying values and principles that can support who we want to be as a species. When we contrast this with who we are in fact, we should get some sense of direction about who we want to be, and how we can get there. More than this, though, there is a need to reconnect understanding with meaning, and to close the culture lag. This will require a foray into ethics because it is here that such connections are made.

The basic argument is that we behave the way we do, and have difficulty changing direction, because the mind has a structure shaped by the external environment and by the social interactions associated with language, myths, art, history, and traditions. These structures literally *shape* our thinking and define what constitutes rational thought. To change behavior, we must change our thinking, and that requires changing the overriding structure of thought. In simple terms, cultural and traditional ways of thinking determine what passes for rational thought in a given time, place, and culture. This is the definition of what is often called common sense. Historically, these structures have been determined by the connection between understanding and meaning provided in a religiocentric culture.

To change our behavior, and to bring it in line with contemporary scientific understanding, requires that we literally change the criteria for what passes for rational thought in the context of scientific understanding. Connect ethics with the new global reality of our situation as a species, and we can find new ways to connect understanding with meaning. This requires probing deeply into how forms of thought are developed and maintained and relating these new forms to understanding and meaning.

---

7   R Buckminster Fuller, *Synergetics, Section 229.02*

In general, we find meaning by finding a sense of *place* in our respective communities. Part of the problem is that current social, economic, and political institutions do not promote a large variety of options for how individuals can find this sense of place. Rather, because we treat our differences as sources of antagonism and aggression, many policies are directed at exclusion rather than inclusion. This is what causes so much alienation and despair. Religious meaning helps up to a point, but it fails to completely fill the void. This failure is aggravated by humanity gradually moving beyond religion as the centerpiece of defining civilization. Of course, there is the alternative trend toward religious fundamentalism that we need to account for. In a general sense, we might argue that we know that we need to found a global civilization on a coherent set of cultural-ethical values, but as a species. Traditionally, we have done this through religion, so there is a tendency to go back to our founding traditions to start the process. My argument is that this is really more of the same, and will not lead us to a new way of thinking or behaving. This approach will simply entrench our traditional values, which are what got us into this mess in the first place.

A proper sense of ethics is needed to complete the shift. Around the world, we are at the end of the religiocentric approach to civilization that has for generations been driving human history and the structure of thought. We need only change the underlying approach to who we are as a civilized species. At the bottom of this approach stands a set of principles and values defined in the context of our various histories, cultures, languages, religious beliefs, and traditions that structure human thought. To change how we think, we need to recast these underlying principles and values in a new global light so we can begin to shift the whole approach to a more positive model that can bring peace, viability and sustainability to the planet. I call this an *Ethical Framework*, and this is what I want to construct as the target state for humanity. More than just a foray into shifting moral values, this proposition encompasses a real look at how we think, and how that thinking needs to change to create a viable and sustainable world. It helps us to accomplish two goals. First, it helps us to grow beyond the primitive power structures that have trapped us in our current state, and second, it will help us to reconnect understanding with meaning. It will define a person in a new way that recaptures the traditional meaning of an *authentic person*. It is my hope that by the end of this book, you would like to live in the kind of new world that I am describing.

Part of how we shift our thinking is to move beyond our limited ideologies and local beliefs to adopt those values and principles we need as a species to promote a viable and sustainable future. In this context, Ethics is needed more than ever. This is the key to realizing our potential as a species.

The Main Arguments

To get at this problem, we need a firm handle on how thinking happens, and how our thinking develops toward truth and beliefs. In other words, to change our fundamental beliefs, we need to be clear about how we form beliefs and the mechanisms available to modify our thinking toward a desired goal. This means that we must tackle two problems: the problem of power structures, and the problem of understanding and meaning. We shall see that the problems are interrelated; so solving one contributes substantially to solving the other.

To answer that question, I must probe more deeply into how we think, and how we become trapped in thought paradigms.

The German philosopher Ernst Cassirer[8] shows that the thinking process happens with *symbols*. He identified three symbolic forms or structures of thought: language, myth/religion, and art. I will outline how the mind is actively formed or structured by specific environmental, collective, and cultural experiences. For example, the *Witoto* tribe in the jungles of the Amazon will perceive the world as a jungle, and will develop understanding in terms of the specific language, myths, and art of the tribe within the context of their environmental experiences. This will produce a similar but different connection between understanding and meaning than the *Bushmen* tribe living in the Kalahari Desert. What is common to both is that understanding and meaning are formed within the public

---

8   Cassirer, E. (1953). *The Philosophy Of Symbolic Forms (Vol.1–2)*. New Haven, CT: Yale University Press.

sphere of their respective environments, which is the combination of a group dynamic of perceiving and conceiving the world. These virtual public structures of mind are called *Frameworks*.

The dynamics of Frameworks involve the specific differences between language, myth, and artistic forms of expressions. What Cassirer shows is that languages are formed on common principles, even though they lead to various results. We symbolize contents of empirical experience such that all phenomena are symbolic of something. Each symbol supports and plays off all the others to structure a system of symbols. Symbolizing extends what something signifies in the system of symbols, such that the meaning of any particular symbol is bound to the specific form or structure of the language. Words not only indicate contents of experience, but also indicate other words. This is the defining characteristic of language. Words are defined with other words—within their place in the system of words that actually evolves. Symbols are the idealizations of conscious apprehensions. Meaning is found in the function of the symbols within the system of symbols. We order our thoughts according to our linguistic terms of reference, and through this, we objectify experiences. Cassirer shows how language contributes to the meaning of space, time, and number. Language forms a structure of consciousness that orders experience in a kind of *Weltanschauung*, or worldview. Differences between languages are more than just phonetic differences, but rather differences in conscious structures that provide differing world perspectives.

Myths provide the first attempt at understanding, but not in the modern sense of laws that are independent of human experience. Rather, myths provide an approach not about *how* the world works, but of *why* the world works as it does. Myths define a magical sympathy for the whole in which any part is tied in with the destiny of the whole. To understand the why, we need to understand its place in the whole. The mythical image is life itself as an undivided whole as part of an undivided cosmos. Mythical thought traces the whole back to the source or reason for an event or action.

Rather than explain space and time, myths explain place and moment: Why this happened to that person at this time. The magical, mythical worldview that is created interpenetrates and inter-accommodates with linguistic forms as part of the overall worldview. Myths are both reinforced and lived through rituals and sacrifices. Over time, mythical, magical worldviews evolve beyond simple spirits and totems to modern gods with modern rituals and prayers. Mythical symbols develop their own form or structure, which is just as coherent and material as language, and just as well grounded in phenomena. Mythical/religious worldviews are not non-rational as the reason versus faith debate supposes, but are simply a different way of experiencing the world—a worldview that is just as valid in its way as is modern science.

Cassirer's presentation of art is a harmonizing expression and representation that renders reality visible by establishing a balance between the world of expression (language) and the world of signification (myth/religion). Art discovers the pure forms of things and renders them accessible to the world.

I extend this view. Language and myths are ways of making contents of experience public by using the forms or structures that make experience explicit and public. Art does the reverse. It uses a content of experience to make the Framework itself explicit or public. This has the impact of reinforcing language and myth in a virtual public structure that literally forms the human mind within the culture that develops in its place and time.

The model I develop explores how we are trapped in our current social, cultural, and political systems because we actually live inside a set of Frameworks that structure thinking in specific ways. A Framework will be defined as more than just an *episteme*,[9] or form of understanding; that is, it is more than just the context within which understanding is possible. I intend a Framework to be the literal, multilayered structure of a mind that is the result of human interaction and that is developed largely through

---

9 Michael Foucault defines an *episteme* as that which is *a priori* to experience. He describes it as more than just a "framework" that contextualizes thought in a given age and geography. Rather, it is the "*a priori* that in a given period delimits in totality of experience a field of knowledge, defines the mode of being of the objects that appear in that field, provides man's everyday perception with theoretical powers, and defines the conditions in which he can sustain a discourse about things that is recognized to be true" (p. 172). What I am referring to is more than just the structure that is *a priori* to understanding, but also includes meaning, and the conditions for connecting understanding with meaning.

language, myths, and art. Once developed, it is a *shared* structure within a community and provides the structure for both understanding and meaning and how these play off each other through environmental and community activity. In simple terms, a Framework is a virtual public mental structure that shapes thought and experience for a given community and culture. We might think of this as a communal or collective worldview that shapes our personal worldviews. I will also argue that Frameworks are specific to a given community in a given place and time. This leads to the idea that there are many cultural Frameworks around the world—all providing different ways to bring people together as a community, and which all provide many ways for meaningful, individual self-realization. For example, the public mental Frameworks of medieval European communities were quite different from today's European Frameworks. Similarly, today's North American Frameworks are quite different from Native American Frameworks of a few centuries ago, and different again from present-day Chinese and Japanese Frameworks. Frameworks specify what counts as common sense within a given community and culture.

With this in mind, I argue that there is an overriding structure to Frameworks that is the result of the division of labor in any complex community. Social divisions create *Sub-Frameworks*, based on power relations within and between communities. In general, there are Tops, Middles, and Bottoms,[10] and the interrelations between these lead to consistent and predictable patterns of behavior, many of which are the source of antagonism and aggression.

By and large, we are each part of a larger system, but we only see our local part from our Top, Middle or Bottom perspective. This lack of vision for the whole system and how things fit together is called system blindness and this causes what Barry Oshry calls a "dance of blind reflex." There are five kinds of system blindness:

1. *Spatial blindness* is when we only see part of the system.

2. *Temporal blindness* is a focus on the present, but without consideration of the past.

---

10 Oshry, B. (2007). *Seeing Systems: Unlocking The Mysteries Of Organizational Life.* Oakland, CA: Berrett-Koehler Publishers.

3. *Relational blindness* occurs when we do not see ourselves in systemic relationships.

4. *Process blindness* comes from not seeing systems as wholes. We miss systemic differentiations and shared responsibilities and complexity.

5. *Uncertainty blindness* is seeing fixed positions battling fixed positions, but missing the uncertainties underlying each position leading to unassailable positions about responsibility, or vulnerability, or dominance.

Frameworks form systems of interpenetrating forms, such as language, myth, and art, which are then further refined within Sub-Frameworks and the various kinds of system blindness. Our thinking tends to become trapped within these forms and substructures, and that contributes to the difficulties in shifting behaviors.

There is a common set of principles that defines Frameworks, and when viewed in a global context provides for a global Framework, which I call Father Culture.[11] Culture is formed from respective linguistic, mythical/religious, and artistic forms that are then refined in power structure terms, which cause us to play power structure games. We are trapped in this way of thinking largely because we have been developing this Framework since the Agricultural Revolution, and because we don't have any other Frameworks to shift our thought patterns to. As this is a global phenomenon, Father Culture is the overriding Framework for thinking in global terms.

Frameworks literally structure thought processes and define how we live, understand the world and ourselves, and how we find meaning in our lives (or not). Again, what passed for rational thought in Europe at the beginning of the first millennium is very different from what passes for rational thought in Europe in present times. Theology, as the prime explanation of how the world works, has been replaced with a scientific approach that is largely indifferent to theology. There are many

---

11 In the book *Ishmael*, Daniel Quinn calls this "Mother Culture." I object to this characterization, as power structures are clearly male dominated, competitive, aggressive, and patriarchal.

Frameworks layered in any culture, from individual thought patterns through to family group thought patterns, to the thought patterns of tribes or nations. Individual tribal/cultural Frameworks do evolve and change, but social evolution to date has always been inside the larger Framework of Father Culture.

Power structures are unviable and unsustainable by definition. They are based on Top–Bottom, master–servant relations that promote divide-and-conquer, competitive have-versus-have-not system blindness behaviors. Father Culture does not and cannot provide a Framework for the kind of thinking that will lead to peaceful and sustainable global systems and institutions. How did we get into this state of affairs?

I begin by clarifying the problem of how the world got into its current state through two stories: Ishmael, and the Parable of the Tribes. Ishmael is Daniel Quinn's[12] fictional creation, an ape that has learned to speak, which offers a perspective on humanity from the animal kingdom. Ishmael argues that humans violate fundamental natural laws of competition that would otherwise ensure the overall stability of global ecosystems and resource availability. Quinn shows how the Agricultural Revolution started humans down a path of war against nature and each other.

Andrew Schmookler[13] elaborates on the theme of the war of "man against man" with a parable that shows how tribal conflicts lead to power structures and to ways of building communities that require playing power structure games. His parable shows how power structures work, and why they are both unviable and unsustainable. These two models—Ishmael and the Parable—define a larger cultural framework I called Father Culture. This is the overriding theme of our current situation and forms the basis for why we are having so much difficulty shifting gears. Of course, whereas the models provide a context for why we think the way we do as a fragmented, ecologically unviable and violent global community, they do not explain why it is so difficult to change directions.

---

12 Quinn, D. (1993). *Ishmael: An Adventure Of The Mind And Spirit*, a 1993 novel by Daniel Quinn.
13 Schmookler, A. B. (1995). *The Parable Of The Tribes*. Albany, NY: State University of New York Press.

To make matters more urgent, there are two historical trends that exacerbate the problem. By about the middle of the 19th century, we became a planet in the sense that activities and impacts became systematically global. We settled into 19th-century balance-of-power games. This is what Buckminster Fuller called the "World War Game,"[14] and this is the game we are still playing.

The second problem is the rise of a science that has provided new knowledge, but also incredible tools to enhance power relations for those who can afford it. When we put these together, it is evident that we are waging 19th-century balance-of-power world war games with 21st-century weapons of mass destruction—a lethal combination if ever there was one.

One of the benefits of secularizing understanding through science is that we also secularize ethical values. I will argue for two perspectives on this front. First, ethical values are different in kind from traditional religiocentric moral values. Traditional religiocentric moral values are based on what is now called Virtues Ethics. I will present Virtues Ethics, along with Consequentialism and Universalism, to provide a more complete list of the three kinds of ethical criteria. I will argue that we need all three to properly form an ethical system. When we put these criteria into a common model, they become the criteria we use to determine the quality of an individual's thinking:

1. Are this individual's decisions and actions virtuous, made with honesty and integrity?

2. Have they thought through the consequences of their decisions and selected actions that promote overall benefits and minimize harms?

3. Have they identified,.and are they acting on, *right* principles?

I will argue that you need to promote all three to pass ethical muster. Any failure in any one kind of criteria opens up the actions for ethical criticism. The next question is, what are the principles of an ethics that

---

14 Fuller, R. B. (1973). *Utopia Or Oblivion: The Prospects For Mankind.* New York: Viking Press.

we need to ensure that we are acting on *right* principles? I will argue that the four values presented above—life, liberty, equality, tolerance form the core foundations of an ethics. There are two rules for morality:

1. You must consider all three kinds of ethical criteria to be ethically successful.

2. When selecting principles to act on, you do not get to cherry-pick your principles.

Our current ethical values are designed to constrain abuses of self-serving, competitive power processes. They are not designed to promote cultural diversity in the sense it has been presented. A slight shift in these definitions to a more positive, cooperative view changes the definition of good governance, and the institutions of power and authority. This will turn out to be a key mechanism for not only solving the power structure problem, but also solving the understanding-meaning problem.

One of the techniques I use in this book is called Goal Analysis.[15] In this methodology, a *goal* is treated as a *fuzzy objective*. An objective properly has three parts: (1) What are we to do (achieve), (2) under what circumstances or conditions, and (3) how will we measure success? Two out of three doesn't count. Any failure of a goal statement to meet the criteria of a proper set of objectives is considered fuzzy, and can only lead to fuzzy results. I have proposed two specific objectives—to increase cultural diversity and harmonization in the world and to do so through the positive implementation of a full set of foundational ethical values as the center of civilized behavior. In short, I am advocating that if we shift our underlying values from traditional religiocentric values to a proper set of ethical values, we shift the Frameworks that constitute rational thought and subsequent behaviors. We need to build a global civilization on these new values if we are to succeed in producing measurable increases in the cultural diversity and harmony needed for a viable and sustainable future.

One of the objectives of this book is to develop an *Ethical Framework*, and how one would think within it. This includes specifying the contents of the Framework and how it is grounded in the four foundational ethical

15 Mager, Robert F., *Goal Analysis*, Chapter 4, p. 23.

values. With an awareness of a set of objectives, and a clear view of the target state, real change can become possible.

This leads me to outline how ethical values translate into moral precepts that guide our actions. In effect, I will outline the guidelines or rules for behaving within an Ethical Framework. With a clear model of how Frameworks and Sub-Frameworks are built, I will then explore a way of creating this new Framework by outlining the underlying founding values that would support the Framework. For example, the foundational values that we shall need to produce a peaceful, sustainable future are the thymotic values: life, liberty, equality, and tolerance. It is through these ethical values that we try to constrain power and its abuses. Liberty, for example, means that each individual is sovereign over each individual's own mind and body. This is in response to the master–servant relation that would enslave individuals under a power structure. Liberty says, in effect, that no one may own another—the power to enslave others is to be curtailed. Liberty also serves to constrain Top behaviors that exploit Bottoms.

Following the work of the renowned sociologist Jane Jacobs,[16] I will outline how Father Culture breaks into political and economic power elites, each with its own set of moral precepts (the rules of being a Top). These precepts form a recognizable pattern, which Jacobs calls a "syndrome," and which I will use to characterize the moral values associated with various Frameworks. In this context, we identify the *Guardian Moral Framework*, which characterizes the rules of behavior for political institutions, and the *Commercial Moral Framework*, which characterizes the rules for exemplary business behaviors. Each moral Framework lists fifteen precepts that amount to the rules for behavior for a politician or business person. The problem is that when we lay out these rules, there is no direct connection between these moral Frameworks and the underlying ethical criteria and values that should ground them. For instance, I will be unable to connect guardian moral precepts with life, liberty, or equality. Rather, in this case, the Guardian Moral Framework will appear to oppose the foundational ethical values. The same argument will prevail with the Commercial Framework. To add to the mix, I will then extend Jacobs'

---

16 Jane Jacobs was an American-Canadian journalist, author, and activist who influenced urban studies, sociology, and economics. She invented the concept of Social Capital.

argument to distribute power across individuals as in a democracy and outline the moral precepts for democratic rulers and citizens. Again, there is no clear connection between the democratic moral precepts and founding ethical criteria and values. From that position, I will argue that we must not sacrifice any foundational ethical values because to do so would literally devalue Ethics. This will leave us in a bit of a quandary. How can we found a modern ethics to promote a viable and sustainable future if we cannot connect our political and economic moral Frameworks to an ethical foundation? In effect, I will conclude that Father Culture is divorced from the modern ethical values and the principles we need to produce a viable and sustainable future. This is a major reason current institutions cannot get us to where we need to be.

To complicate matters, science, as defined within Father Culture, does not appear to be bound by ethical constraints. Scientists produce knowledge but leave it to the power elites to decide what to do with that knowledge. It is important, then, to understand how science works. To that end, I outline both empirical and theoretical scientific methods and explain how these work together to provide scientific understanding. To see how science is changing, I then explore some of the developments in quantum theory, complexity, and how computers are enhancing empirical methods. With a clear view of how science works, we can later explore ethics for science, and how this can impact our ability to embrace new ways of thinking toward a more sustainable future. In this presentation, I will not argue that science will save the day. However, it is so important for the solution that we need to position science in a way that it supports needed changes.

Currently science does not align with ethics, but supports the unviability of Father Culture. Science provides an enhanced knowledge base, but does not provide the decision criteria to use that knowledge intelligently or wisely. Science projects are generally those that the power elites are prepared to fund. The result is that over half of all scientific research is with weaponry and the forces of destruction for political power elites. The other half is for commercial profit. Knowledge is power, and power elites have a vested interest in capitalizing on the knowledge advantage that science can give them to maintain or increase their sphere of control. In Father Culture, science is not only divorced from Ethics, but it can also be used to actively oppose or undermine it. One of the reasons we are trapped in the Framework of Father Culture is that it is well supported by our knowledge base and is poorly constrained by Ethics. When push comes to shove, Ethics always takes a back seat in the proceedings (and then we all wonder why we are not moving forward toward a more sustainable future). Scientists and policy makers around the world all turn to ethics and morality to deal with new technologies that cut to the core of natural processes - such as splitting the atom or re-engineering the human genome. When such dangers emerge, the world turns to ethics to decide how best to move forward. Ethics is universal in the sense of global and trans-cultural in practice. However, there are no real enforcement mechanisms. Compliance is voluntary. This is a consequence of Ethics not developing as an institution under Father Culture. Rather, Ethics has historically been co-opted by our various and sundry religious institutions. These are not designed to practice ethics, but religion, which are not the same things. This is one of the greatest failures of Father Culture.

To shift thinking toward a peaceful and sustainable future, then, requires the development of a new Framework for thinking. Humanity needs to quickly change what passes for rational thought in how we approach world problems. Father Culture is so pervasive that we can hardly imagine what the world might be like without power structures. The idea sounds incredibly idealistic, almost to the point of silliness. However, once we understand how Frameworks are built and changed, we will have the tools to begin the process. The amount of change required to accomplish this task is not as great as might first be supposed. Small changes in thought processes can have widespread positive consequences if we pick the right Framework. Of course, power structures will not magically disappear, but by seeing power relations in their systemic form, we defuse many of the sources of antagonism and aggression. Part of my model must enable you to "see" systemic relations so you can determine how behavior does in fact change when proper context and mutual understanding are achieved.

With the understanding of how Frameworks are built, I can create a new Framework by outlining the underlying founding values of an Ethical Framework. To accomplish this, ethical values must be defined positively— not to constrain power, but to promote a new kind of self-realization.

Remember, we will measure the viability and sustainability of our world by measuring the richness of the cultural and individual diversity that is present. This means that we will need to encourage and promote cultural diversity and develop policies and institutions that provide for self-realization. Again, this will lead to a new set of moral precepts that define moral behavior. Again, I will leverage work introduced by Jacobs.

Jacobs proposes that ecological systems differ from current economic models in that Nature is a closed system. She characterizes *expansion* as "increasing diversity and increasingly various, numerous, and intricate co-development relationships."[17] Energy is trapped and used in ever-increasing ways. This increases diversity, and so the system expands within itself. This is why we can measure the viability of an ecosystem in terms of the richness of its biodiversity. But this natural model is contrary to the political and economic expansion within Father Culture, which grows by conquering more territory to support the production of more goods. We behave as though we are operating in an open system. Because the system is actually closed, this kind of expansion is no longer possible. We have settled into a kind of balance-of-power politics. This is another reason Father Culture cannot get us to a viable and sustainable future.

Jacobs applies this model to economic theory and proposes a model for proper energy and resource accounting in humanity's economic development and pricing policies. I will extend Jacobs' position into *Natural Ethics* to show how natural expansion can ground ethical values.

Natural Ethics provides positive definitions of the four foundational ethical values. For example, instead of liberty being a constraint on power, it is understood to promote individual growth and accomplishment by increasing the range of self-realization options through an increasingly diverse web of personal development opportunities. Tolerance is not just a response to the objectifying of others by power structures in the sense that we will put up with our differences (like it or not), but becomes the active promotion of individual diversity in the positive sense of respect for persons. The idea is to replace the definition of responsible governance in Father Culture, as currently defined within the Guardian and Commercial Frameworks, with a definition of responsible governance that encourages

---

17 Jacobs, J. (2001). *The Nature Of Economies*, p. 42.

diversity and self-realization. Once the foundational values are positively defined, I will develop a new set of moral precepts that define responsible governance that I call an Ethical Framework.

The Ethical Framework is based on fifteen moral precepts that directly tie to the four foundational, natural ethical principles. We will define each of these and outline the specific relationships that make the model work. The precepts are as follows, in Table 1.1.

It is from this way of thinking that we develop policies and institutions that promote and encourage cultural and individual diversity by providing for new ways of finding a sense of place in the world. The idea is to develop a kind of world where we create an increasingly complex web of interdependencies that expands within itself, that facilitates new opportunities where cultural diversity can be explored and expanded, and that introduces a wider range of opportunities for individual self-realization.

Table 1.1: Ethical Framework

ETHICAL FRAMEWORK
Promote peace and harmony
Come to voluntary agreements
Be honest
Promote community
Respect persons
Promote personification
Seek natural justice
Dissent for the sake of the public good
Promote integrity
Promote unity
Promote harmony and inclusiveness
Invest in the global community
Demonstrate moral courage
Seek meaning and understanding
Seek personal spiritual growth and fulfillment

Toward an Ethical Society

My argument is simple. The Framework called Father Culture is ad hoc, poorly thought, and yet still dominates our thinking. When you change the underlying values that determine how you think and set the rules to evaluate high-quality thinking, you have the potential to change everything. An Ethical society is intended to present an example of how such a Framework might look. I presented my case with three arguments. The first outlined the case for what Frameworks are, and how they are formed. The second argument is that the current historical landscape is a world dominated by Father Culture, which continues to subvert ethical criteria and thymotic values. Father Culture manifests itself largely in power structure politics and economics. It is the demonstrable Framework for poor-quality thinking, as ethics defines this. The third argument is that understanding and meaning have become disconnected causing alienation, antagonism, and violence. I argue that we cannot shift gears toward a peaceful and sustainable world because we are trapped in a Framework of thinking that perpetuates Father Culture. With a subtle shift in the meaning of life, liberty, equality, and tolerance, we can redefine what constitutes good governance, embrace a global perspective toward others (overcome system blindness), and rein in science under the umbrella of ethical values and constraints. We can shift to a new Framework to define rational thought in a new way. I am arguing against what I call the "duuhh" principle. This is where we chronically and persistently put ethics on the back burner whenever it is thought to be convenient and we then scratch our heads and wonder why the world is in such a mess. Well, duuhh!

Historians characterize the development of cultural norms based on a transition from existential to self expression values. Existential values are those community values needed when faced with chronic and persistent existential threats, such as war, environmental threats (droughts or weather events), famine, or disease, These values have consistently lead to rigid hierarchical societies with a preference for strong man leaders, patriarchy and little tolerance for deviance from defined roles. These are the values that underpin Father Culture.

When existential threats diminish, self expression values can emerge. These then challenge, patriarchy, the rigid hierarchy, and promote tolerance for alternative lifestyles and identities. If we are going to promote human flourishing we need to understand the underlying values that can lead to a global culture where the collective community not only facilitates but promotes self expression values however these are understood within the context of local beliefs and traditions.

We want to avoid more "duuhh." We need to put ethics on the front burner in our decisions and actions and evaluate our leaders in terms of the new rules of good governance. You would demonstrate good citizenship by promoting the community's values and honoring diversity and integrity, and you would judge community leaders against appropriate ethical and moral criteria. We are looking for leaders who demonstrate quality thinking, who promote cultural and individual diversity, and who give proper due to how people and our world ought to be treated. I propose an Ethical Framework firmly grounded ethical criteria and the underlying thymotic values. The Ethical Framework presents the first Moral Framework that is firmly tied to fundamental values that define who we are as a species.

Proposed Game Plan

First, we must begin to break out of the system blindness patterns of behaviors so that the blinkers of the five kinds of system blindness start to fall away. We all begin to see how actions in our part of the system impact other parts of the system. We see how things got to be the way they are, and how relationships are impacted in ways we did not understand before. We see how processes work, not just in our part of the world, but across the whole planet. We see the larger context and how the system behaves, and this in turn reduces the uncertainty people have about what they can do to positively work for the system. When we do this, the following benefits are realized:

1. People are willing to move beyond their narrow perspectives to see the big picture.

2. People begin to have more understanding and patience with each other.

3. People start to see the context of others' actions, and so take these actions less personally.

4. Instead of simply reacting to others, people put more energy into the work of the system.

5. Problems are identified from the part of the system where they originate.

6. As people gain understanding of others' worlds, they see how their own actions reduce cooperation and system coordination. They can meaningfully participate in strategic plans that promote cooperation and coordination.

From these considerations I develop Mission, Vision, and Objectives statements:

Vision: To develop a robust system of planetary management that is responsible for itself. To live in peace and harmony with our environment and with each other as individuals, groups, and societies.

Mission: To pursue economic, political, cultural, and religious programs that promote diversity within the closed system of planet Earth for peace and sustainability of the human race, and that reconnect understanding with meaning for all peoples.

Finally, I will restate my objective for this study as an objective for humanity moving forward:

Peace and Sustainability Objective: To produce ethically aware and responsible citizens of Earth (to embrace an Ethical Framework). To ensure that quality thinking stands behind our decisions and actions.

The main stakeholders are: (1) all the citizens of Earth—I call this the human perspective; (2) all people engaged in economic activities—I call this the economic perspective; (3) all politicians and people who manage our political institutions and bureaucracies—I call this the political perspective; and, (4) all those who are involved in religious and cultural activities around the planet—I call this the cultural/religious perspective. There are two broad strategies:

1. increase-positive-cultural-differentiations strategy; and

2. reconnect-understanding-with-meanings strategy.

I construct a Strategy Map outlining objectives for each stakeholder for each perspective.

For example, the first strategy would include objectives to: improve human, knowledge, and organizational capital; develop world order strategies along with social stability strategies; and, establish Earth productivity strategies that align with economic stability strategies. Good governance with improved intercommunal relations and transcultural values would address the human perspective.

This leads to a Results Chain where I profile the kinds of activities we might engage in to reach our strategic objectives.

I suggest that we start with human capital—a global inventory of our capabilities and skills. Find ways to increase the effectiveness and efficiency of our social technologies to eliminate silos and induce improved cooperation and coordination between institutions. Increase the number of people we pay to look after global interests and take steps to beef up our support for groups that look out for global interests and see that they are properly funded to do their work. Develop processes and institutions to enhance global citizen participation in the political process, and enhance democratic institutions for all peoples as a way to reduce much of the world's violence.

I have argued that we are already an interconnected global system of systems. I propose that we do this somewhat intelligently so that we improve the efficiency and effectiveness of our resource use and stabilize our economies. We develop more effective and efficient processes that improve communities around the world with a focus on improving local environments, health and safety, and mechanisms to improve intercommunity relations.

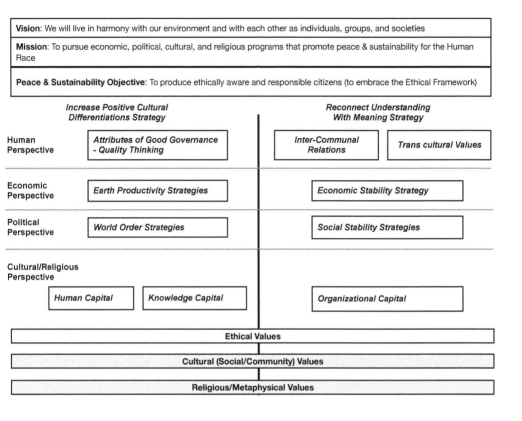

Vision: We will live in harmony with our environment and with each other as individuals, groups, and societies

Mission: To pursue economic, political, cultural, and religious programs that promote peace & sustainability for the Human Race

Peace & Sustainability Objective: To produce ethically aware and responsible citizens (to embrace the Ethical Framework)

	Increase Positive Cultural Differentiations Strategy	*Reconnect Understanding With Meaning Strategy*
Human Perspective	*Attributes of Good Governance - Quality Thinking*	*Inter-Communal Relations* — *Trans cultural Values*
Economic Perspective	*Earth Productivity Strategies*	*Economic Stability Strategy*
Political Perspective	*World Order Strategies*	*Social Stability Strategies*
Cultural/Religious Perspective	*Human Capital* — *Knowledge Capital*	*Organizational Capital*

Ethical Values

Cultural (Social/Community) Values

Religious/Metaphysical Values

Figure 1.1: Strategy Map – Ethical Priority

These initiatives are designed to promote globally responsible leaders, more adequate and peaceful participation in our various political and economic processes, and new innovations to increase codependency webs, thus creating more niches for contributions by members of communities that are healthy, educated, and working with other communities rather than opposing them. These initiatives would result in an enhanced global community with expanded economic opportunities for all (within a properly closed global economic system). It would make it easier for more people to see the system as a whole and work for the system, with many more opportunities for people to find meaning in a modern scientific, global community. We would achieve a more peaceful, sustainable world.

In this book I have argued that the world is a mess. Our civilization has evolved globally in a completely arbitrary and ad hoc way. We are, and always have been out of control as a species.

We live in a time of the accumulated global systemic effects of these ways of thinking and behaving. A new global awareness is emerging, but in an arbitrary and ad hoc way. Traditional thinking holds that we get to a just society by getting people to personally behave in moral and socially responsible ways. When we all do this, we get a just society.

I argue that this is backwards. Our various cultural worldviews determine how we understand the world and find meaning in our lives. I argue that it is here that we must take at least some control over this new and emerging global worldview.

We must see the whole world as a system (to overcome system blindness), but based on proper global universal values and understanding. Rather than wait for a supposed accumulation of personal worldview alignments, we create a kind of global, collective groupthink based on ethics and informed by science. This new collective worldview will structure and shape our respective personal worldviews. This is how we will get personal alignment.

It is time to behave as a species and not just a loose collection of out of control individuals and communities. It is time to move beyond our traditional ways of thinking and behaving to put ethics on the front burner. It is time to build a sustainable, peaceful world – a world that works for everyone.

CHAPTER 2
Symbolic Forms and Expressions

The reader is sitting in a wingback chair in the corner of the room. The chair angles to face the center of the room. To the reader's left and behind the chair is a lamp, which is the main illumination for the reader and the book. To the reader's right is a fireplace. The fire emits an orange glow and a gentle heat. Opposite the reader on the other side of the fireplace is another reading chair facing the reader, which also angles to face the center of the room. You are a spectator positioned in the middle of the room. You can see both chairs, the fireplace, and the lamp. You can read the title of the book, *The Ethical Society*. You see the back of the book, and the reader sees the pages. You can see the reader's face, the eyes moving from side to side as the pages are scanned. Periodically, you hear a page turning. The reader is focused on the book, but if the reader were to look up, the reader would see your face with your piercing and peering eyes.

This description presents an ordinary set of events—one person looking at another who is reading a book. However, even such a simple scene presents some problems for perception. First, as a spectator, you see the room and its occupant from your unique point of view. You cannot "see" your own eyes. There are things in the room that are hidden from view. In contrast, the reader also views the room from a unique position, and while the reader might share some of your observations, there are also things hidden from the reader's view.

How do we as a species perceive ourselves, and the world around us? How does the everyday fact of unique points of view affect what we perceive? How do we establish common elements in any perceptual scene? For example, how do you know that the reader sees pages and not some other object hidden from your view? How do we determine that there are any objects in view that are common to both perceivers? More than this, how do we do this to such an extent that we can assume there are common objects that we share? How do we know? Are there any differences between how the room really is and how it appears to me to be? Are there any differences between how the room really is and how it appears to you? How could we discover any such differences?

I am trying to connect understanding with meaning in such a manner that I am not dependent on a religiocentric way of proceeding. To do this, I must assume a distinction between reality and appearances—how the world really is, versus how the world appears to be.

A particular environment shapes the kinds of experiences that people might have, and these, in turn, affect how we might think about things. For example, a person living in the arctic conditions of northern Siberia would develop different survival strategies than someone living in a tropical rainforest. Specific environments often have particular features that people may or may not experience or observe.

To understand how people perceive and think about the world, it might be fruitful to see how the structure of thought might shape worldviews or other thought processes. We each experience the world through our senses and from a unique point of view. The sights we see, the sounds we hear, and the smells and tastes we have are fundamental to any experience.

There are many theories about how perception works, but there is little consensus about which approach might be correct. The problems relate to two areas. The first is that we do not really know enough about how our brains work to explain, for example, how we "see" things. Science knows about light and the structure of the eyes and about sound waves and the structure of the ear, but from there to how "I see" or "hear" an object in my mind is not well-understood. How we get from an image on the retina of my eye to me "seeing" a bird or a tree is a complex process. The brain is still much like a black box in this area.

The second issue is that all people can experience illusions. However, it is not clear how this happens. How are our senses fooled by various situations? The problem of illusion is important because if human senses can be easily fooled in such a way that we cannot determine when we are being fooled, then relying on our senses as a source of knowledge and understanding could be severely crippled. We also need to understand when this happens so that such experiences can be tuned out of any serious use as empirical evidence for knowledge claims.

There are two kinds of perception, *real perception* and *phenomenal perception*. Phenomenal perception is the common-sense view of perception. We do not see our eyes or hear our ears. We see the world around us. I see the cup on the table in front of me. You see the book you are reading. In general, we each have no sight of light entering our eyes, and being converted to signals in the brain, or of becoming conscious of seeing. You see the book, and you read it. It is as though your consciousness sees the book directly or hears the music directly. Phenomenal perception is sometimes called *direct perception*. If I can avoid the thorny question of how consciousness occurs and accept that an ego or some such brain activity is what does the seeing, then I can say that the ego perceives things directly.[18]

Direct perception is the view that there is no magic or *medium* to interfere with what we perceive. We see tables and chairs in the room exactly as they are. This is the view known as *Realism*.

Realism is pervasive in Western thought. After all, we each experience the world around us and do not really experience light waves and sound waves as such. It was not until science came along and discovered how light and sound waves work that there was any competing theory of perception. This raises the question about what to do with light and sound waves, since they seem to play no role in realism.

Let's use the example of you looking at a tree and provide a scientific explanation of the process of perception. In the scientific model, electromagnetic radiation in the visible frequency range (light) is reflected off the tree, and enters your eye, forming an image on your retina. This image is converted into electrical impulses by the rods and cones in the retina of your eyes, which signals the brain that processes it. While science has not yet worked out how the processing takes place or how this results

---

18 This is not the view that a little man (or homunculus) is sitting in our brains and viewing a screen with images. Rather, I intend that whatever the process of "consciousness of a percept" is, it appears transparent to the task of perception.

in the conscious seeing of the tree, the first steps are well understood. Further, this process of using electromagnetic radiation to see things has been worked out for devices other than eyes, and these form an integral part of how scientists make observations and even measurements. I will call this *real perception*, as there is much scientific evidence in its favor.

The contrasting view is called *representational perception*. Representational perception is any theory or approach to perception that involves various media (light or sound waves, for example) plus sensory activity to present a perception. We receive information through our senses, and somehow aggregate and assemble all these sensations into a kind of informational map—a representation of the world. Of course, it is not obvious or clear how well this informational representation actually represents the object in question. For example, while I can see objects using specific frequencies of electromagnetic radiation, there might be much information about an object that I cannot see because that information would require that my senses be tuned to frequencies of light that are not currently available. Current evidence suggests that bees and insects can perceive objects in ultraviolet light frequencies, and, hence, they perceive flowers and other objects quite differently than humans do.

It turns out that both kinds of perception are correct. We have a real body that perceives the real world via light and sound waves, and inside my real head is an informational representation of the real world from my unique perspective. The brain is able to assemble all information from our senses, light waves, sound waves, chemicals (smell and taste), and surface texture information into a coherent representation of the real world. We do not just represent individual objects in perception; we form a coherent, perceptual representation of the real world from the information provided by all our senses.

While this idea that perception is representational is a bit odd, it turns out to be the only model of perception that accords with science. For example, all recent research into brain activities indicates that there is a difference between what we apprehend via our senses, and any conscious awareness of what we apprehend. There are cases of patients with brain lesions who are blind. All perceptual apparatus works fine—their brain is receiving appropriate signals from their eyes, but their brain cannot process the information, so that these people are not conscious of what their eyes are actually seeing. If you throw a ball to such a patient, they can catch it. Their brain is processing the visual information, and they move their hand to the right place in the right time, but they have no conscious awareness of what is happening. The more we learn about how the brain works, the more representationalism is being validated.

This theory is important because it explains perceptual behavior and how we experience the world. Real perception explains the physics and physiology of sensing. The other kind of perception is called Apparent or Phenomenal perception which describes normal perceptual experience. We see, but do not "see" our eyes. We hear, but do not "hear" our ears. It seems like we perceive objects directly. Both are needed to explain empirical experience.

But this is only a very small part of a very complex process. You are reading a book, and this is generating ideas and images in your head possibly with associations that I do not have. We can speak to each other and convey information about our relative experiences.

In a very real sense we each experience the world from a totally unique perspective. No one can experience the world from your point of view, but you. Your life path of experiences is totally unique. While our paths may cross and may even intertwine depending on levels of intimacy, we each remain a distinct entity with our own life experiences. But we also share understandings about the world and even what things mean.

For example, you might talk about the book you are reading. This raises questions about how we think. We do not just passively perceive the world; we use perceptual information to act on the world. How do we do this? The answer is that we abstract from our informational representations. It turns out that all representations are symbolic of something. We think in symbols. We represent experiences with symbolic forms. Symbolic forms provide a way for each of us to align and synchronize our respective experiences, and we are so good at this task that we know we are sharing a common world.

There are three primary symbolic forms at the core of our thinking: language, myth and religion, and art. The kinds of questions we need to answer include the following:

1. How do words establish fictional or nonfictional ideas?

2. How do words relate to informational perceptions that are the contents of experience?

3. How do these confirm or refute whether our experiences correspond to the real world or are purely fictional?

I will explore how science works in a later chapter. However, while science is clearly an important activity—I have defined it as the basis for separating understanding from meaning—science is not the only way we come to understand the world around us, nor are scientific theories the only way to understand how the world works. To get to a more general account of understanding and meaning, I need to explore more deeply how we get from perceiving the world to our ideas about the world.

In modern scientific views, the real world is the world of atoms and quarks and energy interactions. In the real world, nothing is solid. The book (or tablet) you are holding is 90% empty space. It is just an assemblage of energy structures (electrons, protons, etc.) exchanging energy in an ever-dynamic world of interactions.[19] How does this energy world get to be solid tables and chairs and cups and people? How do we informationally represent the world as ideas?

To start this account, the case for perception needs to be modified. Perception was presented as a passive process where experience seems to happen automatically. The process to get from perception to ideas takes three steps. The first two are called *abstraction,* and the third is called *concretion.* Abstraction occurs in several steps from experience with our senses through to the ideas we form about what we apprehend in perception. We seem to take the information about the world and abstract from that information to get ideas. Humans create symbolic abstractions, and these become more detailed and complete as the process unfolds. For example, any child can draw a tree. This is usually a green blob on top of a vertical brown trunk. Only later, in the third step, do we learn to distinguish between elm, maple, oak, and so on. We will see that objective understanding is really a consensus about what we collectively

---

19 We grant that there is some controversy regarding whether this is true when we consider quantum mechanics.

experience. In this view objectivity is based on publicity. The process of achieving publicity is the process I will call concretion. The more public, hence, concrete our experiences are, the more objective we think our understanding is. We use various mechanisms, such as language, to communicate with each other, and through such mechanisms as language, we overcome the inherent abstractness and subjectivity of personal experience.

Objectivity is tied to public experiences. These are experiences that we can share. But how does this happen? How can the objective world be understood in terms of shared phenomenal world experiences? How do we know when an experience is shared or not?

Abstraction is the process of how raw sensory inputs enter awareness in such a way as to form concepts or ideas. For example, we do not just see a tree; we have a concept of what a tree is. Abstraction involves two steps. The first is *raw sensory apprehension*. The second is *cognition*.

For example, we draw a generic impression of a tree. There is no real detail as to kind of tree, but it is readily recognized as a tree. This is the most abstract representation that treats impressions as symbols for various phenomena.

Figure 2.1: Symbolic Tree as an Abstract Representation

As we progress through each step, apprehensions become increasingly abstracted from basic sensory inputs toward the symbolic. We think in symbols, and this provides the basis for cognition. Symbolic forms are public structures that we collectively create in a process I call *recognition*. This is really a process that aligns our respective thoughts with the details of how the world unfolds in what we will call public experience.

How the steps in abstraction and concretion lead to understanding happens mostly in step two of the abstraction process, where we begin the formation of symbols associated with the sensory apprehensions from the first step of abstraction. These symbolic forms structure our mind and enable the shift away from purely private understanding.

Symbols are the basis of *ideas*. Ideas are *abstracted common representations* based on specific actual representations or experiences. These common representations are really symbols that we employ to characterize concretions in the third step. All empirical experiences are symbolic of something. The main examples of symbolic forms are language, myth, and art. Symbolic forms align understanding. Other people apprehend the same things that I do, and this leads to the first sense of objectivity. This process is called recognition because it happens with others. Language is not an individual activity, but an activity created and shared among minds. Through our symbolic forms, the mind gets the structure it needs to participate actively in the world. Because of language, myth, and art, our experiences are not just a passive outcome of perception, but are also enabled as active participation.

The Process of Abstraction

Kant understands cognition through concepts that rest on functions. Functions are the action of ordering different representations under a common one.[20] Following the work of philosophers Ernst Cassirer and Suzanne K. Langer, I call these common representations *symbols*.

There is a tendency to consider the determination of an object of cognition in a static way. We either apprehend an object's function, or we do not. But cognition is both a dynamic and iterative process. If I see a purple frog on the table before me, I can perceive the object, but I cannot be cognizant

---

20 Kant, Immanuel, *Critique of Pure Reason*. Translated by Paul Guyer, Cambridge University Press, 1998.

of what it is or whether it is dangerous. I cannot bring the representation under a common representation except to loosely associate it with the form of frog-like creatures of experience, and purpleness. Where such determinations might convey some sense of functionality such as "good to eat" or "dangerous," I might have no way of knowing which except through experimentation, or information from others about this object.

Cognition is a dynamic, iterative process of bringing representations into a coherent, structured common representation. For cognition, all experiences are the combination of information about them and their common representation.

In other words, our experiences are mediated by cognition, which is in turn mediated by the form of the common representation or what is signified in the experience. Events happen in a patterned sequence, which is patterned by the way my perceptual processes are ordered in space and time, including any movement of me as the point of reference.

In logic, this activity is usually introduced as the relation between signs and symbols. Signs present the first real attempt to abstract relationships between events, and these signs lead naturally to more complex symbols. This relationship and development is best described by Suzanne K. Langer.[21]

The primary difference between a sign and symbol is the structure of usage. In particular, a sign has a three-part structure whereby a subject relates an object or event to another object of the event that is of greater importance. For example, a wet road is a sign that there has been rain, or a ring around the moon indicates that it will rain tomorrow. "Stop" is a sign to control traffic, and so on. The structure is:

subject + sign + object   **(1)**

The sign is the common representation of the function, which is the beginning of understanding. Signs are the first step to formalizing or structuring abstractions. Common representations are iconic, so lack substantive content in the sense that they cannot be matched to specific, actual entities of experience; thus, we need an iterative process to

---

21 Langer, S. K. (1957). *Philosophy In A New Key: A Study In The Symbolism Of Reason, Rite, and Art*. Cambridge, MA: Harvard University Press. Chapter 3.

apprehend similarities of form without regard to specific substantive instances. Again, for example, if the object is a tree, the abstracted form does not consider the specific color or shape of the leaves, or the size of the trunk, or size of the representation in relation to other objects, or the pattern of branches. What is conceived is a generic form of object that is tree-like. Yet this formal conception signifies a kind of common representation. This is what Langer calls, "simultaneous integral presentations." These are simple picture-like impressions of objects that any child can draw. We call these *icons*.

This skill of signifying common representations is essential to survival. We each need to perceive gross forms to live in the world.

Iconic signs are the first part of the process of abstracting for the purpose of cognition. This enables each of us to apprehend the myriad relationships presented through the senses, and sort them into relations internal to objects and those that are external to and between objects. It further enables active participation in the world around us. I can focus on this or that tree without having to contend with the internal relations between leaves and branches. I can pick up a cup or walk over to the shore or jump away from a predator. Such activities presuppose that I cognize the relationships between myself and my surroundings at large, including the relations among the objects in my surroundings.

That we see a tree and not just an assemblage of leaves and branches brings a focus on the object at large. It is these objects at large that get related to other objects at large. The cup is on the table. I would relate the cup handle to the cup, and then the cup to all the other parts that make up the room. I perceive the many individual relations between the table, the floor, the walls, etc. Actually, I perceive in gross terms a cup, table, floor, walls, etc.

Concepts or ideas are cognitions of simultaneous integral presentations. They pertain to the formal/relational aspects of what is apprehended, including the relation between the structure or form of a thing and any specific substantive qualities that are simultaneously essential, such as shape, color, texture, and other qualities. As relations change over time, we each learn to conceptualize the patterns of the changing dynamics we are conscious of. Some of these patterns appear causal, and others simply infer.

While signs imply cognition of a sequence of happenings, there are other relations between events that can be understood. There are similarities and differences between objects, and even between conscious apprehensions, or in the order of similar experiences.

Consciousness is a field of apprehensions that mirrors the complex energy dynamics of the world, not at the level of energy interactions, but at the level of things. Experience is more like a patterned sequence of happenings rather than a simple linear ordering. Conceiving, or having ideas about something, is the active apprehension of the pattern of conscious apprehensions. That is, our experiences are partly structured by what is actually perceived, but are also structured by how the mind is able to connect the gross relations between objects in dynamic and complex ways. Some order is given in perception, and in the way in which we each experience the world from our unique vantage point. However, the apprehension by the mind that there is an ordered pattern to experience is based on a consciousness of many possible pattern relations generalized through conceiving, and this is what allows us to order our experiences with a sense of familiarity. This starts with signs.

Rings around the moon do not cause rain, but indicate or signify a pattern of events leading to rain. The sign is a first-order abstraction of the pattern relationships apprehended over iterative events. X tends to lead to or be associated with Y. This type of cognition involves the interplay of memories, presentations, forms of intuition, and the mind's activity of trying to make sense of what is apprehended in experience. This making sense has survival value.

"I" am also part of the flow. I act on the world, choosing to look at X rather than Y, or picking up this book while ignoring that one. My unique position is also relative to any memories being formed of the pattern of events and relations. "Now" is extended in the sense that my experience might also include associations with memories of similar events, and what followed. This leads to more complex associations between the signs themselves.

A further abstraction would be to conceive of the pattern of signs in relation to each other and not just in relation to my perceptual experiences. This kind of further abstraction means that I might envision an association of signs without there being a perception happening at that moment. For example, the rings around the moon indicate that it might rain, but it is not raining now. This gives rise to the phenomenon that I can be cognizant of objects that are detached from current experience. This kind of projection of ideas into a signed order of experience is what separates concepts from percepts. Percepts are contents of my experiences that are present now as a result of perception. Concepts or ideas are of things that I am familiar with, but which are not necessarily being experienced at this moment. What is important to notice here is that the patterned order of events in empirical experience is mirrored in the patterned ordering of signs. The pattern of signs is a direct reflection of the patterned ordering of events in empirical experience. We say that the signs indicate contents of empirical experience.

In the same sense that the child's version of a tree abstracts from perceptions of trees, ideas are further abstractions of signs. At each step of the process from experience to consciousness to associations and signs, more and more of the detailed substantive qualities of objects are removed. While the child's drawing of a tree is certainly tree-like, the concept or idea of a tree is not tree-like. The idea of gravity is not itself gravitational. Conceptions are apprehensions of objects that I can have without requiring a specific instance to be present in perception for such awareness to happen. These more abstract apprehensions or cognitions are referred to by Langer as *symbols*.

To express a conception, we must first identify it. This is the singular common representation of the conception. I conceive a complex form of a type of object (say a tree). While there are many trees, I have one concept tree. Consequently, I note that this is a singular idea that is a common representation of all the internal relations and qualities that make up that object. Moreover, this thing as symbolized can be isolated from its external relations and treated as a "thing in itself" or as a separate entity. This separation of the thing is part of the conceiving that separates the idea or the concept from concrete perceptual experience. Symbols represent types of objects in a singular way. This singular common representation is then named. This is called *denoting*. We denote or name our concepts. Denotations are singular because the form of the concept with its internal relations is considered simultaneously and without a sequence or order of presentation. We have a concept of a tree, not a complex naming of all the parts and their associations. Denotations could be a sound, or a mark in the sand. What makes a denotation a symbol is consistency of use. I must always denote a specific concept the same way. The structure is:

subject + symbol + conception + object (2)

Publicizing ideas is an act of expression. A symbol is associated with the conception of an object. The idea is what is signified by the experience. For example, the object might be dangerous or good to eat. As mentioned, the physical object need not even be present for me to have the idea and to name it.

There are two key points. The first is making a firm and consistent connection between a symbol and a conception or idea. The second, conceiving, involves the process of "stretching" sign relations to a more general form of symbol by adding the conception or idea to the mix. This process makes use of a special class of symbols that provide a richer symbolic inventory based on the signs developed earlier in cognition. These are called symbolic expressions.

Language

Ernst Cassirer's *Philosophy of Symbolic Forms* presents the most in-depth exploration of what our symbolic expressions as forms of thought are, and how these work. Cassirer presents symbolic forms as a kind of "differential calculus," where there is a reciprocal relation between the signifier and what is signified in the formation of the expression.

The heart of his approach is a concept of *symbolic pregnance*. By this, he means, "the way in which a lived perception, as a 'sensuous' experience, contains at the same time a certain non-intuitive 'meaning' which it brings to an immediate and concrete representation."[22] In other words, the meaning of any symbol can only be defined in terms of its relations with every other element of the symbolic structure.

---

22 Cassirer, *Philosophy Of Symbolic Forms*, Vol. III, p. 202.

Where signs' interrelations are patterns mirroring the patterned experience of the world (they indicate empirical experiences), symbols form their own patterned interrelations that may or may not pertain to the ordered pattern of empirical experience. Such symbols form their own systemic structure with its own system of indications. For example, words can indicate a content of experience, but words can also indicate other words. This leads to the possibility that some symbolic forms could be fictitious. They get so wrapped up in their own systemic structure of cross indications that their alignment with the world is lost in the mix.

There are three major kinds of symbolic forms: language, myth/religion, and art. Each symbolic form has its own structure in how it relates its contents to each other, but they can also modify each other.

Each symbolic form constitutes a specific way of seeing or understanding the world. Each symbolic form is its own kind of understanding. For example, how we experience the world linguistically is specific to language. It is similar for myth and religion and for art. They each provide their own kind of understanding. At the same time, each interpenetrates the others to form what we will call an *experiential whole*. Each symbolic form is a kind of moment of *signification* within the whole of experience. Without expressive forms, we would lose what Lofts calls the "concreteness of the lived experience of the world."[23]

Cassirer starts with language. This is the act of linguistic designation. What distinguishes language as a symbolic form is that while signs usually indicate some content in empirical experience, words have the unique ability to indicate other words. This gives language a structure that can be quite independent of empirical experience. We call this denoting in the sense of signifying.[24]

Language begins with the act of making a signifying sound. Cassirer says that we seek to control our situation, and in the process, we sound out a primal "cry"—an explosive rejection of our control over reality. This is the first sense of awareness of the world other than how it presents itself

---

23 Lofts, *Ernst Cassirer*. p. 59.
24 Technically, this is called the *indexical structure* of language. The study of linguistic indexical structures is a subject area of within the study of semiotics

to us.[25] What we are aware of is a sense where we might in some way exert some control over our experiences. This primal cry is more than just a cry of pain or a grunt, because it signifies something beyond the present, beyond the merely personal, and beyond a mere sign of the present, to a significance that needs contemplation—what could be. This function is the beginning of what will later become *meaning*. What is really happening is that my utterance is a sound symbol conveyed to you. It could be a cry of pain, or a sound designating an object that is common to our experiences. I cry out, "Cup." We know from biology and other studies that all higher life forms are extremely good at gestures and mimicry. I cry out "cup" while gesturing to the object, and you mimic me. Our phenomenal-world experiences align on the common object. We are both cognizant that we are both "seeing" an object now denoted as "cup."

To move to the next stage, the primal cry moves toward an ordered sequence of phonetic expressions. We start to associate words with other words and not just contents of experience. This develops a patterned sequence of word indications and associations that is specific to the ordered denoting that is shared across individuals. For example, the tribe joins in with "cup." Each member is consistent in the designation of the sound symbol. This consistency of shared function invests the symbol with a kind of coherence—not empirical coherence, but the coherence of shared experience. The object is common to all members of the tribe, as are its associations and indications. This develops a vocabulary of common objects. Words indicate other words to form a system of word associations that characterizes a language.

Sound symbols are localized to the group or tribe doing the denoting. In the process of developing these symbols through common action across a group of minds, the symbols themselves begin to form an ordered pattern based partly on the patterns of empirical experience, and partly on the ordered pattern of the associations and word indications as these are created by the group. "We" form ordered expressions.

As ordered expressions obtain coherence, they begin to form a symbolic system that contextualizes each phonetic utterance. Words have meaning

---

25 Cassirer is not always clear about this process. We will offer a clarification in the assessment below.

only with other words—within their place in the system of words that evolves. We build on the order of the world as it is presented. Over time, this new ordering process evolves to shift the presentation of the reality from a primary to a secondary role. The world, as presented to us in our experiences, begins to find order, not in its empirical presentation but in the structure and patterned relations of the linguistic process itself.

Symbolic expressions are *functional representations*. Meaning is found in the function, not in the objectifying. Symbols are the idealizations of conscious apprehensions, in and through objectively (or publicly) determined functions. In other words, language makes it possible to recognize ordered events within experience and to demarcate those contents that are public from those that are purely private. We can share experiences and align on their meaning.

Linguistic terms of reference play an increasingly active role in ordering our informational representations. The object there is a "tree." The object here is a "cup." Language starts to form demarcation points that order experience in space, time, and number. Insofar as all symbolic forms present what Cassirer calls structures of consciousness, experiences are stabilized according to linguistic forms within the conscious structure that language provides. Notice, however, that this conscious structure is not an individual structure, but a structure that is common to the group creating the linguistic form. This is what we will refer to as a *virtual public mental structure*.

We collectively systematize common representations as linguistic symbols. Linguistic structures delineate events within the spatial and temporal patterns with increasing signification as common or public conscious structures evolve—as language gains in sophistication.

Language, then, forms a virtual public structure of consciousness that orders experience in a kind of *Weltanschauung* or worldview. Differences between languages are more than just phonetic differences, but differences in conscious structures that provide differing world perspectives. I call these virtual public structures Frameworks.

Symbolic expressions, then, serve two purposes. First, they provide a measure of the commonness of experiences (the function or form), and second, through publicizing, they objectify and provide an order for these experiences. What is important to keep in mind is that language is a virtual public mental structure. It is created and developed among minds in a group. Language is a team sport. Second, each individual's mind within the group is shaped or structured according to the public structure that develops. I think as an English-speaking 21st-century Canadian, which is different from how I would think if I were a French-speaking 12th-century Frank. Respective, virtual public mental structures are the basis of what we call *culture*.

Myth and Religion

What if we tried to understand the world not using science, but in a way that includes our respective uniqueness as part of the understanding? This would inherently include a strong connection between personal meaning and understanding. Such an approach would provide a kind of meaningful understanding of the world. It would be less of an approach about how the world works, and more of an approach of why the world works as it does. This is the essential structure of myth. Myths are not a less rational form of thought; they are simply different, with different objectives and kind of understanding. It is humankind's first attempt at understanding the world, and it presents its own criteria for objectivity. It has its own modes of necessity and its own view of reality. For example, science tries to understand the world in terms of universal causal principles, such as gravity. It is enough to know that the reason the apple fell is due to gravitation. But mythical thinking wants to know why this or that particular apple? Why did this event happen to that person? Universal causal laws in and of themselves simply do not meet those requirements. We need something else—something more.

While science seeks to understand how the parts work, for mythical thinking, there is no distinction between wholes and parts. The world is a coherent system and cannot be reduced to a whole-part–part-whole set of relations. The destiny of any so-called part is tied in with the destiny of the whole, so we need to understand whole destinies to understand the why for this or that element of the whole. Cassirer calls this sympathy for the whole, which is a magical sympathy: "All things that are united by this sympathy, all things that 'correspond' to one another or support one another magically coalesce into the unity of a magical genus."[26] Myths are an esthetic fantasy, where the principle of *post hoc ergo propter hoc* (before this, therefore, because of this) forms the primary sequence of experience. Anything can connect to anything else in a given place or moment. Animals that come out of their burrows in spring bring the spring with them. The swallow "makes" the summer.

Mythical thought is permeated with the objective character and force of a symbolic form, which is the result of the shared experience that makes it a virtual public mental structure. We call this magic. Magic is such an integral part of mythical thought that Cassirer usually speaks of the magical/mythical consciousness. Word magic comes from the fact that words indicated other words detached from empirical experience. This detachment forms the basic activity for mythical thinking. Mythical thinking is based in the distinction between the ordered structure of empirical experience, and the ordered structure of language, which can be independent of empirical experience. Mythical thought tries to bridge the gap. Mythical thought is concrete, because it fuses the object with its signification. In Equation 1 above, sign and object are fused such that when we add the third term from Equation 2—symbol—we are adding it to a fused conception/object.

subject + symbol + conception/object   (3)

This means that the magical worldview is saturated with an atmosphere of efficacy. It becomes the translation and transposition of the world of subjective emotions and drives into a sensuous objective experience. Historically, this is the first sense of a personal subject in the sense of an "I." It is the first attempt to place the "self" as an independent being opposed to the world. Man no longer simply accepts the world as given, but builds it up with his own view of reality—his own worldview (*Weltanschauung*): "This is man's first and most primitive form of consciousness of his ability to give form to reality."[27] Life is an undivided whole as part of an undivided cosmos.

---

26 Cassirer, *Philosophy Of Symbolic Forms*, Vol. II, p. 182.
27 Ibid, p. 157.

Mythical thought traces the whole back to the source or reason for an event or action. For the mythical image, this is simply life itself. Cassirer states, "Mythical fantasy drives toward animation, toward a complete 'spiritualization' of the cosmos, but the mythical form of thought … leads to … a kind of materialization of spiritual content."[28] All mythical thinking is impregnated with spiritual significance. In other words, all contents of experience are not only symbolized linguistically, but there is spiritual signification in all common representations. This is what all contents of experience are symbolic of. This is the joining of the conception/object. Mythical symbols develop their own form or structure, which is just as coherent and material as language, and just as well grounded in our experiences. As with language, mythical symbols indicate other mythical symbols to form a systematic web of mythical thought that has its own structure based on empirical experience and language but which is separate from both. This produces a mythical indexical structure that brings all mythical symbols into a coherent systematic whole. Each community develops its own virtual public mythical mental structure.

There are two dimensions of mythical thought. The first is narrative, and the second is the *reality of actions* or rituals, which are part of the expressive, symbolic form. Mythical symbols are developed as narratives for the source or reason for an event in experience. These symbolic forms are then acted out or lived in ritualistic actions. The narratives and rituals are not intended as an allegorical explanation of the world. They are much more like lived events.

When we see the shaman put on the bearskin and do the bear dance around the fire, we, from our modern scientific perspective, tend to be rather condescending. "Oh, look, isn't that cute. He's pretending to be a bear spirit."

We need to understand that for the shaman, this is absolutely false. He is pretending nothing. He can and does *become* the bear spirit.

In primitive mythology, all forces are anthropomorphized as spirits. In this sense, spirits are *in* everything. They are in rocks, trees, flowers, animals, and so on. The whole world is understood in the context of the function of spirits, which are symbolized to explain not just why the world

---

28 Ibid, pp. 55–71.

works, but to expand on the meaning of the world itself. Through the role of spirits, experience is explained. But such explanations then become inseparable from our perceptions of the world; that is, spirits become part of what is represented in experience. Percepts and concepts become simply two sides of the same coin (the conception/object). The shaman experiences life this way. So integral is this process of felt, integrated symbolizing to the basic process of thought that it forms the essence of experience itself. This shapes understanding and meaning. Through the symbolic expressions of group ritual action based on narrative, these spiritual forms have the same objectivity as all other experiences. They are just as real. The shaman is of the bear clan, and his life force is explained and is meaningful in and through the narrative ritual of the dance. In and through the ritual activity as lived, he *is* the living expression of the spirit. He cannot understand the world in any other way. It is what he *means* by understanding.

The heart of ritual activities is the *sacred*. The mythical image of the sacred is a kind of structural schema or template used to construct and organize the world. All reality divides into the sacred and the *profane*. The difference pertains to mythical illumination. To the extent that an action or event is not meaningfully explained within the schema, it remains profane and outside the need of ritual action or intervention. We do not need to explain mundane activities such as eating or drinking in the same way that we need to explain birth or illness. I eat because I am hungry. No further explanation is needed. But why is Bob ill, and not Harry? What spirit has impacted Bob to cause such an event? A general law that applies across all mythical thought is the "law of concrescence or coincidence of the members of a relation."[29]

Mythical thought forms a virtual public mental structure in which all differences are reduced to a kind of spiritual reality. For example, mythical space is not space as we think of it in empirical terms. It is more like a sense of *place* than space. The meaning of a thing pertains to its place within the whole and in its proximity to the sacred. Mythical space is created from a kind of repeatable place structure, which is defined by the schema of the sacred. Each mythical form, of course, presents its own schema of the

---

29 Cassirer, *Philosophy Of Symbolic Forms*, Vol. II, pp. 64–82.

sacred. As each language is developed within the local tribe, each mythical form develops according to its own group and experiences. Each culture is constructed according to its own worldview. The sense of place defines the meaning of why A is here and not there.

Mythical time is bound up with life as an activity. It is less about temporality than about the moment and proximity to the sacred. This gives rise to the idea of the *holy*, in the sense of holy days, for example. Holy days are life days: when to plant and harvest the crops, birth days and death days, battle days. Mythical time is really about the anticipation of holy events and consecration in preparation for these moments. The past is an absolute past that lives in the present (sympathy for the whole of the universe unfolding) and is lived as the sacred meaning of the present. The source or reason for an event is found within the whole of the cosmos in relation to the sacred in this place and moment. Again, these moments are reinforced through narrative, and lived through ritual actions. Myth is not about space and time, but place and moment. The universe unfolds according to a divine plan, and we are part of the fabric of that unfolding. In a modern Western Christian society, we might say that I have a place and moment in God's creation as part of His plan. All myths and religions have a similar idea or expression. There is no modern sense of past or future that can indicate empirical causal chains or predicted events. The cosmos unfolds as it was meant to in what Christian scholars called "the great chain of being".

Mythical thought has its own form or symbolic structure and yields its own combination of understanding/meaning. However, mythical forms are not static structures, but rather embodiments of life energy. We are all active participants in a cosmological unfolding. We are all in this place and moment for a divine reason. The cosmos is invested with a kind of life force or *manna* that connects all things within the unfolding whole.

The overriding intent of mythical thought is to get at the unity of everything. Within the individual, this develops into a strong desire to identify oneself with the community and with spiritualized nature in a way that is not possible with scientific understanding. For example, cult actions center around the desire to connect with or communicate with gods or spirits via an offering, intercession, thanks, or atonement.

This is the origin of the ritual of *sacrifice*: "The sacrificial service is fixed by very definite objective rules, a set sequence of words and acts which must be carefully observed if the sacrifice is not to fail in its purpose."[30] Sacrifices are a form of magic spell. Magic, at its core, is little more than wish fulfillment. Demons and gods have a will that can be made to serve the individual or group, but only if the proper observances are made. This entrenches ritual across the community and engages all members in the virtual mythical mental structure. The feeling of self is fused with the feeling of community, and this provides the drive for the unity of family, tribe, and community.

Cultic expressions are derived from the unifying drive of tribe and community to both create and reinforce devotion to the gods and spirits. When Cassirer puts these considerations together, he traces the evolution of mythical/religious forms from the primitive to the modern. His explanation of the transition to modernity is a rough guide, but hits the salient points. From the idea of the sympathy for the whole and place and moment in the unfolding of the cosmos comes the common representations of the forces of nature in the form of the spiritualization of the world. These spirits are the bringers of the seasons, and of night, and the unifying forces of the place and moment in the cosmic unfolding.

Spirits behave as subjects, not just as objective observances or significations. This break from the primitive and vague objectivity of spirit forms toward subjective participation marks the break between myth and religion. Cassirer refers to this as a transition from *mythos* to *ethos*—from spirit cult to the distinctive spirit or character of a culture. We progress from primitive spiritualization to a more significant cultural form of shared feeling of community. We represent the spirit forms in a more concrete and objective way. The mythical virtual public mental structure is reinforced and enhanced.

All religions begin in cultic, mythical thinking but break away to form a different religious attitude of individual relations with the cosmic unfolding. Religion incorporates mythical thought, but adds sensuous images and signs, which it then recognizes as the means of spiritual expression.

---

30 Ibid, p. 121.

Early religious forms develop *totems*. Totemism is the magical connection between humans and animals, usually expressed in terms of the hunt. The real hunt is preceded by a mythical hunt. Such magical thinking makes the hunt successful. This experienced and felt magical relation leads to clarifying the character traits of the various animals that are identified culturally as clans. Clans are not just descended from animals but really are these animals. The ritual eating of the animal in the communal sacral feast is the means of renewing the blood kinship that "binds the individual members of the clan with one another and with their totem."[31] The sacral feast is one of many community activities, along with drinking and sex, that have sacred significance.

As our religious symbolic forms became more sophisticated and abstracted, we represented these in ritual manifestations such as masks and costumes, and then in statues called *idols*. The mythical image was given a concrete form. Idols did not represent the spirits, but became the embodiment of the spirits, similar to the acts of the shaman, but with an objectification of place and moment. What is important in this development is that the spirits took on an objective form with specific characteristics. Idolatry is a characteristic of all polytheistic religions. It is their defining characteristic. The idols become the focal point for the ritual actions. The main activity in the relation between human and spirits remains sacrifice, although we now sacrifice in the presence of the idol. A key development is a growing hierarchy of connectedness with spirit forms. Rituals become increasingly complex and require greater specialization. Local shamans give way to priests.

Under the priesthood, spirit forms coalesce into the gods. But there is a break from polytheism to monotheism, which is more than just a break from idolatry. From gods to one God requires a sophisticated transition to combine characteristics among gods. There is an evolutionary trend from vague spirits that coalesce into totems, which then coalesce into gods, which coalesce further into God. God can have no idol, so all idolatry must be banned. Modern religions are not banishing representations of gods, but the gods themselves in the face of God.

---

31 Ibid, p. 227.

Cassirer points to epic poetry as part of the evolutionary steps from primitive myth to religiosity. Poetry evolves into prayer and the cadences and meters of songs and religious expressions, and becomes *prayer*. Prayer is the same manifestation of magical wishful thinking that is the basis of sacrifice: "*Prayer*, like sacrifice, aims to bridge the gulf between God and man. But in prayer, the means is not merely physical but symbolic and ideal: the power of the word."[32] The power of prayer contains the magic to compel the godhead with words. Prayer, like sacrifice, has an "infallible and irresistible power."[33] The actions in religion are not so much the power of dance with appropriate costumes, or ritualistic sacrifices in the presence of an idol, but the songs and meters that govern the objective world. The *Weltanschauug* of religiosity reaches its current peak. From this it is easy to see why religion forms the core of culture, and eventually civilization.

Frameworks

First, symbolic forms provide a worldview from which to think about the world. Symbolic forms that present a virtual, public mental structure literally shape our thinking, be it through language or myth/religion. Second, these structures are systematic in nature. That is, our symbols form a system of thinking; they are integrated. Symbolic forms inter-accommodate, interpenetrate, and support each other. Symbolic forms draw from the patterned interactions of empirical experience, but form their own pattern of interconnections. Once we have the word, the word can have symbolic power in prayer, which provides support for the language we use to express understanding and/or meaning.

To develop a systematic structure of language we need only two rules: First, there must be a tacit agreement about the sound symbol and what it symbolizes. Second, we must be tacitly consistent in symbolic expression.

When I call the object of experience a "tree," I am denoting the concept plus object. I am attaching a symbol to the concept plus object, as in Equation 2 above. I have used an expressive form to designate a content of

---

32 Ibid, p. 229.
33 Ibid.

experience. The sound transmits the signal, with its information, to you. The consistency rule is formally called the Principle of Mutual Exclusivity. This term comes from psychologist Ellen Markham's studies on how children learn a language.[34] Simply put, this means that objects cannot have two different names. She has discovered that children have difficulty believing that an object can have two names. Markham argues that if an object is given a second label, then that label must refer to a secondary property or attribute of the object: "A child who learns the word elephant knows, with absolute certainty, that it is something different from a dog. Each new word makes the child's knowledge of the world more precise."[35] If the child learned that each elephant could also be a dog, the world would get very complicated very quickly.

The idea emerges that "I" do not create a language, but rather that "we" do. Language is a communal event by definition. Language is not developed by an individual based on innate language modules in the brain or intuitions or preferred grammars, but is developed among individuals in a dynamic, iterative process. It is an inherently public activity.

Language shapes each individual mind according to the structure of the symbolic form that the group develops. The structure is, therefore, virtual in the sense that it is not physical, and public in the sense that it is not the purely subjective structure of any one individual mind. Symbolic forms are shared structures of mind that virtually shape the thinking patterns of each member of the group. We think in English or French or Japanese or Assyrian. Each language is created among the tribe or group.

Mythical thought works the same way. We think as Christians, or Muslims, or within an ancient Egyptian mythical cult. When we do this, we publicize subjective experiences within the shared Framework of the group or tribe. Our participation also shapes the Framework itself, as we introduce new ideas or experiences. Because Frameworks are public structures, and it is through these that we align and synchronize subjective experiences, I argue that publicity and objectivity are the same thing.

Frameworks are the collective joining of our symbolic forms. So far, we have language and myth/religion. These inter-accommodate with each

---

34 This material is reported by Malcolm Gladwell in *The Tipping Point*, page 196.
35 Ibid, p. 113.

other to form a systematic whole. Once we understand Frameworks, we can begin to understand why we think the way that we do. Frameworks can and do evolve under mechanisms.

1. **Expanding the scope of public action.** By and large, the more people who share in the Framework, the more public it is. This implies that a greater tacit agreement of terminology across a larger group will provide clearer designations of what the words mean. It improves the absolute certainty we have that an elephant is not a dog.

2. **Translation.** Group A meets Group B. They have developed different linguistic forms. But when A denotes "tree," and B denotes "*arbre*," they observe that the designation is the same object. This improves the absolute certainty that the object's properties are not secondary.

Expressive forms, such as language, publicize experience through group forms of expression. When these are validated, certainty regarding the object's properties improves. What else could we call this but understanding? What we have done is to make an object's properties public and clear. We have objectified experience in a way that is impossible as an individual mind. We have provided a public reference for what was, previous to language, a purely subjective and personal event. The symbolic form of language provides the first basis for objective understanding. Insofar as certainty improves with public scope, so too does objectivity. Mythical thought enhances the linguistic Framework. Myth provides the first sense of explanation and meaning about why the world is the way it is. Myth, and later religion, develop an entire *Weltanschauung* as a virtual public structure. As a symbolic form, myth literally structures our thinking about the why of the world. This brings us to art as a symbolic form. Mythical/religious structures follow the same rules as for language. The more people who believe the more objective the belief is. The more commonality we find between group myths, the more objective those beliefs appear to be.

Art

Word magic and picture magic stand at the center of the magical world-view and are the basic forms of objectification as a cultural esthetic: "It is the sensuous embodiment of cultural meaning and cultural identity that is found in tastes, smells, sounds, tactile impressions and visual gestalts."[36] Art is the equilibrium between the world of expression and the world of signification. Art renders symbolic reality visible by harmonizing expression and representation—subject and object—in an esthetic imagination that discovers the pure forms of things and renders them accessible to the world. Cassirer distinguishes three dimensions of the work of art—physical existence, objective representation, and personal expression. These are three ways of understanding the same reality. The artist weaves the artist's own formed sensuous material "into a differentiated but organic whole that represents the living form of nature or spirit."[37]

Art deals with the forms or structure of experience – both empirical and symbolic. In the same way that language is detached from empirical experiences, art expresses the forms of thought independent of content. It seeks meaning in the virtual mental structures themselves.

As the real world brings order to our experiences, and as the mind enhances that order with symbolic Frameworks, art delineates and expresses that abstract form. Art moves through the media of space, time, and all other forms of symbolic expressions. A spectrum of artistic expression and activity flows from the spatial, through language and myth, to time. For example, painting and sculpture are essentially spatial in the mode of artistic expression. Literature and poetry relate to linguistics and often seek to express the form of the mythical, whereas music has its origins in ritual and is primarily temporal. In fact, music might be the only purely temporal symbolic form that we have, thus revealing the nature of temporal symbolic forms across many kinds of experience. Even poetry has a rhythm, and so approaches the form of music.

Art provides order to our apprehensions as it also raises the level of abstraction from myth and religion. Art is universal, often springing from

36 op cit, p. 185..
37 Ibid, p. 196

language and religion in an attempt to express the forms themselves, or at least to clarify the expressive nature of the symbolic forms. The pure sense of form characterizes art as a symbolic expression. All art is symbolic. But rather than being symbolic of empirical world contents as language or mythology, art does the reverse. Art uses an experiential content and *expresses an element of the virtual, public symbolic structures of language and myth.* This is why art reflects and articulates the collective consciousness of the community that shares the worldview as derived by language or myth. Art is determining and reflexive of the community and the culture from which it springs. Art does this through its choice of subject matter. This is why art is cultural. There is Egyptian art, European art, Greek art, Anasazi art, and so on.

Art reveals an aspect of the cultural Framework while clarifying the deeper meanings. Art always seeks to express the universal (the Framework) in its purest form, and because art is intrinsically expressive, it objectifies these universal forms. This is why art appears so ethereal. It uses contents to reveal symbolic forms in contrast to normal thought, which uses symbolic forms to reveal content. It is important that both reveal meaning, and that both objectify and clarify that meaning. This is why art resonates within a culture in a way that craft does not.

Art objectifies the forms of thought. It expressively reveals the structure of Frameworks. Through art, the members of the community can shape the collective forms themselves. Each culture has its own forms of art, and expresses its pure forms in its own way. For this reason, art as a form of expression is ubiquitous, but as individual to specific groups as are language and myth/religion. Like language and myth, art adds to the collective dimension that can reflect back on the community, and on the individuals within the community.

Frameworks

Frameworks are virtual public mental structures that are formed through the specific interactions we each have with others in how we form our languages and beliefs about the world. Of course, our choice of language contributes to our beliefs and vice versa. They are both reinforced with artistic expressions that serve to publicize the structure of the Framework itself. A codependency web across each symbolic form is built up over time. This results in a system of forms within which thinking happens. The group Framework characterizes the culture, and because it is built up over time, forms the traditions of any tribe or group. Frameworks develop iteratively and over time in various layers or levels, from individual subjective thinking to individual objective expressions, to familial thought through to tribal or community structures. At each stage, the Framework grows in structure, comprehension, and objectification.

The objectification of the Framework is achieved through the simple process of including other persons. Two people who share a particular way of doing things pass this way on to others, their children, or other members of the community. In the absence of such others having a personal or cultural biography of "why we do things this way," such ways are objectified as the way things are. For example, a newly married couple will develop ways of doing things that are particular to them as a result of learning how to live together. They will share a biography of how these ways of doing things evolved. Their children will learn how to do things their parents' way. But without the biography of how these ways developed, children accept them as the way it is. The same principle holds true with tribes and communities. As Tribe A shows Tribe B how they do things, they broaden the Framework of Tribe B. At the same time, they enhance the reach of their own ways, and because Tribe A does not share a tribal biography with Tribe B, Tribe B objectifies their way as the way things are.

This simple mechanism helps to explain how the Framework itself grows and evolves and becomes entrenched. Within any historical time or space (period or geography), how things *are* can be determined. Egyptians believe in x and y, and Assyrians believe in w and z. Each developed their own ways of doing things. However, to each group, these were not simply the way we do things, but were the way things are! To behave differently or to understand differently would require that each person either adopt a new Framework, or sufficiently modify their own Framework to assimilate the ways of the other. Of course, in the latter case, the Framework is modified, but not replaced.

This helps to explain why it is so difficult to change people. The Framework actually structures our mind, such that we think within the Framework. All understanding and meaning is found in the objectification inherent in such a public context. In short, the Framework defines the cultural and epistemological context that we each use to understand the world as we experience it. However, the Framework is so complex that moving people outside of their Framework to be purely objective (in the sense that they understand the world independently of cultural context) is extremely difficult. We all live and experience the world around us within some Framework. Without such a Framework, no understanding would be possible. Further, the Framework we live within defines what understanding is objectively true for each of us. Objective understanding is all about the way things are. We can each dream of changing the world, but the reality of the Framework will always impose on such dreams. The most we can hope for is to understand enough of another tribe's Framework to assimilate their perspective into a new understanding. With this method, we might make some sense of these strange views, but until our Framework is modified, these new ideas will never really be our own. We might, though, be tolerant of such strangeness given our newfound understanding.

In this sense, the Framework is multilayered. There are natural forms provided by our environment, as well as many layers of personal, cultural, and tribal forms involving the state, our local community, our place of work, and our family. We each have a place within the hierarchy of the community. This sense of place contributes to the Framework, and our respective understanding and meaning in the world.

For example, consider someone who travels from a tropical climate to a winter climate. Such a person, who has never experienced extended periods of snow, ice, and cold winds, would have to relearn many habits, from how to walk on ice without slipping, to how to dress to keep warm. Of course, the reverse would be true for the person from a winter climate moving to the tropics. There are survival techniques that are formalized and learned in childhood, and reinforced throughout life regarding how to live safely in a specific geography and climate. Family, tribe, and other social structures might set and uphold these forms, especially where the safety of members of the community is concerned.

In addition, societies are arranged in hierarchies such that roles for family and work can vary significantly for individual members. This then means that there can be different expectations regarding how we must act within the community, as well as how people understand and find meaning in their lives. These hierarchies define one's sense of place and moment within the community. It is these hierarchies that we need to explore next.

Social Patterns Within Frameworks

Barry Oshry is the founder of Power + Systems Inc., a not-for-profit educational corporation operating out of Boston, MA. In his quest to understand the mysteries of power and powerlessness in social systems, he developed a large-scale organizational simulation called *Power Lab*. In the simulation, participants role-play within a defined set of structural parameters. Observers record behaviors, and then they analyze the results with participants. The simulation methods and results are recorded in his book, *Seeing Systems*. The title comes from an observation that social systems are systemic structures, but that we tend not to see the whole system. Rather, we focus on the part of the system we are in. Oshry contends that this failure to see the whole system and our part and place within it is an underlying causal factor in many of our behaviors.

Over the many years and many Power Labs, several consistent and pervasive patterns have emerged. These results provide a way to understand the finer details of how people think within Frameworks. Symbolic forms provide a high-level overview of virtual, public mental structures, but we play out our thinking within hierarchical and often complex societies. I argue that more than this, these patterns are the result of Sub-Frameworks (Framework levels within the system of symbolic forms) that are part of how our thinking is structured.

Oshry creates a society of Tops, Middles, Bottoms, and Customers. These can either be construed as positions within society or as conditions that we all face within our communities. Tops have responsibility for all or part of the action. Bottoms are at the receiving end of initiatives over which they have no control. Middles are caught between conflicting demands and priorities. There are also Customers, who look to another person or group for products or services. Whereas these differentiations define simulation roles, the intent is that we all play some or all of these roles in various situations and at various times in our lives. These are not intended as hard and fast distinctions or to simply mirror social stratifications. These roles are intended to be generic enough that they can apply across a wide variety of social structures from families to corporations to tribes and whole societies. The roles could be political, commercial, social, economic, or cultural.

Oshry claims that when we do not see systems, we miss partnership opportunities, misunderstand and possibly hurt one another, become antagonists rather than collaborators, remain strangers, and generally squander much of the potential of the system. There are five kinds of *system blindness*.

Spatial blindness is when we only see part of the system. We see our part but not other parts, let alone the whole. We do not know what is happening elsewhere, and we act on incomplete information. We do not see how our actions impact other parts of the system, or how our part is impacted by actions happening in other parts. We miss how all parts influence each other. This can lead to developing stereotypes and taking things personally even when actions are not really personal at all.

Temporal blindness is a focus on the present, but without consideration of the past. We focus on the now, but we do not take into account what has led to the current situation. This can lead to misdiagnosis, or to fixing what does not need fixing, or missing what *does* need fixing.

Relational blindness occurs when we do not see ourselves in systemic relationships. We feel burdened or oppressed, disappointed, or indignant. There is much personal stress and pain, and we fail to develop partnerships. System contributions are lost.

Process blindness comes from not seeing systems as wholes. We miss systemic differentiations and shared responsibilities and complexity. We miss opportunities for coalescing or sharing vulnerabilities. Relationships tend to deteriorate over time.

Uncertainty blindness is seeing fixed positions battling fixed positions, but missing the uncertainties underlying each position; the conditions for which there are no obviously correct answers. We escape uncertainty into unassailable positions about responsibility, or vulnerability, or dominance. This blindness leads to righteous battles.

Failing to see systems leads to predictable results. Oshry calls this the *dance of blind reflex*. Each part of the system operates with its own rules and its own reinforcing behaviors. We become entrenched in the part we are playing. The Sub-Framework of each role dominates our thinking and sets the patterns of our decisions and actions.

1. Tops feel burdened by complexity and overwhelming responsibility. They have too much to do and not enough time to do it, and everything is changing too fast. They have incomplete information, and are not sure how effective their decisions are, or even if they have been properly carried out. They look to Middles to support them, but Tops do not think they get adequate support. They are isolated and out of touch with much of the system.

Tops are responsible for the whole system, but they divide responsibility among themselves to manage the complexity. This leads to each Top specializing in their area of responsibility, and to concern for their area even at the expense of other parts of the system. This results in functional silos, where each part of the system works for itself rather than for the system overall. Tops feel a lack of support from each other. Of course, some Tops are more "top" than others, leading to control battles and resentment. Relationships break down.

*

2. Bottoms feel oppressed in and by the system. Higher-ups make decisions that affect their lives, over which they feel they have no control. They are unseen and uncared for. Bottoms never get to see the whole picture, so they do not see any leadership vision they can commit to. They add little value and are largely uninformed.

Bottoms develop an intense sense of groupthink. Members identify with one another based on common causes. The situation becomes "us" versus "them." Bottoms reinforce this division with peer pressure to maintain group unity, which gives the group an inflated sense of value, along with an intense pressure to conform. Those who fail to conform are exiled. Failure to reconcile opposing positions can lead to splintering factions. Those who do not splinter submerge their differences.

*

3. Middles are torn by the system. The Tops and Bottoms pull them in opposing directions. Middles tend to be loners, neither connecting with the Tops nor the Bottoms. Others often see them as indecisive and wishy-washy, with no firm opinions of their own.

Middles tend to one of four behavior patterns:

- They identify and align themselves with Tops, alienating themselves from Bottoms;

- They identify and align themselves with Bottoms, alienating themselves from Tops;

- They bureaucratize themselves to create hurdles to make it difficult for anyone to work with them; and/or

- They try to please all parties and burn out.

Middle groups are non-groups. There is no sense of "we," or any common purpose or mission. Middles are isolated from each other. They are each unique, with little in common with their peers. Middles are competitive, and quick to make judgments, generally based on surface characteristics. They have no collective power and show little interest in being together.

*

4. Customers are righteously done to. They are surprised to discover that the system sees them as a problem rather than an opportunity. They are ignored and inadequately attended

to. Customers make reasonable demands that are greeted with hostility. They feel angry, betrayed, and powerless.

*

These patterns are the direct result of how power relations fine-tune and configure Frameworks. We think in symbols, which provide the high-level forms of virtual, public mental structures. These explain how we develop diverse cultures, each with its own language, myths, and art forms. Symbolic forms explain the intrinsic patterns of community and culture. But communities are also structured in organizational hierarchies. Frameworks also have hierarchical patterns within communities, and these forms structure our thinking within the community. They also then contribute back to the larger culture. The Oshry system defines the intrinsic hierarchical properties of our virtual, public mental structures.

If we think of social configurations as thought forms, the patterns of behavior begin to make sense. Tops think in terms of responsibility, and how to deal with complexity. Bottoms get stuck in integration. And Middles are alone, unstructured, and without cohesion. Any organizational system only works when all parts of the system work well together. Hence, Tops, Middles, and Bottoms must see the whole system and their place within it. At the end of the day, the system needs all its parts working together, not just this or that part partially cohering. All the issues of alienation, feelings of responsibility, failures, and isolation are the result of a mental focus on a particular part of the system as though it were isolated. This leads to very specific behaviors from each group. Because they are not well supported, Tops tend to take on even more responsibilities (take charge to do for themselves), which increases complexity and leads to further directional and functional differentiations. They then complain that their policies and visions were not properly understood or carried out by others. Bottoms increasingly reject responsibility, passing it off to higher-ups because it is "them" who must lead "us"; then they complain that they have no control and are oppressed. Middles align themselves with Tops or Bottoms, alienating themselves from both, then complain about their isolation.

As with the larger symbolic forms, Top, Middle, and Bottom Frameworks in a community structure thinking. Each organizational role falls into its own version of groupthink. Tops learn to think and behave as leaders and take greater charge. Bottoms learn to think in their own version of groupthink to fight oppression and perceived leadership failures. Middles remain as unique individuals and fail to cohere to intermediate properly between Tops and Bottoms. Each part of the society thinks and acts in isolation of the others and in their own conflicting manner. We then all wonder why we cannot get our act together as a society—why there is so much antagonism and potential for violence. Add to the mix competition between tribes and communities, and we can readily see how difficult it is to change behaviors toward a peaceful, ecologically sound, and well-managed world. In all of this, we find that social structures and hierarchies are the direct result of power structures. Social elites take charge and divide up social responsibilities. They control energy and resources to keep people in their place. They decide when and where to challenge competing groups or conquer more land.

In systems terms, power structures are inherently unstable (dysfunctional), and this is the source of their unviability. They become dysfunctional because communities lose their sense of the whole, and break into the social thought patterns that are endemic to hierarchies. To make matters worse, elites or Tops must ensure their sphere of control, so they implement controls that constrain social development toward systematic harmony. Power structures become based on divide-and-conquer strategies. Tops control the masses by placing controls that ensure hierarchies and ensure their place as Tops. They oppress Bottoms, and they create social silos to keep Middles isolated from each other. Tops divide and conquer both vertically and horizontally across the society, creating social classes or castes. They do so by controlling energy and resources, and maintaining control on force mechanisms, such as laws and military. In most societies, law is a force monopoly by definition, and only the state gets to have a military. Non-state militias within a community are called rebels. All of this creates and sustains the hierarchical relations that define societies as power structures under Father Culture. In other words, they create the conditions for their own failure to be viable and sustainable.

The result is that we are all trapped in various kinds of groupthink that constrain our ability to change - including changing for the better. We are constrained from seeing the whole system, and so are trapped in various dances of blind reflex.

Meaning

Frameworks can be defined as virtual public mental structures composed of the explicit linguistic, religious, and artistic symbolic forms established by any tribe or group. When combined with specific contents of experience of the natural world, they provide the context within which we can understand our experiences and objectify that understanding. Within the social context of the public community structure, we also find a sense of place and significance. These Sub-Frameworks are formed out of the hierarchical structure of society, as characterized by the Oshry model. As these are virtual, public mental structures, they are also objective. Thinking within Frameworks leads to truth. This is why Oshry's behaviors can become so entrenched. It is not just that as a Bottom, I don't see my place in the system. I, as part of the we, am oppressed, and this shared oppression is objectively true and therefore real. This is a publicly reinforced truth (groupthink). I must behave this way because that is what the system demands of me.

Through such objective understanding, we each as individuals find a sense of *place* in our environment and in our community. Place can refer to position or status in any social unit, and can vary with social units. For example, a man might be head of the household with his family, but on the low end of the pecking order at work or in the community.

How we each interact with others, given the specific nature of the Framework in which we live, provides social meaning. We must each find our place in the world, and through finding such a place, meaning becomes possible. In a very real sense, we are individuals living and thinking in a sea of objective/public forms. The natural environment, combined with our social and cultural environment, forms the context within which we live. Our religious beliefs provide the context within which we understand the why of the world. Science provides understanding of the how of the world. Art reinforces Frameworks by rendering them public and explicit. Social position provides the form for how I interact with my peers and other parts of the system. Within these Frameworks, we need to find our role both in contributing to the community and in benefiting from the joint efforts of all members of the community. We might be a great hunter, or shaman, or artist, or healer. The point is that we perform these tasks within the context of the understanding that is provided by the Framework itself. Meaning is found in what we do and how we live.

To maintain a sense of meaning, we must do more than contribute to the community. We must contribute to and maintain the Framework. The Framework is the public structure of mind that determines how we think and therefore live. It provides the form of understanding, place, and meaning in our lives. Should our Frameworks be destroyed, all understanding and meaning would be destroyed with them. Frameworks are public sources of objective understanding. As objective knowledge is what we use most to survive and to enhance our lives, we cannot underestimate the significance of our Frameworks for providing meaning. Most individuals find meaning in their family or in their work, through which they make their contribution to the community. A testament to the strength of our Frameworks is that such meaning can be found directly within these narrow public contexts. Indeed, Frameworks provide the only public context for approval or rejection, for success or failure. This is part of the reason groupthink is so attractive.

When we as individuals accept and live within the Frameworks and hierarchies of our community, we have a responsibility to promote, protect, and maintain those Frameworks. After all, if they were destroyed, so would all sense of understanding and meaning. The power of public perceptions and ideas can override even the most basic of our instincts. Consider the woman who has suffered the horrors of female circumcision, yet feels bound to the Frameworks of the community to pass on the atrocity to her daughters even to the point of overriding her feelings of love and a natural instinct to protect her offspring. Frameworks objectify her existence and her understanding and meaning in the world. This is not just "how we do things"; it is the way it is, and we might add, the way it must be. In this way, traditions are maintained even against the most personal and tragic aversions to such behaviors. How can one fight against reality? How can one conquer objective understanding with personal aversions? How can we find meaning in a world where there are no communal, public, and objective Frameworks within which meaning could be found?

We are each obligated to support and promote our respective Frameworks and defend them because, without them, we are reduced to solipsistic subjects, alone and divided from the world and from each other. Frameworks structure the mind itself. How could we think any other way than that which is determined by our Frameworks? Surely, such thinking would be aberrant or questionable. For example, a modern scientist placed in the 16th century would be burned at the stake for heresy. Even simple tools such as artificial respiration would be viewed as witchcraft. There were no Frameworks for any (what we now think of as) rational understanding of how such a technique could possibly work. People living in that time would, however, have a Framework that would explain what happened, and what the consequences should be for the perpetrator. Likewise, while it would make sense to want to grow up to be a shaman if one lived in 14th-century America, it makes little sense in the 21st century. However, to want to be a priest or a corporate executive or a scientist makes very good sense.

Frameworks, then, are multilayered assemblages of communal thought patterns that form the basis of understanding and meaning. While there is a common Framework in the sense of a nation, there are *Micro-Frameworks* in families, local communities, age groups, peer groups, work groups, special-interest groups, common-interest groups, clubs, associations, teams, and so on throughout any community. Each of these promotes a tendency to see only their local part at the expense of the whole.

CHAPTER 3
Ishmael and the Parable of the Tribes

Ishmael

Ishmael is a 2,000-pound gorilla who has studied human history and learned to communicate with humans. He is a fictional character, created by Daniel Quinn in his novel *Ishmael*. Ishmael represents a look into our times from outside our species. He considers that humans are destructive, and that we are heading for self-destruction. These trends include nuclear and biological weapons, ecological destruction, famine, war, and the many ways that people destroy the garden we call Earth.

Ishmael asks two questions: "Why are things the way they are?" and "How did they get this way?"

The answer provides a new perspective on how to approach ethics and civilization. I will explore how things got this way in greater detail than Quinn does in *Ishmael*, and will then challenge that detail.

Homo sapiens, as a species, evolved pretty much as we are today by about 100,000 years ago. About 10,000 years ago, we began what is now called the Agricultural Revolution. All ideas about civilization begin there. To historians, what comes before this is prehistory, and nothing much happened.

Ishmael points out that for 90,000 years, humans lived in small tribes, and completely in harmony with nature. There were tribal disputes and challenges to the animal kingdom, but overall it was a peaceful and prosperous time. Disease was rare, food was plentiful, and the workload needed to survive was light. There was time for culture and art, and many tribes produced great works of art. There was also a great sense of human spirit, and a connection to the world. We know this because we have studied primitive peoples still living this way.

About 10,000 years ago, in the Fertile Crescent in the Middle East, a new kind of culture emerged. Humans discovered agriculture. This meant that there were genuine food surpluses for the first time. It also meant that people had to settle to manage their crops. This is the beginning of towns and cities, and the opportunity for a group of tribesmen to focus on special tasks outside of survival skills. For example, tools were needed, as were vessels to store food, and a method of distributing food. These tasks were not directly related to feeding the tribe, but were essential for the survival of the city. This was also the introduction of a hierarchical society, and of a method of exchanging goods.

Generally, more readily available food means that there can be more people. More people means that you must grow more food. More food means yet again more people, which means even more food is needed— and so on until the present day. To grow more food requires more arable land. But the process is static. That is, the land is used until it is depleted (bleached), and then the farmer must move on. But farmers must settle in the area they move into, to develop the land. They must protect arable land in any area to be cultivated.

This introduces the first new concept in human development: that it is acceptable to dominate an area of land, and to deprive others of access to it. Ishmael refers to this as a violation of a fundamental law of nature—the Peace Law, or the *Law of Limited Competition*.

Humans violate this law at all turns. First, we exterminate our competitors. Second, we destroy our competitors' food to make room for our own. Third, we deny our competitors' access to food. In short, we wage total war against nature.

No other species behaves this way. No species kills just to destroy competition. No other species denies another species food or access to food. Animals kill for food, but only take what they need. A lion that is sated does not prevent another predator from hunting a herd. The herd does not belong to the lion. In addition, lions do not set up barriers to deny their competitors access to a herd. In the natural world, all creatures obey the Law of Limited Competition. This promotes diversity, which increases the richness of the ecosystem, as well as the survival options for all species.

Ishmael points out that the Agricultural Revolution was not a radical innovation, but an occurrence that happened over time. For example, it does not take a food scientist to notice that seeds dropped in a spot of soil grow to produce the same kind of plant that the seed came from. From there, tribes might simply plant seeds for food they found particularly tasteful or enjoyable. As they grew more and more of these foods, and as these new quantities dominated their food sources, they would naturally continue the process. Over time, a way of thinking was formed. This process became objectified from "how we do things," to "this is the way things are."

The introduction of agriculture marked the point in history when humans began to violate the Law of Limited Competition. In an agricultural community, the community owns the land for as long as they can use it. Possession is nine-tenths of the law. The land must be defended from all competitors. As the need for more land grows, land will become unavailable to competitors, and so they will be denied access to food. Any competitor who fails to comply with the new rules would be fair game for extermination. After all, this was war, and there could be no exceptions.

The Agricultural Revolution is still unfolding today. It is what I refer to as Father Culture. Before agriculture, there were only *leavers*, people who obeyed the Law of Limited Competition. Agriculture introduced *takers*, those who own the land at the expense of those who would otherwise have the need of it. In modern parlance, these might be referred to as primitives versus sophisticates, or as ancients versus moderns.

Of course, our sophisticated modern culture is self-destructive, and as a species we have convinced ourselves of our rightness through centuries of rationalizations. We have gods who gave the Earth to humans for human dominion. We have historians and anthropologists who praise those takers who succeed, and who point to the lost cultures of those who failed.

In addition to our failures with nature, humans introduced a new concept about how to treat other humans. Ishmael points out that the rule to "lock up the food that is produced" by agriculture applied not just to other animals, but also to humans. In modern times we would broaden this idea to include resources such as energy, raw materials, and even ideas. Controlling resources is necessary to maintain the division of labor that keeps the community prosperous and well-defended. This was particularly necessary in the beginning, when confronting another tribe that had not embraced a full dependency on cultivation. The issue centers on the amount of labor required to grow food versus simply going into the jungle and gathering it. The former process is very labor-intensive when compared with the latter process. To be absorbed into the conquering tribe would require that the conquered embrace the new reality of how food is obtained. In other words, they must help grow it. Perhaps they will make up the labor force that grows all the food for their new masters. In any case, the only way to force people to work for food is to lock it up so they cannot simply gather what they want. Such masters effectively hold people hostage in exchange for food.

Ishmael introduces several layers of concepts into his presentation. For example, leavers would readily understand that agriculture is non-sustainable and goes against the Law of Limited Competition. Depending on what is grown for so much effort, and against so many opportunities for natural disasters, agriculture must have seemed intuitively wrong-headed. Further, the whole sense of community and the natural support of the community for each individual would have been torn apart. This, too, would have been something to rebel against, or even to fight against.

Consequently, to understand what Father Culture really is, I turn to a parable that outlines how modern sophisticated thinking has worked for 10,000 years. It is a parable by Andrew Schmookler called "The Parable of the Tribes."

The Parable of the Tribes

Imagine a group of tribes living in close proximity in the Fertile Crescent. Tribe A is surrounded by five other tribes: B, C, D, E, and F. In normal tribal interaction, there is some friction. These disputes are settled in a variety of ways, some more violent than others, but overall territory and tribal integrity are preserved. Tribes need to exchange goods, and so depend on each other to some extent. For example, tribes would find mates in surrounding tribes. Generally speaking, they live peacefully together.

Tribe A evolves the dominance of agriculture and all that this entails for social development. Now, disputes must be defended with greater vigor. No other tribe can be allowed to poach on Tribe A's land. Further, Tribe A has resources that the other tribes do not have. It now has the resources to conquer the others. The Parable of the Tribes asks what options the other tribes have in the face of such aggression. There are four possible responses:

1. They can withdraw;

2. They can allow themselves to be conquered or absorbed;

3. They can fight back and be destroyed; or,

4. They can fight back and win.

If there is no place to run, option one is a nonstarter. In any event, even if they run, they still lose their territory, and must start again elsewhere. If they do not move far enough away, they will be constantly challenged.

Options two and three entail losing their identity as a tribe, being absorbed or ceasing to exist. This leaves only option four as a possible solution. They must fight and try to win. To do this, they must wage war with Tribe A, and they must try to do so on A's terms, because A has defined the victory conditions.

This leads to power as the central force in any tribal order. Those who are bigger and stronger win. Might means right. To lose is to lose both quality and quantity of life. It is the cult of power. It is a way of thinking that we call *the master–servant approach to living.*

It is evident how this will work in practice. Tribe A attacks Tribe B, or moves in and denies Tribe B access to their territory. Tribe A has resources that Tribe B does not have. It can support an army, a group dedicated to protecting their land and conquering to gain new land. With a hierarchical leadership directed at such a narrow goal, and marshaling resources for just this purpose, Tribe A would be almost invincible.

This invincibility is catching. The only effective way to beat Tribe A or even hold it at bay, is to adopt its methods. Primitive, simple life must become modern and sophisticated. What is worse, the situation defines the criteria for survival.

In a very real sense, the value of life is sacrificed to the cult of power. What is interesting is that Tribe A is not an evil tribe bent on the destruction of their neighbors. Rather, they are driven to such actions by the very nature of the agricultural society they have formed. To keep the fruits of their labors, they must expand to feed the new populations created by food surpluses, and they must defend their land against all takers. Of course, as all tribes adopt or are absorbed into the agricultural society momentum, they will bump into each other sooner or later, and thus war will ensue.

Ishmael points out that many of the stories in the Old Testament are really the stories of primitive leavers being conquered or absorbed by the moderns—the takers.

The Cult of Power

Andrew Schmookler proposes that natural systems vary from civilized systems in two key ways. A system is sustainable only in terms of wholeness, and wholeness requires two parts—synergy and viability. For Schmookler:

> *Synergy* is as the optimal pattern of interaction in which each part functions in a way that enhances the welfare of the other parts as well as its own.

> For a system, *viability* is maintaining whatever it is on which its continued existence depends.[38]

Nature is a synergetic whole. Whereas competition is normal, intra-specific behaviors are part of the strategy for the preservation of the systematic whole. In this sense, all pattern interactions between or among species serve the survival of the whole. Schmookler says that *corruption* occurs when parts serve their own interests at the expense of the whole.

Civilization forms an ecological whole, but unlike nature, it is also inter-social. As man dominates; this domination corrupts the natural

38 Schmookler, pp. 216-217.

order and reduces the viability of the system. The corruption comes from *unregulated conflict*. It is the nature of the conflict that I will discuss in terms of master–servant relationships and in the antagonism of those at the top of a society and those at the bottom. In Father Culture, war against all competition is unregulated and without regard to long-term consequences. However, domination is not merely a function of coercive force. Given the Parable of the Tribes, and that fighting back is the only viable option, greater force or stronger power yields greater resistance.

What history tells us is that people are reluctant to be simply absorbed and placed in servitude. Further, people hold on tenaciously to their traditions and cultures. This is understandable given current knowledge of how public/objective knowledge is formed. The symbols and the various ways of thinking within which reality is comprehensible in any objective form are structured in and through the community that forms such *ways of thinking*. For a whole community or tribe's way of thinking to be shattered by a conquering force is to shatter the basis for any meaningful understanding of reality. Such use of force robs all individuals of any sense of being a meaningful person.

A simpler way of wording this is that the system in which we live frames our understanding. It also frames our choices. For example, living in late 20th-century Toronto, it would be absurd for me to want to be a shaman when I grow up. However, 300 years ago, for natives of this part of the world, such a goal was both laudable and meaningful. When civilization with its Father Culture descends on my shamanistic community and forces me to abandon such meaningful and objective goals, it would be hard for me not to resist.

The Parable of the Tribes explains Father Culture. It also provides a context for historical views on the origin of so-called master–servant relations (more on this below). It turns out that the evils of mastery are not just the results of a few megalomaniacs using force to enslave others. Rather, it is the result of the seemingly innocuous process of growing food. It is, to paraphrase Hannah Arendt,[39] the *banality of evil*. Mastery and force do not originate in the minds of evil men, but in systems of survival that

---

39 Arendt, H. (2006). *Eichmann In Jerusalem: A Report On The Banality Of Evil*. London: Penguin Classics.

require that all peoples participate in the power struggles the Agricultural Revolution spawned. Mastery is not about evil people. It is about a system of survival that challenges the viability of natural systems by replacing the Law of Limited Competition with the unregulated dominance of a single species or, at a lower level, a single tribe. Further, dominance is not even limited to intra-species competition, but applies to all competition, even within the human species.

The origins of what is called civilization are the result of the need to use more land, or to use land more efficiently. This leads to new technologies, which in turn lead to divisions of labor, as well as new ways of making things. Schmookler's rule is simple: *open-ended possibilities create new necessities.* This rule stands in stark contrast to natural systems that are open but not open-ended. All possibilities in natural systems must follow the laws of synergy and viability. They are constrained by the whole system, and the promotion of the welfare of the whole system by each of their parts. Human culture, by contrast, is constrained by the whole system (in this case, power systems), but is not constrained to promote the whole system. Power is inherently corrupt in the sense that the parts can opt to promote their own well-being at the expense of other parts or the whole. In other words, Father Culture is unviable by definition.[40]

There are wide-ranging consequences of this power system called Father Culture, and Schmookler illuminates many of them. First, the Agricultural Revolution does indeed spawn a culture. It produces its own symbolism, and objective view of the world, and defines reality in these terms. Personal and collective meanings are found within this Framework.

Second, both history and how we think are shaped by the powerful non-alternative of seeking power. All players must play by the same rules toward the same victory conditions, or they are not counted as players or are eliminated as non-players. Consider the way that modern Western communities do not consider primitive communities as serious players. They are ripe for conquest and absorption, and that is precisely what we do to them.

Using my terms, Schmookler defines Father Culture as the Framework within which choices are made. This Framework is communal and defines

---

40 Until quite recently, this hasn't mattered ... now, however, we face an immense problem.

both public and objective understanding. Schmookler adds that this Framework determines our choices both as individuals and as communities. Inter-social evolution has transpired within this Framework, which means it is very difficult to break out of the reality that this Framework defines. And, indeed, much of our destructive behavior is explained as human nature, evil leaders, inherent violence in our genetic makeup, and so on. A clearer answer is to examine the Framework itself and see where it works and where it does not.

For example, cultural survival depends largely on the ability to transmit knowledge down through the generations. If evolution applies at the social level, then it would be expected those social qualities would be selected that could enhance survivability in the face of present or competing power structures. In terms of the fundamental values we could adopt, courage, strength, and fighting skill, and so on would be preferred. These values understood as precepts for correct behavior present most of the preferred values for most of human history under Father Culture. Indeed, these are the values and moral precepts adopted by successful master states throughout the ages.

History, then, is shaped by several factors. Withdrawal in the face of a powerful assault assumes that there is room to move. History is full of examples where there was no room to move, and societies were conquered. Further, destruction of the enemy serves the purposes of the conquerors. What they want most are the resources, not the people. If people can become resources as slaves, then they need not be destroyed; otherwise, destruction is preferred. This is the source of hatred in organized atrocities. With this as a ground rule, the stakes are always high. Only power can resist power. Further, as situations escalate, the difference between defense and offense blur. The maxim that the best defense is a good offense is well-practiced throughout history.

To complicate matters further, cultural evolution is not a random process. At least it is not as random as natural evolution. Cultural evolution occurs at a breakneck speed when compared with natural evolution. There are teleological processes at work. These are the human purposes governing the origin of cultural alternatives. Although the constraints of power limit the choices available, there are choices. Further, there is a selection process that determines the spread of some of these alternatives at the expense of others. In short, we must select for power. While there are many ways to structure our communities to serve power interests, they all reduce to the main rules that work. Singular command structures, ruthlessness in the face of the ever-present enemy, divide and conquer, and take no prisoners stand as the guiding principles of choice for successful communities.

How masters achieve this is through the strong central control of the community at the expense of the individual. Thymotic values like liberty and equality get submerged in these master–servant relations that typify historical communities. The costs of seeking power are high and affect everyone equally. For example, Schmookler points out that power structures must constantly recreate servants to maintain their power base. There must always be haves and have-nots. Within the Framework of power that determines such choices and thinking patterns, we appear to be natural creatures.

All power structures work on the military model. This is why aristocrats are always officers, and why they maintain a strong martial tradition. Part of the role of the leaders in a power structure is to provide the Framework within which individuals will serve—even to the point of death. This manipulation of a values is the complete Framework within which people will find meaning in their lives. It becomes the objective reality that defines the values and principles of good living. What better honor could there be than to serve or to do our duty?

Inter-social controls serve to promote public good, but they are imposed on individuals who start life with a primary loss of wholeness. This is the overriding source of existential angst. Angst, however, is not a modern or postmodern problem. It has been the source of much anger and confusion throughout history.

Consider this in light of the choices that are available to each of us as individuals, and in light of our current understanding of the true nature of objective knowledge. Shared feelings and a common or shared understanding largely define what we count as objective knowledge. They certainly define public experience. Personal meaning is derived from the public Framework. If power structures define that Framework, then they also define our choices. We can only be fulfilled by choosing in line with what our masters provide. Masters, in turn, are not free to choose. They must choose within the parameters that select for victory in the never-ending game of power playing. If they choose wrongly, it is the whole community that suffers. But the whole community suffers anyway as the masters muster the community to their game plan. They maintain the social infrastructure that sustains the power structure that sustains the community. Life is basically about sacrifice. Masters sacrifice unlimited choice, while servants sacrifice whatever is left after the masters have taken their turn. In the world of power structures, the masters tell you, "You can go first after me." Unfortunately, we are all part of a power structure, so we are all either masters or servants.

Controlling Resources

Ishmael points out that the primary distinction between pre-modern leavers and modern takers centers around the concept of ownership. In early communities, there were certain items that were part of a person's or a family's belongings. But, by and large, the tribe shared in most things. For example, each individual had their own clothes and perhaps a family unit had a hut. All else was largely communal. The whole village shared tools, weapons for hunting, and all fruits of labor. A successful hunt would bring too much meat for a single family. Failure to share would waste what could not be consumed. Moreover, while I might be successful today, I might fail next time. If I share with the tribe today, they will share with me tomorrow.

As in the true communal nature of socially constructing reality via symbolic forms, security was found in communal activity. When a child was ill, all would seek to care for the child. All emotional bonds were with the community, and were shared as much as language, myths, and art. Indeed, they were formed in the context of such communal activity. This is what was lost in civilization.

For Ishmael, this loss began with a single idea—lock up the food. When a community had been created that was dependent on specialized skills, those skills took on a value above and beyond all members of the community. Some skills were valued more than others. For example, special skills in growing the primary source of food will clearly be valued. So, too, will the skills of those who can store food for lean times. However, those who can take more land to support the burgeoning population will be most highly valued as they secure the land, protect it from all competitors, and are the source of new growth. Such leaders who are specialists in defense and offense do not produce directly, but live off the surplus created by the producers. These are the guardians. Fail to provide for the guardians, and the whole system would collapse.

Over time, increased specialization across the community had two very real effects. First, it took comprehensive producers from a leaver society (those who could hunt, gather, create art, commune with nature, etc.) and forced them into a specialized function. From then on, they would only produce pots for storing food, or clothes, or tools. These people were kept from providing for themselves by the guardians who locked up the food. To get food, one could not just go into nature and gather some. One had to pay for food with service. Ownership began with the idea that primary resources such as food and shelter were not simply there for the taking but were to be earned.

Ishmael points out that leavers spent less time on daily necessities than civilized people. Primitive people did not work 40 or 60 hours a week to get food or shelter. Further, they shared resources, including labor, so that all could benefit from the diverse skills in the tribe. This brings the second effect of civilization to the fore: it forces individuals to be individuals. If I cannot depend on the community for support simply because I am a member of the community, then I must look after myself. Clearly, self-interest is the only viable alternative. From the point of view of the guardian, and in military terms, this is the classic strategy of divide and conquer.

Over time, as individuals lost their generic skills, they became more dependent on the community to survive. But, unlike people who depended on the community in primitive societies, in civilized communities, support is rarely given. It must be earned. In other words, there is dependence without the support structure. Each must work for the masters who set the rules, and the structure of the community is in the masters' favor. Community support is only for those who serve, for those who earn the right to such support.

Such rights can be earned in only one way—with service to the community by playing your specialized role in community affairs—to find your place. This applies to guardians as well as servants. Guardians protect the order and viability of the community. Servants produce and provide for the community. Each must play their role. However, the spoils and surpluses are controlled by the guardians, so they can reap the lion's share of what gets produced. After all, they set the rules. The order they maintain is the divided specializations of the individuals they have conquered. Leave or challenge the order at your peril. Such was—and still is—life in civilized communities.

Civilization effectively changes what might be called the conditions for survival. In primitive communities, survival is tied to quality of life. It was closely tied to the survival of the tribe or the community. This intercommunal spirit was so strong and brought such strong qualitative values to each member of the community that exile was commonly understood to be the worst punishment. To live without the community was unthinkable—it was not life.

Civilization shattered this inter-accommodation between the individual and society. In civilized communities, survival is not so simple. It is true that if the society is unsuccessful, individuals will suffer. However, they suffer in different ways. First of all, they lack the generic skills needed for basic survival. They might know how to spin a pot, but they would not know how to grow food, or defend themselves. They might be wealthy merchants, but would be lost in the wild. Second, in the loss of community, they lost their sense of person. The very individuality that marked their success in the community was useless without the overriding guardian structure. Third, they have been taught by the system of civilized living that success is marked by position and wealth in the community, and not by the appreciation of the individual talent they brought to the tribe. It is this third inward-looking perspective that points to the real loss of community in civilized communities. Each individual is manipulated by the system of power and prestige as the only guarantee of any sense of meaning. Indeed, it is power and position that largely define meaning for individuals.

*

This brings us again back to power as the centerpiece of civilized life. Insofar as our forms of thought determine our concept of reality, and insofar as communal life determines our forms of thought, the structure of the community plays a very large role in determining what we mean by reality. This, in turn, provides the source of meaning for any life.

In primitive societies, meaning was found in the natural order as presented by the natural world. In short, nature provided the communal Framework or structure that determined the forms of thought that defined reality and meaning. Humans had 90,000 years to develop the type of society that worked best in nature for both survival and quality of life. Most primitive communities lived pretty much the same wherever we found them. There were cultural and linguistic differences, but the generic structure was much the same. Ninety thousand years of social evolution has taught us common principles of community and social interaction with nature. Civilized society replaces this natural framework with an artificial Framework of power and competition that pits the individual against all individuals and against the whole of society. It divides society into Tops, Middles, and Bottoms. Life without some Framework of values and community (a social contract) is nasty, brutish, and short. However, this is also true if one picks the wrong Framework or signs into a poor or bad contract. All primitives think that civilized community is a bad deal.

To complicate matters, the four choices Schmookler left to tribes confronted with power structures must be followed. The vanquished must become power structures themselves or perish. The need to win to survive is the primary condition of survival for the community. The individual is subjugated into a life structured by power.

The Role of Morality in Community Relations

The simple consequence of civilizing people is that it destroys the natural community of people and replaces it with an artificial *sense of community*, which is a mere shadow of the natural order. It is an incomplete Framework within which we must each define reality and find meaning.

Master–servant relations do not work, yet this structure remains the essence of civilized communities, and power structures produce their own moral precepts. Consider, now, how these tie together.

Simply stated, morality is an attempt to preserve natural, communal values in a society that only provides a sense of community. This means that civilization only approximates the natural, communal order that worked so well for 90,000 years. The major losses are the values of life, liberty, equality, and the person. Master–servant relations deny the value of life and the person, and subjugate all other values. It is the nature of ideologies that the forceful subjugation of any value does not mean that it disappears. On the contrary, these values come back to bite the ideology that has repressed them. Many historians see human history as largely the fight for freedom, or equality in the face of ongoing oppression. It is the war of the haves against the have-nots. One master dies, and another takes his place. We seem unable to escape the ideology of power. As a species, we are trapped inside the Framework of Father Culture and the values it prescribes, regardless of whether they work over the long term. How did we get into this state?

Our language, myths, and art form the Framework within which experience takes place. Objectivity emerges from publicity. In this case, there is a gradual transition from "this is how we do things" to "this is the way it is." In the formation of civilized communities, this process happened quickly if the specialized knowledge was understood in terms of myths and practiced as an art. The rules to be followed were not just practical statements, such as "plant such-and-such seeds here." These rules had to have a mythical dimension. It was important that the knowers understood that nature was giving up its secrets to a rational man who could use these natural laws for the benefit of the community—in this case, the power structure. Initially, there were magical relations between the whole and its parts. Sympathy for this whole led to the ideas of ritual and sacrifice. Because knowledge was power, the knowers had to idealize their knowledge. Such rules were beyond the pale of this or that tribe, but pertained to nature itself. As Stanley Diamond points out in *In Search of the Primitive*, "as Civilization accelerates, its proponents project their historical present as the progressive destiny of the human race. The political component is obscured by deterministic arguments from natural law, natural history and natural science."

The traditional arguments that expansion was required to secure new sources of land and materials are not quite complete. Oppression need not have been the central motive for why this occurred. Diamond states, "Even if we acknowledge the necessity—due to population pressure, scarcity of land, water and other resources—for political constraints in the earliest stages of state formation, there is no inherent reason for it to have taken the oppressive form that it did—except for the burgeoning anxiety of those removed from direct production about their economic and political security."[41]

In other words, bringing the process of increased dependence on agriculture to an increased dependence on those who rule the community was simple self-defense of those rulers to ensure that producers will not cut them off from their food supply. Those at the top included the shamans and priests who understood the special rituals and magic incantations to exert their control over nature. The anxiety that those at the top might be cut off not just from those at the bottom, but from their mythical/magical rituals, required them to defend their position from their own community, as well as from outside competitors. The rulers had to convince the masses of their special place and moment in the mythical/magic order of things. They had to shape the language, the magical and sacrificial rituals (which only priests could perform), and sponsor the reinforcing art that tied the community to the system. It was this total ownership and compelling Framework that made them takers. They took from nature and their fellow community members, alike.

Notice that what rulers perceive to be at stake is life itself. It is this with which they gamble, and which they are prepared to lose if they are defeated. The moment they win at this game, a master–servant relation is formed. The value of life is the first natural value to be sacrificed to the new power structure. It constitutes the origin of the power structure. The success of the guardians (as Tops get to call themselves) guarantees that the have-nots (the Bottoms) will be their servants. And so the cycle of civilization begins.

---

41 Diamond, S. (1981). *In Search Of The Primitive*. Piscataway, NJ: Transaction Publishers. Page 8.

Whereas this explains the source of the division of labor and the gap between the rich and the poor, Tops and Bottoms, it does not explain why this gap continued to widen. Diamond perceives that this trend was primarily due to increased exploitation. The rulers must continually exploit their environment, including all natural and human resources, to expand and consolidate their position. Guardian precepts are primarily rules of conduct to ensure a continued and relatively stable order over an extended period. They also serve to prepare each generation of rulers to the thought processes that ensure success. These rules are not simply "how we do things around here." They define "the way it is," and the "the way it must be."

If my discussion is correct, recorded history is not really the fight for freedom or equality. It is the process of the re-emergence of the basic thymotic values that were part of the natural community prior to their submergence in civilization. This re-emergence is based on need for recognition—to be valued. The primary difficulty with this is that as a species, we have effectively defined these terms within the power Framework we are seeking to get beyond. Consider liberty in this context.

Liberty, in a modern context, is predicated on the idea of the individual. That is, the individual is sovereign over their own mind and body. In this context, servitude is wrong. The whole point of liberty is to be free from powerful and oppressive forces (such as guardians). But, the idea of individual realization is quite different from that found in primitive cultures.

There are two main contrasts to be illustrated here. The first is that Father Culture requires that power structures be dynamic. In particular, they must always progress to a higher or newer form. There is an inherent imperative to be constantly expanding and growing. This is a violation of the nature of viable systems.

The second point is that power structures politicize the individual in a way that did not exist in natural communities. The very definition of an individual is different in civilized versus primitive societies. Let's explore each of these in turn.

Power Structures and Progress

The idea of progress is so ingrained in civilized thinking that it functions almost as a mantra. Diamond puts it this way:

> Faith is the dominant idea in Western Civilization. In its name, Western man rationalizes not only his self-interest, but also his failures. He does not perceive his failures as the result of his goals, nor of his motives, but rather of the means at his disposal, or of his human limitations. A guardian cannot surrender his notion of progress without destroying the rationale for his entire civilization … . It is the notion of progress that mediates his alienation, and makes it possible for him to construct a reality which he does not actually experience. But his commitment to progress is really less a faith than a compulsion … . For the idea of progress is not based on a rational analysis of our civilization. It springs from the disequilibrium of the system in which Western man finds himself … . The idea of progress is, above all, the precipitant of unresolved social and personal conflicts in modern civilization. It is the awareness of this conflict along with the effort of resolving that creates the sense of unresolved movement toward specific goals which are defined as progressive.[42]

In other words, we are out of control.

The point here is that required progress is mostly absent in primitive communities. Again, Diamond describes the situation, "the structure of primitive societies is perceived as permanent. Progress is a reality of personal growth, a progress *through* society, not *of* society, as the individual moves from experience to experience on what the Winnebago tribe called the *road of life and death* [italics his] … . 'Progress,' in primitive societies, if this Western conception can be applied to them at all, would be a metaphor for spiritual transformation. The contradictions of growth through the various phases of the life cycle are socially recognized, ritually expressed and dialectically resolved."

---

42 Ibid.

Individuality is defined differently in primitive communities. Such societies are inherently *person*-oriented rather than *power*-oriented. This fundamental respect for the personification of the individual is a key element in understanding the Framework within which primitive individuals seek and find understanding and meaning in their lives. Here, the individual is just that—an individuated part of the whole community. The fundamental recognition of this individuated person leads to the idea of respect for an individual life. Individuals are a distinct part of the community. Their relationships and contributions are all judged in terms of the life cycle of the individual. Because such communities do not progress as such, self-fulfillment is a spiritual process through life itself. The whole process is completed through the integrity of the language, myths, and art of the community. Yet each contribution is from each individual's unique perspective.

Primitive communities are not really communistic in a political sense. People own things. Property is not fully communal. Yet each person knows that their very meaning and being are intimately tied to the community. Again, for such people, the worst punishment is exile or banishment from the tribe. This is a greater horror than loss of life. It constitutes a loss of recognition, and this entails a loss of affirmation of being and of meaning.

In a civilized society, the very structure of power creates a chasm between those at the top and those at the bottom; masters count and servants are reduced to objects. The process of constructing a power elite is based on the breaking down of all processes of social recognition that lead to meaning and affirmation in the sense just described for primitive communities. In objectifying the individual, each becomes cut off from the community. Individuals are merely units of work or servitude. As such, people become individuals in the modern sense that they are separate entities. Power alienates individuals from each other and from participation in the community. This is why those at the bottom develop groupthink around the us-versus-them patterns. It is why they think those at the top are uninformed and oppressive. Collective action is the only way the servants can form a social unit within a power structure. This is also why Tops take on more and more responsibility and divide their responsibilities to more easily manage the increasing complexity that such individuation creates. It is what leads to social silos, and the eventual turf wars between those at the top.

Rather than a community that develops according to the patterns of natural, viable systems, social evolution is replaced with social engineering. We are born alone and die alone. All that is in between is reduced to a search for recognition and meaning. This is why we can only gain a sense of community. Of course, such sentiments are alien to natural persons.

Tops take the responsibility to control the language, rituals, and art, make people earn their keep, reduce the person to an object, and create a separated individual. After all, the best power strategy is to divide and conquer. In civilization, individuality means "divided from." Divided from each other, we cannot be truly free in the sense of spiritual transformation. Personal progress is *of* society, not *through* it.

This divided self is precisely the abstraction of subject and object that defines reductionism. Rather than being a subjectivity that affirms objective understanding and meaning through social coherence, the divided individual must seek meaning and understanding as dictated by the Framework that has been engineered by their masters. It is the masters who set the rules and structure the Framework within which reality is experienced and defined. They control the language and the mythical-magical rituals, and they promote the artistic forms to reinforce their behaviors. It is an engineered Framework, based on motives and goals that are driven implicitly through the power structure itself.

Ethics

I must caution the reader not to idealize primitive culture. The idea of the *noble savage* is a myth of modern times. There are many examples in primitive communities of cannibalism, human sacrifice, slavery, and servitude. Indeed, warfare among primitive tribes was a chronic state of affairs.

At the same time, I want to be careful to learn what we can from such people. For example, John Keagan in *History of Warfare* points out that primitive warfare was not an all-out battle to exterminate the enemy. This kind of fighting is a modern invention. Rather, primitive fighting was more a display of courage in a ritualized way. There was much shouting and banging on shields, much gesturing, and some contact with intent to harm. People were killed and seriously injured. But such raids were often to obtain women or defend a hunting or agricultural ground. The goal was to drive off intruders or to expand the gene pool. While such groups fight today, tomorrow they would trade goods and behave much as friends. There would be vendettas, and retaliations, but they were part of the large interaction between tribes or communities. One of the ways of expanding the objectivity of one's worldview is to interact with others. Socialization as a process is not always a positive or a peaceful activity. In fact, almost any form of interaction will contribute to the process. The Framework, therefore, includes rules of conduct that are informally enforced by the community. I have defined such rules as the basis of morality. The values or principles that ground morality is called Ethics.

Ethics, then, stems from social processes as terms of reference of an individuated or authentic person in the context of their community, and the system of communities with which they interact. Affirmation is not just for the person but for the community as well. The process is the same for both. Since individuated persons contribute to and define the Framework within which experience, understanding, and meaning are found, any person's interaction with any other person is also an interaction with that person's community. The reverse is also true. Any interaction between communities is also an interaction with the members of each community.

This communal authentication process actually holds true whether we are in power-structured communities or primitive, natural communities. The difference is that in power-structured, civilized communities, the community itself provides only a sense of authentic identity. By creating divided individuals and repressing persons as objects, guardians can engineer a Framework that objectifies others, whether they are people or creatures of nature. All are eligible for the status of enemy or servant.

By creating divided people, personhood is diluted or suppressed. Guardians decide who is the enemy, and direct meaningful activity in accordance with their goals. People who fail to participate are eligible for punishment. In such a state, guardians must both exercise and maintain control. As such, vendettas, or personal retaliations, must be controlled. Divided people must not seek retribution for themselves, because such retribution does not also represent the community, as would be the case for an individuated person in a natural community. Guardians must, therefore, formally enforce rules of conduct. Thus, the idea of law was born.

While some have tried to define law as natural, they fail primarily because the concept of rule politicizes proper conduct. Such rules cannot be left to individuated persons to define a contribution to a natural community. They certainly cannot be left to the groupthink of those at the bottom. Rather, they must be engineered. In the same sense that the individual is divided from their community, the rules are set above as abstracted concepts to be symbolized and formed accordingly. Thus, we arrive at the concept of the *good*. Of course, this concept is difficult to define in civilized terms precisely because it is really a symbolic sense of natural communal affirmation. It is an objectification of an experience that in natural communities is both subjective and objective as part of genuine recognition, affirmation, and personification.

Consequently, power structures provide a poor sense of genuine good, and genuine right and wrong. Because divided people cannot define and contribute to the forms of such experience and understanding without entering into groupthink patterns of behavior, divided people must rely on guardians to fill in the gaps. Historically, guardians have engineered the rules that favor their control mechanisms. People are expected to feel honor and duty, and courage and sacrifice, for the guardians. These are the rules that define and keep people in their place. Combine moral precepts with economic and political controls, and the guardians can define a public space that objectifies the reality of one's place in the world. Goods and rights can be further defined, accordingly. And so we have done.

The key issue here is that the moral precepts that have evolved as "systems of survival," as Jacobs calls them, are divorced from the authentic grounds of ethical criteria or thymotic values. This means that it is not possible for guardian or even commercial moral precepts to be properly grounded in Ethics. Frameworks fail to meet real ethical status because they cannot connect with the ethical criteria and the underlying thymotic values that ground an ethics. Insofar as power structures are unviable, they demonstrably fail in the quality of thinking that ethics is designed to provide. They fail in virtues. They fail to promote overall beneficial consequences and mitigation of harms. The entire system is designed to support those at the top at the expense of anyone who gets in their way. They fail in the values or principles of ethical conduct. They deny life, liberty, equality, and person almost by definition. Because civilization is artificially engineered toward specific values that serve guardian or commercial interests, self-realization is not possible. Ethics becomes a fight to emerge in the face of the "moral" Frameworks that define survival for the class or community.

Underlying the artificial sense of community exists a more real community spirit. People do interact as persons, and social recognition and community take place at a lower level than the political or economic. For civilized people, this occurs most in the family unit. At this level of social interaction, people are indeed persons, and until they are removed from their family in maturity, they remain individuated within the family unit. This is the essential naiveté and innocence of children. This is why we often refer to primitive peoples as childlike. This recognition, often confused as dependence, is the root of childlike behaviors. But children define the family as much as they are defined by it, and so they remain as individuated persons. Part of the education process in civilized communities is to objectify children and divide them from key social units. This is explained as a virtue, and, indeed, in civilized communities is a mechanism for survival, if not success. Individuality as a self-contained independent spirit reaches its peak value in the commercialism promoted by American-style capitalism. The rugged individual or cowboy is held up as the ideal for liberty and freedom. In this moment, civilization reaches its peak and begins to retreat in the face of ecological realities. Nature, it seems, is not composed of rugged individuals but of individuated components that work harmoniously together according to their place in the natural order. The myths have it right. True, viable systemic order is found in the sympathy for the whole and the place and moment of each part within that whole. The promotion of individuality as the definition and measure of freedom reveals the true poverty of civilized notions of freedom.

We seek to expose this undercurrent of real relationships that go beyond those imposed on us by our civilizing guardians. We need the freedom to seek out those with whom we can have meaningful relations at this deepest level if we are to have any meaning in our lives. This sense of freedom is what liberty really provides and is what we seek.

In this context, history is the struggle against power structures. The struggle has been maintained in the undercurrent of the authentic self that the guardians have not yet been able to crush or control. Our true nature as individuated persons has never been eradicated, and now that life, liberty, and equality are making headway as key values, this proper sense of culture is beginning to emerge. This proper sense of culture is not yet redefining liberty and equality, but is peeking out of the shadows through movements that are based on holistic and spiritual values. It is found in the movements toward whole medicine, and the rebirth of interest in what we can learn from the myths and magic of Indigenous peoples who were closer to nature. Ecology and new methods of naturalism are starting to break into popular culture. Of course, there are those who cling to the old ways, with mass genetic engineering and political ideologies that seek a better world through engineered solutions, but these are being challenged for the first time in a serious way.

CHAPTER 4
Ethics as Quality Thinking

Religions originally had the purpose of providing understanding, meaning, and values to life. In modern times, science has replaced religion as the source of understanding and positioned religion in the realm of meaning and values. However, in the face of growing globalism, religions have remained largely regional and culturally specific. The result is that there are few values or sources of meaning common to the world's great religions. Modern religions are global in scope but not in any sense of global values or meaning. They each remain competitive rather than cooperative, and this competition is not what is needed. A religiocentric approach to founding a global civilization is no longer workable.

Humans, as a species, need to establish a set of underlying values, which cut across the various world's religions and which can be embraced by all peoples and cultures. The task of this chapter will be to identify what these values might be, and how they might work. Philosophy has a long tradition of working out the principles of ethics and morality, so I will draw on that rich history of ideas. There are two parts to this chapter's goal. The first part is to define the criteria for what I will call *quality thinking*. These are provided by the various ethical systems that have been proposed. Second, following the discussion on how we develop Frameworks that structure thinking, I explore the underlying values we might embrace as a species and illustrate how these values are to be used to form a Moral Framework for all people.

In general terms, rules of conduct are usually described as a *morality*. Ethics systematizes these to provide a coherent, rational set of rules or values—how we ought to behave. I will start by outlining five of the key ethical theories and exploring what works and what does not in each model. We begin by defining some basic terms and explaining how to tie a morality to its underlying ethical values.

*

To distinguish between morality and ethics, morality is the study of those rules of conduct that are considered necessary to promote peace and order in a community. Ethics pertains to the system of values that underlie the reasons or rationale for moral precepts. Logically, ethics precedes morality. The latter is really the implementation of ethics as understood by the community in question.

Morality is the set of rules that we, as a community, *informally reinforce* through praise and blame. That is, we praise or condone "good" or socially desirable behavior, and chastise or condemn "bad" or socially undesirable behavior. These rules are often called *mores*, or *moral precepts*.

Legality, on the other hand, is the set of rules that we, as a community, *formally enforce*. This usually pertains to those behaviors that are so important for the well-being of the community that informal reinforcement is not enough. Formal rules are called *laws*. Laws come from and are answerable to morality. For example, we can have an unjust law, but there is no such thing as an illegal moral precept.

Ethics pertains to the principles or values that form the basis of moral precepts. When we group moral precepts under a common set of rules pertaining, say, to a particular class within a society, we refer to a Moral Framework. Ethics is usually defined in terms similar to the definitions of rational behavior, but put into the context of the community as a whole and over a long term. For example, when an individual seeks to take an unfair advantage over another, such as when a stronger male uses force to make a female submit to his sexual desires against her will, that behavior would be classified as unethical. How unfair is defined leads to the moral rules that we should follow in how we interact with other persons. Ethics pertains to the underlying values that set the criteria for what constitutes unfair or immoral behaviors.

Another way of explaining this involves the concept of *prudential advantage*. Prudential advantage is a fancy way of referring to self-interested actions. The idea is that we each endeavor to act in such a way as to maximize self-interest, but with an appropriate amount of prudence regarding whatever advantage we can gain for ourselves. The point of ethics is that when we construe prudential advantage too narrowly, we lay ourselves open to be blindsided by factors that are extrinsic to our decisions or plans. We also miss opportunities. For example, a young male in a slum area, raised by abusive parents, sells drugs to get money to get out of the slum. He does not consider the damage he does to the community. However, the community does not just idly sit by and let such damage happen. The drug dealer's actions have consequences. Because society is bigger than one individual, we can readily see that in his effort to pursue his own advantage, he does not take into account all the forces that can be brought to bear to stop and punish him. When we compare his sales skills selling drugs with what he could achieve if he were to get a job selling legitimate goods, his chances of success would go up exponentially if he chose the legitimate option. His chances of becoming a "drug lord" are slim in comparison. Not only does he construe prudential advantage too narrowly to avoid punishment, but he also misses a larger opportunity. This is the kind of thinking that characterizes ethics. We do not trade off long-term overall benefits for short-term local/personal gains. We all succeed when the community succeeds. We do not tolerate disruptions to group success from individuals who play by their own rules to the detriment of other members of the community.

Ethics requires that we *universalize* our descriptions of various behaviors to assess whether the community benefits or is harmed by such activity. In our example, we assess what kind of community we would get if all males could behave like our drug dealer. In this case, we might conclude that this behavior would totally disrupt the family unit and undermine the basis of communal life. Whether it is decided that this harm to society is a moral precept or a law depends on how important to the well-being of society we assess the harm.

Ethics, then, refers to those principles and values of how individuals ought to behave toward each other such that over the long run, the community benefits by all its members adopting those principles and living by them. This "ought to" is defined as a normative evaluation in contrast to a descriptive evaluation, which describes how we actually behave. In an ideal world, normative evaluations have a descriptive counterpart. For example, someone who trades off the long-term benefits of a great inheritance for the short-term pleasures of wine, women, and song might be described as unreasonable or a bit stupid. Whether this is also unethical in a normative sense is often the focus of any evaluation of the behavior.

The key ingredients of an ethics are that these principles are perceived to be of great value to the members of the community because their adoption promotes community well-being over the long run. That is, each individual gains significant benefits through communal life, and all members understand that these benefits are accrued by riding on the coattails of the success of the community overall. Because success is measured over the long run, the benefits are perceived as long-term benefits.

Historically, the idea that ethical principles ought to apply to all members of the community was referred to as *universality*; that is, a principle or value is a candidate for inclusion in ethical discussion if and only if it applies to everyone.

The idea of universality has led to much confusion about ethics over the centuries. Some thinkers have used universality as a criterion for inclusion, and others have tried to limit universality to single communities or even classes. Some have suggested that only individuals can decide such matters, and that universality as such is not an ethical criterion at all.

For my purposes, I assume that universality is a property of an ethical value, and not a criterion to select ethical principles. The goal is to show that ethical values underlie morality in a way that suggests that all communities benefit from ethical guidelines, and these benefits are the same independently of a specific language or culture. Ethics is about "a way of being human," not about rules and edicts on behavior.

Following normal conventions, I will refer to how people ought to behave as *normative*, rather than how they actually behave, which is *descriptive*. Again, reasonable behavior is defined by accruing long-term benefits even at the expense of short-term gains. For example, in business, a company that fails to deliver promised goods will soon lose the capability of finding new clients, and the business will be short-lived. If the goal of a company were to be in business for a long time, say for the lifetime of the owner, then it would be unreasonable to behave with such a short-term outlook.

Once a descriptive understanding of rational behavior is established, we can prescribe how people ought to behave in normative terms. Normative prescriptions are the flip side of rational descriptions. In the case of our company, we would prescribe moral rules that the owner should adopt strategies and policies that lend themselves to the long-term success of the business, even at the occasional short-term cost.

Ethics, then, is the study of proper thought and conduct, or how we *ought* to behave. While morality involves the standards of behavior by which people are judged, ethics, in contrast, is a system of beliefs that supports a particular view of morality. That leads to the question, are there objective, universal principles to construct an ethical system of beliefs applicable to all cultures at all times? As we shall see, we tend to think so.

I have illustrated a high-level view of the relation between morality and the law, but it is not clear how this works in practice. For example, the law is a set of rules to govern behavior, and laws seem to reflect collective moral judgments. If this is true, can we use laws to form *right* and *proper* decisions when faced with choices between economic gain and social obligations? In other words, should we rely on law? This might be worded as: If it is legal, it is right, or if it is illegal, it is wrong. All of this asks, can we use the rule of law to balance economic and social performance? There are good reasons to think so.

The definition of *law* includes that it is a consistent set of universal rules that are widely published, generally accepted, and usually enforced. Law describes the way people are required to act. It enforces consistent behaviors in that the requirements to act or not to act must be consistent to be considered part of the law. Laws are universal as they must be applicable to everyone with similar characteristics facing the same set of circumstances. Laws are published—legal requirements must be in written form, accessible to everyone. Laws are generally accepted, including the acceptance that laws have to be generally obeyed. Finally, laws are enforced. Members of society have to understand that they will be forced to obey laws if they do not voluntarily choose to do so. All of this provides compelling support for the idea that we can rely on laws to enforce moral standards.

But, the relation between law and morality is more complicated than might first appear. First, most laws are *negative commandments*—you are required *not* to act in a given way. Second, the requirements of law overlap but do not duplicate probable moral standards. The overlap is not complete. Some laws are morally inert, with no ethical content, while some laws can be morally repugnant. That is why some laws can be called unjust. Not all moral rules should be laws. For example, should lying be illegal? The requirements of laws tend to be negative, while morality tends to be positive, such as a moral requirement to give aid to those in need or despair. Finally, the requirements of law tend to lag behind moral standards. Many laws are out-of-date, and the process for changing laws can be onerous and time-consuming.

For our purposes, we consider that the law provides a meaningful guide for action because it represents the combined moral judgments of all members of society, but the law forms a *minimal* set of standards. For example, we cannot require you to go beyond the law, where morality might suggest such a requirement. In a democracy, solely relying on the law could lead to tyranny of the majority by ratifying some rights at the expense of others.

There are also problems getting from moral standards to legal requirements. For members of society, these include:

+ lack of information;

+ dilution of moral standards in the formation of small groups;

+ misrepresentation of moral standards of members of society in the consensus of large organizations;

+ misrepresentation of moral standards of members of society in the formation of laws;

+ legal requirements formed through political processes are incomplete; and,

+ moral standards require judicial decision or administrative agency.

All in all, there are good reasons to suppose that morality and the law are different, and that we need both. Law will not substitute for moral reasoning or vice versa. We could consider that the relation between morality and law is less like a Venn diagram, with potential overlaps and distinctions, and more like a threshold model, where behaviors are bounded between mandated actions established by external forces, including laws, government regulation, and other mandates, and a voluntary boundary defined by public commitments, social values, cultural obligations, and other voluntary policies. The issue for an ethics is to establish the parameters of the boundaries, while the issue for each individual is to decide where they choose to be within the boundaries. For example, we must each choose how altruistic we will be above and beyond mere compliance with legal regulations. This brings us to the idea that we can bind our moral reasons together into an ethical system. There are several approaches to ethics, but I will show below that all but two of these are actually complementary. The first approach is ethical relativism.

Ethical relativism is the view that there are no objective universal principles. Moral standards differ between cultures and times; therefore, beliefs supporting moral standards of behavior differ. Each group can provide logical reasons for their behavior as a clear explanation of the basis of their actions. The question that arises regarding ethical relativism is this: in the mix of differing standards, can we derive any commonality that overrides the differences? In other words, is there a set of minimal standards that we can derive, regardless of cultural or temporal distinctions? The moral philosopher P. F. Strawson thought so.[43]

For example, is it the case that each (all) member(s) of a group bears some responsibility for the well-being of other members of the group? If so, that suggests there are positive duties of mutual care and reciprocity, and some form of obligation for mutual aid. Are there negative injunctions against violence, deceit, and betrayal? If so, there are or should be rules regarding abstention from injury, as well as norms for rudimentary procedures and standards for what is just. All of this suggests some abstract virtues of justice and honesty. If these considerations are reasonable, then

---

43 Strawson, P. F. (1970). Social Morality and Individual Ideal. In G. Wallace and A. D. M Walker (Eds.), *The definition of morality* (pages 101-3) London: Metheun.

the question is not whose morality is better, but whether your moral standards are as good as mine in benefiting society. This, then, forces a justification of our standards against standards that are transcultural. What we *believe* is right does not mean that our moral standards *are* right. We can say that our definition of what is right is different, and we can act accordingly, yet the way we determine right would be the same across time and cultures. This, in turn, leads to four ethical systems:

- Eternal Law

- Virtue Ethics

- Consequentialism (Utilitarian Ethics)

- Universalism (Deontological Ethics)

Eternal Law theories take the view that there are self-evident truths, usually incorporated in the mind of God and revealed by Holy Scripture, or apparent in the state of nature. These truths lead to inalienable rights. Such laws are unchanging, and associated rights and duties are self-evident in the sense that they are obvious. For example, the first rule is often stated, "Do unto others as you would have them do unto you."

The problem with eternal law theories is that no two natural law theorists agree on the exact provisions revealed by God, scriptures, or nature. Each religion provides moral standards, but these differ from each other. Moreover, religious rules tend to be situation dependent and vary with individual circumstances. They were formed in largely agrarian societies and do not translate well to modern industrial communities.

The second moral system, Virtue Ethics is a branch of moral philosophy that emphasizes *character*, rather than rules or consequences, as the key element of ethical thinking. A system of Virtue *Ethics* is only intelligible if it includes an account of the purpose (*telos*) of human life, or in popular language, the meaning of life. This idea was first developed by ancient Greek philosophers who characterized a state of *eudaimonia*. Eudaimonia is a state variously translated as "happiness" or "human flourishing." It is not a subjective, but is rather an objective state. It characterizes the well-lived life, irrespective of the emotional state of the person experiencing it. Eudaimonia consists of exercising the characteristic human quality—reason—as the soul's most proper and nourishing activity. Having offered an account of the good life, a system of Virtue Ethics identifies those habits and behaviors that will allow a person to achieve that good life. These habits and behaviors are the virtues.

For the virtue ethicist, eudaimonia describes that state achieved by the person who lives the proper human life, an outcome that can be reached by practicing the virtues. A virtue, then, is a habit or quality that allows the bearer to succeed at whatever the bearer's purpose is. Thus, to identify the virtues for human beings, one must have an account of what the human purpose is. This is often the stumbling point for a system of virtues. That said, there is some agreement regarding what the virtues are. We can form a list, such as:

+ Integrity—discerning what is right and what is wrong, and acting on what you have discerned; saying openly that you are acting on your understanding of what is right and what is wrong;

+ Veracity—telling the truth, including transparency, clarity, and honesty;

+ Fairness (Justice)—understanding, quite simply, that one human being is not better than another and recognizing the basic value of all humans;

+ Accountability and responsibility – answerable and accepting liability for your decisions and actions over events that you can control; meeting your obligations to the community;

+ Respectful of others (Human Dignity)—recognizing the intrinsic worth that resides in every human being and that each person matters, every person counts, everyone is fully informed, fully awake, outspoken, and questioning, and everyone is engaged in key decisions;

+ Commitment—binding yourself (intellectually or emotionally) to a course of action; you are dependable and reliable, and faithful to known values;

- Social Responsibility—living in a manner that meets or exceeds the ethical, legal, commercial, and public expectations of society; considering the good of the wider communities, local and global, within which they exist in terms of the economic, legal, ethical, and philanthropic impact of their way of life and the activities they undertake; and,

- The Common Good—a catchall phrase that describes creating and maintaining an environment that is supportive of the development of human potential while safeguarding the community against excesses.

The difficulty with Virtue Ethics is in establishing the nature of the virtues. Different people, cultures, and societies often have vastly different opinions on what constitutes a virtue. Therefore, Virtue Ethics does not focus on which sorts of actions are morally permitted and which are not, but rather on which sort of qualities someone ought to foster to become a good person. While this can be a useful exercise, it tends to suffer from the kinds of problems we found with ethical relativism. If, however, we can agree on a basic list of virtues, such as the list above, Virtue Ethics provides a good starting point for thinking about ethics.

The third moral system, *Consequentialist Ethics* (sometimes called *Utilitarianism*) places emphasis on the outcome instead of the intent of individual actions. The moral worth of personal conduct can be determined solely by the consequences of that behavior. For example, right acts result in benefits for people, whereas wrong acts lead to damage or harm. The goal for ethical thinking, then, is to create the greatest degree of benefits for the largest number of people, while incurring the least amount of damages or harm.

The first problem, of course, is what do we mean by *benefits?* Do we mean material goods, friendships, knowledge, health, pleasures? A focus on pleasures tends to promote hedonism or self-centered approaches. Furthermore, benefits are not all positive. There are negative costs and adverse outcomes associated with each action. Outcomes could include pain, sickness, death, ignorance, isolation, unhappiness, and so on. How do we establish a balance? To make matters worse (or more complicated), costs and benefits tend to aggregate over time. That means that aggregate harms or costs need to be balanced against benefits. This, in turn, suggests a computational approach to net consequences.

One calculus is Utilitarianism, where we calculate costs and benefits as Utility, which is defined as the degree of usefulness. Our perception of the net benefits and costs associated with a given act need to be calculated equally for everyone. When we do this, we find that an act is right if and only if it produces a greater net benefit for society than any other act possible in the circumstances. This leads to two versions: Act Utilitarianism and Rule Utilitarianism.

Act Utilitarianism only considers the consequences of a particular judgment or action. What good and bad consequences will result from this action in these circumstances? Moral rules are only "rules of thumb" to guide actions.

For Rule Utilitarianism, particular judgments or actions appeal to moral rules such as do not kill, or do not steal, or do not lie. Such rules are justified by the principle of utility: the good and bad consequences tend to result from this sort of action in general, in these kinds of circumstances. Therefore, an act's conformity to a rule makes it right. Beneficial consequences of individual acts do not alone make them right, and rules cannot be disregarded because of the exigencies of particular situations. Therefore, rules have a place in a general code of conduct. To see how this works, we must assess the system, as a whole, in terms of overall consequences. We can do this because we already accept codes and laws as an integrated body of rules, none of which stands in isolation. So particular judgments and actions can lead to moral rules, which can lead to a moral code or a whole system of rules, all of which if followed would maximize utility for the whole community, however this is defined.

There are some problems with consequentialism. First, a rule's acceptability depends strictly on its consequences. But some actions are simply wrong, regardless of calculated overall benefits for a majority. For example, what if killing someone maximizes overall benefits—such as killing Hitler before he started his acts of aggression? Of course, such pre-emptive actions could lead to the possibility of exploitation. In such cases, the model would fail to balance the benefits of the majority against the sacrifices of a minority. In a democracy, this could be construed as a tyranny of the majority. While consequentialism on its own could be problematic, we will see below that when combined with other ethical models, many of its shortcomings can be overcome.

The fourth and final moral system, *Universalism* or *Deontological Ethics* was first developed by Immanuel Kant and referred to duties and obligations of an individual. In this view, the moral worth of an action cannot depend on the outcome, because those outcomes are too indefinite and uncertain at the time the decision is made. Rather, moral worth depends on the intentions of the person making the decision or performing the act, but not in the sense of a list of potential or actual virtues. For example, if I wish the best for others, my actions are praiseworthy even if my actions are ineffectual or clumsy. Good intentions normally result in beneficial outcomes. That means that we can equate good intentions with personal duties.

To see this idea in action, suppose that you oppose abortion on religious grounds. That is, based on your faith and religious beliefs, you believe that it is okay to override the liberty of a woman to decide over her own mind and body in these matters. On a subsequent issue, I come along with a different religious view and seek to persecute your church. The Kantian question would be, what would be the basis of your complaint? Presumably, you would object to my actions based on freedom of religion. But this suggests that you should be free to believe according to your conscience. This is your *complaint*. Kant asks, what is the *basis* for this complaint? You think the right way to treat others is to override liberty when it is convenient to your religious beliefs. If that is the right way to treat others, on what basis would you complain if others treated you the same way? Given your behavior, you have effectively set yourself up to be a victim of your own policy.

What Kant has revealed is that moral actions need to be viewed as matters of principle. In principle, is this the right way to behave? If we think it is, we can have no basis for complaint if others treat us the same way. A proper ethical stance would consider this in advance. I would recognize that my personal and perhaps unique point of view or beliefs is irrelevant to the *principle* of my actions. The biography of my church does not exonerate unprincipled decisions and actions. All our decisions and actions need to be considered as matters of policy as well as practice. This is where the idea of universalism comes from. Ethical principles must be universal in the sense that they apply to everyone in similar circumstances. For example, when we victimize others, we consider this as setting a policy such that we could have no complaint if others treated us the same way. To fail to think this through is not the act of a rational human being. In Kant's view, part of the whole point of moral reasoning is that we consider our actions and decisions to avoid self-victimization, and we can only do that by understanding our decisions and actions as matters of policy and principles and taking care not to victimize others. In other words, Kant has effectively defined what we mean by *good intentions*.

Good intentions entail duties that are incumbent upon us, such as to tell the truth, to not steal, and to honor contracts. Unlike virtues, which pertain to individual character in the context of how best to achieve the good life, duties are universal and apply to everybody.

The main principle includes the *categorical imperative*: treat others as ends rather than as means. The general idea is that individuals are persons worthy of dignity and respect. Individuals are not impersonal means to achieve our own ends; therefore, no action can be considered right if it disregards the ultimate worth of any other human being.

This presents the idea that there are universal principles of right action. We take any action and consider it as a principle of behavior—would you be willing to have everyone in the world, faced with similar circumstances, forced to behave the same way? In particular, if others treated you this way, would you consider yourself a victim of wrong behavior? An act or decision can be judged good or right or proper only if everyone, without qualification, performs the same act, or reaches the same decision, given similar circumstances. It is unfair for me to do something that others would not do, not because of adverse consequences, but because I have a will, I have a duty to act consistently, or I would have a contradiction of wills. Rules are right for me only if they are right for everyone else, so moral rules are based on logical consistency. Again, if I think that action X meets the conditions of a correct principle of behavior, I would have no basis for complaint if I were treated the same way—that is, according to the principle of right action.

Like consequentialism, universalism has an act and a rule version. For Act Universalism, rules do not bind an agent in new situations. Rather, new situations may prompt a need for new rules. For Rule Universalism, the heart of morality is the set of binding rules and principles that classify acts as right, wrong, or obligatory. While it is true that some rules depend on previous acts, the issue is, which rules are primary? The philosopher John Rawls gives us an example he called *distributed justice*. As the primacy of justice requires greater equality or fairness, according to Rawls, rational people would accept social and economic inequalities only if these resulted in compensating benefits to everyone, particularly the least-advantaged members of society. He supposed that to get at proper ethical understanding, imagine that you are not yet born into a society, and you do not yet know where you will be in that society. In particular, imagine that you might end up a least-advantaged member. You must decide, under a veil of ignorance, what rules you would consider fair if you did not know whether you would end up advantaged or disadvantaged. What rules or principles of conduct would you choose?

In this approach, ethical reasoning is based on a single value: justice. For Rawls, truth is the first value for a system of thought. You would want to know truthfully what would work best for all. This, in turn, would lead to justice as the first virtue of social institutions. Society is an association of individuals who cooperate to advance the good of all, such that collaboration comes from recognizing that joint efforts produce greater benefits than solitary efforts. The issue for deciding on universal principles is how to distribute benefits across society. Rawls maintained that, with this in mind, we would arrive at five principles:

+ Public education is based on equality;

+ Welfare is based on need;

+ Payment is based on effort;

+ Public honors are based on contribution; and,

+ Salaries are based on competence.

The major problems with universalism, as is evident from Rawls' example, is that there is no method of prioritizing and no degrees of stringency in how we must follow or be guided by our principles. What rules are absolute or relative? How do we balance absolute rules with personal freedom? For example, can we treat all others as ends and never as means? What happens in those situations where we treat some as means? It is not clear that we do not end up in some form of relativism. What actual principles of behavior emerge may depend on my personal situation. It is not clear that just treating others with dignity and respect will help.

*

Each ethical system brings a valuable perspective to moral reasoning. Except for ethical relativism and Eternal Laws (which historically are difficult to implement), the three remaining theories all bring clear positive benefits. Consequentialism provides one of the clearest definitions we have of unethical behavior—when we trade off long-term overall benefits (for the greatest number) for short-term gains. This also indicates the basic relation between ethics and reason insofar as this also makes a pretty good definition of unreasonable behavior (i.e., stupidity).

The idea of ethical principles also provides direction for reasonable behaviors. Each principle can have weight without assigning a priority weighting or ranking. We can try to find the greatest balance of right and wrong in the circumstances. For example, *prima facie* duties could indicate that duties are, on all occasions, binding unless they are in conflict with equal or stronger duties. Also, we develop a sense that duties might always be relevant and provide strong moral reasons for performing the acts in question.

Of course, with all rule-based prescriptions, we need to ask whether the case in question falls under a rule, or whether a rule leads to competing and equally attractive alternatives. Do other factors or values (religious or professional obligations) compete with the rule? Notice that we could refer to consequentialism or virtues to help decide these matters.

Another benefit of universalism is its emphasis on duties and responsibilities. This relation leads to the idea that there are rights. A *right* is a justified claim, or entitlement, validated by moral principles or rules. It is usual that rights violations refer to an unjustified action against a right, and that infringement refers to an unjustified action overriding a right. All rights entail obligations on others. There are two kinds of rights in terms of the duties they impose—negative and positive rights. A negative right imposes a duty on others to not interfere with something (negative). For example, if I have a right to this pen, you have an obligation or duty not to interfere with my using the pen. The main restrictions involve constraining behaviors that would harm others, such as using the pen as a dagger, or writing hateful and inflammatory letters. A positive right imposes duties or obligations to provide something (positive). For example, if I have a right to food, you would be obligated to assist me to obtain food were I unable to provide for myself. These rights lead to what is called the *correlativity thesis*—a right entails that someone has an obligation to act in certain ways, and an obligation similarly entails a right. We distinguish between rights and right. X has a right to do Y, or X acts rightly in doing Y.

So, morality and ethics prescribe criteria we use to determine duties and obligations, as well as right or wrong behaviors. This leads to several criteria that are required if we are to make moral rules enforceable:

1. In morality, the focus is on general rights and obligations that bind all members of the community;

2. Everything true of positive rights is true of positive obligations;

3. Everything true of negative rights is true of negative obligations;

4. Any valid claim that constitutes a right is an enforceable claim—the question is the mechanism; and,

5. Special rights and obligations hold only in virtue of special relationships, such as professional relations or identified stakeholder interests.

There are issues to be worked out in detail. Rules and criteria often conflict, so how we implement an ethics or moral system often determines its effectiveness. A powerful set of negative rights and obligations is antithetical to a moral system composed of a powerful set of positive rights and obligations. For example, rights of privacy can conflict with enforceable obligations to assist others. This forms the basis of many of the moral conflicts in moral discussions.

We can get around many of these issues in practice by combining Virtue Ethics with Consequentialism and Universalism. These present three kinds of criteria we can use to evaluate the ethics of someone's behavior. In this context, we suppose that ethics is really about two things. First, ethics is about holding someone's character up to public scrutiny and *evaluating their actions and decisions against a set of ethical criteria*. These criteria can stem from:

1. Virtue Ethics—such as what kind of person (organization) are you?

2. Consequentialism—do the consequences of your actions and policies promote overall well-being for the greatest number of stakeholders and minimize harm?

3. Universalism—are you treating others as means rather than as ends? Would you be willing to have everyone in the world faced with similar circumstances behave the same way (and, in particular, toward you)?

Second, and in broad terms, ethics pertains to what I will call *quality thinking*. Ethics is about taking the time to put some quality thinking behind your decisions and actions. Ethics provides the criteria for how we evaluate quality thinking. Are you being honest and fair to others? Are you acting with integrity? Have you stopped to consider the consequences of your actions and selected courses of action that result in beneficial consequences and minimize harm? Notice that with these criteria, the quality of your thinking regarding what you decide, and *how* you decide to act, can be evaluated. You may well select actions that should bring about beneficial consequences, but how you go about it actually results in greater or avoidable harms. Finally, have you correctly identified and acted on the right principles?

We need to consider how all this works together. The general rule is as follows: I can criticize your behavior on ethical grounds on any of the three kinds of criteria. I can question your virtue (your honesty and integrity), I can question the results of your actions (and whether you even stopped to consider the consequences of your actions), or I can find fault with the principles of your behavior. To fail the ethical test—to be found that your decisions and actions are ethically questionable or wrong, you only need to fail on one kind of criteria. To pass ethical muster, you must pass all three kinds of criteria. I call this *Rule #1*. Rule #1 explains why it is easier to criticize the actions of others than to get things right yourself—not to mention, how ethics works in practice. Ethical failures are character failures that publicly praise or condemn individual or organizational decisions and actions. When we act on right principles, we pay attention to the potential outcomes of our actions, and at least strive to benefit rather than to harm, and act honestly and fairly toward others. When we do that, we all get the benefits of high-quality thinking and acting. However, when we fail to act on right principles, we fail to properly consider the consequences of our actions, and we fail to treat others honestly and fairly. Consequently, we are usually punished for our failures either directly or in how people treat us in future endeavors. Ethics works.

Ethical Values

Universalism presents the idea of the categorical imperative, that we should treat others as ends-in-themselves rather than as means. This imperative is often thought of as ethics promoting human dignity. It would not be much of an ethics if it did not do this. In this sense, we can refer to this principle as the *moral value of a person*. But are there other moral values that are needed for an ethics?

The answer is yes. There are at least three other ethical values that we need to embrace to avoid the criticism that we do not have much of an ethics. In addition to the idea that we must meet the criteria of virtues, consequences, and principles of action, we also need to include these underlying values. I refer to these as values rather than principles (they could be either or both) to stress that these values underlie ethical reasoning. To miss out on these values would literally devalue any ethics or morality that is based on the incomplete list. This leads to a need for *a second rule* for high-quality (ethical) thinking.

Over the 2,000 years of philosophical discourse, the Greek basis for ethical reasoning continues to stand as the ground of our thinking. As mentioned in Chapter 1, the Greeks considered that man is the only animal that places a value on things. They called this *thymos—man, the valuing animal.*

The first thing that people value is their own life. I have added that we must also value other persons as part of the process of creating Frameworks and symbolic forms. After these fundamental values, we tend to focus on family, possessions and so on.

For most of history, ethical struggles centered on the thymos of life in what Hegel called the master–servant relation.

The master conquers an individual and determines to take that individual's life unless the individual pledges servitude. As valuing one's own life is a supreme value, the individual agrees. At that moment, the real value of life is lost—it is passed over to the master. The two enter a relationship that formed the basis of most tribal communities over the centuries.

The servant loses his self in the struggle for life. The master now owns that self, which means that the master no longer recognizes the servant as a fellow subject of any intrinsic value. What was once a person is now merely an object for the master's use.

As life and personal identity are critical to objective understanding and meaning, to give up one's life and person to another is to give one's *being* to that other. In this sense, the servant does not exist for himself, but only exists *for the master.* The servant's very existence is now dependent on the master's whims. Any sense of meaning or personal value can only come from him. There can be no self-worth, nor self-esteem that is not directly tied to the master's life goals and actions. In many such ancient societies, all slaves and servants were expected to die when their master died, so they could be buried with them to serve in an afterlife. All servants who failed to do so on their own were killed.

When the servant gives up the values of life and person to enter servitude, of course, all qualities associated with life and person are lost. The servant gains quantity of life, but a life that is miserable, with a complete loss of self. The master has no respect for the servant, who is seen to be weak and cowardly. The servant sacrifices any will of his own. His will becomes a tool of the master's will.

But the master–servant relationship that forms is complex and takes on long-term consequences unforeseen by the master in the quest for dominance. In this relationship, the servant is dependent on the master for his life (there is no longer any person), but the master is dependent on the servant for his position and his person—which is what the master values over life itself and gambled for in the first place.

The sweetness of the master's victory is that the master is also master of all that the servant lost. All sense of person, freedom, and all such qualities are objectified and passed over to the master. His power is complete. The servant is no longer human, but becomes a nonperson—an object for the master's use. All force and violence are primitive attempts at mastery.

It becomes easy for the servant to understand the dual nature of this dependency, and the limits of the codependency. The moment the servant chooses freedom from bondage over life itself, the relationship is broken. The master no longer has any power over the former servant. There are limits to power.

As the servant comes to realize these limits, he attains in principle what made the master a master—personal identity in the form of the willingness to sacrifice everything, even life itself, to attain ascendancy in a power relationship. In this realization, another can limit the power of any one individual. But the master cannot acknowledge that the servant has been raised to his level, so fails to see the truth of his own dependency on his servants. After all, the servant is not a person but only an object to use. The master is overthrown by his own blindness.

For the servant, who is now the master's equal as a person, a revelation is put forth: mastery requires servitude.

But the servant-as-master cannot ignore the dependency on any servant, and cannot really ascend to replace his former master. He must rise above the master–servant relation and seek a new and more productive relationship with his peers. This is grounded in the ontological basis of the development of any social Framework.

In overthrowing the master–servant relation, in the freedom from bondage, Hegel reveals how communities progress to a higher order of tribalism that we associate with civilization, or, at least, civilized behavior. But, in the process of the development of human societies, there are other thymotic values that stake the claim for progress. Hegel identifies these as liberty and equality. Liberty and equality follow quite naturally from rising above the master–servant relationship.

In rising to personhood as the master's equal, the servant is liberated from bondage. This freedom is the first taste of victory. But the servant is now equal not just to the master, but to all persons. The real liberty is not an individual freedom, but a liberty from all master–servant relationships.

There can no longer be any master–servant relation that works to divide people into distinct categories, some who are persons, and some who are not. *All are persons and all are equal.* Consequently, liberty and equality are now valued above all things, for without these, people might succumb to attempts at mastery.

Here, we see the first glimpse of the character of ethical values, and the need for all people to embrace ethical values as a way of being in the world. All those who fail to recognize and live the values of liberty and equality also fail to recognize others as persons and are seeking some form of either mastery or servitude. These values (or their absence) define the *character* of the person, or how they relate to others in the world.

Life and person were the first thymotic values that came from simple communal interaction with others. These were the first values that were shattered in the formation of the master–servant relationship, and these are the first values reclaimed when the master–servant relationship is overthrown.

With the reclaiming of life and person as basic values in human relationships comes a new understanding that liberty and equality are required along with life and persons to avoid the master–servant relationship failure. As such, these values come to be understood as fundamental to how people *are*, and how they ought to be and behave. This expands the basic list of thymotic values to four: life, person, liberty, and equality, which form the basis of modern Ethics. From these, all our modern moral precepts and laws are derived. In the face of the failure of our various religions to provide common foundational ethical values for an increasingly global community, we could adopt these values as, at least, a starting point for moral considerations. The thymotic values can be the foundations or foundational values of any ethics of a global scope. All peoples around the world either have been in or are currently struggling in some form of master–servant relationship. In fact, the world's communities are largely defined in terms of power structures. We must rise above these power structure relationships if we are to form a global community committed to long-term survival. In these terms, it becomes important to understand what these values are, and how they contribute to the kinds of moral precepts that can guide modern behaviors.

Before I get into details, I need to position these values in a more focused context. First, all religions include a set of moral values in the core of their belief systems. That does not mean, however, that all theological concepts derived from that moral center are somehow magically moral. *Theology and morality are not the same things.* They have different goals and agendas, and not all moral principles can be firmly placed in line with the sacred. Whereas theology and ethics can clearly be related, we need to keep their separateness firmly in mind.

Second, we have selected the following values to explore based on two factors—the history of ideas and a simple rule of thumb. I state the assertion, "It wouldn't be much of an ethics if it didn't …" The reasoning here is that if ethical principles and values are to be systematically formed to ground morality, they must be more than just a loose set of principles or values. They must be mutually supporting in a systematic way. What I have in mind here is that in producing a moral fabric of a community, we need to weave several principles or values together. The final design is based on how our chosen values support each other in the weave. The moral fabric of a community is greater than the sum of its values and principles.

Rule #1 provides the criteria for quality thinking. It measures whether someone has taken the time to think through proposed decisions and actions. But how do we relate these criteria to the underlying ethical values? The key comes from looking at universalism in a slightly different context from above.

Kant defined *practical reason* as the faculty or capability to ignore the uniqueness of individual perspective. This is how reason is able to derive laws. With science we can describe *A* causes *B* causes *C*. This description is independent of any one person's unique perspective or point of view. *A* causes *B* causes *C*, regardless of whether you, Albert Einstein, or I observe it. The same applies in normative matters. How we ought to behave is based on behavior that is independent of individual perspective or biography. In situation *X*, it should not matter which of us is in the situation. *A* is how we ought to behave or what we ought to do. This is the basis of the *categorical imperative*. Considered along with the value of life as we rise above master–servant relations, promoting human dignity is our second underlying value.

It wouldn't be much of an ethics if we could not hold people to account for their decisions and actions. As such, we need to grant at least a minimum of freedom of decision and action. It makes no sense to deny anyone freedom to decide and hold them accountable for the consequences of their actions. This freedom is called *liberty*. When we consider liberty in the broader social context that was provided by Hegel, we can derive many of our fundamental rights and freedoms. Liberty refers not just to individual freedom, but also to political freedom—and that is the sphere where most of our rights are enacted.

Finally, in our complex and hierarchical societies, it wouldn't be much of an ethics if those in authority could act arbitrarily and indiscriminately, without fear of recourse or recrimination. This principle is called *equality*.

Notice that these underlying values meet the grounding conditions for our three kinds of criteria in deciding ethical matters, as well as providing a slightly different take on how to proceed. We explored the rise of liberty and equality from the master–servant relation, and we can now see that these pertain as founding principles or values across our three ethical approaches. A virtuous character should promote positive, long-term, overall beneficial consequences, particularly in the context of values that promote life, dignity, liberty, and equality. Considered as matters of policy and principle, we are looking for founding moral values that minimize victimization and promote not just reasonable behaviors, but an ethical basis for how we ought to behave. We are looking for values that provide a strong basis for complaint if they are not taken seriously.

Let us begin by exploring the nature of each value in greater detail. In the same sense that I can evaluate behavior using criteria from all three approaches, the whole point of an ethics requires all four values considered together. It will become evident that each value plays off and supports the others, so that all values must be considered in a balanced way if we are to form a proper ethics.

Reverence for Life

In rising above the master–servant relation, life is no longer the primary value. At a minimum, the servant is prepared to sacrifice life as a value to enter servitude. But, as with all basic values, life does not simply or magically disappear. It cannot really disappear because it is a foundational value needed for community with others. We might observe at this point that slave states are often thought of as rather backward, politically and economically, as they fail to really capture the value of all members of the community in a constructive way. They tend to expend a great amount of energy and resources in keeping their slaves in line. These are energies that could have been used to the greater success of the community. In the long run, slave states do not appear to work as they cannot maintain mastery indefinitely. It is this new understanding (usually by slaves) that brings the first real limits to the master's power over the servant.

Because the value of life does not magically disappear in the master–servant relationship, it resurfaces later in a new and exciting way. Albert Schweitzer in his *Philosophy of Civilization* best presented this, defining civilization in terms of ethics as a *"reduction in the strain of existence"* [emphasis added].

This reduction in the strain of existence results from the sheer physical well-being of individuals. This is a twofold process: man against nature, and man against man. The underlying basis of our success is the ability to *reason*. Reason first triumphs over nature, then over man.

Today, people are experiencing a real triumph of man over nature brought about by science and its application—technology. More people now live at a higher standard of living than the richest kings of only 100 years ago. Furthermore, this standard of living is both increasing and becoming more pervasive.

For example, despite the obvious differences between the rich and the poor, when we look at the extreme poor—those who are confronted with starvation on a day-to-day basis—there is hope for the future. According to the World Game Laboratories, the extreme poor represent less than $1/7^{th}$ of the world's population. Whereas this is a substantial number of people, it represents the lowest percentage of such people compared with the world's overall population than at any other time in history. This reduction in this group's size has been accomplished while the world's populations have been exploding. Given our current agricultural capabilities, there is no reason for the existence of this group. As a species, we produce more food than is needed to feed the world's population. Our mastery over nature is almost complete—although there are substantial long-term costs in how we have gone about this.

This brings the second aspect of civilization to the fore—man's triumph over man. This is the basis of the ethical dilemma now faced. From this point of view, we are not yet civilized. As a species, we have begun to realize that ethics stands at the root of the solution. So far, many solutions have been tried with various ideologies rather than with a real understanding of the underlying values and principles that are needed to succeed. But these values are reasserting themselves. They did not magically disappear, as the masters had hoped.

Again, my approach can help us to understand and provide a worldview that connects our experiences of reality with ethics. Under power structures in the master–servant relationship, basic questions about the meaning of life and our purpose in the world (both as individuals and as societies) are lost. Worse, master–servant relations lead to shallow thinking, which undermines the basis of recovering any sense of meaning for large portions of populations. This has resulted in two attitudes that became prevalent over the last two centuries.

The first is a positioning of ethics as somehow above the facts of science arrived at by reason. Man against nature has been divorced from man against man, such that science does not really answer to ethics or morality. In this sense, science has been divorced from its own rationalism, and simple facts have been placed in the predominant position over what these facts mean, and how they should be understood and used.

Schweitzer's claim is that this kind of thinking undermines any real understanding of the role of reason in science, and in the process divorces the power of reasoning from the empirical facts themselves.

Schweitzer goes deeper into this criticism of empiricism by pointing out that in divorcing facts from explanations, such ideologies undermine the power of explanations and their usefulness. This leads to skepticism about rationalism in general and a discrediting of reason and its role in finding meaning.

Second, Schweitzer finds that old ethical values are being replaced with new ideas that reflect a disjointedness between ideas and the material environment. Schweitzer is referring to the rise of materialism as an ideology. Materialism is the direct result of the increase in the mechanization of work, and of the mechanical structuring of institutions. Our whole society has become less personal and humane as a result. Society has been objectified and dehumanized and made somewhat antiseptic.

What further aggravates this problem is the increase in specialization in work without any suggestion that a worker comprehends the whole process. That is, no worker sees the whole production process through from beginning to end, let alone participates in more than a small part of the process.[44] This again tends to dehumanize our environment.

Against these trends, societies in general have failed to prop up the larger values of civilization, and so civilized values have been slowly eroded.

Schweitzer's evidence of the extreme dehumanization of the world rests in the way that wars were fought in the 20th century. These are characterized as worldwide conflagrations that had no regard for life, either as civilians or as armies. Both were treated as simple objects or pawns in the larger quest for victory at all costs. In this quest, all moral legitimacy that could justify any victory was also lost. This is the importance of understanding the role of reason in the face of empirical facts.

Ethical values are not factual in any empirical sense. They are normative by definition—not descriptive. Consequently, real meaning can only be derived by reasoning correctly – with appropriate quality. More importantly, a proper relation between reality and ethics brings a living philosophy to the table. Philosophy is not something you just think about; it is what you seek to experience in life, and is based on your life experiences. I might also add that it is based on and is needed for a viable and sustainable community.

Such a living quest for understanding and meaning is the essence of being human. It calls for a community where we each reason and act

---

44 Notice that this is a form of system blindness and contributes to the dance of blind reflex.

appropriately, as opposed to collecting facts and prioritizing objectifying agendas. For Schweitzer, this is the key to connecting reality with ethics. In my terms, implementing proper values is the key to connecting understanding with meaning.

For Schweitzer, *life* is the key value at the center of all human relationships. It is man who connects ethics with reality in and through the act of living in the world. It is man who connects understanding with meaning and values. This is a reaffirming of thymotic man. The first and most basic value is life itself. In the context of human interaction, recognition, and the connection between understanding, meaning, and value, life has intrinsic value in and of itself.

In the moment of the master–servant relation where life is forsaken as a value, there is a rift between reality and ethics, between understanding and meaning. Power comes from divorcing the world from ethical values. The master can do as he pleases to his servants. Might makes right.

But in rising above the master–servant relation, the rift between reality and ethics needs to be repaired. For Schweitzer, this amounts to rehumanizing man, and requires the value of life to be reaffirmed. In the moment that this happens, we reaffirm our self, our personal identity, our community, and our relationship with the world at large. Here, we can find meaning and purpose. But how does this reaffirmation take place, and what does it entail? To answer this, we must first profile the other ethical values mentioned above. We will see that the answer lies in how they support each other.

Respect for the Person

When the master–servant relation was overthrown, the servant reclaimed not only life, but personal identity, as well. However, in the first moments of the fall of the master–servant relation, the servant's sense of person is buried deeply within symbolic processes. It is a given and not yet a self-conscious realization.

In Kant's dictum that we always treat others as ends-in-themselves rather than as means, we are asked to refer to others by name and recognize that they have the same fears, ambitions, feelings, and capabilities as we do. We do not dehumanize them by ignoring those qualities that we would want recognized in ourselves. We do not *depersonalize* them. We do not replace names with derogatory or slang descriptions. The thymotic value of the person is often expressed as a golden rule—do unto others as you would have them do unto you. Note that personalization can be a negative if within a power structure you take personal offense at the systemic blindness of others. It is not this kind of personalization that we are referring to here.

Depersonalization is best expressed in military terms. The key objective of basic military training is to deprive the individual of their person. That is, all personal qualities are suppressed in favor of the military unit. In battle, each life depends on the actions of others, so personalities must be suppressed for the good of the unit. Further, it is easier to make the supreme sacrifice for your country if you do not have a sense of self or person that is not intimately tied to the unit.

This latter deprivation is the key to how to train people to kill. Targets are designated as *objects* rather than as *persons*. They are monsters, or "the enemy," or (insert any derogatory term). Euphemism is the vanguard of the master's training. Governments do not commit mass murder or genocide. They have "final solutions" or conduct "ethnic cleansing." The point is that all recognition of the humanity of the victims is suppressed.

The fastest way to end a war is to make the soldiers "see" the persons they are killing. It is okay to kill an object, but to take a person's life is murder. Personhood defines the moral status of any individual. Deny the person, and you deny moral status. With the recognition of the value of the person, we establish a *respect for the person*. This is often called *tolerance*.

Tolerance is a thymotic value. We must respect the person because this is the source of moral status. Only persons are eligible for moral status. But an individual must have the capability to exercise a choice of actions or non-actions. Only those who can choose a course of action from among alternatives can be held morally accountable. For example, those who are forced to commit crimes or moral wrongs under duress, as in a war, are not considered morally responsible for their actions. In general, morality is concerned with the consequences of a choice made by a person who is free to choose from among alternative actions. Any individual so identified is called a *moral agent.*

Moral agency is the normative by-product of how we build Frameworks. Symbolic interaction with others affirms *fellow subjectivity* and equates the same normative status to that individual that they want that individual to accord back to them. In this regard, respect for persons is the key to a moral attitude toward others.

The idea that a person is a moral agent pertains to the idea of free will and responsibility. The point here is that respect for the person, or tolerance, is a thymotic value that must be present in any ethics. In practice, tolerance is directly tied to liberty and equality, so these now need to be defined.

Liberty

Liberty is concerned with the condition in which coercion of some by others is reduced as much as possible in society.[45] When we put this into the context of a person, we can define liberty as "no other person can lay a claim to sovereignty over his or her self or person." There can be no master. Each individual is sovereign over their own mind and body. Each individual is recognized as a person.

This means that no person can own another. This is not just a descriptive claim in the sense that no one can live another's life for them; it is a basic tenet of how each of us actually *is* in the world. If there are no masters, and each individual is at liberty to live their own life, then all people are free to act as they think best. They are free from coercion by others.

Or are they?

In any geographic area, people will have to interact for food, shelter, warmth, and so on. These exchanges cannot be made without some regard for the well-being of another. Simple acts of brutality take everyone back to the master–servant relation, which is now known as an unviable model. It appears that there must be some limits on individual behavior.

45 This presupposes that individuals are free to act as prescribed.

Each individual is not at liberty to seek mastery over another. Rather, individuals are only a master over themselves. This is the true sense of personal identity in the context of community with others. All moral rules centered on violations of this sovereignty are derived from this understanding. If I kill or rape or enslave another, I have violated their sovereignty over their mind or body. I have violated the value of liberty. When considered as a universal act—what if everybody behaved this way—it becomes easy to see that such behaviors cut to the core of community life and rank as the worst offenses any person can commit. Such conduct requires formal enforcement, and so murder, rape, and slavery constitute crimes. Indeed, these are so important we designate them as capital crimes—as the worst crimes (kinds of coercion) a person can commit.

The idea behind liberty is that we are each surrounded by a kind of *moral space*. We are each free to act as we choose within the moral space. However, this is not an unlimited freedom. We are only free within the similar rights of others to their freedom of choice and action. We are not free to enter into or deprive others of their moral space. We are not free to harm others. Harm usually refers to coercive physical or mental damage or to the use of force to make others do our bidding as though we are a master over that person.

The whole point of liberty then, is to protect members of the community from the arbitrary use of force. Remember, liberty emerged from master–servant relations where the master's power is based on the willingness to use force to control or kill wayward servants. All servants are understood to be objects or things for the master's use. Servants are their masters' property. This leads to further characterizations of liberty as a foundational value.

The value of liberty stated as a principle of conduct has a corollary: we should use the least amount of force or coercion necessary to achieve our ends. The idea is that we must interact with others, but as liberty is designed to protect us from arbitrary force, we should always strive to avoid using force if at all possible. If force is necessary, its use should be minimized. Notice that law is usually defined as a force monopoly—no one may deprive another of their liberty or property except through the due process of law. With this in mind, we should only resort to laws and the use of legal force when absolutely necessary.

Furthermore, liberty means that no one may own another. This is the basis of the above-mentioned political freedoms or rights. For example, more positively, we say that I own my own mind and body. This becomes the basis of all property rights. If I own my mind and body, I am entitled to the fruits of my labors and whatever property I can gain from those labors.

Liberty as a value is designed to provide a principle of conduct in how we each relate to other persons in our community. However, we each relate both to each other and to the community at large. This brings us to liberty's companion, equality.

Equality

While liberty refers to the individual in terms of freedom from coercion, and how people ought to treat others with respect to their person and property, there is also the idea of how we should relate to the community as a collective, and more importantly, how that collective should behave toward each member as individuals.

Equality comes from the recognition that there can be no ascendancy of one person over another. This refers to the primary relation between the individual and the community overall. Communal living requires contributing to the greater good, but most communities are structured in authoritative hierarchies as a way of organizing. As a natural development of the division of labor that collectively enhances the well-being of the community overall, these structures provide some sense of hierarchy of some individuals or groups over others. This kind of organization of communities appears to violate the thymotic value of equality. But it need not do so.

Equality refers to how those in authority treat others. This depends on the understanding of the difference between *power* and *authority*.

Power is the result of genuine coercion to obtain mastery. Power is based on objectifying others and denying their person. In contrast, authority is the result of the division of labor as part of communal organization.

Authorities always respect others as persons and take strong steps to avoid objectifying them. Authorities who treat others as though they have power over them (i.e., with mastery) violate equality. We say that they have abused their position.

Authorities have a duty to treat others as equals in the sense of persons; that is, as they themselves should be treated if the situation were reversed. This directly ties the value of equality to respect for the person as in the above-mentioned maxim, "Do unto others as you would have them do unto you." Equality is a normative term that does not imply that people are equal in skills, ability, intelligence, and so forth. It is not descriptive. Equality means that people should not be treated differently based on arbitrary reasons. The issue for ethics is that we do discriminate against others all the time. We select friends and form relationships based on individual preferences. We hire people based on specific skill sets and capabilities. We judge others based on opinions of their presentability or character, and so on. The issue for equality is whether a particular characterization or preference is relevant to a form of treatment by the whole community and by those who are in authority to represent community interests.

For example, in matters of collecting taxes or matters of capital offenses, skin color is irrelevant to any kind of person in a normative sense. To treat people differently based on such a reason is to be arbitrary in a way that would objectify them, in the sense of seeking a sort of mastery over them. As master–servant relations do not work over the long run, such behavior is now seen to be unreasonable (in descriptive terms) and unfair. To collect the same taxes from all members of the community, and then to deny certain members the benefits derived by paying those taxes simply because of a characterization or preference that is unrelated to the benefits to be derived would clearly be arbitrary.

Equality, then, refers to how people should treat each other in situations where one person has some authority or position over another. This authority should recognize that there is no mastery here, and that all are to be treated equally. In modern Western societies and in the United Nations, there is usually some declaration of the rights and freedoms that specify what constitutes arbitrary treatment. For example, the list usually includes race, sex, color, creed, and religious belief. Some lists also include sexual orientation and other characterizations. The point is that no one in a position of authority may discriminate against any member of the community if the reason for that discrimination is based on any of race, sex, color, creed, religious belief, or any other of a number of reasons, if they are arbitrary. To engage in any form of arbitrary discrimination is said to be a form of corruption, and the authority in question is said to have failed to meet the moral standards of the community.

This brings us to an illustration of how these values are to be used to form a moral framework for all people.

An Ethical Framework for Moral Precepts

Any ethical view must promote all four thymotic values in as balanced a way as reasonable and possible. *This is Rule #2.* The idea is that to build up the moral fabric of our community, we need all our foundational ethical values balanced toward the greater good—the long-term well-being of the community. Any view or argument that would reduce the foundational value set or forget about or suppress one or more thymotic value would literally devalue any morality.

If a theory ignores or suppresses liberty in favor of a political program or agenda, that theory would be morally suspect. A genuine suppression or subversion of liberty for political ends would literally devalue the moral fabric of the community. The same might be said of equality. Any law that fails to uphold equality—which would prevent those in authority from discriminating against members of the community for arbitrary reasons—would be an unjust law. If a law were to permit and promote arbitrary discrimination, it might also promote intolerance and perhaps even a loss of life and liberty.

The idea is that we should not throw out or suppress any foundational value just because promoting it would be inconvenient to some other objective we want to make predominant. Foundational ethical values do not magically disappear whenever they become inconvenient. The whole point of these foundational values is that they are not easily ignored or suppressed. Again, we need all our foundational ethical values, not just those that are convenient to this or that point of view.

I call any theory or position that promotes all foundational values in a balanced way an *ethics*, while any theory or position that suppresses or sacrifices foundational principles and values is called a *mere ideology*. As mentioned in the first chapter, ideologies can be more or less vicious. For example: someone might argue for a political or social reform that should improve the moral fabric of the community. However, they might inadvertently or by mistake fail to balance one or more thymotic values. Such a policy would still have the consequence of devaluing morality, but it would be unintentional. This stands in contrast to those who would actively subvert foundational values to promote their policies or programs, without regard to the harm or suffering such policies would cause. Someone might suppress a value for personal gain without regard for those who would be harmed. Such intentions are clearly vicious. Ideologies, then, come in a range from mere to vicious depending on the intent of those advocating the policy or program.

With this in mind, we can characterize the meaning of ethics. We harken back to the idea from universalism that when we victimize others, we set ourselves up to be victimized in return. I call this getting your *just deserts* or what Americans call a comeuppance. Ethics as quality thinking promotes this sense of poetic justice. In the long run, people get pretty much what they deserve. People who do good deeds and are fair, principled, and promote the public good deserve just rewards, and those who are unfair, unprincipled, and cause harm deserve some form of punishment. It is very satisfying when a harmful person gets what's coming to them pretty much in the same way they dished it out to others. This is the real meaning of ethics and serves to explain both how and why ethics tends to work. When a large number of community members actively seek the satisfaction of seeing people get what they deserve, more often than not, the good people are rewarded, and the so-and-so's get what's coming to them. Ethics works. Overall, and in the long run, people tend to get what they deserve. This is the basis for our ideas about *justice*. This does not mean, of course, that there is no injustice in the world. People do not always get their just deserts. Many people deserve better and do not get it. Many people escape their just deserts. But, overall, people do tend to get what they deserve. As we improve the moral fabric of our communities, more often than not, justice tends to prevail, and this is a true measure of progress.

Justice is only possible if we can balance foundational values. When we treat others with respect for their life and person, and grant them appropriate liberty, and treat them with appropriate equality, justice tends to prevail. Injustice is often defined in terms of the direct omission of a foundational value; for example, when liberty is denied, or someone is a victim of intolerance. A common source of injustice is prejudice, when we prejudge someone's character based on arbitrary criteria, and then actively suppress their liberty as a result. Much of this kind of thinking comes from current power structure institutions that perpetuate master–servant values.

In Rule #2, we do not get to cherry-pick underlying ethical values. A properly formed ethical position promotes all our foundational ethical values in a positive and balanced way. Failing Rule #2 is another way to fail at ethical reasoning.

But, to pass ethical muster, we must pass both rules. We must meet all the criteria of quality thinking and balance foundational values in the process. When we put these together, we can derive moral precepts that describe the rules of behavior for a given situation. Unfortunately, not all moral Frameworks pass the two rules.

Justice

In any world of extended tribal relations, an individual is more than a tribal unit but has some status as a person. In short, the values of life, liberty, equality, and tolerance depend on recognizing persons. All thymotic values depend on recognition of others as fellow subjects and rail against objectifying others.

We credit both the collective and the individual with moral responsibilities. Much moral discussion centers on the relation between collective and individual responsibilities; for example, how a corporation should treat its employees, and how the employees should treat a corporation. Many of the debates surrounding environmental issues suggest new responsibilities for corporations, as well as new responsibilities for individuals toward corporations that fail to be environmentally responsible.

A community that prospers is a community that values life, persons (promotes human dignity), liberty, and equality, where justice occurs more often than not, and where there are increased opportunities for personal growth and material well-being. This shifts the focus from the amount of liberty and equality to the quality of the values as manifest in the community. This requires that we recognize the person and not just a tribal or social objective unit.

In morality, responsibilities and duties are ascribed to each member of the community as the chief enforcement mechanism. For example, we saw that the value of liberty can be implemented in two ways, referring to positive and negative rights. These two kinds of rights, negative (duties of noninterference), and positive (duties of assistance), come from the thymotic value of liberty. All related moral precepts and rights ascribed to members of the community depend on the recognition and the valuing of liberty as the basis of moral reasoning.

The notion of *valuing* is the essential ground of ethics. As mentioned above, the universal thymos does the grounding in the concept of a person and our recognition of that person.

The value of equality brings us our idea of *fairness*. To objectify others toward an unwarranted mastery is to be unfair to them. In the relationship between the individual and the community, there is a moral expectation that designated authority should not abuse others. When abuse occurs, we say that an injustice has occurred. This adds to our definition that justice means "fairness" (as per Rawls), but there are two senses in which this realization happens.

Justice as fairness occurs when individuals are treated fairly by those in authority. Justice prevails when abuses of authority are stopped, and corrective action is initiated. Justice is clearly based on the value of equality understood in its proper context.

However, violations of liberty can also be described as an injustice. Individuals can unjustly interfere with another's person or property, for example, or fail to assist others in basic necessities. Justice also pertains to the value of liberty.

When the two are put together, a stronger sense of justice emerges that is more than their sum. To produce justice requires recognition of and upholding and supporting both the criteria of quality thinking and thymotic values. Justice can now be defined in these terms—justice is the long-term manifestation of both values of liberty and equality.

But what happened to the values of life and person? Recall that the whole point of the master–servant relation depended on the value of life and of denying the person. Surely, these are also part of any definition of justice?

Indeed, this is the case. When life, liberty, and equality merge, moral order is achieved. In this third sense, justice requires all three values, and not just liberty and equality. A just society promotes and protects all three. However, improved social order permits a deeper self-realization. This adds tolerance as a key component of justice. Recognizing persons is the first step to moral agency. Only persons can be held responsible for their choices and actions. This means that there is a direct relationship between the structure of the moral fabric of a community and how well personhood is integrated with the values of life, liberty, and equality. Reverence for life leads to respect for the person. We each regard the other as capable of being held morally responsible for their actions. But this, in turn, only works if we grant that person enough freedom of choice and action to decide for themselves how to behave. Consequently, we grant the person some moral space within which they are free to live as they please. Of course, there are restrictions on how much freedom is permitted, but the value of liberty is basic to any sense of moral judgment.

The same applies to the relation between respect for the person and equality. If those in authority do not respect the person in their own right, they will behave arbitrarily toward them. This might even include the level of support a community will provide to protect and support the life of that person.

The point is that respect for the person requires that we each recognize the life of the other as a person with the same capacities for emotions, thoughts, and actions as ourselves, and that we grant liberty and equality as foundational values for how we treat each other. This means that we are tolerant of others in their opinions and actions up to the point that we can identify a definite wrong or harm. It is this ability to relate to others in a normative way—how we each ought to behave—that leads from foundational ethical values to specific moral precepts. Respect for the person also introduces an additional characteristic to moral debates. Ethics is always intensely personal. What we are really doing is holding someone's character up to public scrutiny and evaluating their actions and decisions against a set of ethical values or criteria. The question always asks, what kind of person are you? In the context of a global community, we might ask if this is the best you can be as a human being or, if this is the best you can be as a member of the human race.

In this context, ethics mirrors the way in which we establish objective understanding and meaning. The whole point of ethics is to make normative considerations public—to objectify ethical values and principles. Once the foundational ethical values achieve a significant measure of objectivity, we can move forward to establish the moral rules and laws that are based on these foundations. The idea is that with objectively valid foundations, the moral rules and laws that derive will also be objective and public and available for public scrutiny.

The inclusion of respect for the person also provides a fourth sense of justice. Justice is only possible when all four foundational values are promoted in a balanced way. In a real sense, all four values support and promote each other. The trick for getting to morality is to instantiate specific moral precepts or rules that people can follow to act correctly in various circumstances.

The first question to be asked in any moral discussion, then, is which of the four foundational ethical values is at stake? The idea is to promote all four in a balanced way. This might not always be easy in practice. Let us consider a couple of examples.

In contemporary media-rich society, there are often publications that are offensive to some members of the community. An example would be publishing materials with explicit sexual content. To some, this is art, or at least, free expression, whereas to others, this is offensive as pornography. There is often a call for censorship.

This is not necessarily a life or death issue, so the value of life appears not to be at stake. However, the value of liberty is clearly at issue. If individuals freely engage in producing, distributing, and purchasing sexually explicit materials—that is, if there is no overt harm that can be identified—then liberty requires that there be no constraints on such behaviors. In contrast, in cases where someone is coerced into engaging in explicit public sexual acts for someone else's profit, a clear harm can be identified. Getting a person hooked on drugs to perform in so-called X-rated movies is clearly a case of using a person as a means to an end. Such people are objectified and used without regard to their person or their liberty. But what if all parties consent to the behaviors?

The issue centers on how to define harm. For example, women often complain that they are generally harmed because such materials objectify them in all areas of social interaction. Others retort that people have the ability to distinguish between a woman in a sexual context and other nonsexual contexts. Factual data regarding the truth of either claim may be needed to support one position over the other.

The point is that in the absence of a clear definition of harm, censorship does not promote foundational values in a balanced way. Groups that argue for censorship are really arguing to outlaw such materials. The problem is that law is defined as a force monopoly, and so censorship is really arguing to curtail individual liberty with the use of force. For one group in society to use force to make others toe their line is precisely the kind of activity that the value of liberty is designed to protect us from.

The issue is clearer if we put it in universal terms. If one group of the community can use force to make others conform to their moral precepts, why is it not acceptable for other groups to behave the same way? In the absence of a clear definition of harm, there would be a growing use of violence to settle differences of opinion. Again, liberty is designed to protect us from arbitrary and accelerating violence. If it could be argued that the group advocating censorship is really promoting a political or social agenda at the expense of liberty (which is often how such groups appear), then the consequence of censorship would be to devalue morality. Again, if we are going to build a solid moral fabric for a community, we need all our foundational values, not just those that are convenient to this or that point of view. To opt for censorship requires more than just an opinion that such materials are harmful. It requires further reasoning or proof that force is the correct response.

One way of moral reasoning is to ask what would happen if everyone behaved as you are advocating. If your position clearly devalues morality, the direct consequent would be to devalue the moral fabric of the community. This is often worded, "If you think it is acceptable to use force to make others toe your line, then on what basis would you object if others treated you the same way?" The focus of the discussion shifts to how universal your moral proposal would be if universally adopted. It also shifts the discussion directly to the persons involved. Does your position objectify anyone or treat others differently based on arbitrary reasons? Would your position objectify others if adopted as social or moral policy? What kind of person advocates the use of force to settle differences of opinion?

The last question asks directly, what kind of person are you? I advocate that you ask this question of anyone posing a moral argument. What kind of person treats others in the proposed way? Would they agree to being treated that way themselves? Using the censorship example, a church group advocating censorship needs to recognize that they are arguing for a principle of moral conduct. In this case, it might be simply that they are promoting a view that it is acceptable to censor anyone who publishes materials that are not evidently harmful, but offensive. If this principle were adopted, would they feel that justice was served if some other group treated their materials the same way?

Note that if morality is really devalued by the proposal, the greatest justice that the community could hope for is that the advocating group be victimized by their own policy. Justice tends to prevail when all foundational values are upheld in a balanced way. A position that fails in this task should expect treatment with the same imbalanced policies. After all, they thought they were advocating a right way to treat others, so they would have little basis for complaint.

It is not always possible to balance foundational values. The best example for this is the issue of abortion. Here, the value of the life of the fetus is at odds with the liberty of the mother to decide over her own body. Life and liberty need to be both promoted and balanced to achieve a moral result. There are currently four arguments for or against abortion:

1. The anti-abortion position advocates that the value of life is supreme and must be protected at all costs. Abortion is, therefore, wrong and should be outlawed.

2. The pro-abortion position advocates that liberty is the value that should reign supreme, and that all decisions must be made by the mother. Society has a responsibility to honor her choice in the matter and provide whatever assistance is needed for a safe abortion, should that be her decision.

Notice that both of these views are rather extreme. Both simply ignore or suppress a needed thymotic value. Both literally devalue morality. Life and liberty are not promoted in a balanced way. Rather, one value is sacrificed to the other. I argue that these views are morally wrong and fail to meet the standards required for an ethical approach to the issue.

3. The pro-life view holds that in this case, the value of life counts for more than the value of liberty, but that liberty must also be protected as much as possible. With regard to resorting to the force of law, we should use the minimum force consistent with protecting the life of a fetus.

4. The pro-choice position advocates that in this case, the value of liberty weighs more than the value of life, but that life must be respected, so there must be clear constraints on the choices a mother has available.

These moderate views try to promote a balanced approach. Both try accommodating as much as possible the concerns of the other. For example, pro-life groups often provide for education on birth control to prevent unwanted pregnancies in the first place, and advocate social-support systems for adoption. Certainly, pro-choice groups would applaud such measures. Pro-life groups also often permit exceptions to the rule that the value life should take precedence. They might permit abortions, for example, in cases of rape, or incest, or when the mother's life is in danger.

Pro-choice advocates would agree with these permissions, but would tend toward a longer list. The constraints would be on avoiding an uncaring approach to abortion, such as using abortion as a method of birth control.

In general, pro-life groups offer a short list of exceptions to a general rule that abortion is wrong, while pro-choice groups tend to offer a greater list of permissions based on a rule that abortion is permissible if the individual makes that their choice. Notice the difference in language. Pro-life advocates assume that life takes precedence over liberty with some *exceptions*, while pro-choice advocates the value of liberty over life, and so opts for *permissions*. It does not help the debates that both groups use different language, as this often obscures areas of agreement and pushes discussions to cross-purposes. However, if we compare these contrasting views, we can see that while they disagree in principle about which value should predominate, they do agree on underlying social systems to support education and adoption and related social programs. The real disagreement, outside of the matter of principle of which value counts for more, is how long should the exceptions/permissions list be?

My point is that there does not appear to be any answer in principle. That is, there does not appear to be any way to decide who is right in principle. We need both values, and because both values are foundational, it is a serious matter to suppress one or the other. How could we possibly decide?

The answer is one that is not a happy answer for many. The correct answer is that there is no answer. There is no theoretical position where it is acceptable to suppress one value over the other and still promote morality. In short, we can't decide on whether abortion is right or wrong—at least, whether it is *always* right or wrong.

To resolve the issue, we need to acknowledge that balancing these values is not easy and might not be possible even in theory. It might require understanding specific circumstances that a theoretical right or wrong solution would not consider. It turns out that we have a very good mechanism for working this out—our adversarial legal system.

In the legal system, issues are decided by an impartial adjudicator (judge), such that each case is evaluated on its own merits, and these merits are established following structured guidelines for what constitutes acceptable evidence. I suggest that we use this system to find out what situations people actually find themselves in when abortion becomes an issue. Then, evaluate each situation on its own merits and come to a judgment. In general, in these kinds of situations, we tend to permit abortion, and in these other circumstances, we do not. Over time, we can at least strike a balance between life and liberty in practice, and in a way that permits us to decide when one value should take precedence over the other. This does not answer to any absolute moral theory. It does, however, provide a practical balance and does promote both values in a balanced way. In this sense, it is the right way to proceed.

Conclusions

The values just described can apply to any culture or religious faith. They have no religious or cultural dependence, yet can be used to evaluate the moral worth of cultural institutions, including how religious institutions behave. This is vital because religions tend to promote themselves as moral authorities in the community. It is critical that while life is often considered a key religious value, tolerance often is not. There is no major religion today that embraces liberty and equality as core values. These are often viewed as secular ethical principles, derived from European enlightenment philosophies. This is not to say that there is no enlightened thinking in our various and sundry religious groups, but this is a far cry from a faith that adopts these values as core values in their moral frameworks. In short, whereas major religions agree on some form of Virtue Ethics, they have, for the most part, failed to embrace Consequentialism and Universalism. No moral groups that I know of have advocated an approach to ethical thinking that uses all our ethical criteria and values in a positive way for the benefit of all. So much for moral leadership from the core of civilization.

The point is that ethical criteria are no longer based on the religious or cultural values of a tribe or community. They have an objective status above any one tribe or culture or religion. Yet, these are the values we use to evaluate the decision and actions of our institutions and those who run them. If traditional moral authorities cannot promote foundational values in a balanced way, we might have grounds to consider whether there are other political, social, or theological agendas that are taking precedence. If so, we might want to re-evaluate how effectively our religious institutions provide moral guidance.

One of the ways we might do this was presented by Hanna Arendt. In a modern society, people tend to say that they have no personal responsibility since it is the system, or the institution that determines their decisions and actions. Arendt points out, though, that our legal systems hold individuals responsible for the actions of any system or institution.[46] People run all organizations, and their character can be held up to public scrutiny and their decisions and actions evaluated against objective ethical criteria. Religious institutions need to take note that this is now how their behaviors are being evaluated. We are not judging character on theological criteria such as faith and doctrine, but on ethical values, and these are mostly different in kind from traditional, theological moral criteria.

Finally, when we put it all together, a proper ethical approach considers ethics as a way to evaluate the character and quality of thinking of any individual or group. We have three broad kinds of criteria—virtue, consequentialist, and universalist—and four foundational values to be considered. I can criticize you for a failure in any one area. You can fail in virtue, consequences, or fail in principle. Or conversely, you can indicate that you have put some quality thinking behind your actions and decisions by paying attention to virtues, consequences, and principles, and showing how you promote foundational ethical values in a positively balanced way.

Ethics works. The key lies in the meaning of just deserts. It is thinking honestly and fairly for the long term and acting with integrity in such a way as to avoid the mistakes that could be made whereby you promote harm or whereby you could become a victim of your own policies and practices. Promoting these values for everyone, regardless of culture or religious beliefs, can provide a basis for a common set of moral precepts that we can all embrace. If this promotes a moral approach to how we live on our planet, and how we behave toward each other, man might finally overcome man. Promoting these values in a balanced way would be more than just reasonable—it would be wise.

---

46 Arendt, *Eichmann In Jerusalem*, p. 13.

CHAPTER 5
Moral Precepts

I will now examine our current political and economic systems to see how these compare with my ethical model. While ethics and morality pertain to how we should each behave as individuals, there is also a need to characterize the rules for the community as a collective. This provides the guiding fabric for individual and group behavior. We will start by characterizing the moral rules associated with the governance of political and economic aspects of a community, and how political and economic individuals should behave. This will set the ground rules for how to think about the moral fabric of a community at large, as well as individual compliance. In the process, I hope to expose the difference between competitive rules and cooperative rules—the rules of the master as opposed to those rules that rise above the master–servant relationship.

The best description of political morality is presented by Jane Jacobs in her book *Systems of Survival*.[47] In this work, Jacobs presents a post-thymotic view of values or precepts, and shows how these divide into two kinds of moral syndromes—those of the masters, whom she calls guardians, and those of the populous, who have risen to a set of economic relations, which she calls the commercial syndrome. Because each group uses all the precepts, Jacobs calls each of the two sides a moral syndrome. A "syndrome" is condition characterized by a set of associated symptoms. But sets of moral precepts are more than just a set of symptoms but are a virtual

---

47 The first two kinds of descriptions of moral precepts are drawn from this book. I have not noted specific page references since these pervade the book.

public form that structures our thinking and guides our behavior. Given the definition of a virtual public structure provided above, I will outline each as a Framework and then consider the implications for civilization.

The Guardian Moral Framework

The Guardian Moral Framework defines the rules of behavior for those at the political top of society and is composed of 15 moral precepts, which will be detailed below. To understand these precepts as a system of moral values that promote and support guardian or master systems, we should consider historically what it was like to be a member of a ruling aristocratic class. This body of ruling elites created and sustained these precepts. These are the rules to which members of the aristocracy or ruling elites must adhere, to ensure the survival of the class system, and in particular their class and ruling status in the community. Let's briefly examine each precept in turn.

1. **Shun trading**. Aristocrats do not engage in commerce. They are above petty affairs such as business relations. Guardians hire people as their agents to engage in such lowly behavior. Every ruling elite for most of recorded history maintained such a rule for its members.

Jacobs suggests that this precept originated in the idea that a master (my terminology) is above "servant" behavior. More than this, the precept protects against treachery. Trading military secrets is still trading. It is simply not done if you want to remain a master. All who share your class must at least rely on your integrity in this regard. The precept guards against corruption and provides a basis for maintaining mastery by focusing on master activities rather than on commerce, which requires some equality. This precept is often referred to as *honor*.

2. **Exert prowess**. This is the main precept for being a guardian. A master gets to be master by exerting prowess and defeating the servant. Prowess means bravery (even to the death), and skill in combat. This precept also marks those who seek power over authority.

3. **Be obedient and disciplined.** This precept maintains the status quo of the master–servant relation, which is the primary responsibility of a guardian. All other personal values and beliefs must take a back seat to supporting your class. Obey the rules (e.g., of chivalry) and have the discipline to overcome your emotions to do the right (i.e., masterful) thing.

4. **Adhere to tradition.** Tradition serves as an alternative for conscience in guardian work. It reassures a scrupulous or doubting individual that obeying orders is the right thing to do.

5. **Respect hierarchy.** All guardian organizations are based on the principle of hierarchies. To get ahead in a master society, you must "move up the ladder." These hierarchies form the chain of command that is the Framework for obedience, discipline, and tradition. The military is the best example of how the first four precepts combine and reinforce each other in this respect. Hierarchical law reinforces prowess.

6. **Be loyal.** Governments regard treason as the wickedest crime, worse even than murder. (Of course, slavery or servitude is okay.) Loyalty reinforces obedience and provides a basis for masters to dispense largesse by rewarding and demonstrating their loyalty to their followers. Jacobs points out that many of Machiavelli's precepts center on loyalty. Most guardian activities are about how to get and keep loyalty. After all, without loyal followers, there can be no power structure, and no masters.

7. **Take vengeance.** The emotional drive to retaliate seems to come naturally and does not need to be taught. Basically, master behavior requires that any slight that might demean a guardian's position must be dealt with harshly and quickly. A guardian cannot allow anyone to inflict a harm (physical, emotional, or psychological) without making some retaliatory move. After all, a guardian cannot lose face, as this would undermine the guardian's position at the top.

8. **Deceive for the sake of the task.** Deception is an integral part of any successful hunting expedition. Hunters use deception to kill or capture prey just as the military uses it in combat operations. This precept points to the importance of deception to ensure a victory. After all, victory is the

primary goal of any master—to become a master by defeating opponents. Deceit is valued as part of the guardian arsenal.

However, a guardian must not deceive another member of the guardian class. That would be disloyalty. Deception is valued to establish and maintain a master position when used against the enemy (read, servants who might be able to undermine mastery).

9. **Make rich use of leisure.** Hunting is not a continuous activity. There are spurts of energy between long periods of boredom. War is similar. A guardian must use this time well to keep fit as a guardian. Master behavior requires that the whole person be up to the task of guardianship.

Leisure is available because guardians shun trade. They tend to develop their community through art, science, and literature. Historically, the elite have always been responsible for sponsoring and creating the arts. They have the means and the time, and usually the education and tools needed for such tasks. However, rich use of leisure has another purpose for the elite. It affords an opportunity to display their superiority—not only to the masses, who must grovel at their feet, but also to those who should wonder at the marvels their superiors can create. Rich use of leisure demonstrates superiority.

10. **Be ostentatious.** This is the impersonal guardian display of prowess. It serves to "evoke awe, fear or reassurance."[48] It also expresses pride, tradition, continuity, and stability. Ostentatious tradition is the highly visible continuity with the past. Ostentation provides the mechanism for displaying both the power and the sheer mastery of the guardian.

11. **Dispense largesse.** The guardian form of investment—in power, influence, and control—is the art of calculating who in society needs persuading, placating, or threatening at a given time.

12. **Be exclusive.** Guardians are elite and do what they need to do to maintain their status as such. This is the pride of mastery.

13. **Show fortitude.** "Accept hardship with uncomplaining stoicism."[49] This precept demonstrates that guardians are tough, which is the source of

---

48 Jacobs, *Systems Of Survival*, p. 83.
49 Ibid, p. 90.

macho mentality. In my view, masters are willing to sacrifice life to become masters. This willingness to risk everything makes them masters (or so they think). This is fine for those who create the guardian class for their community. But what of those who are born to the class? These members must display the same backbone or grit as the founding masters. Courage and valor are the stuff of guardians.

14. **Be fatalistic.** This precept links with fortitude. Those who live high-risk lives need to have a sense that when they must lose, it is not because they are not masters; rather, it is because of something else. Their luck ran out, or their number was up, or whatever superstition explains the failure.

15. **Treasure honor.** Jacobs describes honor as the Western equivalent of "face" in the Far East: "It is the recognition of status and the respect owed to status... . The respect is owed, and the self-respect earned, because honor implies moral obligations, and its possession certifies that the obligations attached to a position ... are admirably fulfilled."

That "master" values linger in our communities and are pervasive throughout our political systems is evidenced by this list of moral precepts. It outlines the values of the ruling elite, be they aristocrats, governments, or political leaders. Further, it is how they expect to cohere as a group and expect to be treated by the lowly masses.

The Commercial Moral Framework

The Commercial Moral Framework is also composed of 15 precepts, which are discussed below. Consider, historically, what it would have been like to be a member of the commercial class. This will aid in developing a thorough understanding of these precepts as a system of moral values that promote and support commercial systems. These precepts were created and sustained by the body of traders. As a result, these precepts are the rules that members of the business community must adhere to, to ensure the survival and prosperity of their community, and in particular their class and community status. Let's briefly examine each precept in turn.

1. Shun force. Without this primary precept for all traders, they would live in constant fear that force would deprive them of their goods or profits. Further, if violence were tolerated, it would preclude the ability to come to an agreement that would benefit all parties. This leads naturally to the second precept.

2. Come to voluntary agreements. This is a definitional matter for trading. When force or intimidation enters the picture, it is no longer called trade.

3. Be honest. Honesty gives substance to any voluntary agreement. Without honesty, there can be no way to ensure that a bargain will be carried out as agreed. Because traders shun force, they must rely on the integrity of others to conduct business.

4. Easily collaborate with strangers and aliens. Honesty leads naturally to the idea of trust. We must each trust those with whom we deal to honor their agreements. Historically, traders would be the community members who would have to deal mostly with strangers because goods and materials were shipped to and from many places. No trader could know in advance who to trust, and traders could not rely solely on locals to provide ready markets. At some point, a trader had to rely on others to complete the transaction. Even today, we trust in systems of people to do their jobs, even in such simple matters as depositing money to our bank accounts. We can now do this from almost anywhere in the world. But to rely on such a system is to trust that the many people and organizations involved (whom we never meet) will act with integrity throughout the process.

Honesty is a primary ingredient for success in business. As indicated earlier, the trade-off of long-term overall benefit for short-term local gain defines unethical behavior. When the banker takes my money rather than depositing it in my account, it will not be long before no one will trust him, and his bank will close for lack of customers.

5. Compete. Jacobs supposes that voluntary agreements require effective choice. That is, if we are to trade honestly, no one party can hold a monopoly. This precept also links with honesty and shunning force. We all need a choice of banks if we are to find one that will deal honestly with us. Jacobs views competition as the guarantor of overall long-term benefits—that is, of an ethical system of business.

6. Respect contracts. Contracts mark the terms of any agreement. This restates the idea of coming to voluntary agreements, and then sticking to them honestly. Contracts, whether formal or informal, state the details of the agreement in such terms as can be well-understood by all parties.

7. Use initiative and enterprise. This precept ensures prosperity through growth and diversity. To have real competition and to avoid a monopoly entails encouraging new ideas either in products or services.

8. Be open to inventiveness and novelty. Enterprise and initiative require openness to new ideas. But commerce requires more than just traders coming up with new gimmicks. For trade to work well, buyers must also be open to novelty. An appreciation of inventiveness is required for the whole commercial system to work.

Inventiveness and novelty also relate to competition. Diversity stands at the heart of competition, so the appreciation of novelty and inventiveness is a core method of ensuring that the competition is lively.

9. Be efficient. Competition also requires that goods and services are sold in a way that is profitable. Anyone can build any product or provide a service. But those who are most efficient in *how* they do this will gain an advantage. It is not just what you do in business that counts; it is also how well you do it, and efficiency is a measure of that effectiveness.

10. Promote comfort and convenience. A central ingredient of commerce is the idea of progress. Innovation leads to more than just the exchange of essential goods; it leads to the trade of non-essential goods as well. This latter group of goods and services promotes a higher standard of living. Remember that trade grew up with the wealth of the landed aristocracy as the measure of material well-being. Trade is another way of achieving a similar result. However, when commerce works well, the whole community benefits, and this leads to an overall increase in the standard of living.

It should also be noted that trade was often regarded as crass by the aristocracy, who shunned it. Historically, there was no way for commerce to improve the lot of the gentry. It could, however, improve the lot of the lower classes as more of them began to participate in commerce. Many of the caste systems imposed by the aristocracy were to prevent just this occurrence. After all, you cannot call yourself superior if any Tom, Dick, or Harry can live as ostentatiously as you can! Maintaining a strong hold on wealth and its distribution is one of the ways that guardians maintain their power.

11. Dissent for the sake of the task. As new ideas come along, we must give up old ways to be able to embrace the new. This is a common contemporary experience, given the current pace of advancements in technology. To promote new products and services that would compete to replace older methods requires dissent from the old methods. This often means getting rid of the "dinosaurs" that cannot or will not keep up with the rate of progress.

12. Invest for productive purposes. The idea of dissenting for the sake of the task leads to the idea that investment efforts should be for productive purposes. New products and services require investment. Investing in old technologies, for example, could mean that you would lose the competitive fight and lose profits and other benefits. To compete well, a business must constantly be improving. This kind of attitude is central to any successful commercial enterprise.

13. Be industrious. For trade to work well to everyone's advantage, all members of the community must participate in commercial processes. Traders frown upon freeloading, which amounts to a violation of trust. Consequently, traders value industriousness and condemn idleness. This is the source of the modern work ethic, the idea that only those who work hard deserve to succeed.

14. Be thrifty. Investing in new products or services requires experimenting, and the willingness to accept risk. Bringing new ideas to a practical commercial end requires time, money, effort, and much more. Only those who are thrifty can afford the investment in such activities. Spending all profits on "wine, women, and song" (idleness) not only uses up the resources needed to remain competitive, but it also shows a complete lack of industriousness.

15. Be optimistic. Jacobs points out that traders are fearful of violence and its associated loss. They hedge their bets with formal contracts, insurance, forecasts, pledges (e.g., of collateral), letters of credit and introduction, and so on. Much of the administration of running a business is the paperwork of managing risk and of reducing these fears. These are all steps to forestall surprise and misfortune. Jacobs notes that people who take such steps are always optimistic for positive results.

Commercial life is full of failure. But, if traders were not optimistic about the next deal or their new product (which they spent much effort inventing), they would give up on trading altogether. Traders do not, as a matter of practice, behave as depressed people. Rather, they are always optimistic that business will prosper, and their efforts will be rewarded. Jacobs points out that this is not just a behavioral observation, but also a moral precept. Traders praise those who try and try again as it promotes and encourages long-term faith in the viability and success of the commercial system overall. Sure, there are setbacks, but in the long run, trade brings prosperity, and a better life to all. This is the source of the belief that progress is a way of life, and a normal expectation.

Politics and Economics

It is evident from the Commercial Framework that we live in a commercial world. Many of our common sayings and guidelines for behavior are based on how we interact with others in the business arena. It is also evident, without going into a detailed comparison, that commercial precepts can conflict with those of the guardian class. Each set of precepts leads to different moral values and behaviors.

True commerce as a widespread activity has always been with us, but was repressed by guardians as a way of maintaining mastery. Masters keep the real wealth because wealth is a source of power. Wealth provides leisure. It funds the activities needed for ostentation, dispensing largesse, and for maintaining the forces needed to be true wielders of power. Historically, most wars have been fought between guardians who sought an advantage over each other, or in response to some slight. History reads like a veritable who's who of princes and kings exerting prowess, exacting vengeance, loyalty, and obedience, deceiving, and showing fortitude, and demonstrating honor—all to gain the resources to maintain hierarchy, ostentation, leisure, largesse, and exclusivity (i.e., to demonstrate and preserve mastery).

In contrast, commerce reveals values of cooperation through competition. Whereas both traders and guardians value competition as a way of improving positions of strength, they each restrict competition to the members of their own class. Guardians compete with prowess, ostentation, largesse, and other precepts that serve to promote mastery (including mastery over each other, if that is appropriate at the time). Traders compete not for mastery but for profit. Agreements must be voluntary, and benefits must be mutual. Commerce is primarily a cooperative activity where competition places second as a means of offering new products and services that are of interest for others. This is why others enter agreements to conduct trade in the first place. For guardians, competition is primary, and cooperation is only for servants, who must cooperate with (read, obey) their masters. Any cooperation between guardians is solely for some personal advantage or gain in "mastery." When viewed side by side, commerce really shines in the post-master age where servants (traders and the like) rise above the guardian (master) relationship.

Jacobs finds that both Frameworks are needed to conduct affairs in the world. Governments need guardian values to be successful, and modern traders need commercial values. However, historically, we have not always been successful at mixing the two Frameworks in ways that promote peace and order. Jacobs focuses on what she calls "monstrous hybrids" to explain many of the political and economic systems that have been tried across the world. Communism, fascism, and socialism are all hybrids, where governments either enter commerce to "run the show" or allow commercial values to provide guiding principles for laws and policies. All such attempts fail.

From my point of view, monstrous hybrids are examples of mere or vicious ideologies, and Jacobs' views help to illustrate how they fail. In Jacobs' view, hybrids confuse the morality of guardians or traders, and the confusion undermines the basis for success. For example, guardians who are involved with commerce open themselves up for corruption. If payment for services is acceptable, they cannot dispense largesse or demand loyalty, or exert prowess. They are compromised by their commercial activities. Conversely, traders who behave as guardians tend to use force, be ostentatious, and promote vengeance and idleness—all values that undermine the basis of honest commerce.

In Jacobs' train of thought, both Frameworks are needed. There is a place for leadership as well as commerce, and as long as we do not mix the two, we should get a system that works. For example, traders expect that all should honor their contracts and be honest and hardworking. But, how do we deal with those who are not honest or hardworking? Traders must shun force, but sometimes force is necessary to bring about a just resolution of disputes. Guardians fill this role, provided they are not compromised by a conflict of interest (i.e., have a stake in commercial transactions).

The state provides the role of protecting commerce from those who do not obey the rules. In my terms, the state enforces the laws as moral rules that are too important to be left to informal reinforcement.

On the face of it, some form of government or ruling body with the force capacity to enforce laws is needed. But this is because there are those who do not honor or obey the rules. Ideally, a just society is only possible if all members of the community obey the rules. In the absence of true and reasoned consent from all community members, we need some ability to discipline offenders whose crimes are too serious for the community to ignore; thus, the need for *laws* and an enforcement mechanism. As a species, we seem to need a system to deal with offenders. But notice that this requirement is different from the requirements leading to masters or guardians. Mastery arises out of force and violence. However, there is a distinction between the need for a ruling order, and mastery.

Earlier, I distinguished between power and authority. Power seeks mastery, whereas authority grows naturally out of the division of labor needed to organize a complex community. Jacobs' guardian precepts are the marks of masters, not authorities. However, there is much to be learned from this.

Democracy

Most forms of government are power-based. They are variations of mastery. However, there is an alternative. Karl Popper points out that the only system we know of that is different from traditional guardian states (as I have defined them) is democracy. Democracy is the only system that allows us to remove incompetent or tyrannical rulers without resorting to violence. As indicated, the need for violence stands at the core of mastery, and is the usual way that servants overthrow their masters. In the absence of a way to peacefully overcome mastery, violence is the only recourse servants have. Totalitarian and communist systems are modern versions of guardianship. Jacobs provides the precepts for Popper's sense of historicism and presents how these systems became confused in the face of the success of commercialism. Totalitarian and communist systems were all formed in violent methods (the ruthless subjugation of all opposition), and provided no peaceful mechanisms to remove incompetent rulers. In this sense they are just variations of traditional guardian ways of ruling, and the guardian precepts applied to both.

This leads to a need to understand why democracy is different in moral standing. Why is democracy not just another monstrous hybrid? How should it work in the sense of how should people behave in a democracy such that those running the community are not masters disguised as authorities? How does democracy constrain or prevent mastery? Does it constrain or prevent mastery?

Democracy distributes power across the community. In theory, at least, all members of the community participate in the system, although participation is from their relative positions in the social hierarchy. This means that everyone in the community has a political role in addition to any economic roles they might have.

A comparison shows how each guardian precept conflicts with its commercial counterpart. But there is something different about a democracy. Traders and guardians have different motives, behaviors, and values, and these provide a source for the contention between the two groups. In a democracy, there is no real contention between the government and the people. Indeed, these are idealized as the same thing. However, a democracy still needs a capability to enforce laws, so there is some contention between rulers and the ruled.

Table 5.1: Comparison of Jacobs' Guardian and Commercial Moral Frameworks

GUARDIAN FRAMEWORK	COMMERCIAL FRAMEWORK
Shun trading	Shun force
Exert prowess	Come to voluntary agreements
Be obedient and disciplined	Be honest
Adhere to tradition	Collaborate easily with strangers and aliens
Respect hierarchy	Respect contracts
Be loyal	Compete
Take vengeance	Use initiative and enterprise
Deceive for the sake of the task	Dissent for the sake of the task
Make rich use of leisure	Promote comfort and convenience
Be ostentatious	Be efficient
Dispense largesse	Invest for productive purposes
Be exclusive	Be open to inventiveness and novelty
Show fortitude	Be industrious
Be fatalistic	Be optimistic
Treasure honor	Be thrifty

Rulers in a democracy[50] (democrats) must behave in a way that is similar to guardians. But where guardians rule through mastery, democratic rulers achieve order by way of representation. That is, they represent those interests that the people of the community have presented to them, in governmental institutions. The interests of their citizens temper how they behave. Consequently, where guardians act out of self-interest, democrats must act on behalf of the interests of others. Their role is more altruistic as a result. This requires that democratic rulers tone down power to mere authority. In a democracy, authority is achieved by distributing power to every member of the community, rather than placing it in the hands of a small elite group (although, in practice, this might seem hard to distinguish). Rulers in a democracy are not elite in the sense of a privileged group; rather, they are higher on the social scale by virtue of their position

---

50 I shall refer to authorities in a democracy as democrats (lowercase *d*) to distinguish the generic form from any specific party or affiliation.

relative to the overall hierarchy of the structure of the community. They can represent the will of the people (as opposed to their own selfish will), but the people can remove them easily if they fail to do so effectively.

Democrats' behavior is determined by the moral precepts that guide their conduct. As with guardians and traders, these precepts reinforce each other to form a moral Framework. Let us examine each of the 15 precepts in the democrats' Framework.

1. **Minimize the use of force.** Democracy as a system is based on the value of liberty—that no one enslave another as property—wherein each person is sovereign over their own mind and body. One of the corollaries of liberty is to use only the amount of force required to achieve the desired end, and not at all if not needed. The idea is to protect ourselves from the arbitrary and indiscriminate use of force (even the force of law). This precept comes from long experience with the whims of masters and their excessive use of violent means (such as vengeance).

2. **Obey the law.** In a democracy, no one—not even the king or president—is above the law, which marks the difference between master–servant political systems and a democracy. There are no masters, and certainly no one who is master enough to proclaim themselves a god.

Police are agents of the law, not the state. These agents can (and do) prosecute anyone (including the president) who breaks the law. In guardian systems, the state employs "secret" police who are the guardians' agents. These agents work explicitly outside the law in the sense of law derived from moral rules. (They often make up their own "laws," which are based on guardian interests rather than community interests.)

3. **Promote the rule of law.** It is not enough that rulers should themselves obey the law. In a democracy, there are no secret police, or agents of the state who use the law as a means to a master's end. Rulers who behave this way seek mastery and abuse their authority. Recall that law comes from morality. If it is okay for a democrat to use the law to gain some advantage, a precedent is set that it is okay for others to do the same. Democracy is based on liberty, but it embodies equality both in principle and in practice. While equality is not as evident in a democracy as is liberty, it affords the same opportunity for all to become authorities in principle. If it is okay

for a ruler, it is okay for the ruled. There are no sharp boundaries between the two, as in a master–servant system.

As a principle of democratic conduct, a democrat's using the law to gain an advantage would lead to a breakdown of law and order. Rulers in a democracy must not only be law abiders themselves, but also promote law and order throughout the community.

4. **Collaborate with the community.** Democracy is not a dictatorial process (by definition). Democrats must not issue edicts, but work with the community as a ruling process. In most democracies, regions within the state send representatives who represent the interests of the local community to the governing body. This representation is real and requires an ongoing communication and collaboration with the community to make ruling effective.

5. **Respect persons.** Recall that the best way to ensure servitude is by dehumanizing individuals. When rulers see their community members as objects rather than as constituents, then there is a danger of abuses of authority. Democrats, then, must not allow any such objectification to take place. Each citizen is an important member of the community and should be treated as such. The rise of democracy goes hand in hand with the rise of tolerance as respect for the person.

6. **Cooperate with each other.** In the guardian realm, competition is between fellow guardians. Indeed, this is the source of many wars. Traders push competition to second place in favor of cooperation and voluntary agreements. Democratic rulers need to push competition even further, into third place. While there is competition for votes and competition to pass various legislation, the overall enterprise is one of first collaborating with constituents, then cooperating through voluntary representation, and only then does competition come to the fore. Competition to promote special interests serves the same purpose as cooperation, and democratic institutions support both.

7. **Demonstrate authority.** Because a democrat can be scrutinized for effectiveness on the job (i.e., be removed for incompetence), they need to demonstrate their position, and the success of their position. This involves two activities.

a. Democrats are authorities, not masters (with power), and they need to demonstrate that they understand the difference. They hold their office not because they have rendered their subjects subservient, but rather because they are filling a position in the hierarchy of the division of labor as members of a complex community. Failure to demonstrate their knowledge of this could bring charges of abuse or corruption.

b. It is the role of a democratic institution, as a state, to create and enforce laws. Without this capability, anarchy would result. For example, traders often need some resort to force to ensure that contracts are honored. This is one of the roles of law, and of democrats. However, without a clear demonstration that they are competent to create and enforce useful laws and regulations, democrats quickly lose credibility. They must ensure that their constituents take them seriously by behaving with authority (i.e., forcefully) when this is called for.

8. **Trust in the system.** In a democracy, there is no one-power center, and so it is often the case that particular interests do not find a clear representative. Such groups that support these special interests can fail. This failure and the frustration associated with it provide a primary source for confusing authority with power. The system ensures that no one should use force to make others toe their line. This is basic to both liberty and equality as thymotic values. Democracy deploys a system of checks and balances to ensure that no one group gains mastery over others. Overall, this system works in the long run. However, it also often appears to be flawed in the short-term in that some specific required and focused action is difficult to achieve (hence, the source of frustration).

For example, democracy makes for poor generalship in a war. A war requires clear lines of command to a central authority. Indeed, war is a favored activity of guardians, so this structure should not be a surprise. Democrats who fritter away resources or focus on in-fighting instead of the crisis at hand cost focus and energy that distract from the objectives needed to deal with a situation. This is why guardian types often try to seize control of a democracy. They claim that without such a central command structure, community goals cannot be easily achieved.

Real democrats trust that the system will work things out over the long run, and all such controversies will resolve themselves as they should. This is a form of justice in the community. Recall that justice is a kind of long-term moral appropriateness. It is appropriate to seek justice, and so democrats must trust that justice (in this context) will prevail.

9. **Promote community well-being.** Democrats represent the interests of their constituents. They can be peacefully removed from their posts if they do not. Success depends on how well they do their job. But democracy borrows a faith in progress and the future from commercial values. Tomorrow will be better than today because democracy promotes justice, and justice works over the long run. If society does not trade off long-term benefits for short-term gains, then over time we will each reap ongoing benefits.

Democrats must behave in such a way as to promote these benefits, and to ensure that these benefits continue to be ongoing.

10. **Be tolerant.** Respect for persons requires tolerance. For a democrat, this goes beyond personhood and includes their opponents as well. Democracy is primarily a cooperative system, and so democrats must be tolerant of those who disagree with them. For example, most democracies incorporate many parties, who represent diverse community interests. Each party vies for votes to be positioned as representing the majority of the community's members. All parties in such debates must be receptive to the views of their opponents.

Tolerance in this context derives directly from liberty and equality. Each member of the community has a right to disagree with others, and one should not use force to modify opposing positions. Democrats must, therefore, be lenient and engaging toward those with diverse views and opinions, and not react as a master in squashing such attitudes and permissions.

11. **Promote your community's interests.** Because democratic processes usually require that local regions or constituencies send representatives to the government, democrats must represent their constituents' interests. This often poses a dilemma for democrats. They have a responsibility to promote the well-being of the community overall, yet must also represent the specific interests of their constituents. These can oppose each other if a local region does not share the larger community interests.

Part of the democratic process is to prioritize and evaluate the consequences of any action (or lack of action). Where the community's interests
coincide with a local constituency, then the representation requirements
are clear. But, when these stand in opposition, the constituency should
receive appropriate consideration. The democratic process guarantees
that disagreement is permitted and normal. When a local constituency
disagrees with the majority, democratic principles require that dissenting
voices be heard. That is the point of representation.

Further, there is a danger in a democracy that people might confuse
majority will with what is right (in a moral sense). The majority could
be morally wrong in their choice of actions, so dissent functions as a
safeguard against the tyranny of the majority. Representing the interests of
constituents means that democracy presents the views of the many diverse
groups in the community. All voices are given fair and equal representation.

12. **Be fair and impartial.** In a democracy, all are equal as described
in thymotic terms. Democrats must revere equality. For example, legal
authorities such as judges and arbitrators must hear both sides of any story
and be impartial in the sense that conclusions are based on principles and
evidence, rather than on prior opinions (which would be called pre-justice
or prejudice). A democratic legal system is based on such a view and is
characterized as an adversarial system.

Democrats, as authorities, must treat all community members with
this kind of fair representation. Even though a democrat belongs to the
majority party, they must recognize that not all their constituents voted
for them. A particular voting status does not entail differential treatment
in official matters.

13. **Demonstrate moral courage.** One of the failings of guardians is
that they get to make their own rules. This leaves the community at the
whims of their masters. Democrats are constrained by such behavior.
They are the "guardians" of the community's moral precepts as well as
their laws. In this role, they must demonstrate that they are moral agents.
Often, this requires courage to do the right thing as opposed to doing the
popular thing. Authority is a property of a position in a complex society
and is not the result of a popularity contest. Maintaining the distinction

between effectiveness and popularity is a criterion used by the community to determine who should be removed as incompetent. Democrats must display that they are effective at representing the values of the community.

14. **Be competent.** To remove an incompetent master requires violence or the natural death of the master. To remove a democrat requires that no one vote for them. The whole point of a democracy is that citizens can remove incompetent democrats, so democrats must demonstrate their competence at performing their duties. This is often through community events and representation. It is the democrat's version of largesse.

15. **Be moral.** As guardians treasure honor, and as traders are thrifty, democrats are moral. They do not just represent moral values. They are moral agents. It is who they are, by virtue of their position in the community. Note that all three kinds of ethical criteria bear on a democrat's moral standing. They can be ethically criticized for failures of virtue, consequences, or principles.

Democrats are guardians without servants. They are not masters. Rather, the community is the master, and democrats just represent or promote community interests. This leads to the idea that the rest of the community is part of the democratic process in a way that servants are not part of a ruling guardian state.

The precepts of how citizens in a democracy should behave are the converse side of the democracy coin. This is called the *Citizen Framework*, and it includes 15 precepts that provide the counterpoint to the democrat Framework. Let's examine these in more detail.

1. **Oppose the arbitrary use of force.** Citizens must always be wary of those in authority who would turn their position into mastery. One of the signal marks of guardian behavior is a failure to obey *moral rules* or *laws*, or a failure to be fair and impartial. As noted, they use prowess to seek vengeance.

The role of a citizen, as opposed to a servant, is that a citizen has real power—not in the sense of mastery, but in the higher sense of a power distributed equally across all members of the community. Whereas guardians concentrate power in the chosen few, democracy maintains a broadly distributed power, which is the main safeguard against mastery.

Democracy, therefore, is doomed to failure when power becomes concentrated in the hands of an elite group. All efforts at preventing this serve to conserve democracy. Because focused power is arbitrary across the community, all such arbitrariness must be opposed.

2. **Promote those who best represent your interests.** Because a key feature of a democracy is the ability to replace incompetent or corrupt democrats peacefully, citizens should select those who are competent. Those who can best represent a citizen's interests are the preferred choice. Consequently, citizens vote for those who can do what they are hired to do—represent their interests in a competent and moral way. Citizens are obligated to not confuse this with popularity.

3. **Fight corruption.** Corruption can entail many forms, from the attempts at mastery to failure to uphold *laws* or *moral rules*, to failures of moral courage. When there is corruption, individuals are not treated fairly and impartially, or with proper respect and tolerance. They are not treated as persons.

Basically, an abuse of authority is a failure of a democrat to honor their position, which is the result not of mastery, but of the division of labor in the community. They seek power (mastery) rather than authority, or they confuse the two and behave as a guardian. All such behaviors or attitudes are a corruption of the democratic ideal. The whole point of distributing power across the community is to constrain such tendencies. The responsibility of every citizen becomes to identify and oppose corruption wherever it is observed. This attitude provides the vigilance needed to prevent concentrations of authority into power structures, and which prevents mastery. Identifying corruption and a vigilant attitude are also a measure of the freedom of persons who are not servants but citizens—equal partners in the running of the community.

4. **Collaborate with your peers.** Democratic structures require constant communication between their parts. In a democracy, these parts are usually referred to as constituencies. These are local areas, from which each sends a representative to the legislature or parliament. Determining which representatives are competent and which are not requires that constituents assemble on a regular basis and evaluate a democrat's performance.

Further, many issues need to be addressed, which require some measure of consent between constituents to avoid confusion and anarchy. In this regard, citizens need to collaborate regularly to discuss issues and points of view. A democracy demands the expression of different perspectives and opinions as part of the process of governing. Collaboration facilitates this process.

5. **Respect the rights of others.** As noted, a right is a duty or obligation placed on others to avoid doing something (such as not interfere) or to do something (such as provide assistance). Respecting the rights that a community has identified is an integral part of the moral fabric of a democracy. If I respect the rights of others, I am entitled to a similar respect from others. Part of a democrat's job is to facilitate disagreements arising out of violations of others' respects. However, it is every citizen's responsibility to show such respect to minimize the need for a facilitated response.

6. **Assemble peacefully.** Democracy provides for the peaceful removal of incompetent or tyrannical rulers. A key word here is peaceful. With power distributed throughout the community comes the responsibility to keep the peace. This means that just as democrats must minimize the use of force, so, too, must all citizens. When either party resorts to force or violence to achieve its goals, democracy as a process begins to break down.

7. **Seek justice.** As stated previously, justice is a kind of long-term moral appropriateness. This does not mean that there is no injustice, or that justice always prevails over the long run. Justice tends to prevail when we revere the thymotic values of life, liberty, equality, and tolerance. Democracy as a system at least facilitates these values as living values, and, in its ideal form, treats them as moral goals for the community. As a result, each member of the community is responsible for the protection and promotion of these values. When citizens understand this, democracy is strongest.

8. **Dissent when you disagree.** One of the points of democracy as a system is that people can disagree, and most democracies provide different forums to facilitate these disagreements. Forums range from an adversarial legal system to school and community debating clubs.

Unlike servants, who may never express opinions contrary to the master's will, citizens are at liberty to do so. This implies that each citizen should respect the opinions of others (even if they disagree with those opinions) and respect each person's right to express their views. It also means that each citizen who needs to be heard speaks up, especially when they disagree with a majority opinion.

9. **Participate in the system.** Democracy requires the active participation of all members of the community. At a minimum, this means casting votes where these are required. But, more than this, democracy requires active participation in debates, fighting corruption, selecting representatives, and so on, which are really in the self-interest of the citizens. Through direct participation, citizens are really helping themselves, which is much of the point of any democracy.

10. **Personify.** Guardians objectify their enemies as a way of dehumanizing them. Democrats must avoid doing this because to do so would amount to mastery, and that is corruption in a democratic system. Democrats must promote personhood for all members of the community.

The same applies to citizens. Each citizen must respect others as persons and avoid any tendencies to objectify opponents. This is the citizen version of the democrat's precept to minimize the use of force. When citizens resort to force and violence to promote their views, they are acting to the severe detriment of democracy as a workable, practical system.

11. **Invest in democratic processes.** Just as traders invest in economic affairs so, too, must citizens invest in their political system. This investment involves community work and public interest.

12. **Fight against exclusivity.** Whereas guardians seek exclusivity, distributed power systems must shun this. No one group should master another. While democracy is based on rule by a majority, the majority should not seek to be a static group but a dynamic one, which shifts with changing situations and events. Exclusivity leads to a tyranny of the majority. This is not only not moral (moral principles are not decided by majority vote, but are universal and apply to everyone, regardless of their status relative to a majority group), but it also leads naturally to corruption in the sense that the majority group masters the community at the expense of the minority.

Responsibility for avoiding a tyranny of the majority rests with all citizens (including democrats), and not just with a ruling party.

13. **Promote the community's values.** Promoting community moral and cultural values is the responsibility of all members of a democratic community. This mirrors the attitude and behavior of masters in a guardian system. They promote their exclusive community's values as a measure of self-interest.

The same holds true for democracies, except that the self-interest distributes across the entire community, and not just across an elite group.

14. **Be informed.** The citizen's version of competence, this precept forms the basis of active and meaningful participation in democratic processes, from debating, to voting, to communicating.

15. **Honor integrity.** While guardians treasure honor in and of itself, and traders honor thrift (and profits), citizens honor those who display proper public spirit and active participation. This is a community's way of acknowledging its members who make meaningful contributions to the well-being of the community.

It is evident from this list that the Citizen Framework mirrors the democrat Framework in such a way that both are needed to describe democratic attitudes and behaviors effectively. While democracy involves an emergent set of values from rising above master–servant relations, it also significantly alters the playing field and the rules for a ruling order. The goal of distributing power across all members of a community is to prevent an exclusive and arbitrary special-interest groups from dominating the political landscape. This marks the major success of democracy as a system. But what is more interesting is that democracy is not really competitive as are guardians, or even traders. Rather, democracy is a true cooperation between members of a community whose self-interests lead them to promote their community in a peaceful and moral way.

Given the current capability to destroy all life on earth, we should begin to appreciate why the Guardian Framework is no longer a tenable way of behaving—especially now that there appears to be a viable alternative.

Jacobs' assessment (which does not include the Democratic and Citizen Frameworks) leads to the rise of commercialism as an alternative to master–servant relations. It also points to recent history as the rise of the Commercial Framework (or commercialism) begins to dominate guardian systems. Of course, historically, we are conditioned to shun commercialism as crass and unworthy of a serious place in our political thinking. The legacy of aristocratic values continues to taint our views.

However, democracy with its own precepts and moral values provides a direct competitor to guardian systems. Given the thymotic values as a basis for rising above master–servant relations, the rise of democracy is really the rise of thymotic values themselves. In particular, democracy, in its modern form, is based on the values of liberty and equality. While democracy presents a single alternative to the various guardian models (fascism, communism, etc.), the rise of democracy and the values of life, liberty, equality, and tolerance present a view that the various guardian systems are really just attempts to preserve some form of mastery in the face of a real and substantive morality. Guardian behavior is nonmoral when compared with democratic behavior. Any claims to the moral superiority of guardian systems are empty forms—mere or vicious ideologies. Tyrants and would be masters often charge that democracy doesn't really work. There are too many factions in-fighting for control to provide effective governance. However, as Winston Churchill once pointed out, democracy is the worst system we know of – except for all the others. Like it or not, it appears to be the best system we have.

It should be evident to the reader that commerce and democracy might be mutually supporting Frameworks, but are not necessarily required for each other in any particular way. This is in contrast to a guardian system, where commercialism and its values are shunned. Democracy can embrace commercialism for the same reason that guardians seek wealth, namely that wealth facilitates power. In a democracy, the power, however, is distributed across the members of the community, and that serves commercial interests. The more people who contribute to commercial success, the greater will be the wealth of the community. But this wealth is dispersed throughout the community rather than being captured by an elite group. In this sense, there is no group to control economic progress. Such progress is up to the community. If such a group honors commercial precepts, they, too, can be successful traders. The more successful traders there are, the wealthier the community.

While it was in the self-interests of guardians to control wealth— control being the operative word—pure self-interest motivates citizens to control the economy. But this is a distributed control in a democracy. By participating in commerce, citizens not only ensure a higher and growing standard of living, but they also ensure that wealth does not concentrate in the hands of an elite group. Participation in commerce is part of defending the democratic ideal. This is why politics and economics go hand in hand. Guardians always knew that wealth was a source of power; now citizens and democrats know this, too. We need only guard against a monstrous hybrid, where commercial values start to replace democratic values to ensure the mutual support of both. This is often manifested in communities that strive to ensure that all members of the community contribute to their full ability. The community invests in infrastructure and services such as currency and banks, roads, and infrastructure, education, and health care to facilitate widespread community engagement in commercial activities. In democracies, these ideas are frequently enshrined in constitutional rights and freedoms. We do not see this kind of behavior or attitude in guardian cultures.

The challenge for modern humans is that our economic systems are not necessarily tied to the Commercial Framework. This is because commerce has developed in contrast to guardian precepts. The Commercial Framework appears to support thymotic values, but it is not a requirement that it does so. To see how we might proceed, it would be useful to see all these precepts side by side.

On the face of it, democratic precepts are opposed to guardian precepts. There is also an appeal to democratic alignment with commercial precepts. Both seek honesty, obedience to the law, free association, and collaboration, etc. But there are some stark differences, as well. Citizens demand justice and fair representation; they seek information and participation in the system, and shun exclusivity. There are no appeals to these values in commerce. Rather, commercial values stress initiative and enterprise, investing for production, industriousness, and optimism. These values are not the same.

Table 5.2: Comparing Guardian, Commercial, Democratic Ruler and Democratic Citizen Moral Frameworks

GUARDIAN FRAMEWORK	COMMERCIAL FRAMEWORK	DEMOCRATIC RULER FRAMEWORK	DEMOCRATIC CITIZEN FRAMEWORK
Shun trading	Shun force	Minimize the use the force	Oppose the arbitrary use of force
Exert prowess	Come to voluntary agreements	Obey the law	Promote those who best represent your interests
Be obedient and disciplined	Be honest	Promote the rule of law	Fight corruption
Adhere to tradition	Collaborate easily with strangers and aliens	Collaborate with the community	Collaborate with your peers
Respect hierarchy	Respect contracts	Respect persons	Respect the rights of others
Be loyal	Compete	Cooperate with each other	Assemble peacefully
Take vengeance	Use initiative and enterprise	Demonstrate authority	Seek justice
Deceive for the sake of the task	Dissent for the sake of the task	Trust in the system	Dissent when you disagree
Make rich use of leisure	Promote comfort and convenience	Promote community well-being	Participate in the system
Be ostentatious	Be efficient	Be tolerant	Personify
Dispense largesse	Invest for productive purposes	Promote the community's interests	Invest in democratic processes
Be exclusive	Be open to inventiveness and novelty	Be fair and impartial	Shun exclusivity
Show fortitude	Be industrious	Demonstrate moral courage	Promote the community's values
Be fatalistic	Be optimistic	Be competent	Be informed
Treasure honor	Be thrifty	Be moral	Honor integrity

While some precepts between the commercial and democratic Frameworks appear to be in line (shun or reduce force, be honest, obey the law, fight corruption, etc.), there are many points of conflict. For example, being industrious does not necessarily entail looking out for the community's interests. Investing in production is not the same as investing in the community.

Next, consider whether capitalism promotes commercial values. In this sense, the word capital means different things. There are at least three definitions. The guardians promote political capital, commerce promotes economic capital, and democracy promotes social capital.

Communities need to develop as much capital as they can to be successful at promoting a just society. Capitalism per se references only one kind of capital. Democracy promotes social capital by focusing all parties on what is best for the community, as determined by the community, and not some elite group—political or economic.

Consequently, while capitalism promotes economic capital, it fails to promote other kinds of capital, regardless of what the economic elite would have us think. When democrats hand over political authority to a corporation in the interests of economic efficiency, they are really counting on the corporation to promote and build social capital in the sense that the corporation will actually look out for the best interests of the community. However, without allowing the community to be the arbiter of the results, they have really handed authority over to an economic power elite who can use modern marketing methods to control the citizens and limit their active participation.

A good example of this in action is the Framework within which we conduct agriculture. We have designed a system for food production that is heavily dependent on machinery, pesticides, and chemical fertilizers, as well as genetically controlled plants. We know that these methods are unsustainable. The soil loss alone is alarming. Add to this the tainted foods themselves, and the chemicals that are running off into the drinking water, and it is evident that our current methods are a recipe for disaster, and that disaster is imminent.

The response of industry in the face of citizen pressures to find alternate methods has been to accelerate research in genetics to produce better plants. However, the word "better" has been misapplied. Many genetically modified strains of plants require more pesticides and fertilizers than non-genetically modified plants. Most strains of grain now in production require chemically enhancing the soil. Most of these plants would be extinct in a few generations if we stopped such artificial enhancements. These plants have been designed to work in chemically enhanced soils, soils that actually cause environmental damage. Further genetic research is not designed to reverse dependency on chemical supplements. Therefore, better is a misnomer. No major agricultural corporation has addressed the issue of non-sustainability in the methods of agriculture in the Western world. Rather, they are seeking ways to profit from the genetic research that perpetuates current methods. They are locked in a Framework of thinking that cannot envision any other way of farming.

The hidden hand of capitalism is supposed to correct this problem. If enough people seek organically grown foods, with little or no genetically manipulated plants, then industry would respond to the demand. But the situation is a catch-22. We can only purchase what is offered at competitive prices. Because the majority of agricultural corporations have no interest in responding to community concerns, companies continue to offer what they decide consumers can have. Further, they use their size and power base to ensure that alternative farming methods do not really compete, and so remain expensive and not readily available. Modern marketing will convince consumers that their interests are being served. The guardians of agriculture have spoken!

In this way, the Framework of modern capitalism determines how executive Tops think. They know that what they are doing is wrong for the environment and for the community, but they must compete on terms that do not address those issues. It is a shame that chemicals destroy the environment, but corporations are not charities. They must move forward and progress to compete. Citizens are Bottoms, fighting a system that does not have the mechanism to permit care and proper representation. The hidden hand is indeed hidden, and is much too slow to be considered politically responsive. Capitalism is not tied to democracy. It is tied to guardian values, and that is the mistake democrats make when they hand authority over to such power structures. When this happens, it is called Corporatism.

The Unconscious Civilization

The real point to understanding our moral precepts is to see how they compare and how to clarify who and what institutions operate under which banner. Remember, the question is, how should we be ruled? It's not "Who should rule?" For example, it is clear that dictatorships are pure guardian Frameworks, whereas Western political systems at least aspire to democracy. The dark horse in all this is the ever-present Commercial Framework. This set of moral precepts is pervasive and gaining in ascendancy even over democracy. It appears that as a society, we are unconscious of how progress takes place.

To explain how this works, consider how we approach the massive changes occurring throughout the world and the speed with which these changes are occurring. The argument is often referred to as the *technological imperative*.

Generally speaking, we observe that there is a rapid pace to developments in the world. The pace seems to be driven by the pace of technological change in the marketplace. For example, product life cycles are less than a few months for many industries. Communications and travel systems have made the world much smaller. Television and news systems bring the world into our living rooms every day.

We are undergoing a revolution in the world—what is referred to as the Information Age. We are leaving the Industrial Age, where material goods marked the measure of productivity, and entering an age in which information itself is the primary commodity.

This is not surprising, given the failure of 19th- and early 20th-century ideologies. These were ruled under Guardian Frameworks that continued to promote competition and power structures that dominated information resources. But, under democratic rule, science has flourished and information has become pervasive. Today, more resources around the world are put into science and engineering than are put into developing political capital. This probably marks the first time in human history that something other than political or economic power has ascended to first place in what we do as a species. Knowledge is power, and science brings knowledge, so the power elites have funded a massive scientific and engineering effort.

There are more scientists and engineers in the modern world than there are soldiers and politicians, and their ranks are growing. They all have one thing in common—to push forward a frontier of knowledge.

This investment has brought great change and power to some, but, overall, it is backfiring on the guardian elites. Science works for everyone, not just the elites, and science does not work if access to that knowledge is restricted.

Democratic systems have understood this and built the infrastructure to make knowledge available to all. The current development of the internet proves that knowledge systems can bypass all old-school economic and political systems.

The question is, who is in charge of all this change? It is easy to see that the political institutions and power elites cannot control all the aspects of the system they have unleashed. Perhaps the market will control these forces? However, the marketplace cannot determine or guarantee a positive sense of progress for all people. It favors those who can earn profits and is ruthless to those who cannot compete.

The technological imperative suggests that no one is in charge. Rather, the pace of technology has taken on a life of its own, and now sets its own pace and direction. We either keep up or fall behind (to our peril). The problem with this theory is that it fails to offer any sense of direction. Rather, it states that we are now victims of our own systems of information. I offer another hypothesis.

The technological imperative really does tell us once and for all that no one is in charge. As a species, we are out of control. As a species, we have no common agenda, nor common direction. We are constantly being pushed about by whatever forces happen our way. This is the essence of what Buckminster Fuller calls World War Game, and we are still playing it.

However, modern communication does provide a new way of seeing ourselves. Global information and communications exchanges provide much to reflect on. It seems that being out of control is the natural order of humans. In reality, we have never been *in* control. Our whole history has been a series of almost random events, with everyone simply reacting to others and to circumstances. We have never really behaved as a coherent species, with a common goal, or direction. So far, all history has been the story of how out of control we really are.

This leads to a self-consciousness of how we really are in our world. I am using the word *self-consciousness* in both its popular senses. We are conscious of how little control we really have over our destiny, and we are not comfortable with who we are.

For example, we know that we cannot go on destroying the environment. We know that we cannot go on with nuclear arms and terrorist methods of resolving disputes. But, how can we change ourselves to overcome these problems? We are trapped in a system that goes nowhere in particular, when we need real leadership and direction—as a species, and not just as tribes or nation states. This condition is called the *malaise of modernity,* and it is from this malaise that we begin to correct who we are. All the moral precepts in the world will not help us if we continue to behave as we always have. We need something different instead of more of the same.

Corporatism

One of the mere ideologies that is emerging is a rising belief in the power of commercialism in the form of capitalism that is called corporatism. In Jacobs' terms, this is a new monstrous hybrid based on the belief that economic structures are more efficient than government structures, so power systems should shift to the economic systems. In particular, capitalism is the system inspired by Adam Smith to facilitate free development and flow of goods and services.[51] This economic system is supposed to be self-regulating and requires minimal interference from governments. For example, rather than resort to a guardian to settle disputes, unfair business practices will emerge such that the offenders will naturally lose profits and business because no one will choose to do business with them.

To complicate matters, there is a current perception that democracy and capitalism go together and that they are mutually supportive. With this view in mind, proponents of corporatism have a powerful message.

---

51 Smith, A. (2012). *Wealth Of Nations.* Hertfordshire, UK: Wordsworth Editions Ltd.

Capitalism, combined with democracy, defeated Communism through the sheer power of the market and the ability to freely create wealth. This is why (according to these proponents) communist leaders almost voluntarily shifted their political systems to a democratic model. Communism is a monstrous hybrid that cannot work because guardian precepts continue to stifle economic freedom and growth. Communist nations had to choose between economic prosperity for their people or a continued sliding into increasing guardian control that shuns economic development for all. In the end, something won that was not Communism.

The current situation appears to be a combination of two Frameworks. On the political front, democracy has won, or at least attempted to distribute power and put morality back into the community. Where both democrat and citizen precepts are understood, the program was a success. Where these precepts were not well-understood, the success was more suspect.

But mixed in with this was the need for economic development and the promise of economic prosperity for all citizens. The system to be modeled was capitalism. However, where there have continued to be power structures and elite groups politically, with a failure of the citizens to contribute fully to the democratic process, what emerged were monopolistic economic patterns and less than wealth for all. Mixing the Commercial Framework too particularly with any political instantiation of the Guardian Framework produces a monstrous hybrid. In this case, the hybrid is an economic power elite that behaves as guardians, but which is based on capitalistic principles. The converse occurs in nations where democracy is strong, and this is also a version of corporatism.

In developed countries, the role of government is to represent the people's interests, and this largely centers around infrastructure services, such as roads, communications, health care (in some countries), social-support systems, and so on. Under the guise that capitalism has emerged as the dominant and most successful economic model yet devised, and in the light of its victory over communism, public services are being privatized to gain greater *efficiency*. That is, government agencies are too costly to run to deliver and manage essential infrastructure services. Private interests are more efficient; therefore, they should develop and manage these services.

The gain in cost savings can be passed on to the consumer in the form of reduced taxes.

The problem with this latter model is that private interests are motivated by profits, not representing public interests. The result is a system where representation is deferred to a private individual or group. Under the guise of efficiency, the democratic process is undermined, and representations on issues involving public concern are diverted to special-interest groups that are not being paid to represent anyone except themselves. Rather, they are being paid to profit by looking out for their own interests. The capitalist model foretells that should one private interest fail to offer valued services, consumers are free to shop elsewhere. However, this begs the question of representation. The market force is a hidden hand for correcting problems. The problem is that the mechanism is hidden. We are transferring public processes to interests that can work on hidden agendas. In areas like infrastructure services, such failures could devastate a community long before corrective action could take place.

Corporatism, then, is yet another monstrous hybrid that cannot work because the performance objectives of the system are fuzzy. Do we really want private enterprise to represent us as citizens in all matters of public debate? How can we get at a proper democracy when we confuse the precepts of the democratic ideal with commercial precepts? Both developing countries and developed countries will fail in the same way. Developing countries will fail to train their citizens to embrace democracy as a political process because they will see authority pass to economic interests as economic power structures. Developed countries will also see authority passed to economic power structures, but will maintain the fiction that they are still in control. The results are the same. The political division of power that marks a democracy will be handed over to economic interests that are not obliged to represent anyone but themselves. As such, they can assume mastery over their community, as any guardian state would attempt to do. The language of corporatism makes this readily apparent. Corporatists see themselves as the guardians of economic efficiency for the community and are interested in protecting their own interests in what they think is best. The way to do this is to monopolize the economic environment. As government is a force monopoly, what better way to monopolize a community than to have unsuspecting democrats hand their authority over to a private special-interest group such as a corporation? Corporatism is insidious, by definition.

The main point here is that there are many ways that guardians can protect their interests and keep their power base. As divide and conquer is the key success strategy in warfare, and as democracies are already divided between democrats and citizens, it is not too difficult to usurp authority and turn it into power. The trick is to do so in such a way as to remove the checks and balances that democracy imposes. Communists did this by eliminating rival parties to vote for. Corporatism does it by taking over key infrastructure sectors. The drive for power is at the root of the problem.

The Malaise of Modernity

Throughout history, there have been many changes in the human condition. With hindsight, there has also been what looks like stupidity. At each point of major change, many people seem to know what they are doing is wrong, but do not seem able to effect real change. We are out of control as a species, and always have been.

The clearest example of this evil was provided by Hannah Arendt in her 1963 book, *Eichmann in Jerusalem: A Report on the Banality of Evil.*[52] Adolf Eichmann was the Nazi criminal on trial in Israel as the mastermind behind the Nazi death camps in World War II. Arendt's central theme is that Eichmann was not a monster, or even a particularly evil man. Rather, he was like most of us. His ambitions were to do well for career advancement, pay off the mortgage on his house, provide for an education for his children, and so on. It just happened that his career meant executing (literally) Hitler's Final Solution.

It is not my intention to argue whether this is a valid assessment. What is interesting is how we can all in some sense sympathize with Arendt's point of view. We all want to succeed in our chosen career and be loyal to the company or state or our family or whatever. This dictates that we

---

52 Arendt, Hannah, *Eichmann in Jerusalem: A Report On The Banality of Evil.* London: Penguin Classics, 2006

conform to the rules of employment and good conduct if we want to keep our positions (let alone get ahead). Many of us have seen whistle-blowers ostracized, fired, and financially and socially ruined simply for doing the right thing.

The problem is that in a modern economy, livelihood depends on employment and society's institutions, and it is often employers and leaders (Tops) who do things that we (Middles and Bottoms) should object to. What can we do, other than hope that moral courage and speaking out can stop the behavior? How can we truly effect change for the better from within a system, if we are not high enough up in the social order to dictate the change? This problem is complicated by the fact that in most systems, by the time someone gets to a key decision-making position, they are so indoctrinated by the system that they defend it rather than change it. They become so entrenched in their position that they lose sight of the whole system, and their behavior is then determined by the system. This is one of the reasons large corporations find it so hard to adapt to the pace of change now occurring in our society. The change is not just organizational; it is systemic, and that means breaking out of our Sub-Frameworks to see the system as a whole. Preventing or slowing change is what the "dinosaurs" are defending because they cannot imagine what the new system might be like. To them, it looks like anarchy.

In fact, the problem is much deeper. It is difficult to see how our ethical criteria and thymotic values translate into moral precepts, and how these are adapted—more or less—into various moral Frameworks. It does appear to be clear that guardian precepts are opposed to the underlying values that would ground an ethics. It is also evident that while the moral precepts of guardians are very different from those of a democracy, and these in turn are different from commercial precepts, none of the moral Frameworks clearly and directly ties in with all of our ethical criteria and thymotic values. This is further confused by the way in which guardian precepts dominate authority structures. The key values of guardians are loyalty and conformity. These are at odds with the values of liberty and equality associated with democracy. To make matters worse, guardian precepts intrude in many systems through how they treat their members (Tops versus Middles and Bottoms, etc.).

The many ways in which organizations attempt to rationalize these precepts provide the source for the ideologies that lend themselves to the master's goals. For example, fascism and communism both provided a political/economic agenda for reshaping society. These social-engineering programs required absolute loyalty to the cause from all members, regardless of any claims favoring democracy. It is this forceful requirement that makes these ideologies vicious.

With corporatism, there is the development of yet another monstrous hybrid in the contrast between guardian and democratic values. These present a straightforward conflict, while those of commercial values can be somewhat complementary to either.

The tendency to equate capitalism with commercial moral precepts and with democracy is the formation of a new ideology that has the capability of generating hatred and a breakdown of moral order. Such equations must be qualified as to their truth. It is not obvious that capitalism is the best economic system from a Commercial Framework point of view, let alone necessary to democracy. To justify such claims would require showing how capitalism meets all of our ethical criteria, as well as the thymotic values, when combined with a democratic political system. Further, such proponents would have to determine that a modern economy is indeed a true capitalist system. Finally, they would have to show how there could be no other economic system that complemented democracy as well, to rule out rival economic systems as a preferred system.

My task is to relate how all ethical criteria, including thymotic values, can be promoted and defended in the context of modern systems, and to examine alternatives (if there are any). This task is hampered by the current ideological confusions about what kind of society we are, and how we ought to behave. It relates directly to the problem of who is in control, which is a problem that Charles Taylor refers to as the malaise of modernity.[53]

To understand the crisis of modern times requires pulling together many strains of thought. First, recall the pure moral precepts of Guardian, Commercial, and Democratic Frameworks. These, combined with a need to promote and protect fundamental thymotic values, will be the starting point.

---

53 Taylor, C. (1991). *The Malaise Of Modernity*. Toronto: House of Anansi Press.

Second, consider that communism represents a vicious ideology, and not a philosophy, as such. Again, Jacobs refers to ideologies such as communism as monstrous hybrids. I might also include fascism, and other radical political ideologies of the last 150 years in this category. These hybrids, which combine guardian with commercial values, all have one thing in common. They blend various precepts from each Framework from the political side of considerations, rather than the economic. That is, they each attempt to bring economics under the control of the state for political ends. While they rely on different mixtures of precepts to legitimize their respective agendas, the process of forgetting about or suppressing ethical criteria, including thymotic values, remains the same.

The idea of Frameworks that we have developed further exacerbates the problem. Each of us seeks meaning in and through our community. The Framework of our community structures our thoughts and defines our reality. It defines who we are. We are each trapped in a Framework that is engineered by power elites who dictate that our place must be found within current social institutions and norms, and that we should seek meaning in these institutions. We have seen the patterns that emerge within the Sub-Frameworks that develop, and how these contribute to antagonism and aggression. In such Frameworks, our thinking becomes locked into the agenda of the program. This is the source of the hatred that can occur when the control group commits atrocities against those who are outside the program.

In Kosovo, former Yugoslavia, there were many atrocities committed by Serbian soldiers. History is full of examples of a dominant group committing horrific acts against others, more or less with impunity, and with the support of the guardian elites. Derrick Jensen presents many examples in his 2003 book, *The Culture of Make Believe*.[54] Guardians get people to participate in such atrocities by creating a Framework for opponents as objects (i.e., as nonpersons) such that it becomes acceptable to do whatever it takes to make the agenda succeed. The hatred within these acts lies in the extreme depersonalization, and the viciousness of the ideology that promotes and sustains the Framework that directs "meaningful" thought.

54 Jensen, D. (2004). *The Culture Of Make Believe*. Hartford, VT: Chelsea Green Publishing.

All monstrous hybrids have elements of such viciousness, which is why they are called monstrous. The covert recognition that our political and economic systems do not promote a just or even a sustainable future leads to malaise for a growing number of people.

Ideological systems do not work because the blended precepts undermine the others. For example, when a guardian is permitted to have a financial interest, the door is opened for corruption. At the very least, this removes the possibility of a sense of equality for citizens of such a state. From their preferred position in society, such elites can dominate every aspect of individual lives without regard for honesty, integrity, or beneficial consequences for all, and at the expense of liberty and equality. While there might be benevolent dictatorships, they are dictatorships, nonetheless. Power corrupts. Such systems must collapse in the end because the suppressed thymotic values always reassert themselves, and because conflicting moral precepts undermine the legitimacy and credibility of the corrupt order.

The crisis of modern times is a new ideology that continues to promote power structures. The view that economic factors should dominate even at the expense of political considerations, or corporatism, suggests that our various and sundry political systems have all failed because they put the cart before the horse; they focus on political, rather than economic factors. Economy shapes a society, and politics must follow in its wake. Political values or precepts conflict with economic prosperity, and so should be suppressed. In this view, the political unit is the corporation, because this is also the basic economic unit. The corporation desires progress, and so the road to social progress lies in the economic well-being of the community.

Corporatism blends moral precepts from commercial and guardian Frameworks and tries to bring the state under the control of economics. In the rejection of communism and fascism, we are moving the pendulum too far the other way. Of course, given the failure of communism, capitalism is seen as the economic system to control the state. If this assessment is correct, corporatism will also fail because it is a mere ideology, and because it does not solve the problem. It offers more of the same (blending guardian and commercial precepts) rather than something completely different.

Given the current and rising malaise, there is presently much appeal to corporatism. Political solutions have not been very effective at ending war and bringing order to the world. Also, overcoming economic hardship is most difficult where politics, or religion, or another ideology prevents people from developing prosperity. Economic gain, not diplomacy, ended the Cold War. The USSR could simply not afford its system, so communism failed. More good has been brought to greater numbers of people than ever before through growth in industry. Indeed, industry is a key commercial value, and the basis of progress—not just in the West, but wherever economic forces have been unleashed. Economy shapes civilization, good or bad, and we should acknowledge this and support such values.

Many people are uncomfortable with corporatism. The critic who is most clear in his disagreement is John Ralston Saul. In his 1997 book, *The Unconscious Civilization*, Saul attacks two trends he sees developing in the modern world as corporatism gains ground. He points out that corporatism promotes self-interest as its guiding moral principle, and it is difficult to reconcile this with any sense of altruism. The corporatist response is that in the long run, the hidden hand of the marketplace will right all wrongs. As people fail to support those activities that cause harm, the market will adjust to tune out those activities.

However, Saul points out that all real social progress has not come from the marketplace. The marketplace did not end virtual slavery in the early years of industrialism. It was responsible for child labor, terrible working conditions, and a general increase in poverty across the population. It created and oppressed the working class. What raised moral standards was not some nebulous hidden hand, but real people acting not out of self-interest, but out of disinterest—that is, interest in public welfare, or the common good.

This idea of a genuine altruism, understood as disinterest, is the catalyst for bringing about true social change. Assume for the moment that under guardian precepts, humanity has not really progressed very far in the development of an ideal society. Now follow this with an understanding that self-interest will not work under any system. The problem is whether we can, as a species, really move beyond those value systems that promote self-interest to a genuinely ethical state. Even if we were to do this, we would be a long way away from bringing about this state of affairs.

So how should we proceed? First, all ethical criteria need to be included in the discussion. The hidden hand theory of market economics fails by observing that while capitalist societies are materially better off, the distribution of wealth is very elitist. There is a promise of wealth for all, but this is dishonest because only the chosen few are truly better off. The consequences not only do *not* bring about benefits for all, but they also introduce harms, particularly to the Bottoms. Apparently, the hidden hand favors the self-interest of the elite, regardless of any underlying ethical values.

Further, the goal of a corporation is to make profit. It is not a charity, by definition. The recurring recessions and depressions indicate that corporations do not always behave in their own long-term self-interest. For example, it is now believed that the major reason for the great market collapse of 1929 was that the purchasing power of the consumer was too low relative to the production and output of the system, such that the system could no longer support such incongruities. Yet, no group of corporations modified their behaviors to avert the catastrophe.

That situation appears to be repeating itself on a global scale. With global production lowering costs and moving manufacturing to third-world countries, many industrialized nations must give up jobs to support the new system. However, the people who are now without jobs are supposed to be the people who can buy the finished goods. The system is literally undermining its consumer base by moving jobs to those who cannot afford the finished goods to support the system.

While it is laudable that the poor nations of the world should be included in modern industrial practices, large corporations are not employing these people out of altruism. They are seeking cheap labor to lower the cost of production to increase sales and enhance profits. The question is increasingly becoming, sales to whom?

From my point of view, it is evident that corporations are mixing guardian and commercial moral precepts in a way that focuses on a distribution of jobs, but not on wealth, per se. We are not all at liberty and equal, with the same opportunities for a high quality of life. We are not all persons. Indeed, many modern practices are at the same level as those in the sweatshops that oppressed people at the beginning of the Industrial Revolution.

The malaise, then, arises from the failure of the current moral Frameworks to mesh with each other to provide a system promoting true ethical values and actually moving humankind forward toward a just global community. We all deeply feel our failure to take control and behave in a rational and morally acceptable way. The malaise is made worse by the threats of nuclear and environmental destruction, and it is clear that we are running out of time.

More than this, there is a general historical disconnection between all three kinds of ethical criteria and the moral precepts that founded our political and economic systems. Even democracy maintains no clear connection with the underlying thymotic values. It does try to promote liberty and equality, but it does so as a defense against tyranny, rather than as a positive activity promoting ethical values.

This brings me back to the main question: why can't we change our ways, given the knowledge we have of the catastrophe that is looming for our species? We need to understand that when we rely on the vestiges of guardian precepts, we are thinking within a Framework that has been around for centuries. We are bound by a Framework of Father Culture and cannot envision a world without it. We cannot imagine a world without power elites and their associated values and precepts. Such a world looks like anarchy.

It should be evident to the reader that any solution we find to how best to proceed with world governance will involve the evidence-based approach provided by science. We will now take a short detour into the world of science – how it works and how it is evolving. This will expand our base for incorporating science into an Ethical Framework.

CHAPTER 6
Science

Using scientific knowledge wisely is a prerequisite for a peaceful sustainable world. Science is universal in the sense that it can be done anywhere by anyone trained in its methods. It is the only truly global institution we have. There can be no going forward without taking science into account. Science is, arguably, the most successful intellectual enterprise in human history. We have learned more about the world and ourselves in the past 400 years, than the past 4,000 combined. Science works through a set of procedures and processes that tune out all subjective factors. If you do the math correctly, and follow experimental procedures we call the results scientific. It does not matter what language you speak, or what religious beliefs you hold or what traditions you follow. If you tune this stuff out, we call it science. If any of these subjective factors pertain, the "science" is questionable. This is how science disconnects understanding with traditional meaning. Traditional meaning is intimately tied to the subjective factors that science tunes out.

Science has become so important in our modern world that we need to understand how it works to be able to position it properly in an ethical society. Moreover, scientific methods speed up the discovery process. This is called rapid-discovery science to contrast modern methods with ancient and medieval science. Knowledge is progressing by leaps and bounds and the discovery rate for new knowledge is accelerating almost daily.

Science has become so pervasive and important in modern society that we really need to understand how it works. We also need to explore the kinds of developments in scientific methods that are likely to affect how we might proceed in the future. We need to harness the power of science to properly serve humanity as knowledge capital. No strategy for change would be complete if it did not redirect science to humanitarian objectives, in alignment with other initiatives.

We will explore these methods here, and also explain science as a symbolic form, providing a Framework for modern thought. We will also explore how contemporary science is improving its methods to further accelerate the rate of discovery. If you think things moved quickly in the 20th century, hold on to your hats—you ain't seen nothing yet.

Modern science started with two forms: rationalism—that logic is the basis of all true knowledge; and empiricism—that accurately observed, properly evidenced truth claims are the basis of true knowledge. Science effectively developed by combining both. Rationalists took the view that perceptions were unreliable in this context and chose logical coherence. However, empiricists remembered the "logic" of church authorities and questioned such a "logical" approach. Their response was to specify rules for observation, and they suggested that all truth claims can be verified or not by applying such rules. In short, they claimed that empirical methods were the only guarantee of objective truth.

To accomplish this feat of truth-finding, empiricists generally suggested that common sense should win out over theories based solely on logic. How then does science obtain objectively true results?

We saw in the second chapter that science is a very different way of approaching knowledge than traditional myths. It is almost exclusively concerned with *how* things work and is unconcerned with *why*. Science is a particular form of symbolic reasoning: in this case, a symbolic form that emphasizes precision in symbolic definitions with mathematics and precise logical and empirical methods.

How Science Works

Science grew out of two schools of philosophical thought: empiricism and rationalism. Let us look at each position, in turn, identify their respective limitations, and then look at how science got around those limitations.

Empiricism

The main tenet of empiricism is that *all* evidence for knowledge claims must be sensory (i.e., empirical).[55] Empiricists' central problem is the question, how do sensory elements get to be sensory evidence? That is, how do we select perceptions to count as evidence for knowledge claims? Empiricist philosophy is primarily a search for these processes or criteria.

Some see the problem as psychological. The selection process is determined by psychological criteria that form the process for this to happen. However, in the face of scientific evidence of how perception actually works, a deeper problem comes to the fore. If all evidence for knowledge claims must be sensory, then the question becomes, how do we know when our perceptions correspond with reality? In other words, how do we know both that our perceptions are true, and that they *can* evidence some knowledge claim about the real world?

What would happen if our question were to be answered? I say, "X is how sensory elements get to be sensory evidence." For this statement to be true, the process X would have to involve some knowledge of the correspondence of perceptions with their real counterparts. As such, X would itself be a knowledge claim. However, according to the empiricists' approach, to count as a knowledge claim, X would have to be empirically evidenced.

The problem is that if all evidence for knowledge claims must be sensory, and the question being asked is whether sensory elements are even suitable as evidence for knowledge claims, then any claims to *know* that such-and-such process works would require more sensory evidence if the claim is to be verified. In other words, to say we can empirically evidence knowledge claims requires first accepting that sensory elements can function as evidence for knowledge claims. The whole argument is circular and begs the question.

The solution proposed by Karl Popper seems to be the only way out for empiricists. Popper recognizes that naive realism is false and opts to accept that knowledge claims cannot be evidenced if that would mean that the evidence would verify some claim.

---

55 Quine, *Epistemology Naturalized*. (This is a central argument of the paper).

In the empiricists' model, scientists form a hypothesis about X and seek verification through sensory evidence. That is, they construct an experiment that would provide the appropriate perceptions (measurements) to verify (or not) the hypothesis. Popper claims that scientists never verify their hypotheses—they only refute them. Scientists can have empirical experiences that are true, but the process of verification is not precise. What is precise is when empirical evidence refutes some knowledge claim. In Popper's model, scientists form hypotheses and accept their results until some new evidence rules out that hypothesis. Verification is never achieved.

This model explains quite a lot about how scientists come to reject one theory in favor of another, but it is not complete in two respects. First, it is not clear how to select from among our perceptions those that can count as evidence for knowledge claims and those that cannot. In Popper's view, this is the imprecise process. Second, if we observe scientists at work, they really do think they verify some things, and do not behave as though this is an imprecise process. Indeed, it is difficult to explain how scientists can arrive at "laws" if there can be no verification of any knowledge claims.

The better option would be to say that the second question cannot be answered within the framework of empiricism. The answer to the question must lie in some other method of selecting sensory elements that is not itself grounded in sensory processes. The correct approach that we will adopt here is that Popper is onto something very important—science is self-correcting.

Rationalism

Rationalism was the view proposed by Descartes,[56] Leibniz,[57] and Spinoza.[58] If I present rationalism in the same terms used above, I can say that the main tenet of rationalism is that *all evidence for knowledge claims must be logical (i.e., mathematical).*

---

56 Descartes, R. (1999). *Discourse On Method, And, Meditations On First Philosophy.* Indianapolis, IN: Hackett Pub Co Inc; 4th ed.
57 *Leibniz, G. W. (2014). The Monadology. Oxford: Acheron Press.*
58 Spinoza, B. (2002). *Spinoza: Complete Works.* Indianapolis, IN: Hackett Publishing Company, Inc.

I maintain that logic and mathematics are conceptual in nature and that they can represent the real world. For example, the concept of gravity represents some real force in the world. This is the case of all true concepts that describe empirical experiences.

This leaves us with the question, how do logical elements get to be logical evidence? This is similar to the question posed for perception and truth claims. How should we sort out from all our concepts those that can count as evidence for knowledge claims? Since concepts are representations, this question can be reworded in terms of correspondence truth. How do we know when our concepts represent reality well?

Again, let us consider the answer to the question. Say that Y is how logical elements get to be logical evidence. Again, Y constitutes a knowledge claim, and so it is fair to ask, what evidence supports this claim?

The problem is that if all evidence for knowledge claims must be logical, and the question being asked is whether logical elements are even suitable as evidence for knowledge claims, then any claims to *know* that such-and-such process works would require more logical evidence if that claim is to be verified. In other words, to say that we can evidence knowledge claims logically requires that we first accept that logical elements can function as evidence for knowledge claims. Again, the whole argument is circular and begs the question. Rationalists answered the question, "How do logical elements get to be logical evidence?" by referencing an outside principle such as God or a *pre-established harmony*.

The appeal to logic as evidence follows from the belief that we live in a logical rational universe. If the rules of logic are correct, and if we follow the rules, then we must arrive at truth claims. Further, the rules of logic are coherent by definition. We can readily discover internal inconsistencies, and the absence of internal inconsistencies permits the verification of truth claims.

While this is a persuasive appeal to the nature of logic itself, it does not address the issue of whether such-and-such concept represents any real counterpart, such that it evidences a knowledge claim. In other words, the appeal to *coherence* as a method of determining truth appears to work in isolation of *correspondence* unless one first accepts that logic can be used to support knowledge claims. The problem is that logical arguments are *valid*, but not necessarily *true*. Logic works with conditionals that may or may not apply in empirical experience. Using logic in this way confuses validity and truth, and so we must go outside of logic to make the link.

There seem to be no rationalists who challenge logical realism, as Popper did Empiricism. Rationalists all sidestep the issue and fall back on coherence truth and the coherence of the world. All that is needed is to determine that logical principles accurately reflect the (assumed) metaphysical coherence of the real world, and the legitimacy of any logical knowledge is assured. For example, Leibniz assumed that "all truth is analytic." This is the idea that all predicates follow from the subject, much as a tautology does. All bachelors are unmarried men. From this, he derives the *Principle of Sufficient Reason*. There must be a sufficient reason for anything to be what it is, and that reason is found in the *analytic* of logical deductions. In short, for a claim to be true, there must be no internal inconsistencies. Any conceptual logic must match the coherence of reality.

Again, this begs the question. Like empiricism, rationalism cannot stand on its own tenet. It must appeal to some outside element or process to justify its approach.

Science: Empiricism and Rationalism

I have shown that for each of empiricism and rationalism, questioning the legitimacy of their respective tenets requires that they each beg the question of the legitimacy of their respective tenets. Consequently, each approach on its own merits is untenable.

Science grew out of both of these approaches, but developed in such a way as to be very successful. How did science overcome the limitations of each? It blended the two approaches into a single coherent model.

To understand how this works, I need to begin with an error. I will suppose that there is not one science but *two*. I will correct this impression later. I submit that there is an empirical science, understood as such, and a rational science, usually understood as *theoretical science*.

To begin is the question of how sensory or logical evidence gets to count as scientific evidence. Science answers this by first restricting what counts as a sensory or logical element. Consequently, science has devised sophisticated rules for determining what counts as a candidate for scientific evidence. For example, any old observation will not do. To count as what is called a *scientific sensory element*, a number of procedures and guidelines must be followed. Observations must be made under rigorous conditions—such as a laboratory experiment, and these are clearly stipulated as part of scientific methodology. These, in turn, are based on the idea that observations must *in principle* be repeatable. That is, it must be the case that anyone who follows the procedures as outlined in a scientific report will make the same observations (within an acceptable range of accuracy). This must be true in principle, if not in fact, for any observation to count as a scientific observation.

A similar set of procedures must be observed for scientific concepts or theories. They must be mathematical, using accepted mathematical procedures, and must harmonize with other accepted theories. By and large, these follow a precept for achieving theoretical descriptions of the world: *To describe a cause is to explain an effect.* Theoretical sciences seek to explain the world in scientific terms, and these terms are, in part, specified by the procedures used to get a legitimate theory. Any old method will not do. For example, in the 18th century, Bishop Berkeley suggested a method of explaining by inventing convenient analogies. This will not yield scientific results. Concepts and explanations must be precise, but in a specified way. The use of mathematical methods to generate such descriptions is one of the ways that science restricts the available concepts and theories that might count as logical elements.

Once it is accepted that the procedures described do restrict the range of sensory or logical elements that can count as scientific, we can no longer refer to these in broad terms. I will distinguish these as *scientific sensory elements*, and *scientific logical elements*. When I pose the question about how to select from among our sensory or logical elements those that can count as evidence for knowledge claims, science again reduces the scope of the problem. Science asks, *How do scientists* (those who follow the rigorous scientific methods) *select, from among scientific elements, those that can count as evidence for scientific truth claims?*

I have introduced a new concept into the discussion—the idea of scientific truth claims. These are the truth claims scientists make that are the results of their investigations. There are two kinds of scientific truth claims: theoretical and empirical. How these are evidenced provides the solution to the respective circularities of empiricism and rationalism.

I have already introduced theoretical truth claims. To describe a cause is to explain an effect. For example, gravity causes the apple to fall from the tree to the ground. Bacteria entering a wound cause infection. This means that theoretical truth claims are explanations of observed effects, and that they are explanatory in nature. How does anyone know which theories are true? Scientists evidence them with scientific sensory elements. That is, they rely on scientific observations (perceptions) to evidence their theories.

Figure 6.1 explains how this process works. Scientists assume that in the real world, there are necessary connections between things. The problem is that no one experiences necessity as such. Indeed, in *A Treatise of Human Nature*,[59] David Hume pointed out that the best anyone can do is experience contingency between events, and this is the basis of his rejection of rationalism. This same objection was raised above with the problem of logical realism. Furthermore, if perception is representational as presented, then there must be a consideration that what is experienced empirically in the phenomenal world may not be an exact representation of the real world. In Hume's terms, one of the differences is the experience of "necessity." Helier Robinson puts these together in the following model, presented in Figure 6.1.

In the real world, *A* necessarily causes *B*, which necessarily causes *C*. Robinson postulates an informational representational world where we experience these relations as *Humean* (named after Hume) or *contingent cause*. *A* contingently causes *B*, which contingently causes *C*. To explain these relations, science postulates *logical cause*. This is the logic of theoretical science. *A* logically causes *B*, which logically causes *C*. If the mathematical descriptions hold, scientists claim that their observations of *B* and *C* confirm the hypothesis.

---

59 Hume, D. (1975). *A Treatise of Human Nature*. Oxford: Oxford at the Clarendon Press.

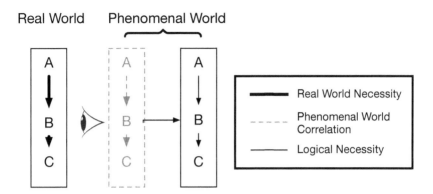

Figure 6.1: Robinson's Model of Science

But science extends this even further, as can be seen in Figure 6.2.

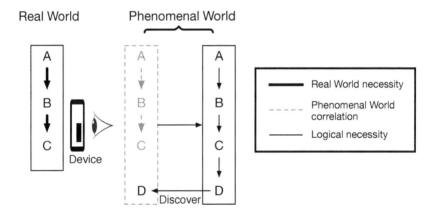

Figure 6.2: Predicting Novelty

Scientists further consider that if A causes B causes C, then D must logically follow. To test the hypothesis, scientists must devise a well-defined test to determine if they can perceive D under the conditions that would link it to A, B, and C, as the theory suggests. If they observe D in the proper place, they conclude that D must exist in the real world such that A causes B causes C causes D.

This is the basis of how theoretical truth claims are verified. However, the process is much more complex than this. To discover D in the correct context, scientists must devise an experiment that will discover D or not. In normal circumstances, such an experiment would attempt to limit the number of sensory elements to an acceptable range of observations, and then to construct the procedures so that if D is found, it is found in the context that would verify (or not) the hypothesis about D.

For example, the scientist might use a device such as a spectroscope to observe D. If spectroscopic analysis reveals D as predicted, then there appears to be a verification of the hypothesis. However, what of Popper's claim, that such verification is not possible on empirical grounds alone?

To answer this, I must now consider the other science I introduced—that of empirical science. Empirical science rests on the idea that there can be empirical truth claims. That is, what scientists observe under the right conditions as specified by scientific methods is *meaningful*. In the example of D above, the question would be, why does observing D with a spectroscope provide meaningful results in the context of the hypothesis? Another way of asking this question is to ask why observations or a measurement using the device in question produce scientific sensory elements? How do scientists know that their observing techniques or measuring devices are doing anything meaningful?

The answer turns out to be related to scientific explanations. In the case of the spectroscope, scientists have a well-defined theory of light, which has been built up from many hypotheses and observations that provide concrete evidence for their theory. Within the theory, they can explain how a spectroscope works. This explanation provides the confidence to use the device in the experiment about D.

In other words, the hypothesis about D is based on consistent and accepted explanations about A, B, and C, and is detailed enough to specify the conditions under which D can be observed. These specifications include the criteria needed to determine what kind of sensory elements can count as sensory evidence to support the claim about D. Provided that the device is used properly, and that it is well-understood, its output is considered relevant to the theory, and scientists can use this device to determine whether D behaves as the theory suggested.

The point here should be obvious to the reader by now. Scientists use perceptions to evidence theoretical claims and use concepts to evidence empirical claims. This latter process is missed by empiricists. However, it is central to science. Consider the recent debates about gravity waves. There is ample mathematics to support the hypothesis that gravity waves exist, and to describe their properties. When scientists produced experiments to verify the existence of gravity waves, the debates centered not on the mathematical models, but on the measuring devices used in the experiments. In general, scientists questioned whether the devices used to detect gravity waves were doing anything meaningful in the context of the experiment. The initial results were twofold. First, it became clear that the theoretical underpinnings of such devices were not well-understood. Second, the hypothesis was neither verified nor refuted.

The first point refers to how science is built up from a series of explanations about the world. When scientists reach a point in their understanding that they can apply that knowledge to new cases, they tend to trust the devices engineered for such purposes. When they do not have enough detail in their explanations, they cannot be sure that measuring devices that depend on such explanations are measuring what they think they are measuring. Scientific sensory evidence depends on the detailed explanatory power of theoretical science.

The second point refers to the fact that in the absence of empirical evidence, theories can be neither proved nor disproved.

Science, then, is a complex activity that involves several processes.

1. There are well-defined rules to determine what counts as a scientific perception or concept.

2. There are theories or hypotheses that are intended to explain observed effects through descriptive methods. These descriptive

methods are the criteria for determining whether the concepts involved are scientific or not.

3. There are observations and measurements made under strict controls such that reliance on these techniques is only possible when scientists have a good explanation of how the device works. This process of explanation forms the criteria used to determine if a perception (such as a measurement) is a scientific sensory element or not.

4. Once science has accepted that the perceptions and concepts are scientific, the relationship between them determines whether they can be counted as evidence for such-and-such knowledge claim. This is accomplished in two ways:

   + If the knowledge claim is a *theoretical* claim, then it must be empirically supported;

   + If the knowledge claim is an *empirical* claim, then the observation or measurement must be supported with accepted theory.

It might seem from this that there is no real foundation to science. This is probably true. Science bootstraps itself into existence. What is built up is a *codependency web* of observations, theories, and explanations, each interconnected to form a coherent structure. Once it is up and running, it seems to be self-sustaining. The coherence of its codependencies stands at the bottom of science. One of the ways of determining whether science is on the right track is to look for inconsistencies in the overall program and its results. If you can find internal inconsistencies or gaps in the coherence of the overall structure, you would have identified problem areas for science to resolve.

Robinson outlines the key components of science as follows:[60]

1. A theory must be logically consistent. If it contains contradictions, it is necessarily false.

---

60 Robinson, pp. 58–76.

2. The theory must not be counterfactual. Its theorems must not disagree with empirical formulas or empirical fact. If they do, the theory is necessarily false.

3. The larger the scope of explanation of a theory (the larger the range of empirical laws the theory explains), the more strongly we believe in it.

4. The greater the density of detail of a theory (the more details that can be accounted for), the more strongly we believe in the theory.

5. If two theories are otherwise equal—they are not false and have identical scope and density of detail—then the simpler is more probable.

6. The harmony of a theory with other accepted theories contributes to our belief in the theory.

7. The elegance of a theory also contributes to our belief in the theory.

8. Symmetry contributes to our belief in a theory. For example, the principles of conservation—of momentum, energy, etc.—are symmetrical with time.

9. Successful theoretical prediction of novelty is the most convincing ground for believing in a theory.

Given my position about empirical science, I can add the following:

10. All reported observations must be public—that is, observable by anyone who follows the same procedures that lead to the event to be observed as reported (plus or minus an acceptable margin of error);

11. The procedures used to observe an event must use techniques and tools for which we have an adequate explanation of how the technique or tool works;

12. The observer must take appropriate cautions to minimize the role of the observer in the observation itself; and,

13. The techniques used to observe an event must seek to control or minimize extraneous influences that could impair the accuracy of the observation.

In general, science works because it can answer the four questions posed by empiricism and rationalism. We determine sensory or logical evidence using well-understood rules and criteria, and then mix and match theories and observations in a codependency web. Both correspondence and coherence truth models are supported by scientific methods. Science imposes a logical structure on our experiences, and builds its success in codependent increments of observation and theory.

This also answers Popper's claim that theories are never verified. In a sense, he is correct, but his empiricist language is misleading. Observations do not "verify" theories as such. Rather, such hypotheses are "accepted" as explanations of observed behaviors. That is, verification is not a step in science, as such. Theories become accepted into the body of scientific knowledge based on their explanatory power, not on their validity in strict logical or empirical terms. When a theory can explain and successfully predict novelty, and explain how measuring devices or observational techniques work, and meets all scientific conditions (listed above), it becomes an accepted explanation. This acceptance involves the inclusion of the observation or theory into the codependency web, which means that other dependency relations can be built upon it. When inconsistency or refuted observations challenge the codependency web, the theory and its associated explanatory power are refuted. Scientists then determine how the failure occurred—was there a misrepresentation of scientific elements due to a flaw in the theory or observation? When this is known, corrective action can be taken, and corrected theories or experiments can produce a model scientists will accept. In this way, science is self-correcting. Notice that there is no authority or scientific priest to decide what is true or false. Scientific truth claims are true within the codependency web of scientific results following the criteria listed above.

Science is not successful because of a single method or technique, but through a mix of techniques and methods. It is science as an enterprise that is successful, not this or that scientific process, theory, or experiment. Since each theory and experiment relies on the whole edifice of science,

science is progressive and increasingly comprehensive. This is why it forms such an important place in any modern understanding of the world.

Quantum Perspectives

I have outlined a model of science that is well suited to classical science. In particular, the model presented so far maintains assumptions that there is necessary cause in the real world. This assumption has been questioned by quantum theory, and so the current model needs some revision.

The main difference between quantum and classical models is that quantum models do not assume necessity in the real world. What science has discovered is that as we probe more deeply into the nature of matter, the treasured necessity or determinism of classical methods has to give way to the contingency or indeterminacy of statistical methods. How this change in outlook took place is a truly fascinating tour de force.

In terms of the model presented so far, the initial point of departure is in the stage of predicting novelty. As physicists probed more deeply into matter, they found that the observed results did not conform to the predictions from deterministic mathematics. Consequently, they had two choices: they could accept necessity in the real world as an assumption and consider that there are severe limitations in the ability to gather empirical data about matter, or they could reject logical cause in the classical sense and replace this with a contingent cause that conforms more readily to the observational successes they had achieved.

As we know, physicists chose the second option. They replaced classical deterministic methods with statistical methods at the level of logical cause. When they had done this, the assumption of necessity and determinism required modification. The model now looks like that shown in Figure 6.3.

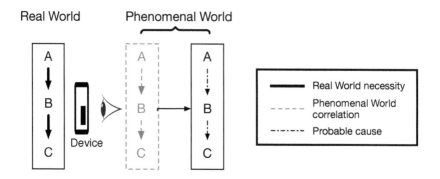

Figure 6.3: Quantum Theory

In this case, at the logical level, *A* probably causes *B* probably causes *C*, and so on. There can be no positive determinations of the causal events. Causal events can only be determined within a range of probabilities. This, in turn, suggests that necessary cause in the real world is not as classical science would have us believe. The statistical or probabilistic nature of mathematical descriptions accurately describes the probabilistic nature of the real world.

The success of quantum theory cannot be disputed. By substituting statistical for classical methods, physics has achieved a remarkable success in predicting novelty, and in confirming the *quantum worldview* that is now in use.

Note that the process of science in the relation between concepts and perceptions remains the same. While quantum theory modifies the view of determinism in the real world, it does not change the fundamental program of science. Science remains a web of theories and observations that finds its success in the enterprise as a whole. This can be seen with a quick observance of Einstein's objections to quantum theory.

First, I should note that Einstein developed much of modern quantum theory. His objection was in the inference of statistical methods to the indeterminism of the world. His famous, "God does not play dice with the Universe," is a reference to the way in which science would proceed under such an assumption. As Arthur Fine points out,[61] Einstein's objection was not at the level of indeterminism on an individual experimental basis, but that the implications for science as an enterprise were not well considered in the quick acceptance of the real-world implications of statistical views. He thought that quantum theory marked a fundamental change in the program of science overall, and because the success of science is grounded in the scientific enterprise as a whole, physicists should not be too quick to make such radical changes. He believed that the success factors of science were in jeopardy.[62]

In the present context, I pose this problem in a different light. In the sections above, I discovered that the difficulty with rationalism is that it carries a large appeal to the experience that there is an order in the world. This is the basis of logical realism. Quantum theory replaced logical realism with a less deterministic model. Reality is not as logically determined as classical science once assumed. Since science picks itself up by its bootstraps, it does not really challenge logical realism. Rather, science assumes realism under the guise of coherence, and as evidenced by empirical methods. This was the change in the scientific program that raised Einstein's objections.

Science as Symbolic Expression

Science moves us beyond language and myth to the same order of abstraction as art, but with the focus on objective content, and not subjective forms. Mathematics is purely symbolic. When Einstein wrote $E = mc^2$, he symbolized not only several concepts pertaining to experience (energy, mass, light, etc.), but also the complex interrelationships between these. Science posits logical relationships and measures results. Science pushes the abstraction process with a special system of symbols that represent relations. Mathematics, for example, is purely relational. Through relating

---

61 Fine, A. (2009). *The Shaky Game: Einstein, Realism And The Quantum Theory*. Chicago: University of Chicago Press. Chapter 6.
62 Heisenberg, W. (2007). *Physics And Philosophy: The Revolution In Modern Science*. New York: Harper Perennial.

mathematical descriptions with empirical measurements, science achieves its objectivity (i.e., in principle, anyone who follows proper procedures can witness the same results plus or minus a specified accuracy range).

The point is that science works in obtaining a worldview that is coherent in the same way that language and mythology do, although it does so through its own language and its own methodology. Science standardizes the meaning of its symbols: d means distance, t means time, v means velocity. These definitional characteristics are uniform and regular in a way that linguistic, mythical, and artistic symbols are not. Scientific symbols are invariant, while the others vary in place, moment, or culture. This invariance is the ground for the objectivity of scientific results.

I outlined how symbolic expressions were standardized first as language, then as mythical forms, and finally as abstracted forms of themselves independent of content. Science presents the other side of the "art" form. It standardizes symbolic representations of contents and determines its own forms based on the actual relationships observed by following common procedures. In general, there are two ways to improve the objective validity of truth claims. As indicated above, we can increase the publicity/objectivity of a claim by making it available to more people for public scrutiny. This works best when it involves diverse groups with diverse languages, customs, and beliefs. Any truth claim that survives such scrutiny must surely be valid. The second way is to get clearer about our terms and ways of experiencing. Standardizing the methods of expression and experience with clearer terms goes a long way to achieving cross-cultural validation. For example, religion does this with ritual and extending authority.

Modern rapid-discovery science puts these two methods on steroids. It both enhances the standardization and clarification and also selects symbolic forms that are literally independent of any given culture and so are cross-cultural by definition. In principle, anyone who does the math correctly, following standard and accepted scientific techniques, will get the same result. The same is not true for other forms of understanding. For example, if you and I are trying to understand why a loved one must suffer a debilitating disease, we could both pray following the exact symbolic meanings and rituals prescribed by our faith. But there is no guarantee that we will in principle have a similar outcome, plus or minus a small variation. Of course, we would rely on an authority (such as a priest) to explain these differences. Science does not work this way. It builds up a codependency web of specific scientific experiences (observations and measurements) and theories and explanations that support each other, regardless of who is making the claim. Science does not depend on the authority of its scientists the way religions depend on the authority of their priests. The difference for science is that the codependency web of theories and observations that is formed is highly structured in a specific and formal way.

Scientists develop understanding in a much more precise way than do non-scientists, priests, or artists. This precision helps to makes science work. The precision in building codependency webs also makes science different in kind from other, more traditional forms of understanding. It is clearly and exclusively focused on how things work. It virtually disregards the whys in the sense of what it might mean for individuals or humanity.

From our modern scientific point of view, we now treat other forms of understanding—those not based on well-defined procedures and concepts that build well-structured codependency webs—as allegorical rather than true or valid. Science changes the rules for how we define understanding. It is not just about improving publicity or referencing authoritative sources that determine the validity of our truth claims. That kind of understanding is allegorical because it is really just a semi-coherent expression of specific symbolic forms. Again, all informational facts are representational, and all representations are symbolic of something. It is how we ground our symbolic expressions—in specific, well-defined procedures independent of individual or institutional forms presented in the context of a well-structured codependency web—that ultimately sets science apart from religion.[63]

However, science and myth are not as distant from each other as some might suppose. The underlying logic of how all representations are symbolic and how we construct worldviews is the same. There is a real

---

63 If the reader wants to experience a contemporary distinction between allegorical and scientific understanding, try a comparative reading of *any religious text or commentary* such as Arthur Lovejoy's The Great Chain of Being (1964), along with *The Road to Reality: A Complete Guide to the Laws of the Universe* by British mathematical physicist Dr. Roger Penrose (2004).

sense in which the medieval worldview of a Benedictine monk was just as legitimate for him as science is for us. It was culturally coherent (including Frameworks with a rich set of codependency webs), had a rich history and development, and followed logical rules that placed religious beliefs in a modern and more objective context than their mythological/magical predecessors. The view was coherent, well-thought-out, and explained why the world worked in a way that everyone at the time understood and agreed with.

That this collective wisdom was not objective in the sense of a modern science is irrelevant to understanding. If Spinoza is correct, and understanding is the essence of man, then any understanding counts. To suggest that science is *better* than religion at understanding the fundamental unity and integrity of nature is false. Like religion, science is based on faith in the fundamental unity of the world, and this is based on the common acceptance of the symbolic expressions selected and the precision of the processes that science uses. Ultimately, we believe science because this standardization and precision feels more real than other symbolic processes.

The reason science feels more real or objectively true is because it clearly focuses attention on the how of the world and not why. Science works by disregarding the uniqueness of individual perspective in experience. We called this *universalizing*. A causes B causes C, regardless of who is observing the chain of events. Science pushes this even further. It disregards anything that considers what makes us human in any meaningful way. It does not matter who or even what produces the scientific truth claim. A human, a dolphin, a Martian, or a robot following scientific methods should all produce the same results (plus or minus an acceptable margin of error). Science is universal in a way that is qualitatively different from any other universal truths (such as religion), and it is this difference that enhances its status to deliver objective truth—to correctly describe and explain reality.

Future Science

There is only one science, but science has two modes or distinctions within it. First, Scientists use observations to evidence theories. Second, they use proven theories as explanations to provide meaning for observations. Scientific knowledge grows with each discovery

For example, science begins with simple data gathering. It then imposes a logical structure to the data with classifications. To classify data, scientists need some criteria to employ to generate the classes. As scientists find that their data do not meet these criteria, they modify the criteria and class definitions to accommodate the new data. Out of this process comes the need to ask how these models work, and the process of theory and observational experimentation begins. As scientists come to better understand these classifications through various scientific explanations, they refine the models even further, and the process of scientific exploration moves into full swing.

What is interesting about this is that there is no point at which the simpler task of classifying types ends, and the further role of exploring in detail begins. From the beginning, the goal is to understand the subject matter at hand and not just to produce interesting classifications.

This process works because the whole is somehow greater than the simple sum of the parts. The explanatory power of a good theory can lead to all sorts of new discoveries, and new discoveries can lead to all sorts of modified and new theories. All are codependent on the others. This is why science's explanatory power lies in the whole edifice, not in just this or that theory or observation. Explanation emerges from the process of scientific discovery. This emergence is most often missed or not accounted for in discussions of science.

For example, the Copenhagen interpretation of quantum mechanics led to the direct result that scientists cannot establish objectivity until they observe a phenomenon. An experiment, conducted by Werner Heisenberg,[64] sent a particle through an apparatus with two slits. The object of the experiment was to predict which of the slits the particle would pass through, given the probability of either event. What was discovered

---

64 Pagels, H. (2012). *The Cosmic Code*. Mineola, NY: Dover Publications Inc. *Page 152.*

was that the act of making such an observation interfered with the process and affected the result. The conclusion was that prior to an observation, the particle existed in a quantum state that was neither projected nor not projected. It could pass through Slit 1 or pass through Slit 2. No determination could be made about any state of the particle prior to an observation after the fact. Heinz Pagels commented, "The Standard Copenhagen interpretation ... showed that indeterminacy ... meant that we had to renounce the objectivity of the world, the idea that the world exists independently of our observing it. For example, the electron exists as a real particle at a point in space only if we observe it directly."[65]

To say that there is no determined reality independent of human experience does not mean that there is not an underlying logic that is deterministic in some way. It means that it is not deterministic in the way in which we have traditionally defined these terms. The concept of traditional determinism needs to be clarified. If temporal flow is linear, then determinism can be defined in terms of a linear progression of events such as causal sequences. However, quantum theory tells us that this is not quite accurate. Pagels concludes that it is "not possible to obtain information without increasing entropy—the measure of disorganization of physical systems." Furthermore, he states, "This increase in entropy implies that time has an arrow—there is temporal irreversibility and physical processes exist which can store information ... irreversibility in time is the principle feature of observation, although that, of course, also entails irreversibility because it involves memory."[66] In short, time-linear descriptions may not provide us with accurate real-world descriptions. With quantum theory, science has reached this limit, and must now explain the world within the parameters of this asymmetry. However, these limitations might not pertain so rigidly at higher levels of complexity, but might be a more straightforward indeterminacy because we cannot control all the variables required to produce a deterministic explanation.

This suggests a re-evaluation of what is meant by *necessity*. In classical models, necessity is perceived to be roughly linear. A causes B causes C, and so on. This predilection comes from ordinary world experiences. Second,

---

65 Ibid.
66 Ibid.

mathematics has historically focused on linear equations because we did not have the computing horsepower to analyze nonlinear equations.

The second point is more immediately relevant. With the growth of the computational power of computers, and their widespread availability, scientists are now exploring nonlinear dynamics. While these are still statistical in nature, they present an opportunity to revise the concept of necessity.

In general, nonlinear thinking implies a multiplicity of events that contribute to a causal effect. The usual example is a butterfly in China flaps its wings, and a tornado results in America. To understand what happened, there can be no concept of a *sequence* of events. The multiplicity of air molecules bumping into each other over such great distances to end in a whirl of air in America is beyond current observational and tracking capabilities. The best science can do is to provide some probabilistic analysis of groups of molecules and possible outcomes over time. The point is that other air movements also affect the sequence of these specific air movements, and this provides the key. We are no longer looking for a sequence of events, but a pattern of activities that accounts for the effect being described. Patterns are analyzed using nonlinear equations.

This approach introduces a view of necessity that is nonlinear. There is a determinacy in the motions of air molecules because their individual movements follow well-understood laws of dynamics. However, when we must account for all of them at once to describe a cause, classical necessity holds little relevance. Patterns of events describe the situation, not linear sequences. Determinism shifts to a new definition: determinism involves the occurrence of a multiplicity of events that are non-simultaneous and only partially overlapping in the sense of a pattern or scenario. The real world is not deterministic in the classical sense. Nevertheless, it is deterministic in the sense of patterns of behaviors. The whole (pattern) has spatial, temporal, and functional properties not found in individual sequences. While patterns may appear amorphous to phenomenal world points of view, that does not mean that they are random or unstructured.

For example, there is a general agreement that there is a hierarchy in the world, from quarks to atoms to molecules to chemicals to substances to cells to organs to organisms. Furthermore, nonlinear techniques are exposing different levels of explanations. The idea that physics could produce a theory of everything by explaining all the basic elementary particles and their interactions is emerging as somewhat questionable. Science is moving to a new way of considering these issues.

These considerations will lead directly to the idea that the program of science is set to change once again. There appears to be a general trend toward moving away from linear reductionist approaches toward more nonlinear methods. An example of this is the emerging study of complex systems. Complexity theory provides an understanding of how systems, grow, adapt, and evolve. It studies the relationships between the key components of these systems: self-organization, continuous adaptation, sensitivity to initial conditions, and nonlinearity, and how these give rise to collective behavior. It sheds light on how a system interacts with its environment.

Computational Science

In general, I argue that traditional notions of cause and effect are too linear and need to be replaced with a more holistic, patterned approach to causal interactions. This is driven by new computational powers, which facilitate computations with nonlinear formulations. The key issue is the overall trend in science.

Science has developed largely with reductionist methods because of the need to focus on linear equations. Historically, scientists did not have the computational power to unpack nonlinear equations. Instead of working with computations that involve hundreds or thousands of variables, scientists reduced the computational load by breaking the world into manageable bits of linear models that work with three or four variables at most. The whole idea of laboratory experiments in science was and is to isolate the key variables presented in the mathematical models, and determine whether various hypotheses could be validated or refuted.

In general, I am arguing that the time has come for science to become less linear in its approaches. Complexity theory is one such example. However, science might take another approach, one that confirms much of the causal analysis presented above and which involves the work of Stephen Wolfram in his book *A New Kind of Science*.[67] Wolfram studied how simple programs behave, and he worked with one-dimensional cellular automata:

> The cellular automaton consists of a line of cells, each colored either black or white. At every step, there is then a definite rule that determines the color of a given cell from the color of that cell and its immediate left and right neighbors on the step before.[68]

For example, if we had taken simple graph paper and looked across the first row, we might find all white cells with one black cell in the middle. We could then construct a rule to get the second row. The rule might say, look at the cell above. If it is white, you be white. If it is black, you be black. For each cell in row two, we would apply the rule. In this case, all cells would be white until we got to the point where there is a black cell above. We would insert a black cell in row two under the black cell in row one. If we then applied the rule to all remaining rows down the page, we would end up with a white page with a single black line running down the middle.

Wolfram studied the one-dimensional cellular automata and determined that there are 256 fundamental rules that can be followed. What he discovered was quite surprising. While we might think that repeatedly applying a simple rule would produce only simple patterns, Wolfram discovered that this is not the case. He discovered that about one-third of the rules produced patterns that are complex and even random.

Wolfram explored other similar-type systems such as Turing machines, mobile automata, register machines, tag systems, substitution systems, systems based on numbers, continuous versus discrete systems, and more, and found that the resulting patterns were the same. About one-third of the patterns exhibit complex or even random behaviors starting from simple rules. Wolfram determined that there are four classes of behavior.

1. Class One behavior is simple, and almost all initial conditions lead to the same uniform final state.

---

67 Wolfram, S. (1987). *A New Kind Of Science*. Champaign, IL: Wolfram Media Inc.
68 bid, p. 24.

2. Class Two has many possible final states, but they all contain simple structures that either remain the same forever or repeat every few steps.

3. Class Three behavior is more complex, where many small-scale structures at some level are always seen.

4. Class Four involves a mixture of order and randomness. Localized structures are produced that on their own are fairly simple, but these structures move around and interact with each other in complex ways.[69]

There are several consequences of these discoveries. The first and most important for Wolfram is that it is a foundational assumption in science that complex systems must have complex underlying rules. Wolfram repeatedly proves that this is false. Because the idea that complex systems must have complex underlying rules is so foundational for science, Wolfram concludes that his discovery alters the foundations of science and leads to a "new kind of science"—hence, the title of his book.

There is enormous potential in Wolfram's approach. For example, it could be that the genetic code is really a set of simple rules that can produce complex organisms. If science could discover what these rules might be, we would have a much clearer explanation and deeper understanding of how DNA works. The same might be true for the structure of space and time, chemical interactions, and many other systems.

Wolfram's first major conclusion is the Principle of Computational Equivalence: all processes, whether they are produced by human effort or occur spontaneously in nature, can be viewed as computations.[70] Wolfram indicates that many systems can be constructed that are universal. That is, they can be used to model any other system. A computer is the most obvious example, but Wolfram explores Turing machines and even cellular automata as universal systems. All that is needed for a system to be universal is a proper encoding system to model the target environment. Wolfram explores his Rule 110 for one-dimensional cellular automata and shows how the rule can be made into a universal system. He concludes that there are many more universal systems than previously thought.

In this sense, computation is defined as something that can be done by a universal system. However, Wolfram explains that no such system could ever be constructed in the actual universe. This leads to a refinement of the Principle of Computational Equivalence: no system can ever carry out explicit computations that are more sophisticated than those carried out by systems like cellular automata or Turing machines.[71]

The Principle of Computational Equivalence leads to a further principle. Wolfram examines many computational systems and relates these to traditional mathematics. He concludes that mathematics is largely reductionist in a special way. Consider the formula for determining where a planet will be in its orbit in three months' time. Such a formula is really just a shortcut or reduction of a great many computations. In practice, we should really compute the position of the planet in a second by second series of computations. The formula allows us to reduce that complex series of computations to a single exercise. It permits us to effectively predict what the answer would have been if we had performed all those computations. In general, science has proceeded on the assumption that if one can find the underlying rules for a system, then this means that ultimately there will always be a way to predict how the system will behave.

However, Wolfram indicates that this assumption is false. He explores many systems where the behavior is so complex or random that such prediction would be impossible. For example, there are many computations in universal systems that do not lend themselves to such simple reductions. In fact, he indicates that most systems might not lend themselves to this kind of reduction. He calls this the Principle of Computational Irreducibility. Computational irreducibility exists when there can be no way to predict how the system will behave except by going through almost as many steps of computation as the evolution of the system itself.

In a general sense, traditional science assumes that complex systems have complex underlying rules. This means that many computations must be more sophisticated than the systems being studied. The principle of Computational Equivalence denies that this assumption can be true. The

---

71 bid., p. 720.

Principle of Irreducibility further reduces the circumstances where we might even think the assumption is true.

Wolfram explores the foundations of mathematics in basic and predicate logics, and shows that mathematicians tend to focus on those theorems that are interesting; that is, those theorems that appear to take a large number of steps to derive. This leaves many simpler theorems unexplored. However, Wolfram has shown that even simple rules can lead to complex or even random behaviors, so the focus by scientists on interesting theorems leaves out many possible avenues of discovery. For example, Wolfram works out the theorems of basic logic in increasing order of complexity to almost 400 lines. Of the almost 2,400 theorems presented, only ten have been deemed interesting enough to be named and extensively studied. These are the theorems that cannot be derived from the preceding theorems in the list without long proofs.

The implications are clear. There are many systems in mathematics and in nature that science has not studied, but which could yield interesting and important results. By confining scientific explorations to those systems that are computationally reducible, science has tuned out many possible sources of research and explanation.

Consequences for Science

From my point of view, Wolfram introduces several concepts that support the approach I have taken. First, Wolfram provides another example of how science might develop to be less reductionist in its approach. The main problem with complexity theory and nonlinear methods is that there is no way to test theoretical results using traditional empirical methods. How can we track and measure thousands of variables in a laboratory? This seems contrary to the very definition of laboratory methods.

Second, Wolfram's response is to use computer models to provide empirical confirmations or refutations. The idea is that once the underlying rules have been established, universal machines can be used to model the consequences of applying those rules. This might require an enormous number of computations (as many systems will not be computationally reducible), but with skill and practice, scientists could learn which consequences match the field of study, and then explore that particular set of computations in greater detail.

In short, Wolfram indicates that science has been overly narrow in its selection of systems to study and has generally failed to look for the underlying rules that generate such systems. This is not surprising. As I pointed out, until recently, scientists did not have the computing horsepower to perform complex computations. Even simple nonlinear equations were beyond their computational abilities. However, much of the literature against scientific reductionism has been directed at empirical methods. Wolfram would now have us include theoretical methods as well.

Third, the good news is that Wolfram provides the basic tools to proceed along the lines he suggests. With modern methods and computational power, scientists have the ability to explore computationally irreducible systems more deeply. The overall structure of science does not change. Theoretical constructs would still be evidenced with empirical observations, and empirical methods would be explained by scientific theory. In the new science, scientists formulate theories based on underlying computational rules, and then run the rules in a model to see if the observed results match what is observed in the natural system being modeled. Overall, the process appears more abstract than formulas and laboratories, but the fundamental principles remain as I have described them. Theories of computation, as well as other branches of mathematics, provide the understanding to explain how computer models work to provide empirical evidence for various hypotheses.

One controversy pertains directly to the limits of scientific knowledge. Postmodernist philosophers have tried to determine the limits of scientific knowledge. Wolfram argues that universal systems can model any natural system if we know what the underlying rules are and have a proper encoding structure. The issue is not that science is methodologically limited in what it can discover or learn about, but it is limited in how it can explore all the consequences of various underlying rules. That is, traditional science limited itself to specific kinds of systems due to historical influences (largely tied to a lack of computation capabilities). In this sense, there are indeed limits to science. However, Wolfram claims, now that the limits of access to computation have been removed, the limits shift from scientific methods to the results of scientific inquiries.

Another approach to the issue of dealing with nonlinear and complex models is presented with synergetic systems. Synergy has several definitions. It indicates that a whole system is greater than the simple sum of its parts. Buckminster Fuller defines synergy as "the behavior of whole systems unpredicted by the behavior of their parts taken separately."[72] Herman Haken provides more clarification: "Synergy means that the cooperation of individual parts of a system produces macroscopic spatial, temporal or functional structures."[73]

The idea behind synergetic systems is that they are self-organizing. New behaviors ultimately emerge from the specific way in which the parts of the system interact with each other to form a whole. Wolfram's Principle of Irreducibility is a further refinement of the definition of synergy, which indicates that macroscopic reducibility is not possible for many systems. Wolfram also suggests that most systems would fall into this category. This means that traditional reductionist methods in science may not always get the results we think are possible. Many systems cannot be studied using traditional reductionist methods, and to do so might result in incorrect results. For example, we might discover how to increase honey production by mating American with African bees, but in the absence of considering other factors such as behavioral characteristics, we might miss a critical component of the offspring, such as aggressiveness. This is how we got killer bees.

Fuller provides a further clue to how science might evolve. A corollary to synergetics is the Principle of the Whole System. This states that the known behaviors of the whole, plus the known behaviors of some of the parts, make possible the discovery of the presence of other parts and their behaviors, kinetics, structures, and relative dimensionalities.[74]

Fuller, Haken, and Wolfram are heading along parallel tracks. Fuller studies geometry, Haken examines self-organizing systems, and Wolfram

72 Fuller, R. B. (1982). *Synergetics: Explorations In The Geometry Of Thinking*. New York: Macmillan Pub Co. Page 3.
73 Haken, H. (2012). *Synergetics: An introduction Nonequilibrium Phase Transitions And Self-organization In Physics, Chemistry And Biology*. New York: Springer. Faceplate.
74 Fuller, *Synergetics*, p. 12.

uses theories of computation to examine simple rules that lead to complex behaviors, any of which could be defined in spatial, temporal, functional, kinetic, or structural terms. Where Wolfram differs from Fuller and Haken is that he indicates that there are always simple underlying rules that facilitate the discoveries to which Fuller and Haken allude. What they all have in common is that codependency webs are inherently synergistic. The whole system, as defined by Fuller, has spatial, temporal, and functional behaviors not found in or which are predictable from any of the parts considered in isolation of their codependent relations.

In general, the debates argue for or against reductionism. The favored non-reductionist approach is called dialectic, which follows Fuller's Principle of Whole Systems. However, if whole systems are not computationally reducible, it would seem that we might have to follow as many steps of the evolution of the system itself to make the kinds of discoveries that Fuller is indicating. How this is accomplished in practice is still to be determined.

The point is that there is a general trend in the evolution of science and its methods. Traditional science, which was outlined in the Figures 4.2 and 4.3 above, examines reducible systems that are largely mechanical and nonsynergetic. The trends in science seem to be toward developing methods to move beyond such reductionist models. This points to a new kind of science that studies nonlinear, synergetic, and computationally irreducible systems using new tools for computation. In this regard, the advent of the computer provides a significant impetus to a new kind of knowledge. Rather than reduce nonsynergetic systems to linear cause and effect models that can be studied in laboratories by isolating a few variables, scientists study irreducible synergetic systems using computational models that are nonlinear using many hundreds or thousands of variables. For example, around 1970, the hard sciences—physics, chemistry, and biology—converged on common mathematical algorithms and normalized many of their definitions. This convergence has resulted in quantum computing, nanotechnologies and decoding genomes—to name a few advancements. This convergence is the direct result of the trends in complexity, synergetics, and computational modeling described above and is leading to new models and approaches to studying complex systems more naturally than reducing them to simple linear models. These models will still need to have empirical verification, but empirical support will be much more complex than with traditional laboratory models, as we have seen with decoding the human genome and with nanotechnology developments.

Conclusions

If most systems are indeed synergetic and computationally irreducible, I can define the limits of science in new and clearer terms. Traditional scientific methods are limited to mechanical, nonsynergetic, and computationally reducible systems. As many or even most (to follow Wolfram's lead) systems are computationally irreducible, science still has much to learn. We are shifting to a new kind of science. However, what might this new science look like?

Wolfram suggests that if science were to move forward with his methods, it would build up a vast repository of information across a wide variety of systems, and over time, scientists would learn which kinds of rules lead to which kinds of behaviors, which could relate to natural or social systems. This would speed up the process of getting close to the underlying rules that might pertain to a particular system being studied, and to a reasonably quick understanding of how its parts interrelate to form the system as observed. Science would begin to leverage the logic of codependency webs in the sense that it could model, say, codependent energy arrays, and produce models that explain the interrelated dependencies using a set of underlying rules.

With such tools, scientists would be able to explore the consequences of many systems in a way that is currently not being tried. Running such simulations or models would also provide enhanced tools to help predict what consequences might obtain from a particular set of rules. While there would always be some need for physical observation and traditional techniques, science would become more computationally based, with more and more models being developed on computers, and where hypotheses developed regarding underlying rules would be empirically tested by running appropriate models and observing and measuring the pattern interactions that result.

How might this work? As discussed previously, determinism is a multiplicity of events occurring that are non-simultaneous and only partially overlapping in the sense of a scenario. The world is not deterministic in the classical sense. However, it is deterministic in the sense of codependencies or patterns of behaviors. The whole (pattern) has spatial, temporal, and functional properties not found in individual sequences. There is logic to the real world, but it is more complex than classical views would allow.

This approach to causal interactions and determinism is now founded in computational theory. Further, it is evident that the principle of computational equivalence provides the theoretical context within which such determinism can be scientifically studied. Classical science uses the causal model shown in Figure 6.4

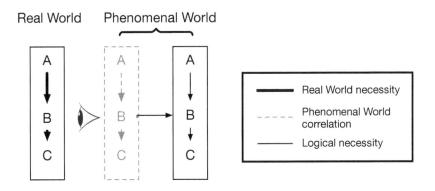

Figure 6.4: Traditional Science Revisited

A new kind of science would follow a model that looks similar but is somewhat different. In the new model, and in contrast with the model of traditional science shown in Figure 6.4, we do not assume a linear necessary cause in the real world. Rather, we assume a patterned interaction of codependent events, producing what R. Buckmonster Fuller called a "scenario universe." Rather than *A* causes *B* causes *C*, we indicate a set of complex systemic interactions between hundreds or thousands of variables. We observe some of the interactions between these variables in an indeterminate way. This is the patterned interaction version of contingent cause in traditional science. In this stage of observation, we notice some of the pattern interactions but not all of them. Much of what we observe is probabilistic.

We postulate a set of simple underlying rules that can generate such complex behaviors, and we follow the computational models to determine if the rules model the scenario within acceptable empirical constraints. That is, we observe both the behavior of the model and the observations made directly. If the model aligns reasonably well with observations, then we accept the results of the model.

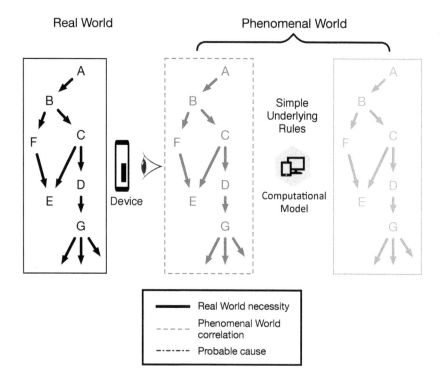

Figure 6.5: Nonlinear Deterministic Model for Science

For systems that are computationally irreducible, the acceptance of the model, combined with a limited set of empirical observations confirming that the computational model accurately describes the behavior of the system being studied, forms the basis for empirical acceptance of the underlying rules that explain the patterned behaviors. Since this would embrace most systems, empirical results are established with confirmation that a proper substitution encoding scheme is in place to generate the computational model. Such universal system modeling shifts the emphasis for empirical science from direct measurable observations in a laboratory setting to direct, measurable encoding substitution rules. In this context, simpler nonlinear empirical techniques would still be valid.

Science, in this new form, expands through a co-development web of computationally derived theories or models combined with empirically measured substitution rules. Like traditional science, which expanded via the complex codependency web of theories and observations, the new science of synergetic computationally irreducible systems expands through its version of a co-development web of models and substitution rules. In this case, the models are computational constructs, and the empirical observations confirm that the correct substitution rules were used. The explanations provided by such models provide a basis for confirming that empirical measurements regarding substitution rules are meaningful. Theories are computational models, and empirical methods confirm that the models do or do not explain the complex pattern interactions observed.

One feature of this new approach to science is that prediction of novelty can cross hierarchical boundaries in a way that traditional science cannot. Recall that a key feature of science requires it to be able to predict novelty. However, traditional science is poor at predicting novelty across the various microscopic to macroscopic levels of the world. For example, there is no method in traditional science to predict the properties of water from combining two hydrogen molecules with one oxygen molecule. This inability is even more pronounced between chemical and biological or biological and social. For example, molecular modeling should be able to predict how a chemical will behave within the complex chemical interactions within an organism. This has obvious and important repercussions for medical research. Moreover, computational models that explicate the simple rules for DNA coding would reveal new areas for research and development in such a way that mitigates much of the trial and error "let's see what happens" approach now being used by traditional scientists.

This new kind of science further enhances the *how* of the world. But more than this, it provides new means for understanding how things behave in complex systems. A key element is to standardize scientific terms of reference. For example, scientists have already standardized how to define a molecule. They then discovered that all molecular sciences—physics, chemistry, and biology—were using similar mathematical descriptions to describe how molecules behave in complex systems. The three sciences converged on common models. This is the above-mentioned convergence taking place across all the sciences.

This new science has also led to new discoveries in the soft sciences. Political science, economics, anthropology, psychology, and epidemiology are all converging on common models of how individuals behave in complex systems, such as communities and societies. As with molecular science, this convergence will lead to new and profound understandings of how societies work and to the kinds of values and policies we need to embrace to achieve specific social goals. This is a qualitatively new way of thinking about ourselves and our traditions and values, and will lead to new kinds of institutions and new perspectives that may help us get beyond our current predicament. The traditional ways of thinking, with self-contained traditions, are coming to an end. This is good news for us because we can use some of these new ways of thinking to form a new Framework that is more global and reflective of the specific things we need to do to shift to a viable and sustainable future. This is how science can help us move forward.

CHAPTER 7
World Game

With these newfound insights into Father Culture and how civilized behaviors impact individuated understanding and meaning, let's reintroduce Albert Schweitzer's definition of civilization. Civilization is a "reduction in the strain of existence," a twofold process that pits man against nature, and man against man. The underlying basis of the success of civilization is humankind's ability to *reason*. Reason first triumphs over nature, then over man. In the 21st century, we are experiencing a real triumph of man over nature brought about by science and technology.

The World Game Institute is an organization developed by Medard Gabel with R. Buckminster Fuller to sponsor games and workshops for communities, schools, businesses, governments, and other groups to stimulate learning and discussion on global issues and sustainability. They have conducted an inventory of techniques and technologies for producing food and energy. They conclude that we have more than enough resources to provide ample energy and food for everyone. Their findings support Buckminster Fuller's claim that we can produce enough food and energy (e.g., for production) to raise the standard of living for the entire world's population to that of a billionaire (by 1970s economic standards—the time that Fuller made his assessment).

As a species, we had that know-how in 1970. That is, by 1970, no new technologies needed to be invented to achieve the goal of ending starvation and generally raising the standard of living for all humanity. We needed only to apply what we knew effectively across the planet. Herein lies the rub. We are too busy with our World War Game/Nation State mentalities to do so. We are too busy in competition, trying to master each other. We are still tied to the Framework of Father Culture and the guardian values and the institutions that support it.

This introduces Schweitzer's second aspect of civilization—man's triumph over man, which is the basis of the ethical dilemma we now face. From this point of view, humans are not yet civilized. But civilization is waiting in the wings. We have begun to realize that ethics stands at the root of the solution. So far, we have tried to solve the problem with various ideologies rather than with a real understanding of the underlying values and principles that are needed to succeed. But these values are reasserting themselves. They did not magically disappear, as the various ideologists had hoped.

With the rise of the value of life, we are back to our thymotic starting point, but with added ethical criteria and the values of liberty and equality. We are beginning to value persons, and so tolerance is on the rise. Indeed, these values cannot be displaced (only misplaced). Further, we are beginning to understand the basis for applying these values in a well-reasoned way. Schweitzer was right. Reason is the basis of our successes to date and is the basis of any future successes.

From World War Game to World Game

Fuller observed that the world has shifted from what he called the *World War Game* to the *World Game*. In the World Game, we think in global cooperative terms.

For example, on the political stage, we currently describe the president of the United States, or the president of Russia, or the prime minister of Britain, as world leaders. But the reality is, they are only paid to promote the interests of their own principality. They are guardians, and their function is completely provincial and totally self-serving for their own nation. In global terms, there are no world leaders in the sense of people who are paid to look out for the best interests of the whole planet and all its occupants. United Nations diplomats come close, but they are constrained by national interests and prejudices.

Nationalist ideologies provide further constraints that confuse unity with uniformity. The writings of legal theorist Hans Kelsen offer a good example.[75] Kelsen defines the law as "[t]he forceful subjugation of peoples through a duly constituted order (state)." In Kelsen's view, law is a *force monopoly*. No one in a community can rightfully take away your property (by way of fines and/or taxes) or your liberty (by putting you in jail) except the state. The state is pervasive and all-encompassing. No individuals within its borders are exempt from the law. This view represents the legal constitution of a state.

Kelsen then goes on to describe international relations and world order in purely "nation state" terms. Constituting a world order is like constituting a state—except that the subjects of international law are states themselves rather than individuals. International order must be the result of the constitution of a world state. By the above definition, world order is achieved through the forceful subjugation of states.

Normally, the forceful subjugation of states is not considered to be constituting a world order. Rather, it is called conquering. Further, war is now the worst crime in international law. Consequently, for Kelsen and others, world order can only be achieved by a nation or group of nations breaking the law and conquering all other nations. This is clearly an example of the Framework of Father Culture at work.

Being the kind of thinking that Fuller calls World War Game, this view transposes our current understanding of how communities are structured and imposes a wholly provincial thinking on the world as a whole. This leads to such misunderstandings as the idea that world order must bring about uniformity of culture and language under a State-like umbrella. This is how many people think about world unity.

But unity is complex. It defines many things taken together as one. Further, unity and uniformity are not the same thing. In World Game terms, the world is already united. As a species, we are many diverse communities that together make one world. The problem of world unity is not how to unite the world. The problem is one of *recognition*. How do we raise consciousness about the world unity that already exists to

---

75 Kelsen, H. (2007). *General Theory Of Law And State*. Clark, NJ: The Lawbook Exchange, Ltd.

the level of recognition of what unity means? How do we shift from our current Father Culture, power-centered Framework to a Framework that provides true unity for all humans as a species? What would this Framework look like?

Notice that World Game thinking shifts the perspective to global thinking and rises above the provincial or nation state thinking of such views as Kelsen's. It provides that we must all rise above master–servant guardian values, and their associated institutions, and structures. We must see language, religion, and art in global rather than provincial terms. We must see the whole system beyond our Top, Middle, or Bottom perspectives.

This kind of recognition is the key to resolving our self-consciousness that we are out of control as a species. When we can all recognize that the world is a systemic unity, made up of many diverse parts, we can begin to get a glimmer of what could be a positive improvement in the lot of humanity. Through this recognition, as a way of overcoming our self-consciousness, we will pave the way to a new Framework.

Let's Play World Game

The question is, how do we shift 10,000 years of a cultural Framework that has only recently reached its goal of complete mastery of man over nature? Do we really have to initiate such a shift to survive? Can we not master man over man within this Framework? How could we possibly change the thinking habits of some 7.6 billion people in time to save ourselves from destruction? Can we really disband power structures? What would the new order look like? Wouldn't the new order without guardians be anarchy by definition? How can we just throw away 10,000 years of success and go back to a primitive communal order? Is that where this argument leads?

First of all, there is no going back to primitive times. I do not believe that we are going to throw away thousands of years of learning and science and go back to straw huts in the jungle. Second, I believe that we do have to change to survive. On one hand, if we stay on our current course, there are no indications that we can survive as a species. On the other hand, there are many indications that the current course is non-sustainable, and that our current thinking is unviable. Third, we do not have to change human nature to change our ways. It is a common myth of guardian values that people are self-interested and selfish. Guardian values teach us that we cannot change this, and this is part of how they maintain control. However, this is only true in a power structure that requires self-interest and promotes this kind of thinking as a key to success. It is not true in a community of authentic people who share resources in a systematic and viable way.

Fourth, we *can* change some 7.6 billion people and 10,000 years of thinking. All that is required is a minor shift in the Framework. A small shift that leads to another small shift that leads to an avalanche of small shifts to a new and viable Framework. The new order can be described in political, social, and economic terms. The proposed shift does not lead to anarchy, but it does lead to proper definitions of liberty, equality, and person, and it will change many current models. The model I propose is progressive, but not as Father Culture demands progress. It will also be harsh and difficult to follow at times. However, it does lead to a sustainable model where our systems are viable over the long run, and that is what is needed. Let's play the World Game. I will begin by dissecting Father Culture to determine the starting points for the new model.

The main problem hindering a viable and sustainable future is the Framework called Father Culture. Power structures are not viable. The strategy for Father Culture has been simple in its elements. Design a method for controlling resources, including people, then assert mastery to control those resources by controlling the information, rituals, and skills needed for the production model. Increase dependency on these controlled resources and then make people do the work (servants) and pay them with allocations of credits in relation to their contributions to the controlled system. You can now control the population. Those who dissent are destroyed. After a time, you will run out of dissenters to kill, and you can focus on rival guardians to expand your domain and increase your territory. Let the turf wars begin. History is largely about rival claims for land. Land is the basis of aristocracy, and it is valued most in and of itself as a source of power. Allow commoners to own land, and you risk giving up power and control. In other words, keep control of the land and its resources, and you can keep the masses in a state of perpetual servitude.

In modern times, this process has been abstracted through currency and the increased scope of what counts as production. In the contemporary model, money is the scorecard for success, and the drive for progress in terms of all aspects of production, from food to satellites. But the basic underlying principles are the same.

Part two of the old strategy is to set up rules for how future generations will be able to sustain mastery. These precepts are directed primarily at perpetuating the individual as a divided object in the community. The engineered community ensures that only masters contribute to the Framework, and all others are servants of it. Of course, you must give servants some sense of meaning to avoid constant threats to your mastery, so you display your power ostentatiously, and demonstrate benevolence and largesse on the community of servants (objects). The best control of the herd is to make them think that they are contributing and finding real meaning in their place in the community. After all, you make them work hard for it. You make them so dependent on your mastery that they would voluntarily sacrifice themselves—if not for you, then at least to maintain the order you have created. You inspire them with the fear of anarchy and the loss of their way of life, their language, and their culture. Given the number of enemies who have succumbed to such fates, such fears have a basis in reality.

This Framework is how we are taught to think. It is presented as the objective structure of our public mind. It is the Framework within which we must recognize each other as a community. We are long past the "this is how we do things around here" stage and well into "this is how it is." How many generations of young men have rushed off to war for the glory of their masters? How many societies have reduced women to objects or property as rewards to men for their loyalty and obedience to the existing order (not to mention for the pleasure of the masters)? Masters do not just control resources, they control our concept of self and pit us against each other. Divided and conquered, we have little choice but to play the game of life by the master's rules. The moral precepts of the Guardian and Commercial Frameworks are disconnected from the underlying thymotic values of an ethics. Guardians must ensure that even ethics is defined in terms favorable to their position and security.

The trick to changing the model is to not worry about food or wealth. All models and attempts to change the system have so far been directed at the systems of political interaction or at wealth creation. Change the distribution of wealth to make it equitable, and we change the system. Or so we tend to think. In fact, we only end up shifting the power structures without attacking the real source of power—our disconnected self. This is why communism and socialism fail; they do not attack the heart of the matter—the Framework called Father Culture.

The Father Culture Framework is public and presents itself as objective reality—this is how things are. But we have created this Framework, and so we can create another. Power structures are not real in the sense that they are natural or a product of nature (including human nature). Once we dissociate power structures from objective natural order, we can begin to see alternatives for how we might do things around here.

Hegel teaches us that master–servant relationships are codependent. So they are. Masters are only masters when there are servants. But while servants can recognize this codependency, masters cannot acknowledge it for fear of losing their sense of mastery. When the servants connect in their groupthink and join together to overturn their masters, they cannot become masters themselves because they already know that the relationship is codependent. In this moment of realization, liberty as a thymotic value re-emerges in the community. There are no masters; each person is sovereign over their own mind and body. No one is property.

When we come to understand the difference between power and authority, equality as a thymotic value comes to the fore. With no more masters, the division of labor is seen as Tops and Bottoms, such that Tops are answerable to all non-property, sovereign persons who constitute the community (i.e., Bottoms). Each must be accorded an equal measure of treatment, in principle, to avoid falling back into mastery. In other words, each person must be treated, in principle, such that arbitrary treatment is minimized. The whims of guardians are not to be tolerated by sovereign individuals.

Being the true character of democracy as a political system, the new political values have shifted from guardian to democrat and citizen. In the distribution of power from the elite sovereign to each individual as their own sovereign, power shifts to authority, and the skills of war needed to overthrow tyrannical leaders are replaced by peaceful means. As each sovereign individual values their own life above all else, and as each treats others equally in such matters of principle, the thymotic value of life re-emerges. This "reverence for Life," as Schweitzer called it, is a natural condition out of liberty and equality, it being difficult to imagine a world with no masters where life is not highly valued.

The final step is toward the thymotic value of the person. This idea has several key aspects. First, a person is not an object. As Kant pointed out, we are each an end-in-ourselves and not a means to another's ends. Second, no individual in their life, or liberty, should be objectified. As a matter of principle, this is the essence of equality. However, the key element of personhood is that it is a public idea. A person is a person because each person is recognized as such by the community and with the community. A person is an individuated soul—one at peace with the environment and community, and one who seeks fulfillment in and through that community. Personhood requires authentic community values, not the limited sense of community that we have been taught to accept as real by our historical masters.

In modern terms, I am speaking about building social capital. But I am referring to social capital in a special sense. Here, social capital involves making public and real the communal values of authentic personhood as developed by our ancestors more than 90,000 years before the Agricultural Revolution. This value is proven to be correct, because it is what evolved over time and what lasted longest until the great disruption of agriculture and the instantiation of mastery as a social model. It is naive to think that the social model developed at the time of the Agricultural Revolution 10,000 years ago will still work today. It is more naive to think that we can continue to shift balances of power within that Framework indefinitely and survive knowing how unviable the whole system really is.

Fortunately, the elements of the new Framework are at hand, and we need only to stitch them together into a coherent model.

The Elements of the World Game Cultural Framework

The first elements are the criteria of quality thinking and the thymotic values already exposed. These have each re-emerged from their vicious suppression by guardians. Most have been embraced, at least in principle.

The second element is knowledge of the Framework itself. We must choose how to proceed instead of being led by obsolete thinking. In those areas where change is realized, progress will shift from communal progress to individuated progress.

The third element is the knowledge of how to create capital. Historically, guardians have been very good at creating political and economic capital but have been very poor at developing social capital. Of course, it is against guardian interests to develop social capital. The Framework of Father Culture suggests that politics and/or economics present the only valuable ways of creating any kind of wealth. In current terms, the spectrum between communism and capitalism presents the be all and end all of such means. For example, capitalism is the best way to create economic capital in spite of evidence that it is not very ecological because it largely destroys ecosystems. Indeed, this is one of the main reasons for thinking that the current systems are unviable. The question is, how does real economic, political, and social capital tie into a coherent model? The new Framework presents us with the moral criteria, values, and precepts, but we have not been able to put these together in the right way.

The fourth element involves the unity principle. We can unite the world without making everyone the same. As a species on one planet, we are already united. We are many peoples and cultures that together make up humanity. Again, the goal is not to conquer, but to recognize that we are a single species sharing natural resources that we all need if we are to maintain long-term viability and survival.

The fifth element comes from the fourth. We must think in species, planetary terms. The new Framework is not local to this or that culture, but refers to what is common to all cultures on a global scale. It is based on seeing the system as a whole and on the synergies that are necessary for a viable model. Provincialism, which is a key characteristic of Father Culture, is unviable in a global context.

The sixth element is the view that resources are scarce. All nations must defend local resources against all enemies. They attack us because they are short of some resource. Essential resources are worth fighting for. Resources include natural occurrences such as land, gold, chemicals needed to run the infrastructure (oil is the latest addition), and so on. The more essential the resource, the more likely the guardian will fight for it rather than trade for it. After all, a guardian cannot be held hostage to another guardian for an essential resource. Moreover, guardians have calculated that at the present rate of resource utilization, the world will run out of many essential resources, so the competition is likely to heat up.

The prime source of resource scarcity is missing in the guardian view. This is called *waste*. Waste is defined as "taking a resource someone can use and putting that resource where said person cannot get it."[76] An example would be allowing sulfur to escape an industrial smokestack into the air where the chemical company that mines sulfur cannot get it. As a result, the sulfur mining company must mine the soil for more. While this is more expensive than reusing sulfur, the sulfur mining companies are trapped in a system that places waste as a virtue.

The final element is that power structures are not natural. For one thing, they are monopolistic by definition, and nature abhors a monopoly. The point here is that power structures are our own invention, and as such, we can uninvent them.

Natural Economy

In her book, *Natural Economies*, Jane Jacobs begins with a few rules based on the following premise:

Premise 1: Understand generalized principles to understand   how the world works.

---

76 Technically, Fuller says that pollution is nothing but the resources we are not harvesting. We allow them to be dispersed because we've been ignorant of their value.

From here, she presents three rules to understand how economies work.

Rule 1:   Development is "differentiation emerging
            from generalities."

Rule 2:   "Differentiations become generalities from
which   further differentiations emerge."

Rule 3:   "Development depends on co-developments."

These three together provide an image of economy as a web of code-pendencies that makes up an ecosystem or a social system: "An economy consists of interdependent relationships competing and yet also knitting together co-development."[77]

An economy works like any ecosystem. There are generalized principles from which specific differentiations emerge. For example, from the generalized principle of a seed growing into a plant, a differentiation emerges when we deliberately place the seed in a spot to fix its place of growth. This fixing a spot can now be a generalized principle that applies to any seed. New differentiations emerge from the process of planting and caring for crops.

Another example is the process of trading goods. Jacobs states, "Possibly the very oldest generality is the practice of sharing … calculated intended sharing as an institutionalized social institution."[78] The institution of trading is a differentiator from the generalized principle of sharing. It is a special case of sharing. Trading becomes a generalized principle from which new differentiations emerge, such as a marketplace, or medium of exchange.

From these principles, Jacobs concludes, "Economic development is a matter of using the same universal principles that the rest of nature uses … development is a process that yields things."

Development is the process of emerging differentiations from generalities. Development requires co-development. That is, development takes place in a web of differentiations that promote and provide the basis or place for the new development. For example, economic development is

---

77 Jacobs, J. (2001). *The Nature Of Economies*. Toronto: Vintage Canada. Page 22.
78 Ibid, p. 27 & p. 60.

largely a process of improving a thing or service in the community—taking a work generality and differentiating to a new work or product to fulfill a need. The new product or idea comes from the web of existing products such that a need or niche is identified. New products, in turn, modify the web, and this opens opportunities for more new products.

The first major handicap to development, then, is to prevent the development web from facilitating further differentiations from the status quo. This is accomplished by monopolizing a product or service such that no new development can take place.

In my terms, this is the economic method of power structures and of guardian moral precepts. In reality, guardians cannot permit co-development with subordinates, so they must stifle subordinate creativity and initiative to prevent the emergence of real competitors for top spot in the community. They must assume more responsibilities as Tops to prevent others from assuming it. This is much of the source of Top patterns of behaviors and the economic cost of power structures. Power structures are monopolies. Kelsen defines the state as a "force monopoly" in politics and law. In economics, power structures are monopolies.

By monopolizing various kinds of work, monopolies control generalities of various kinds. This is how power structures maintain their power base. By monopolizing various generalities and preventing differentiation and co-development, they stifle energy flows and direct the energy to their focal point at the top of the hierarchy of the community, which is the definition of a hierarchical structure.

One of the mysteries of economy is the appearance of producing an economic order that is artificial rather than natural. Jacobs describes this in two ways. The first way is most common and is most revealing. In nature, processes are really energy transformations, either as energy or as matter or both. Natural cost accounting follows the energy flow. The real cost of any component in an ecosystem is the total of all the energy inputs and outputs, including waste, cleanup, and so on. When these calculations are done, nature appears to be in nearly perfect balance. All the energy is accounted for. Sunlight enters the system and is transformed by plants, which are eaten by animals, which are then consumed, including the carcass. Each part of the system is in a co-development arrangement wherein the web of interdependencies provides growth and stability for all members. There is no waste in nature. Almost all energy is accounted for.

Of course, there is a certain amount of entropy in the system, which is why the sun is needed to energize the system continually. But once entropy is taken into account, all energy is accounted for. In a way, the only monopoly in nature is the sun.

Our economic order has been perverted by Father Culture to a power structure where the power monopolizes various generalities and directs output toward a single point—guardians—at the expense of the whole system. As a result, the current economic order does not follow the natural energy flow and so does not balance. We must constantly draw more resources than we need or can use, and we must prevent co-development to ensure a stable power structure—not a stable economy. Further, we create waste. We deliberately take resources that could be used by others (as part of a co-development effort) and put those resources where those who could use them cannot get at them. The result is an overuse of the natural systems and a toxic gathering of waste. Spread this kind of systematic thinking across the planet over 10,000 years, and it is not difficult to understand why we are in trouble as a species.

Jacobs points out that *expansion* is not the same as *development*. Expansion is determined by what the system does with the energy it receives before it discharges it. "Expansion depends on capturing and using transient energy. The more different means a system possesses for recapturing, using and passing around energy before its discharge from the system, the larger are the cumulative consequences of the energy it receives."[79]

All economies start with the use of natural resources and transform those resources into some product or service. Economies are based on using the soil to grow food, capture salt from the sea, mine ore from the ground, or many other natural starting points. These resources are usually for local use, and then as more resources are captured, they can be exported, or traded with other communities. In these terms, Marx's labor theory of value is essentially correct. The value of a product is the combination of the raw materials and the skills of the person or persons

---

79 Ibid, p. 47.

who produce the product. The actual value is reflected in these two costs. However, these are only the costs associated with part of the energy flow through the system.[80] Resources present themselves as inputs (taken almost for free from nature). Human capital transforms the energy in the resources to a new form (product) for local use or export. The more that human capital adds to the process, the more the whole system expands.

Development is the emerging of differentiation from generalities and works in a web of co-development. When a key ingredient of the web is human capital (knowledge, skill, labor, information, etc.), the whole web expands to provide surplus products. In agriculture, the surplus is consumed locally to facilitate the division of labor, wherein the skills can become specialized to add value to the system. In the context of Father Culture, the generalities that are most monopolized by power structures are those that reflect human capital—skills, knowledge, and information. To the powers that be, the rest of the population must be excluded from the co-development web and treated as grist for the mill. That is, they are merely servants to do their master's bidding. Further, because knowledge is monopolized by the masters, they can rightly claim that the masses need their direction and leadership—that is, guardianship.

There are two points that emerge from this analysis of economy. The first is that ecologies and economies are basically similar in that they take energy and transform that energy into some part of a larger web of transformed energy structures. As the natural world does, economies start with natural resources and transforms these into products. Unfortunately, that is where economies stop in the energy accounting chain. Products that are no longer used are waste to be discarded. Whereas nature will slowly reclaim the materials, the economy does not. When nature cannot absorb the chemicals used in production, the toxic waste by-products move through the natural energy system and infect life forms in the energy cycle (including humans).

Consequently, I can agree with Jacobs that an authentic economy is a system that mirrors the energy flow of an ecosystem, and which accounts

---

80 This is where Marxism fails. It fails to account for the energy throughout the whole process, from mining raw materials to manufacturing, to distribution and purchasing, to disposal and removal from the system.

for all the energy within the system. This model is correct because it not only explains how economic development takes place, but it also explains how economic expansion takes place. Expansion occurs when the resources or energy are captured and passed through the system, such that they remain trapped in the system. As more natural materials enter the economy, the system will naturally expand with new products.

The second point is that the best way to cause a system to collapse is to monopolize some aspect of the energy flow. As Jacobs points out, nature abhors a monopoly. A monopoly captures energy and prevents other plants or animals from getting it. As the monopoly grows, it actively prevents other plants or animals from gaining access to that energy. However, because expansion is a result of diversification, and diversification is what would be most hampered by a monopoly, the system would fail to expand, and eventually collapse as energy would not be used most efficiently. If a natural system behaved in this way, entropy would prevail.

This description of how a monopoly works is very reminiscent of how Ishmael described the origins of the Agricultural Revolution. A species (humans) dominates a land area for specific planting to the exclusion of all else. The group both defends the land and denies other species access to the area (food). Monopoly is another name for the violation of the law of limited competition as outlined by Ishmael.

Ecologists indicate that the current dominant economic model (capitalism) fails to account for all the energy in the system. Rather, our economic system deliberately fails to account for the by-products and discards of its processes. In short, waste is a deliberate component of capitalism, and it fails to account for total real costs. Instead, the economic powers pass the real costs on to society in the form of garbage management, cleanup programs, health care, and other social forms of expenditure. Then, the same corporations rant about the high tax rates governments impose on corporations for corporate negligence. If this view is accurate, then corporatism can be seen in a new light. By passing authority over to corporations as power, they can protect their monopolies, and continue to waste. In other words, corporatism is a fancy way for corporations to maintain the status quo and not be forced into becoming ecologically responsible. Monopolies hate competition, and as 10,000 years of practice has demonstrated, humans are quite adept at monopolizing.

An authentic economy is a system where all the energy is accounted for in the cost and pricing models. It is a system that wastes nothing. In such a system, we begin by taking materials out of the earth, but then recycle all materials. There will be some loss through entropy, but the goal for sustainability is a system where all materials are effectively present and cycling through the economy, so mining for new resources is minimized. For example, the World Game Laboratories have calculated that the United States is the largest net importer of tin. Most of the tin ends up in garbage dumps. If mining companies would engage in surface mining at dump sites, the United States could be a net exporter of tin. In other words, there is no reason to mine for more tin. There is enough tin already in the system to meet all the world's tin requirements, provided it gets circulated. This would also facilitate economic expansion by making more tin available for new differentiations (products).

The issue has become one of infrastructure services. For example, we can define mining as "pulling resources out of the earth." In the current Framework of Father Culture, at least, that's what mining companies do. In the new Framework, mining is capturing resources, wherever they may be, preferably by recirculation. All companies that have by-products to their manufacturing processes are mining companies. They can both capture resources and sell them to add to their profits, or pay someone else to do the capturing and selling and profit-making. The point is that if the capture and recycling process does not happen, the costs of the dumping and cleanup must be added to the costs of the product to reflect the real costs of production.

In an ecological economy, all resources are cycled, and mining for new resources is to replace the resources lost to entropy. No corporation can be incorporated unless it fits into the cycled energy model. Cost for failure is reflected in the real costs of production, and that would make most products too expensive for anyone to purchase. In this case, Adam Smith's "hidden hand" supports the energy flow, to quickly correct failures.

Such an economy would still favor diversification and differentiation. It would also expand as any ecosystem expands. But it would expand in a different way than the current model. Consider agriculture, as an example. More new people are born every year, so we need to grow more food. We then grow more food and get more people. The cycle is repeated endlessly. Grow more food, get more people. Get more people, grow more food. As Ishmael points out, we have been doing this for 10,000 years, so we know the model works. All you need to do to get more people is to grow more food. We also know from the Parable of the Tribes that power requires constant growth, and this requires more and more resources. People (servants) are a prime resource after land. After all, we need more people to staff our armies, and to grow more food, and build special tools, and provide services. Population growth is a major measure of a growing political and economic structure. The grow-more-food model is a guardian way of thinking. Suppose we were to follow Ishmael's suggestion and stop the cycle. Given current replacement rates, it appears that the world's population will level off at around 10 billion people, so we will only grow enough food for 10 billion people. Setting aside that we do not currently feed the entire world's population, what would happen?

With the population stabilized at 10 billion people, the system would expand to ensure that all people are adequately fed. As the system expands again, all people would be well fed. At that point, the energy through the food system would become balanced and stable, and expansion would happen through the introduction of new foods (differentiation).

In the current model, expansion goes to the haves, not to the system. Further, full energy accounting would require using all available *viable* agricultural methods. Current use of pesticides and fertilizers may have to go. More viable and sustainable methods would prevail. Again, food prices would reflect the true costs of production, and not the artificial cost models in the current system (which do not account for soil loss, toxic waste, health issues, etc.).

Democracy

This brings me back to the problem of power structures. It is clear that if we are to shift to an economically viable system of production, guardian thinking must be overcome. Further, it must be overcome in such a way that economic factors prevail in the sense of a natural economy. The first step has already been taken. We have begun the process of democratizing the world. Again, democracy is the only system we know of where we can overthrow tyrannical or incompetent leaders by peaceful means. The more that democracy is really at work in the world, the more peaceful interactions that can take place.

In general, democracy provides the moral precepts for both democrats and citizens to follow for a working system. Of course, these must work in conjunction with ethical criteria and the underlying thymotic values. Democracy, on its own, could easily descend into a tyranny of the majority where the majority favors a course of action that is morally questionable. If the majority reigns supreme, the system could be capable of much harm and cruelty. However, with proper ethical values underpinning its moral precepts, democracy can work quite well.

The problem arises with views that match democracy with capitalism. Commercial and democratic precepts are not the same. The objectives of each are different, and the rules can conflict with each other. How, then, can we decide on the correct moral, economic stance, and be true to democratic principles?

The key is to distribute power in economics as in politics. In general, there should be a full cost accounting on how materials are manufactured, distributed, and consumed. As democracy accounts for all the votes in relation to individual citizens, so, too, must economics account for all money in terms of individual products or services. Although this does not democratize economics, it does balance the books and provide incentives for change. To understand how this would work, I need to explore two other values—the thymotic value of the person, and the true nature of liberty (freedom). I will tackle liberty first.

Natural Liberty

I have defined liberty in terms of a response to power structures. It is a primary rule that no one should be a master. The whole point of liberty is to limit and reduce the power of others over each of us as individuals. But the premise is that we are each an individual, divided from each other physically, mentally, and spiritually. This is a residue of the divide-and-conquer guardian strategy with respect to individuals. We are all ontologically divided, so a rule is needed that captures the freedom of a divided "self."

Guardians teach that we must give up our "self" to the community because that is where and how we find a sense of place and meaning in the world. This is one of the key methods for "divide and conquer"—make each individual think of themselves as truly separate and dependent on a world engineered by guardians.

This thinking is apparent in modern psychology and science. Mind can be reduced to brain, self to subject (of the experiment), spirit to body, values to precepts. Science has become so adept at reducing subjectivity to something else that it barely needs to be counted at all. We are each a divided subject in a sea of objectivity. It is the objective world that counts; therefore, subjectivity can be dismissed as crude or irrelevant. After all, truth is objective and exists independently of any particular subjective mind. We are born alone and will die alone. The world will go on unchanged by our presence after we die. Subjective intuitions and feelings must be subverted to the greater cause of the objective reality of our time and place. Unless we are guardians, we are each merely part of the unwashed masses, the herd that is fodder for life's mysteries and flows. Objective place and time define who we can be, and we can do nothing to change how the world is.

These are the traps of guardian thinking that linger in our language, myths, and culture. Such assumptions can even be found in science. Science is a reductionist method that isolates variables and observables according to a well-defined methodology. But, science questions how the world is descriptively, but not *why* it is spiritually or subjectively. The whole point of science is to get at objective (i.e., real) truth. The method strongly tunes out subjective considerations.

The studies of reducing mind to brain present a good example. Because we are individuated (divided from nature and ourselves) beings, and mind is a rather fuzzy concept, perhaps scientists can gain an improved understanding of how the mind works by studying the brain. In its strongest form, science would reduce all mental terms to brain terms to eliminate the fuzzy language of mentalism. The problem is that the argument proceeds from analogy. An argument from analogy is a logical fallacy—the two things being compared are not similar in the respect required to support the conclusion—in this case, that science can dispense with mind and treat us each as a brain only. Brains have the additional benefit of being local and physical and suitable for scientific observation techniques. Minds are fuzzy and are difficult to observe in fine detail. Most important in the assumption, though, is that brains are individuated in a way that each has no part of another. Individual brains can be treated as isolated events.

A large portion of the structure of the mind is public. That is, part of the structure of the mind is not isolated or isolatable. The structure is public in that it is shared through the symbolic forms of language, myth/religion, and art. It is shaped by our history and traditions. The whole point of any Framework is that part of the mind's structure is public, and part is private. The virtual public mind determines what is objective, but subjectivity does not magically disappear because we chose to focus on objective events.

In this context, publicity is grounded in inter-subjectivity. This means that "objective mind" is not a reference to an isolated brain at all. Rather, it refers to a communal process that requires the interaction of more than one brain for the process to exist. Language does not happen in my divided-from-otherness brain. Language is a process of many brains interacting as a public mind. The structure of this process has a clear basis in the respective similarities between individual brain processes, but the structured result is greater than a single, divided, and alone brain. The mind is not fuzzy. It is synergetic. The objective mind is a complex public web of language, myth, and art, combined with natural experiences to form a structured Framework.

The objective mind is an integrated whole involving many subjectivities. As R. Buckminster Fuller describes the universe, it is "the sum total of all humanity's consciously and unconsciously and partially overlapping experiences."[81] Fuller calls this "scenario universe." The point is that we are connected to each other through our symbolic forms, and this is the basis for any objective understanding and meaning. The idea that "I" am a divided self might have a private truth. However, "self," understood as a real subjective presence in an objective world, is largely a public, and therefore communal event. I am "me" in the context of the Framework within which I live and think and experience. I am an individuated being in the sense that "I" am a distinction within a larger whole—a communal whole. Self has both public and private aspects, but insofar as "I am," I am part of the universe and cannot be divided from it (except perhaps through death). Mind does not reduce to brain, because the two are not the same.

Natural liberty follows from this recognition and refers to the public self as a distinction within the communal whole and not as a divided self. This alters the sense of freedom that is associated with individual actions.

Liberty, as defined by John Stuart Mill[82] and others, assumed a divided-from-others self. I have described this to be the result of the sense of community that pervades Father Culture. I am, therefore, free in my actions within the limits of the similar freedom of actions of others. For example, I am free to work and own property, but I am not free to use that property to harm others. Harm in this context refers to physical violence, as well as restricting similar freedoms to others. The idea of harm is rather broad and fuzzy in this context.

If I reconsider liberty in a communal context, this fuzziness goes away. Natural liberty occurs in a community where symbolic processes are understood to be the systemic ground for the objective status of freedoms. As in mythical and religious thought, place and moment are not based on the progress of society, but on personal or spiritual growth *through* the community. "I" am a distinction within the community, and so my personal growth and development are tied to the web of codependencies that forms the community. As the community prospers by the combined

---

81 Fuller, *Synergetics*, p. 81.
82 Mill, J. S. (2011). *On Liberty*. Northampton, UK: White Crane Publishing.

efforts of all its members, so, too, can I prosper. Moreover, I can grow and develop and find many potential places and meanings as I travel through the various stages of my life.

Natural liberty is tied to personal growth within the community and the contribution I can make to the whole. This is not the same as communism, which is a distribution-of-wealth model (as per Karl Marx's formula, "from each according to his abilities to each according to his need"). Natural liberty, in this context, is not about a place or moment in the community that defines meaning for my life, but about meaning that can be found in several places and several moments. I am free to contribute to the community and free to grow physically, or spiritually, or otherwise within the community. Liberty does not refer to sovereignty in the sense of property and ownership, but to the person in the sense of a recognized subjectivity in the sense of a moral agent—a person. Moreover, this recognition is from the whole community, and not just a few authoritative members. In its most complete and mature form, natural liberty refers to recognition in principle. "Principle" is used here in both senses of the word. Natural liberty is a principal part of recognizing persons, and that in principle any member of the community will recognize others as persons. Liberty is inclusive.

Guardians cannot recognize all persons, so they reduce persons to objects suitable for various tasks. Natural liberty, on the other hand, is not founded on the negative positing of "freedom from" but is positively grounded in "recognition for." Thus, natural liberty is grounded in the person as recognized by other persons and not in an attempt to re-establish personhood in the face of mastery.

This is not to say that given our history and the expansiveness of Father Culture, we should not have developed a concept of liberty to respond to power structures. Indeed, liberty as defined in 18th- and 19th-century philosophy is crucial to re-establishing the idea of a person. However, to progress to natural liberty, which is closer to the true thymotic value, requires transcending the idea of a person as property to the recognition of the value of a person. A person is simply a recognized fellow subject with the same hopes and desires for a meaningful life and the same desire for self-realization through the community. As I am free within the constraints of my community, and as these constraints are structured into the Framework within which I understand and find meaning and within which I think and feel, I am free by definition. Natural liberty, then, is the freedom to be tempered by and to temper the Framework of thought and experience that partly defines who and what I am. But, as a recognized subject, a person is also objectified and is part of the Framework that defines thought for the whole community. This is the real sense of a codependency web that favors differentiation and growth. In this case, I would refer to personal growth within the community. "I" contribute to and receive from the community in which I live. Natural liberty is defined by both processes. Further, this codependency forms and defines the Framework within which I live. But where liberty in the old sense implies that we each wrest from our guardians the right to contribute to the development of the Framework, natural liberty includes each of us in the co-development web of the Framework by the principle recognition of our existence. Natural liberty is ontological freedom—the freedom to be who and what you really are.

The practical consequences for modern society are profound. In the old school, liberty must fight against mastery. But for natural liberty, we must each recognize all persons if we are to be truly free. We cannot permit ourselves to objectify another. We must not avoid subjective considerations in favor of objective truths, but must embrace subjectivity as an integral part of how we will modify the Framework of Father Culture toward a Framework that can achieve sustainability and survival. The key is to be found in the idea of each person properly recognized in principle as an end-in-themselves. Communities become truly inclusive.

The mechanism to make this happen is expansion. As we each contribute to the codependency web of human recognitions, and as more individuals achieve a proper sense of authentic self, there will be a naturally occurring diversity and differentiation that will expand the Framework. Further differentiation and diversity will encourage further expansion, and so on. Change the underlying values of any system, and you change everything.

Natural Life

Natural liberty is a thymotic value in the sense that it is fundamental, and grounded in the ontological connectedness of being and otherness. I have explored natural liberty, and so can easily demonstrate that the reverence for life, or the view that life has intrinsic value, comes from the same ground. Insofar as I am a distinction within the whole of nature, I am one with reality. My life is naturally part of nature, including the living whole of the natural planet where I live.

Recognition does not stop with the recognition of persons, but extends to all life forms. This is the basis of myth and religion and forms the spiritual core of the connectedness we each have with the world around us. Myth and religion make this spiritual connectedness explicit through recognition with various natural spirits within the context of the sympathy for the whole. By recognizing the simple truth that other creatures have a subjective presence in nature, we not only get closer to nature, but gain understanding and meaning of our place in nature. This is an important part of the new Framework.

In this modern sense of sympathy for the whole, the whole is the living planet. A connectedness and sharing are part of the natural order, and in the complex web of codependencies in an ecosystem, we are all in this world together. While Father Culture is focused on power structure management, nature and the underlying connectedness of all life has not magically disappeared. If we can reconnect with nature, perhaps we can learn or comprehend a proper sense of place and moment in the natural order.

For thousands of years of what is deemed prehistory, our Framework evolved to a deep understanding of the natural order and the deep meaning that comes with such understanding. This structure of our mind has not been wholly eradicated by Father Culture. At the core of our myths and beliefs is the understanding that we are one with nature and should be at peace with it. That these beliefs start with intersubjective recognition with other life forms challenges contemporary scientific understanding. Such beliefs are condescendingly referred to as primitive. However, life understood as a thymotic value is really a reference to the natural value of such recognition processes. I refer to this as *Natural Life*.

Natural Equality

In a complex community, a natural division of labor will emerge as a result of the various talents and abilities of the community members. Some will be great hunters, some will be great cooks, some will be great artists or shamans, some will be computer programmers, and others will be great marketers. Abilities are developed within the codependency web of any natural order. The process of capturing energy and differentiating to expand and grow within a system marks a key process in nature, and this best describes *natural economy*.

In a power structure, the system creates a hierarchy that requires Tops, Middles, and Bottoms. The process of mastery has led Father Culture to dominate and expand across the world. In this context, equality is defined as a thymotic value that accompanies liberty as a way of curtailing abuses of power and mastery. Because, with liberty, no one may be master over another, power and authority can be differentiated. A society that values liberty cannot permit a hierarchy based on any divisions (of labor or otherwise) that might constitute mastery. Consequently, people grant authority to others within the community. Those who are in authority must also recognize equality insofar as they do not discriminate between individuals for arbitrary reasons.

Equality, then, was posited negatively as an ethical restriction on the arbitrariness of those in authority. Equality reminds us of what it is like to be subjected to the whims of guardians and masters and serves to protect us from such situations. I defined equality in terms of the responsibilities that authorities have in how they treat the members of the community. Failure to support and behave equitably constitutes harm or a form of corruption where an authority seeks or behaves as though they have power.

As liberty had been first presented, equality was presented as a protection from abuse of authority. I posited equality as an equality from abuse rather than recognition for the intrinsic person as an individuated member of the community. Although liberty presented how to behave toward each other, equality was presented as the way the community should relate to each of its members.

Natural equality posits the recognition for each member of the community. In the negative positioning of equality, I presented how the community acts toward individuals but said very little about how individuals act toward the whole community. The latter now comes to the fore.

In a natural order where energy is trapped and circulated, leading to differentiation, growth, and development, so, too, does a natural community capture and use its energies to differentiate and grow. In primitive communities, the growth is defined as the development of the individual within the community over the various stages of life. But the differentiation that presents the hierarchy in the community must also be accounted for. The Framework is developed in and through the actual interactions between members of the community and becomes the whole communal Framework that emerges from these interactions. Art is the attempt to make elements of this whole structure explicit, as wholeness truly addresses natural equality. We are not all equal in ability and temperament, but we are all part of the Framework that provides the context for understanding and meaning. We each contribute to that Framework, as well as being shaped by it. Contributing is not a quantitative measure. It is largely qualitative, and that is why an art form is needed to reveal it. The community develops and grows, as do each of its members. Part of the growth is the result of the communal growth. The other part is how each individual develops within the community. Primitive communities value personal growth above communal growth because they have learned over 90,000 years that differentiation is the definition of growth, and this requires that we each develop through our life.

Natural equality is positively posited as this differentiation and growth within the community. In spiritual terms, this is called spiritual growth, but this does not have to be the only description. There can be material, physical, psychological, biological, and philosophic growth, to name but a few. Natural equality is grounded in the recognition of each person in the context of his or her growth and potential. We each affect the whole community and are each affected by the community. Place and moment are personal as well as group-oriented. These affections are equal between the whole and the part. In a real sense, we are each individuated beings within the whole of the community. Natural equality is grounded in the ontological presence of a person in the objective Framework.

Natural equality, then, refers to more than just how our authorities behave toward individuals. It is a positive affirming of each person within the community in the context of their contribution to the structure of the Framework, and the personal development that occurs within that Framework. There is a natural "e-quality" of the effects between individuals and their community. These effects work both ways—from the community to the individual, and from the individual to the community—and are qualitatively equal.

In practice, natural equality is grounded in how we treat each person as a community member. Father Culture subverts individual growth and development to the growth and expansion of the whole. Guardian power structures must constantly expand to maintain their power and perceived viability. All energies are directed toward communal growth, and individuals have a duty to sacrifice their personal growth to the community, even to the point of death. Guardians proclaim the honor of such sacrifices and keep the masses eager to fulfill their "destiny." Usually, this means to die for some cause that the masters have engineered for their own benefit. What we have received for our efforts and sacrifices is the cultural denial of personal growth within a viable and sustainable community. We have been taught that this is normal. Indeed, so it has become. But it is not natural.

Natural equality combined with natural liberty presents the key values to personal growth through differentiation within the community, and you do not have to be a guardian to achieve such growth. Natural equality, like natural liberty, is also about how we treat each other, and how we recognize with each other in finding understanding and meaning. In this desire and quest, we are all equals.

Natural Tolerance (Respect for the Person)

It should be evident to the reader that all natural thymotic values are grounded in recognition of persons.

The interconnectedness that results in virtual public mind, and the structure of our respective Frameworks, is based on the individual person, recognized as such by others. Thymotic values break down when recognition of subjectivity is denied or suppressed, such that others are perceived and understood to be objects, rather than persons. Natural life, natural liberty, and natural equality are all founded on the ontological reality of the person as a subject, and not just as an object. The person stands at the core of thymos, which is the basis of human dignity. For more than 90,000 years, we evolved communities that learned these values more or less well. We know that these work because primitive communities are all basically structured the same way. Each varies in their specific Framework, which accounts for the differences in language, beliefs, and art, and each Framework is structured around the environmental conditions of the tribe. However, in the breaking of natural law, our species lost its natural sense of values and replaced them with guardian precepts and mastery.

The key to breaking mastery, then, stands in the process of recognizing persons. The more we each recognize persons and do not reduce others to objects, the greater the potential for natural thymotic values to emerge.

In contemporary terms, this is what happens when communities are treated as nation states. Other nationalities are viewed as objects in the sense of foreigners or even aliens. Such people are clearly outside of the true (i.e., local) "cultural Framework" that defines the reality and thoughts of the nation. Foreigners are not "one of us." Their languages, beliefs, and customs are "not ours." Even where similarities abound, the differences mark the focus of attention. Such people (if they are granted that status) are not persons, but objects. We can never really be sure that we understand them. To this extent, foreigners are objects, outside of the groupthink that marks our community. We can prejudge their behaviors, actions, and values. Of course, such prejudice is not posited blatantly. They are positioned negatively by affirming the Framework that we share as a nation and as a people. The term for this kind of group think in modern times is *nationalism*.

Nationalism is the modern tribal view that *our* community is where real understanding and meaning are to be found. Others outside of our community are objectified. A small objectification might admit differences, but these might be deemed irrelevant to commercial activities or other interrelations. A large objectification might lead to the others being perceived as potential enemies. They are "Huns" or "Gooks" or some other derogatory designation that marks them as "unavailable for recognition as persons."

The cult of power and its guardian precepts, which seek to protect mastery, is based on the denial of the person outside of the selected group (i.e., outside of "my culture"). As each culture must protect its land and its people from assault from others, there is much value in combining resources to fight as a community. The tighter the community, the better is it able to resist pressures from outside. Masters organize the community around this simple principle. They divide the community into a hierarchy that enables control of the masses. Masters can then feed the masses their views on place and duty, and point out that dissension weakens the community. They must remain loyal and do their duty to the community in the face of the onslaught that will come from those pesky foreigners who seek to secure their own advantage at whatever costs their masters are willing to bear.

Father Culture is a set of interdependencies that require this constant vigil against destruction. The interdependencies are not just within any one community, but include all communities. We are all locked in a perpetual battle for dominance against the objects that populate the other nation states, and against the guardians who disregard life, liberty, and equality in their positions of mastery. It is no wonder that we have a global system that is unsustainable. The entire process is unnatural and wrong-headed.

Even democrats fall prey to the fallacy of this kind of thinking. They believe that distributed power gives them an advantage over tyrants because their people are "free" to choose their fights, and citizen support is truly forthcoming. Tyrants believe that distributing power is a sign of weakness to be exploited. Democracies are weak and easy prey. Of course, both models are locked in the same Framework of Father Culture. Natural values are based on the person-as-recognized by all, not on this or that master's view of what is strong or weak. Democracies that fight for dominance are in the same trap as the dictators. They are no freer than the servants of the tyrant. They must fight to survive, like everyone else. The system deems this to be their reality.

Previously, I posited tolerance negatively as a response to power structures. We need to respect all individuals and not objectify them to be able to overcome differences that lead to hostilities. Tolerance, described as respect for the person, is how we should behave. We should tolerate differences because *we* are different from *them*. If we can recognize others as persons, they can recognize us as persons, and then tolerance becomes a way of building community. But this is a negative view. We still grant our own community's enhanced standing, and others are still different, but we will accept the difference such that we will not judge them prematurely, or objectify them without cause. We will tolerate their presence.

Natural persons are not tolerated. They are recognized completely as persons in their own right. To be sure, their language and customs are different, but that does not make them inherently different. How many times do we see a person in another nation and recognize that they are like us, with similar aspirations for their family, and with similar attachments to their friends? We all want to provide for our family, we all need friends, we all need healthy foods, and we all want the prospects for a long and fulfilled life. We all need a measure of safety and some protection from harm or disease. We all need help in times of injury or illness. When we reach out to others who are not of our clan or tribe, we recognize that they are like us as persons.

This is the key to peace, as objectification is inherently hostile, a refusal to recognize another person. When this is a group refusal, the group adopts a hostile attitude toward others. When this refusal passes from "this is how we do things" to "this is the way it is," the refusal is institutionalized in the cultural Framework and becomes how such people think. Natural tolerance, then, is how we think without our masters. It is easy for servants to see the codependencies that exist between master and servant. However, masters must deny such codependencies, and so overthrowing masters under such terms leads to liberty and equality. Life and tolerance emerge to join with liberty and equality in the moral fight to free ourselves from mastery. Without the presence of masters to engineer our thoughts and to promote and maintain hostile objectifying attitudes, we naturally fall into recognizing persons. Even at the height of hostilities during World War I, officers had to prevent the British and German soldiers from fraternizing and playing soccer between bouts of offensives, particularly around Christmas when both sides would rather have been home with their families. History abounds with tales of hostile peoples fraternizing with each other when their masters were not looking.

This is not to say that we never have disagreements, or that we never quarrel. But such behaviors are not dependent on objectifying the other completely. Jealousy, for example, can lead to hostile behaviors. However, these kinds of disputes between individuals need not be institutionalized as a form of reality. They remain part of the biography of the two or three individuals. When these biographies shift from "this is how we do things" to "this is the way it is," they are called feuds.

Feuds are different from wars because they are specific to groups within a community, or between communities. What guardians do under Father Culture is to engineer the whole community to a stance of feuding with their neighbors to the point of death, conquering, or destruction. Life is reduced to a commodity. Natural liberty and natural equality are suppressed, and natural personification is sacrificed to the community structure as part of the divide-and-conquer strategy of the masters. Violence and hatred are abstracted and removed from concrete experience. As technology continues to depersonalize such tasks, it becomes easier and easier for guardians to recruit willing servants.

Natural tolerance is how we naturally recognize others, regardless of cultural differences. We see a person, not an object. We do not simply tolerate their differences but embrace those differences to further objectify our own beliefs and understandings. Recall that the main process for increasing the objectivity of our beliefs is to include more people in the pool of those with whom we share and exchange symbolic forms. The larger the pool that confirms understanding, the more objectively true our beliefs appear to be. This is how further differentiation naturally expands a Framework.

There is an existential interest in pursuing relations with others. In the absence of contact with others, understanding remains isolated, and our Framework is merely personal. Objective truth and meaning are found in and through sharing our symbolic forms of thought with others. Guardians arrest and pervert this natural process for their own purposes. However, the fundamental need does not magically disappear because we find ourselves in a system that refuses to acknowledge it.

Natural tolerance is a thymotic value in its full and proper sense. We must value others because this is a primary source of objectively improving and expanding the truth of our beliefs, and what we find meaningful. When there are differences in beliefs and customs, we are witness to the natural differentiations found in nature. Combined, these differences lead to new generalities that in turn lead to new differentiations. This process describes the natural order between species, and within species. Natural tolerance is required as, without it, all differences in beliefs would not merge to new generalities, which could lead to new differentiations. Cultural evolution and improved understanding and meaning over time would not be possible.

Why, then, did primitive cultures remain essentially unchanged for thousands of years? Why did culture not really evolve until the Agricultural Revolution? The answer lies in the balance with nature and ourselves that did evolve over time. Societies evolved until we settled into a balanced condition where enough differentiation took place to balance the evolutionary changes in nature. Certain values and principles emerged as generalities that were comprehended as necessary for survival and for life. These principles stated in normative or ethical terms are the thymotic values that I have been exposing. Social evolution was progressing, but at a natural pace and in conjunction with nature. The Agricultural Revolution disrupted that balance and broke all the rules. We have been at war with nature and ourselves ever since. However, as mentioned, thymotic values did not disappear because they were inconvenient for the masters. They have been suppressed and subverted to the interests of Father Culture. These subversions have been so complete that we live in a world of mere and vicious ideologies, all trying to engineer our thinking to perpetuate power structures. Guardians need to be increasingly forward and explicit in how they engineer thinking because technology is pervasive, and Father Culture is now global. Moreover, because liberty, equality, and life are re-emerging as necessary values, there is an increasing need for guardians to clothe themselves in new garb. Using tools of mass education and propaganda, they continue to hold sway over our fundamental thought processes and continue to keep us trapped in a system that spreads violence, hatred, and unsustainable methods. Even as I write, 50% of the world's scientists are engaged in military research paid for with the support of guardian wealth and often with the support of the mere servants of the system.

Natural Ethics

A philosophy is a view that promotes and upholds all the values and principles needed for comprehension and meaning. That is, it is a worldview or *Weltanschauung* that is comprehensive in both senses of depth and breadth of understanding. This view can now be amended slightly. Ethics, as a philosophy, and unlike a mere ideology, does not just promote and uphold all essential thymotic values, but presents these values positively, and not just in response to guardian precepts.

Natural thymotic values are grounded in (1) the criteria of virtues and consequences, and (2) the quality thinking behind the positive values that lead to harmony with nature and ourselves as a species. Natural ethics involves the kind of thinking that stands beyond the mere ideologizing of Father Culture. Where power structures can provide only a sense of community, natural ethics seeks real community in and through how we interact with others and the world around us. It is not just *what* we do that counts; it is *how* we do it. I have been asking whether our current thinking represents the best we can be as a species. I am asking whether objectifying others to support Father Culture is the best we can do in our treatment of those others. In short, what kind of persons are we?

From an analysis of the ecological and sociological impacts of the current system, we are not a very nice species. We are destructive to nature and ourselves, we constantly disregard others in our ambitions to gain an advantage over them, and we are greedy, violent, and deadly. Our only recourse for change appears to be that nature is bigger than us, and if we do not change our ways, nature will solve the problem. Of course, we might be stupid enough to pre-empt nature from rendering humanity extinct.

We think within the context of our Framework. If we do not challenge the Framework, our thought processes can appear quite logical. Consider the Chinese leadership who decided to shoot their own people in Tiananmen Square. Any thinking person who has studied history knows that shooting your own people is a sign of moral corruption. It might present a short-term solution to a temporary problem, but it fails to deal with the root cause of the problem. As more people come to understand how corrupt and empty their masters are, the less respect they have for their guardians. The less respect people have for their masters, the less understanding and meaning people can find in their place, and the more they come to resent their masters. This leads to the groupthink of the Bottoms, who then aspire to the overthrow of their masters. Any rational, educated individual knows this. The actions of the Chinese government, seen in this light, amount to stupidity.

However, it was not a stupid action to the leaders at the time. Their Framework is tied to a history of emperors and a tradition of guardians that requires absolute obedience from their servants. To permit such a show of weakness would violate their self-esteem as guardians. They would lose face. All opposition must be crushed. This thinking leads to spiritual combat, as well. The follow-up actions were to arrest housewives and normal citizens because they wanted to meditate. Heaven forbid that calm, peaceful people should exist in the community. However, to the guardians, Falun Gong or the Chinese spiritual discipline was a real challenge to the existing order, because it promotes respect for the person, and this violates the "divide, conquer, and treat the masses as objects" strategy of the masters. Again, heaven forbid that people should refuse to see others as objects. This is, indeed, a serious threat to the guardian order. Spiritual growth cannot be permitted within or through the community but must be dedicated to the progress of the community. Individual personal growth must be sacrificed for the community's growth.

This display presents the world with Father Culture at its finest. It is a blatant exposure of how guardians think. I know of no other action that exposes Father Culture *so well*. Most people understand the waste and stupidity of such actions but would not understand that they think much the same way. We are all trapped in Father Culture.

Another example is the current debate over genetically produced foods. Farmers have been genetically manipulating foods for generations. But previous manipulations were about developing strains of plants that could produce increased yields in poor soil. Many of the chemical fertilizers and pesticides in use were designed to protect the newly modified plants. Across the planet, our species is now in a degenerative cycle of agriculture. We grow plants that need chemical fertilizers and pesticides to grow. Remove the artificial aids, and most plant strains could not survive. The chemical fertilizers and pesticides cause increasing rates of soil runoff, further depleting the soil. This, in turn, requires heartier plants, more fertilizers, and more pesticides, which produce more soil runoff. These chemicals now pervade our food and water supplies and are ingested by millions of people daily. There is a marked increase in cancer and disease rates, and scientists suspect a correlation. There are increasingly higher costs of food, environmental cleanup, and health care.

Scientists tell us that such a system is unsustainable. In the end, the soil will be depleted so completely that no amount of genetic modifications or chemical supplements will help. The system is inherently unsustainable when compared with other methods of agriculture.

What is the agricultural industry's response to this problem? They advocate more genetic engineering. In particular, they want to add trans-genetic engineering, where animal genes are added to plant genes. Not to produce plants that need fewer artificial chemicals. Not to produce plants that can work in conjunction with soil-development techniques. The aim is to pretend there is no problem and to produce genetically modified plants that can help to cure some of the problems that the chemical fertilizers and pesticides created in the first place. This is what passes for rational thought in the industrialized world.

I might ask, how can these people be so stupid? What kinds of people think like this? Of course, from the point of view of the industrialists, they are behaving quite logically. They must answer to shareholders, and they must pay for the genetic research they have spent so much money on. Typically, industrial leaders are not scientists. They are business people. Their job is to take what commercial advantages they can gain from their research departments and exploit these for profit. This thinking is based on the commercial values of industriousness, and competitiveness outlined above. Their position is logical within the Framework of their current economy and within the moral precepts of the Commercial Framework. These are not vicious, or evil people. They are like the rest of us, doing our jobs.

I can complain, "So was Eichmann!" But that begs the question. The issue involves the Framework that determines thought processes. The Framework is flawed. It is missing the quality criteria that a natural ethics provides. If these people are stupid, they are taught to be stupid, and they are following the beliefs and values of the community that they live in.

Hannah Arendt has studied this issue extensively and determined that the issue is neither malice nor stupidity. She argues that while there are malicious and stupid people, this is not where the majority of evil comes from. She suggests that there is a difference between knowing and thinking. While we can know things more or less in conjunction with other activities, thinking requires that we stop what we are doing and focus on the thought activity itself. People such as Eichmann simply did not stop to think about what they were asked to do. While most Germans grew up with such rules as, "Thou shalt not kill," Hitler replaced this rule with a variation, "Thou shalt not kill unless they are Jews or Slavs, or communists, etc." These new rules were adopted by the average person, without any thought about what they really meant. Meaning comes from thinking, and Eichmann proclaimed that he was just a "cog in a big machine." If he did not do what he did, some other cog would have. It did not actually mean anything. Of course, this presents a total denial of any sense of person or humanity. How do you hold a person responsible for their actions if there is no person? Arendt applauds the legal approach, which deals only with persons, and so ignores the implied missing personhood. Systems are not responsible, people are. Arendt concludes that evil is really banal in the sense that the most horrific evils seem to be the result of not thinking, instead of true malicious intent. It is precisely this kind of not-thinking that ethics is designed to prevent. Eichmann not only missed the ethics of his actions, but he also missed the whole point of ethics as criteria for quality thinking. He failed to stop and think about honesty and fairness, the consequences of actions, and the principles of his behavior.

A shift of Frameworks without quality thinking can lead to unintended and entirely negative consequences. Reconnecting understanding with meaning is so important for the future for this reason. The risk of picking the wrong Framework—one not based on quality thinking and led by a malicious ruler—could lead the whole world into disaster even faster than the current course we are on. Of course, this poor quality, unthinking approach is much hoped for by those who are truly evil. If Arendt is right, quality thinking is our best defense, and our ethics provide the best criteria for what counts as quality thinking.

Beat the System

World Game is an attempt to beat the system called Father Culture. We need to raise consciousness about what we think, and how we think, and how we behave. Buckminster Fuller believed that the way to beat the system was to teach people about what was possible, given the current knowledge. For example, he showed that all people could be living at a billionaire's standard. He showed that starvation and war are obsolete because we do not have to compete for resources. He taught that everyone could understand science, and through science, new methods would liberate all people from the confines of Father Culture (World War Game).

Although these understandings need to be developed, simply knowing what to do does not lead to a solution. We still have to have the will to do it (whatever "it" might be). We are trapped in Father Culture, which requires us to logically defend our own resources and compete for others, regardless of peripheral considerations such as who starves to death today. Each day is consumed with the logic of power structures and maintaining a haves versus have-nots scenario that keeps the guardians in place. Solve the problem of have-nots, and how would the haves be at an advantage? Permit us to see the starving as persons, and we must all be treated as persons. This means that objectifying others (such as the enemy) would become increasingly difficult. Besides, without guardians and power structures, who would lead the masses into the future? To save the starving and poor sounds more like anarchy to most people. Such a course of action would violate the deep logic of Father Culture by shifting priorities and thought processes to natural values rather than to the engineered precepts that guardians need to maintain their status as masters.

The solution, then, must follow in stages. The first step is truly to understand how Frameworks determine thought processes and structure their own logic. Our leaders are not stupid or necessarily belligerent. Rather, they are caught up in a system of thought and emotion that tailors their thinking with 10,000 years of experience. This stuff has always worked. Humans always seem to survive. Science and knowledge and human ingenuity always seem to bail us out of our dilemmas. Of course, we conveniently forget about the failed civilizations and lost tribes. Superior forces defeated them. We are superior, are we not?

Comprehending the Framework challenges this logic. But, moreover, we become self-conscious of how our thoughts are structured by our environment and our community. We actually see the system we have created. As the world grows smaller, we will each experience more and more interaction with other cultures at all levels of our respective societies. Institutions, individuals, organizations, and governments are all becoming more involved with others. To engage with others while comprehending and respecting differences between our respective cultural Frameworks automatically facilitates a move toward world unity. We see the other as a person because we comprehend that they are just as trapped in their culture as we are in ours. By determining common ground through the person, and by avoiding objectification, we each become self-conscious of the process of interaction. Differentiations become generalized, and further differentiations can develop. We see the system and change our behaviors accordingly. The content of the interaction gets objectified, not the person. This is where we must focus. Recognition will happen naturally when we are self-conscious of our interactions in this way.

In this process, our respective Frameworks are challenged and affected by the new objective truth of the other. The processes occur self-consciously, and so we can include specific values in our judgments and behaviors. The first step is natural tolerance—recognizing others as persons. In communal relations, each person is naturally alive, and respect for their life is critical to the recognition process. Deny the person and their life, and you are mastering. Grant the person and their life and remember natural liberty and natural equality in your judgments.

The question is always the same. *What kind of person is this who behaves in such a way?* We must each learn to ask this question of everyone. When the leader of a nation makes a comment on another nation, we must ask,

"What kind of person is this who can think such things about others?" The answer might be positive or negative, but it is through the answer that we judge the person. It is a critique of the quality of their thinking. Are they acting with virtue? Have they considered the consequences of their actions and made decisions that promote overall benefits and minimize harms? Have they identified and are they acting on right principles?

The same applies in any situation. When leaders of the industrial-agricultural community propose genetically engineered products that perpetuate the non-sustainability of the system, we need to ask, "What kind of person or corporation is this who could propose such a thing?" The more we each ask this question, the more self-conscious (in the sense of embarrassed) we become about the Framework we are trapped within. The answers begin to look like this: "They are the kind of person who objectifies others and is content with the false logic of their Framework." If they cannot or will not recognize you as a person, how can you recognize any quality in their thinking? Do you really want to associate with such a creature? Will you support their platform or their products? Will you challenge the quality of their thinking, their Framework?

Fuller's World Game begins here. With knowledge, self-consciously applied to modify an obsolete Framework, we beat the system. Pascal had it wrong that knowledge is power.[83] Knowledge is only power within the Framework of Father Culture. Shift the Framework, and knowledge is what will break power.

The key is to always consider the situation in personal terms, in terms that are based on the criteria of quality thinking. We have all been taught by the logic of Father Culture that we should be objective in our judgments. Objectivity, in this context, means "independent of human subjectivity." But human subjectivity does not magically disappear because a would-be master asks everyone to disregard it. In almost every case involving the unsustainability of our species and our world, the issue is intensely personal. My body will suffer if genetically modified foods cause

---

83 The phrase "knowledge is power" is commonly attributed to *Sir Francis Bacon*, although there is no known occurrence of this precise phrase in Bacon's English or Latin writings. However, the expression *"ipsa scientia potestas est"* ("knowledge itself is power") occurs in Bacon's *Meditationes Sacrae* (1597).

harm. My body suffers when chemical toxins in the environment invade it. My dignity suffers when I am the victim of corruption in business or government. My children will die of plague or nuclear war. My grandchildren might not have enough food to eat if we continue to destroy our environment. I am not an abstract object that can be dismissed.

What is our place? In contemporary terms, it is defined by the rules and available roles in our community. It is shaped by our language, beliefs, and art, which make explicit both the contents of our experiences within the Framework and the Framework itself. Our thought patterns are virtually public and objective. I can no more be a shaman living in contemporary London or New York than I can escape the need to have a source of income in any modern community. We are all trapped in our collective worldviews. The concept of place is decided by the masters who engineer the community. Part of the problem with the modern world is that this process of engineering a community is not a structured, well-thought-out process. Rather, it is haphazard, the result of many masters exercising their power, usually in competition with each other, and as part of their patterned turf wars. Politicians write and pass laws, judges make decisions, business power brokers invest in new technologies, entrepreneurs build companies to exploit a market opportunity, military generals plan campaigns, medical doctors decide who will live and who will die, executives of large corporations decide how they manufacture their products and who will be able to afford them, and so on. No one is in control. There is no plan, no direction, and no thought about where we are going as a species. Humanity is out of control, and the lawlessness of our behavior is now reaching the proportions where extinction of our own species is a real possibility.

And the Band Plays On

The general response to our predicament is to do more of the same, and to work harder at it. After 10,000 years of Father Culture and guardian values, we don't know any other way. To make matters worse, guardians will fight to the death to protect their position—even though that also means all our deaths. We cannot look to them for solutions.

CHAPTER 8
Natural Civilization

Question: What is the difference between a congress of world leaders and a classroom of primary school students?

Answer: The primary school students have adult supervision.

The emerging Framework is currently based on three activities in the world. On the intellectual front, there are science and its sister, technology. On the political and social front, there is the United Nations, and on the normative front, there is the rise of thymotic values and ethics. These apparently disparate activities are linked in the way that Frameworks are modified and formed.

Power structures need to be challenged directly to save our species. We need to divert the trajectory away from annihilation toward a sustainable future. Guardians believe that science and knowledge will save us, but, as indicated, knowledge by itself is not enough. Science must be applied in ways that increase sustainability and reduce the damage of the current unsustainable systems to be valuable. For example, genetic engineering or nuclear energy are not evils in themselves. The danger is in the context within which we apply the knowledge—the Framework within which such thinking takes place. The current Framework has its own logic, which perpetuates the dangers rather than reducing them. Scientists do not engineer plants to rely on better-prepared soils; they continue to engineer plants to fix the medical problems caused by poor soils and chemical pollution in our environment. Business and governments avoid deploying alternative energy sources because the cartels that run the nuclear power industries are tied to a thinking process that defends their technology even in the face of pollution and waste management issues. Buckminster Fuller noticed that electrical energy could be transmitted across a distance. If several water-based hydroelectric plants around the world could be tied together to form an energy grid, we could transmit electricity to where it is needed. Needs are based on times of the day. Peak hours occur at morning and evening. A global energy grid could provide needed supplementary electricity at peak times per geography. In effect, energy would flow around the world as the earth turns with respect to the sun. Fuller points out that some electrical power sources in Asia would need to be added to complete the grid, but that with these additions, nuclear reactors could be eliminated. The generation of tons of toxic waste could be stopped.

Guardians would not permit such a grid as it would place national interests at a disadvantage. What if a group of nations restricted the energy flow to their neighbor? The neighbor would be at a disadvantage. It would be the job of the guardian of the neighbor to protect his or her nation from such disparities. Provincial thinking prevents the energy grid from being built.

Scientific knowledge is hostage to Father Culture. Over half of contemporary scientific research is conducted for military purposes to serve guardians.

One of my challenges has been to prove that scientific methods are not as objective as scientists think they are. Moreover, I find that scientists themselves are part of Father Culture, and their choice of project is largely determined by the Framework within which science takes place.

So, the challenge is to take on the provincial thinking inherent in Father Culture. To do this, I need to examine global forces, such as the United Nations, and the contributions such activities bring to our species. When combined with natural thymotic approaches to values, and a properly understood scientific program, I will be describing a new Framework that is emerging almost in spite of the efforts to contain it.

Father Culture Politics

We live in a world of great potential for global destruction. Nuclear devastation, biological and chemical weaponry of mass destruction, the breakdown of the world's ecosystems, mass starvation, depletion of the soil and other natural resources, and many other issues confront our species on a day-to-day basis. We have suffered through two world wars that left millions dead, and we are now confronted with terrorism on a global scale. Yet, in spite of all this, there has never been a congress of all the world leaders. In the history of our species, our leaders have never met as a group to attempt to solve world problems, or plan for solutions, or a common future.

This is the failure of Father Culture, which promotes a guardian divide-and-conquer competitive strategy that steeps leaders in a Framework that is purely and solely provincial. It is beyond the mental thought processes of our current provincial leaders to promote a genuine world congress. In short, our species does not have any world leaders.

Our provincial leaders are paid to look out for the interests of their particular province, even at the expense of others. This is World War Game at its finest. The closest to "world" leaders we have are the executives of the United Nations. The United Nations representatives are not the decision-makers of their respective provinces, but represent those decision-makers in their respective provincial agendas. In short, the United Nations is largely a forum for the assembly of provincial thinking to approach global issues. The secretary-general is one of the only people in the world who is paid to be concerned with global well-being. The provincial leaders have made this small concession to global politics. They permit (when they actually condescend to pay their promised bills to support the United Nations) a group of diplomats to pretend that they are moving the world toward a peaceful and sustainable future, while constraining their activities to perform real and meaningful action. The Security Council is constrained by a veto that permits token assent to global solutions while providing a convenient out should the proposed solution be inconvenient or contrary to a provincial agenda.

Provincial leaders cannot meet to deal with world issues as they are not interested in solving the problems they themselves are creating. That would amount to accountability and a genuine desire to be responsible in their policies and actions. There are no guardian precepts that include responsibility other than to the guardian class and their province.

This is not really surprising. Until the 20th century, the average life expectancy of any individual was between 30 and 40 years. For most of our history as a species, middle age, therefore, was about 20 years old. Think of the current generation of 18–25-year-olds and ask yourself if you think they have the wisdom or the skills to run a planet. The world was less complex for most of history, but this does not change the adolescent nature of our behaviors. Think of the wars caused by spurned love, or the politics of mating appropriately, or the inherent greed to own what others have because you are not smart enough to create it for yourself. Guardian precepts are the morality you get when you let adolescents set the rules.

Our current outdated, needing-to-be-reformed Framework contains the vestiges of adolescent guardian thinking that is the basis of Father Culture. No wonder our leaders cannot get together. They are too caught up in their adolescent emotions. Arabs cannot sit with Jews; Muslims cannot sit with Christians. The British hate the French; Iranians hate Americans. All feelings are reciprocal and reciprocated through policies and actions that serve self-interests at the expense of the group. As a species, we are and always have been out of control. I suggest that what is needed is adult supervision.

Natural Civilization

In general, ethics is largely the struggle to contain and hopefully overthrow power structures. In my model, it is the attempt to tame and rid ourselves of the destructive power structure called Father Culture. Ethics provides the criteria for the kind of quality thinking we need if we are to get out of the mess we have created for ourselves. That the Agricultural Revolution coincided with a power structure appears to be a quirk of human history. On the face of it, there was no inherent reason to develop a power-structured community to take advantage of the benefits of agriculture. There does not appear to a logically necessary connection between cultivation and having a select few hoarding resources at the expense of others. In fact, without power structures, there would have been more to go around, and less need for competition for food resources. Why then did we develop a power structure to support cultivation?

The simple answer is that we needed to protect our crops from natural enemies. But determining who these enemies might be was not readily apparent in the context of a tribal people who commune with natural spirits, and who sympathize with the whole of nature. That is, to proclaim another as an enemy, that other must first have been objectified in the sense that we chose *not* to see them as persons. But we must also have failed to see the whole as a system in spite of our sympathy for it.

Of course, there is also the relentless need to expand to produce more food to support an increasing population. In the absence of a clear idea of how expansion works in the natural world (natural energy accounting), defending crops took on a simplistic form. The whole basis of power structures, to divide and conquer, provided the conceptual leap that was made to defend crops. This metaphysical principle led to the violation of the first law of nature. Once objectification was accepted, fellow humans and natural resources all became grist for the power-hungry mill.

Ethics seeks to make its stand against this division. Many modern thinkers cast a fond eye back to primitive communities, where individuated spiritual growth and respect for others and the planet were natural. They suggest that we throw away our complex society and go back to a simple hunter-gatherer lifestyle. In short, they advocate going back to the Stone Age.

If my assessment is correct, they may get their wish. It will not be through choice, but via the collapse of the global ecosystems, or via a biological, or nuclear catastrophe. The Stone Age is a real possible outcome of the current thinking and methods under Father Culture.

We cannot go back (except through continued stupidity), but we can go forward. To do this requires applying what we know as a species and directing our actions in a concerted and qualitatively responsible way. It has been said that we need to learn from history, so as not to be condemned to repeat it.[84]

The Aboriginal values that seem to hold such appeal for some modern thinkers would have evolved over centuries among tribe members, neighboring tribes, and the natural world around them. As objective understanding of the natural order began to emerge in a common sense of natural spirits and fellowship, rules for recognizing persons would have emerged. These metaphysical rules would have been:

1. *Always see the other as a person in the world.* This is the categorical imperative. Treat others as ends-in-themselves rather than as means, which is the basis of human dignity.

Recognition comes through mutual interaction among persons via the symbolic forms of thought, as shared between those who are recognized.

2. As we are each part of the natural order and whole, *we are each a distinction of our community in our life.* Therefore, life itself is of intrinsic value, because without life, there would be no understanding or meaning.

The uniqueness of each person makes understanding and community possible. There is intrinsic value to individuality as a natural distinction within the whole.

The entire tribe shapes and provides the collective mechanisms for forms of thought via language, myth/religion, and art. In this whole, each individual relates and contributes to the recognition process from a unique point of view. Although skills might differentiate between individual functions (shaman, hunter, gatherer, artist, etc.), all members have their role and find meaning in the context of the whole.

3. *Recognition of persons increases diversity,* which results in the natural expansion of the social system.

There are no objects in a community. All members are persons.

---

84 "Those who do not learn history are doomed to repeat it." The quote is most likely from George Santayana, and in its original form it read, "Those who cannot remember the past are condemned to repeat it."

If these basic rules emerged out of survival as values that people understood and reflected on in the sense of seeking meaning within the tribe or within nature, then the origin of thymotic values is found in this social and cultural evolution. Quality thinking evolved out of 90,000 years of cultural evolution and experience.

The Agricultural Revolution and its twisted power structure, which introduced divisions between people, interrupted this evolution. Master–servant relations were born. In these moments, primeval values were lost. Our species has spent thousands of years reclaiming them.

Our species has now reached a point in history where we can begin to reintegrate true values into our community structures. The evolving Framework pulls together various principles and values and creates its own precepts. I call this the Ethical Framework.

The Ethical Framework

Natural economies expand and develop. Expansion is the result of using and passing around energy to produce cumulative consequences, while development is based on the emerging differentiation from generalities within a web of co-development. Moreover, differentiation develops niche opportunities that enrich the web causing further expansion and more opportunities for differentiation and further development.

While Father Culture expands by adding people and resources to the mix, and by developing these expanded resources as though it was an open system, natural economy expands and develops within the confines of a closed system. Nature is a closed system, and this is why Father Culture is failing.

The key to an Ethical Framework is the web of co-development within which development takes place and which drives expansion within a closed system. Wealth can be expanded, and new products and services can be developed without adding people or resources. This requires an adherence to an ethics that is fundamental and direct. The Ethical Framework has fifteen precepts.

1. **Promote peace and harmony.** This is more than just a rejection of the use of force, but is the opposite of resorting to violence to achieve our goals. It is the foundation for moving beyond Father Culture and its guardian precepts. It is the promotion of a way of thinking that is not antagonistic, aggressive or violent. It is a kind of thinking that seeks integration and harmony in the face of diversity and individual interests. We attend not just to **what** we do, but **how** we do it.

2. **Come to voluntary agreements.** Because we are promoting peace and order, we need to use peaceful means to act in concert as a community. This precept applies to economic, social, and political policies, as well as to individual interactions.

3. **Be honest.** Honesty as the best policy is a requirement for voluntary agreements and promoting peace and harmony as a means to our ends. As the basis for fighting corruption in politics or commerce, honesty protects us from the psychological trappings of guardian manipulations.

4. **Promote community.** Frameworks are public and communal. All objective understanding and meaning come from communal interactions. Because each individual is a distinction within the communal whole, it is in our best interest to promote and care for that whole. This requires harmony and inclusion for all members. We care for more than just individual members of a community, we care for the collective whole community as well. We promote community interests to build a Framework that is harmonious and inclusive.

5. **Respect persons.** As the direct link to all ethical criteria and thymotic values, respect for persons means we never treat others as objects or objectify others as a means to an end. From here, the values of natural liberty, natural equality, and natural life are promoted and protected within the community.

6. **Promote personification.** It is not enough that we simply respect others as persons. To move to natural ethics, we must actively

promote differentiations within the community. This, in turn, provides additional sources of understanding and meaning, whether in science, art, or religion. This moral precept appeals most directly to the ontological basis of ethics.

7. **Seek natural justice.** Justice is a kind of long-term moral appropriateness. A just society is one that is viable and sustainable over the long term. Policies and actions that prevent or hinder long-term benefits are unjust by definition, and thus are to be challenged by all members of the community. Further, justice is not just a negative concept to correct injustice. Natural justice achieves long-term appropriateness by promoting persons and real recognition.

8. **Dissent for the sake of the public good.** A public good is defined as that which promotes justice in the community. Whether we fight corruption, abuse, or harms done to individuals, we are each tasked with questioning those in authority, and challenging the quality of the thinking behind policies or actions where an individual or the whole community takes unfair advantage over individuals.

9. **Promote integrity.** Justice is only one aspect of community well-being. The development and expansion of economic and social capital are part of the responsibility of each citizen of earth. Social integration – making a whole community, is based on adherence to the ethical values that promote the kind of community we want to have. None of us as individuals can reach full spiritual growth or personal potential in a community that does not attend to this. This means that we are each responsible for adhering to the values that would nourish and preserve a peaceful and sustainable world.

10. **Promote unity.** Unity means "many things taken together as one."[85] We are a united planet with diverse life forms, cultures, and ecologies. The more diverse are the parts of the co-development web, the greater is the expansion potential of the whole system.

85 Fuller, *Synergetics*, p. 81.

While supporting development, we can develop new meanings and understandings, but only within the integrated whole of a united community. Promoting unity is part of how we increase harmony.

11. **Promote harmony and inclusiveness.** It makes no sense to promote diversity if we are not balancing this with harmony and inclusion. This balance is how we build and sustain robust communities. If we are going to encourage diversity to help people to find new kinds of meaning we must also include them in harmonious ways to play an active part in the community.

12. **Invest in the global community.** If all people are to have enough food and energy and comforts to have the time for spiritual growth and development, the economic and social capital of the community needs to expand and develop. We must each invest in this process.

13. **Demonstrate moral courage.** Promote and uphold all the criteria for quality thinking, including the thymotic values, and do not suppress those that are inconvenient to a goal or agenda. This pertains to the virtues of accountability and responsibility.

14. **Seek meaning and understanding.** This precept embodies the Ethical version of being competent and informed. Science and art are constantly improving the knowledge and understanding of our world and ourselves, and we are all obligated to participate in and keep up with current understandings. This is how to shape responsible knowledge generation and contain irresponsible applications of knowledge.

15. **Seek personal spiritual growth and fulfillment.** Personal growth is individual and achieved through the community rather than by the community (as with Father Culture). We are each responsible for finding our own sense of place, moment, and meaning. The other precepts set the conditions where personal spiritual growth is possible. This precept encourages the idea that we each take advantage of the opportunity.

The Ethical Framework is the only moral Framework that is fully grounded in quality thinking. More than this, it is grounded in the positive positing of thymotic values. Ethical thinking is not just a reaction to Father Culture. It involves the active promotion and encouragement of a new Framework for thinking. In a real sense, the Ethical Framework provides moral rules to organize and consolidate the three kinds of ethics. It characterizes the virtues (veracity, accountability, respect, justice and social responsibility), but in line with attention to consequences and the four thymotic values (Natural Life, Person, Liberty and Equality).

From this basis in quality thinking we can evaluate our leaders, and decide how to proceed towards our sustainability and viability objectives. By putting ethics on the from burner, and by promoting genuine moral precepts based on the three ethical systems and principles, we have clear and measurable criteria to evaluate the quality of our thinking and actions. This in turn, provides a basis for an appropriate response to compliance failures.

Table 8.1: Ethical Framework

ETHICAL FRAMEWORK
Promote peace and harmony
Come to voluntary agreements
Be honest
Promote community
Respect persons
Promote personification
Seek natural justice
Dissent for the sake of the public good
Promote integrity
Promote unity
Promote harmony and inclusiveness
Invest in the global community
Demonstrate moral courage
Seek meaning and understanding
Seek personal spiritual growth and fulfillment

How can we promote an Ethical Framework in our current Father Culture World War Game-approach to solving the world's problems?

The only political system we know of that permits the peaceful overthrow of incompetent or corrupt leaders is democracy. To progress to an Ethical Framework requires an understanding of how this would work in a democracy. Democracy was envisioned largely as a response to the guardian precepts of Father Culture. This negative positing of a distributed power structure needs to be modified to a positive positing in the light of an Ethical viewpoint. When these are viewed side by side, there is obviously a readier fit between democracy and an Ethical Framework than there is between democracy and commercialism, both from the perspective of democratic leaders and citizens. Let's directly compare the current models to see where this might lead:

Table 8.2: Ethical Framework – Comparison of Current Models

DEMOCRAT RULER FRAMEWORK	DEMOCRAT CITIZEN FRAMEWORK	ETHICAL FRAMEWORK
Minimize the use the force	Oppose the arbitrary use of force	Promote peace and harmony
Obey the law	Promote those who best represent your interests	Come to voluntary agreements
Promote the rule of law	Fight corruption	Be honest
Collaborate with the community	Collaborate with your peers	Promote community
Respect persons	Respect the rights of others	Respect persons
Cooperate with each other	Assemble peacefully	Promote personification
Demonstrate authority	Seek justice	Seek natural justice
Trust in the system	Dissent when you disagree	Dissent for the sake of the public good
Promote community well-being	Participate in the system	Promote integrity
Be tolerant	Personify	Promote unity
Promote the community's interests	Invest in democratic processes	Promote harmony and inclusiveness

DEMOCRAT RULER FRAMEWORK	DEMOCRAT CITIZEN FRAMEWORK	ETHICAL FRAMEWORK
Be fair and impartial	Shun exclusivity	Invest in the global community
Demonstrate moral courage	Promote the community's values	Demonstrate moral courage
Be competent	Be informed	Seek meaning and understanding
Be moral	Honor integrity	Seek personal spiritual growth and fulfillment

Each precept is the active positing of an activity of being a good citizen or a positive ruler. The Citizen Framework was introduced as a negative positing of values to contain democratic rulers and keep them from turning authority into power. An Ethical society does the opposite, which is to positively posit citizen values not against power, but for community well-being.

For example, minimizing force and resorting to voluntary agreements helps to sidetrack issues away from confrontation. Promoting community is the combination of ruler and citizen collaboration. Promoting community is more than just collaboration; it is an active development of community through the development of increasingly diverse co-development webs. Respect and recognition are active versions of cooperation and assembly. Dissenting for the sake of the public good is a positive value and not simply a containment of abuse or a checkpoint against a tyranny of the majority. Rather, dissent is a natural outcome of increasingly diverse points of view that must be acknowledged and recognized by the community at large. Dissenting for the public good involves the active encouragement of increasing diversity within the community. Dissent, in this context, pertains to an attitude of disinterest that promotes altruism.

Investment in the community pertains to all forms of capital, not just political capital. Democratic rulers are fair and impartial because their role is to facilitate the conditions for individual spiritual growth and fulfillment. Facilitating meaning and understanding and honoring diversity is how democratic rulers demonstrate competence and moral courage. This means that it is the job of a democrat to encourage and promote the conditions for increasing diversity and to increase diverse co-development webs. We remove rulers who fail in this activity as incompetent or corrupt.

Overall, these moral precepts align fairly well. There is still some need to guard against abuse and corruption, but notice that corruption is now defined more explicitly in terms of failure to promote community well-being, justice, diversity or inclusion. In this sense, democrat and citizen precepts are still needed, but both are ethical in attitude, understanding, and action, rather than guardian or commercial.

In the Ethical Framework, politicians do not seek power because to do so would curtail the development and expansion of political, economic, and social capital. The co-development web defines community and individual relations such that the democratic rulers are codependent on citizen support groups. The view of the whole system is ever-present in their thinking (there is no system blindness). With a well-informed citizen group and leaders who honestly seek advantage by improving the community overall, there is less negating of guardian values and a more positive approach to global and natural concerns. Leaders are paid to represent all people first, and their local communities second. While this ideal is not a precept in the Democratic Framework, political capital is expanded by developing increasingly diverse co-development relations with other political and social groups. This is how a democrat best represents constituents and expands authority.

Rulers are responsible for the regulation of economic capital and to enforce co-development where force might be required. Because natural liberty is a positive act of recognition, politicians have the job of creating and maintaining the infrastructure that promotes and safeguards natural liberty. Of course, with due respect for persons, politicians do not objectify others, and so also promote and protect natural equality. Natural equality is politically defined as all persons having a relatively equal opportunity for spiritual and personal growth and fulfillment through the community. The political system is designed to protect and promote all such opportunities.

While this model sounds idealized, it should be remembered that I am now thinking within an Ethical Framework and have finally cast off the shackles of guardian values and thought patterns. Of course, politicians will be corrupted, but corruption itself takes on a new meaning. Not just when someone tries to turn authority into power, but corruption occurs when a ruler fails to recognize community members and so fails to promote and protect community interests. In particular, corruption interferes with co-development relations, and so curbs expansion. Social and political capital are measured in these terms, so corruption is defined in terms of the competence and fairness and collaboration that the politician has with the community.

Let's see how the Ethical Framework compares with the Commercial Framework, in Table 8.3, below.

Table 8.3: Comparison of Commercial and Ethical Frameworks

COMMERCIAL FRAMEWORK	ETHICAL FRAMEWORK
Shun force	Promote peace and harmony
Come to voluntary agreements	Come to voluntary agreements
Be honest	Be honest
Collaborate easily with strangers and aliens	Promote community
Respect contracts	Respect persons
Compete	Promote personification
Use initiative and enterprise	Seek natural justice
Dissent for the sake of the task	Dissent for the sake of the public good
Promote comfort and convenience	Promote integrity
Be efficient	Promote unity
Be open to inventiveness and novelty	Promote harmony and inclusiveness
Invest for productive purposes	Invest in the global community
Be industrious	Demonstrate moral courage
Be optimistic	Seek meaning and understanding
Be thrifty	Seek personal spiritual growth and fulfillment

By and large, the Ethical Framework specifies how the commercial precepts work in a positive environment (rather than as a reaction to the Guardian Framework). The first three precepts agree fairly closely, but the Ethical version is designed to promote co-development webs and expansion in the natural sense. Collaboration is the economic version of promoting community. By shifting commercial values to community interests rather than collaboration in the face of guardian divide-and-control mechanisms, economic capital is measured in terms of community well-being and expansion and not simply in terms of profits.

Respecting contracts is the formal, commercial version of respecting persons. Competition is limited to direct corporate competitors with similar products and services. Corporations are not competing against nature or against the community as a whole. The whole planet is commercially integrated, and all energy accountings are made and included in all pricing schemes.

The by-products of any commercial processes are the raw materials for other's processes. Ensuring that these materials are available to those who need them is the commercial version of promoting personification. Initiative and enterprise are constrained by the overall long-term benefits this would yield. Injustice in commerce occurs when a company knowingly produces a product that would cause long-term harm to individuals or the community. However, it also occurs when a corporation creates waste. This dumping of resources that others could use fails to account for all energy transactions and fails to compete with others in honest terms. A failure in virtue and consequences, it is also a failure of principles. Poor accounting practices have always been a measure of corporate incompetence or malfeasance.

Dissent for the sake of the task means that if the task is defined as a potential harm to the public good, corporate leaders refrain from engaging in the activity. This is despite potential profit. Industry leaders are seen as community leaders, and so are responsible for community well-being. Because ethics is intensely personal, asking what kind of person so-and-so is, corporate leaders who fail in this responsibility are personally accountable.

Comfort and convenience are the commercial contributions to community well-being. As the community expands through increasingly diverse co-development webs, commercial opportunities will arise in the emerging niches that develop in the marketplace. Economic capital is increased when all members of the community gain the opportunity for personal growth. In economic terms, this is achieved through increased comforts, leisure, and personal opportunities.

Efficiency is the commercial version of personification, or how a business person presents themselves in community actions and relations. Investment in productive purposes is understood as investing in the community. Spiritual growth and individual meaning will find an outlet in new forms of commercial activity. Natural economic development and expansion must be open to novel ideas for services and products. This also applies to those who participate in commercial ventures. In a natural economy, a possible source of personal meaning and accomplishment is in community development through economic activities.

The work ethic that defines industriousness was initially posited as valuable as a response to the guardian precept of making rich use of leisure. In the Ethical Framework, this takes on a new meaning of having the moral courage to support the community even at a cost of reduced profits. It is the precept against greed.

Optimism comes from improved understanding and meaning. Again, as opportunities for personal growth and meaning emerge within a community that is expanding naturally, many people will be optimistic that positive meaning can be encouraged and achieved at least in part through the economic well-being of the community. Corporate leaders and entrepreneurs would not engage in business if they were not optimistic that they, too, could find meaning and growth in their contribution to the community.

Thriftiness is how commerce honors diversity. It does not engage in waste or ostentation for profit's sake.

Nature is a closed system. In an ethical society, there are few mining companies. All resources are distributed through the co-development web of an expanding economy. Pricing is based on all energy transfers, so the way to keep costs down is to recover material costs (previously called waste) through the greatest diversity of co-development relations that a company can develop and support. Competitors can also be customers. Product development maximizes the knowledge from science to produce products or services that promote diversification and community well-being. No product is produced for profit alone. The spiritual growth of commerce takes the form of a clear understanding of the contribution that the product or service makes to the comfort and well-being of the community. Long-term costs to the community are minimized.

Corporate structure and products support natural diversity and development and blend in with nature as much as possible. Naturalism and the contribution to community well-being are the key marketing appeals on a product-by-product basis. Companies compete in resource efficiencies to control costs as much as they can. Successful companies develop the co-development web and directly contribute to diversity in nature and the community and so to economic expansion. Corporate liability has narrow limits. Persons run companies, and if they make decisions that harm people or the environment, the corporation is as liable as the board members and executives who direct the policies and run the company. Penalties include stock devaluation, outright removal of shares from trading, or loss of ownership. Finance is not based on artificial compounding of interest for capital's sake, but is based on diversification and the direct contribution to economic expansion. It is based on the strength of a firm's position in the co-development web. The greater the web of codependencies, the greater the value of the company to the community. In an Ethical society, this is understood because the population is stable, so new customers come from the existing pool through economic diversification.

Commercial leaders understand that the relationship between a company and its customers is one of codependency within the co-development web. A stable economy comes from maximizing the number of people who earn wealth to provide the largest possible customer base. The idea that wealth should flow exclusively to a select few at the expense of a large consumer base undermines co-development and economic expansion. If economic expansion stops, development opportunities occur less often, and valuation and profits decrease. When each company is tied to a co-development web, then devaluation of the economy overall translates quickly and directly to a devaluation in company profits and market opportunities.

To make this work requires knowledge, not just for knowledge's sake, but for humanity's sake. It requires an ongoing ability to see the system as a whole and to sympathize with it in practice. Science must work for our species and not just for an elite group of guardians. Let's explore science in this context and see if it can be humanized.

Science in an Ethical Framework

Objectivity is determined through virtual public Frameworks. There are two key ways that objectivity can be enhanced. More people can be included in the Framework, or clearer or more exact concepts can proliferate across a wide population base. Under normal circumstances, understandings and beliefs are challenged by interactions with other tribes, such that new concepts and understandings emerge, or existing beliefs are strengthened or improved. In religion, for example, if my tribe believes in the power of the bear spirit and we encounter a neighbor who has noticed such power and also believes in it, our belief will be understood to be more objectively real or true. Another tribe may not worship bear spirits, but may also worship different animals. In a general sense, the logic of our two Frameworks is similar. We might add their spirits to our belief set, as they add our spirit set to their beliefs. Further, we might generalize to animal spirits or totems to include all animal spirits in principle and from there, further differentiate into kinds of totems. In this scenario, totems would be a general concept that could be, in principle, shared across a wider population base. Understanding and meaning would lead to more generalizations and further differentiations, as each tribe seeks to further its understanding of the animal spirit world. We would be closer to our understanding of why the world works as it does, which would be much more comprehensive, and, hence, objectively true. This is how knowledge expands.

Science introduces a new concept to traditional symbolic forms. It establishes precise definitions for each symbol, combined with very precise rules for how these symbols interact. When combined with a structured and well-defined process for observing the world, science makes a large leap to enhanced objective truths. In science, all symbols are well understood, in principle, by all scientists. Empirical observations are made such that anyone who follows the prescribed methods will make similar observations (within an acceptable margin of error). Consequently, scientific truth is most objective because it, in principle, includes anyone who understands the symbols and follows the prescribed methods. In principle, it includes all people, wherever they are. Scientific truths are universal in a way that linguistic and mythical beliefs are not (or, at least, so our scientists think).

Religious beliefs are also universal but are universal in a different way. Religious beliefs place a universal spirit at the core of the belief system. All who meditate and pray, following the prescribed rituals, will experience the revelation regarding this universal spirit. In principle, this should be true for any human. However, given the variety of religious beliefs, it is not clear that such faith or revelation or enlightenment can occur outside of the cultural Framework that such beliefs require. There is ample evidence of missionary conversion to another faith that requires more than just following prescribed rituals. In general, a convert must embrace the cultural norms of the religion to be truly included in the revelation. Hence, while there is clearly some objective truth to these enlightenments, it is not clear that each experience is the same for each individual. This fuzziness about what the experience is and what it means is what science seeks to avoid. Rather than being fuzzy about a universal experience, science seeks precisely defined and understood universals. For science, the process is universal, and not necessarily the content of the experience. With clear and distinct methods and meanings, science attempts to remove fuzziness from its processes.

One kind of fuzzy experience that science attempts to dispense with is subjective experience. Subjectivity is considered fuzzy because it is so individual and dependent on the unique context of individual experience. Each of us experiences the world from a unique viewpoint. Science seeks to remove individual viewpoints from the equation (literally). It does not matter what my perspective is, per se. If I follow procedures, and understand the symbols correctly, I will come to similar results as others did. Perspective or points of view are irrelevant to the process. Scientists believe that this is key to enhancing the objective validity of their claims.

Recall that scientific theories become accepted into the body of scientific knowledge based on their explanatory power—when they can successfully predict novelty, explain how observational techniques work, and meet all scientific conditions.

This consideration fits well with my version of scientific truth claims. Scientists make claims using methods that enhance the objectivity of their processes when compared with other symbolic forms, such as religion and language. Science is precise and structured to avoid the fuzziness that is inherent in the various Frameworks that make up the general population with its diverse cultures, languages, and beliefs. In a real sense, science constructs its own Framework. However, science is *not* necessarily describing a reality that is independent of human experience. Let's explore this idea in more detail.

There are two ways of describing the universe. The common way is to define reality as that which exists independently of human (or anyone else's) consciousness. Reality exists without any conscious observers. The less traditional form is the definition by Buckminster Fuller, cited in the previous chapter: "Universe is the sum total of all humanity's consciously and unconsciously partially overlapping and communicated experiences."[86] There is nothing that can be identified about the first reality that is different from the second definition of reality. As soon as something is discovered about objective reality, it enters human consciousness (or unconsciousness) and is included in the second definition. The two definitions appear to define the same universe or reality.

There may be aspects of the real world that cannot be experienced. Unfortunately, we cannot name or know these, because as soon as we do, they become part of human experience.

In contrast, there is a logical necessity that human experience of the real world includes some subjectivity. We cannot escape our inherent personal perspectives. The sharing of experience through our symbolic forms universalizes human experience and that is where objectivity comes from.

I am actually contesting the view that science provides any knowledge of an external reality that is independent of subjective experience. I have outlined a process that shows how science achieves such high levels of objectivity in its truth claims. However, I contest the view that science has purged all subjectivity from its truth claims. There are limits to science, and I can begin to identify what these limits are.

Science works with a method called reductionism. What I wish to explore here is to show how science produces its own Framework. We saw how science grew out of the combination of rationalism and empiricism. Rationalism provided the logical/mathematical method of defining precise symbols and their rules for interaction. However, the mathematics

---

86 Fuller, *Synergetics*, p. 81.

and logic of the times were limited. Science did not have the computing resources to calculate what are now called nonlinear equations. Empiricism contributed to the precise method to be used for making observations and measurements.

Historically, then, science was confined to working with non-irreducible systems with linear reductionist methods and so developed its processes with linear thinking. This limited the number and kinds of variables that could be used in describing the world mathematically. Of course, empirical methods had to follow this logic. The result is that science does not really explore the pattern interactions of whole systems, and so misses the opportunities to properly expand its knowledge codependency webs in ever more diverse ways.

This has lead to some major gaffes in how science gets applied. For example, scientists mixed genes from African and South American bees to produce a species of bee that would produce more honey. The result was a bee with a heightened sense of aggression. These are called killer bees. Aggression as a variable was not considered in the laboratory experiments and so was not accounted for in the observations. This kind of omission is common in biology, where the interplay between systems and species is complex and involves the whole system. Much of the point of ecology is to get scientists to understand the complex and systemic interrelationships that occur in nature. These complexities are only now being considered in the science of complexity. The move toward computational science is the move to correct these kinds of failures.

The issue comes to a head with the relationship between levels of scientific observation. W. O. Wilson describes the unity of scientific knowledge as consilience.[87] He breaks the world into levels of study, from the subatomic to the macro level of civilization. This characterization is not new. As he moves up the levels of complexity, from particles to atoms to molecules to chemicals to compounds to organics to biology to anthropology to sociology to civilization, each level is dependent on the lower levels. Each level is more complex than the lower levels. Wilson points out that science is very good at predicting novelty within a level, but is almost hopeless at predicting novelty between levels. For example,

87 Wilson, E. O. (2014). *Consilience: The Unity of Knowledge*. New York: Vintage.

science can predict certain properties of oxygen in a limited number of circumstances. However, it could not predict from the properties of hydrogen and oxygen, understood separately, that mixing them in a 2-to-1 ratio would produce a liquid with completely different properties. Hydrogen is usually combustible in the presence of oxygen. But when combined in a 2-1 ratio, the resulting molecule has completely different properties. Combined as H2O, they produce water, which is an excellent substance for fire suppression. Predicting this new property is not something that science does well in its current form.

The problem with this limitation is that we are living in a world where science can easily cause major damage to the ecosystem by not predicting systemic effects correctly. For example, science still does not know the long-term effects of many of the chemicals industry pours into the environment. Scientists can suspect that they might produce toxic effects, but until these effects can be observed and measured in a controlled environment, they tend not to validate such suspicions. The widespread use of PCBs and DDT are good examples. We tend to apply our scientific knowledge in a vacuum regarding the long-term effects because science has no way of predicting what these effects might be. This is particularly true if the effects are systemic. In the area of transgenetic engineering, scientists cannot predict the environmental, let alone social, impacts of genetically manipulating plants and animals. When the effects do come, and they will, we tend to be surprised, much as we were when the killer bees emerged. Science constantly fails in this area of prediction. Industry deploys a new technology to contain an oil slick on the ocean, and the new method turns out to be worse than the oil slick in terms of measurable damage. Farmers add a new chemical to their fertilizers and find that it is toxic downstream in the food chain in ways that could not have been predicted.

There are two reasons for this limitation in science. The first is that the reductionist methods of science tend to be linear and mechanical. The view is that to study something, we need only to break it down to its simple construct, study each simple construct in isolation, and put the thing together again. But nature is a complex nonlinear synergetic system that is not always computationally or mechanically reducible. New scientific methods go a long way to correcting this problem.

Science in its traditional form is not designed to observe the complex interactions of synergetic systems. This is why scientists often make things worse when they apply one theory to solve a problem caused by another application of science. Generally, science tunes out systemic variables, but these variables do not magically disappear because they do not fit into the scientific Framework. When these variables are not accounted for, the systemic effects invariably surprise us.

The second reason is that science has not magically dispensed with subjectivity. Subjectivity in the sense of our personal predilections continues to play a part in scientific understanding of the world in two key ways. Science does not happen in a vacuum. It happens within the context of the larger linguistic, religious, and artistic Framework of the community. This context affects expressions, and the kinds of questions scientists ask about nature. For example, Einstein believed in God to the point that he rejected the program of science presented by quantum theory: "God does not play dice with the universe." Einstein's quest for a unified field was largely determined by his search for a program of science that would account for determinism in the face of the evidence in favor of natural randomness. The whole question of unified field derives from the belief in the unity of nature—a belief that has religious origins that can be traced back to the fundamental spiritual connection with nature.

The cultural Framework also determines the kind of scientific research to be done. It is no accident that 50% of scientific research is for military purposes. The guardian precepts of Father Culture dictate which projects will get funding and which results will get applied. Scientists believe that because they are seeking objective truth in the absence of subjective considerations, they are working for knowledge for knowledge's sake, and that this counts as a good in itself. But in the context of power structures, knowledge is power. Knowledge for its own sake sounds laudable, but it is a fiction. It denies that we are each part of a cultural Framework that conditions our thinking and our choices. Science may provide its own Framework to some extent, and it may seek to get beyond specific cultural Frameworks, but it cannot be completely free of these considerations.

The Scientific Moral Framework

In his 1986 book, *The Logic of Writing and the Organization of Society*,[88] Jack Goody points out that literacy produces clerics and bureaucrats. Literacy started with scribes as specialists and led to broader record keeping, such as a census for taxation purposes. Literacy then led to social customs not found in preliterate communities. In preliterate communities, the spoken word and the rituals of storytelling dominated how information and tribal histories were passed on from one generation to the next.

When literacy came along, knowledge became objective both in the sense that it is public and in the sense that it is external to any one individual. This objectivity gives power to the written word. Once the thought is written down, it is available for public scrutiny. But, moreover, it objectifies the thought in a way that storytelling cannot. Add to this, a very precise system of symbols and specific and detailed prescriptions for observing the world prior to recording experimental events, and you have exposed the real power of science.

Science as a social institution regularly produces powerful objective results. Further, these results are only refutable within the scientific Framework. Science sets its own ground rules for what counts as a knowledge claim, then very precisely manages how scientists behave in contributing to scientific understanding. The idea that "in principle, anyone who follows the prescribed methods will arrive at similar results" is the appeal to objectivity, as Goody describes it.

I have shown that this is not the real key to scientific objective truth. Rather, the power of science to be objective in a way that cannot be achieved in language, art, or myth is what sets it apart. However, this power is rooted in the institution of science as literate. It draws on the "magic" of formal expression (writing) to enhance the objectivity of the whole enterprise. This kind of objectivity is a systemic or synergetic property of science. It is also the key to bringing moral values back into science.

Science as a symbolic form achieves objectivity through precise symbolic definitions, precise methods of observation, and the formal articulation

---

88 Goody, J. (1987). *The Logic of Writing and the Organization of Society*. Cambridge, UK: Cambridge University Press.

of its results, which then become independent of any individual scientist and open to public scrutiny. The general public does not scrutinize the scientist because the science is judged and not the person doing the science. But why should anyone accept this?

The scientific response is that science is objective in the sense that it is designed to tune out subjective influences. To reintroduce subjective influences in the public scrutiny would violate the spirit and intent of science. In this view, knowledge is a good in itself and should be pursued within the pristine methodology of science.

The limitations of science to predict the systemic effects of its findings present an inherent limitation that applies to science itself. Language, myth, and art as truth-generating symbolic forms do not disappear from public scrutiny because they are inconvenient to the scientific program. Scientific results, when applied across the community, must be open to public scrutiny, whether that scrutiny is scientific or not. Science is either completely isolated from the community as a *divided* activity, or it is merely a distinction within the whole community. As a distinct activity in this context, it pervades community interests. It is, therefore, also subject to public scrutiny from all quarters.

I pointed that out when the president of the Monsanto Corporation made the decision to proceed with trans genetically modifying agricultural materials, this individual was not evil or mean, but merely caught up in a Framework of thinking that does not permit success in his job if he did not pursue the path that science had laid open for him. In the same sense, I could say that scientists who work for the military are not evil but are simply trying to gain knowledge for knowledge's sake. The Framework of science suggests that it is not for the scientist to decide how that knowledge is to be used. Science reaches its limits here and relates with the larger cultural Framework of the community—in this case, Father Culture.

To challenge Father Culture, the key question is always, "What kind of person thinks this way?" What kind of person can see the damage their research contributes to their community, and yet continue to believe in knowledge for its own sake? Scientists base their projects on several factors: a reasonable hypothesis, available measuring devices, resources, funding, and their personal compensation for their work. No scientist that we know of works for free. Scientists must feed their families, provide homes, and do all the other tasks required of members of a modern community.

To think of science as just a job would be to objectify science in a way that distorts the true objective value of the scientific enterprise. Science is about persons discovering about our world (hopefully) for the betterment of all. Again, the key here is persons. Scientists are people. Their children will suffer the effects of toxic waste or transgenetic manipulations, as will their neighbors.

Science does recognize that scientists are persons. There is a series of 15 moral precepts that constrain a scientist's behavior. Let's outline these here.

1. **Shun force.** Scientists must not use force to get other scientists to accept their results. If science as an enterprise permitted aggression to settle contentious issues, it could not achieve the level of objective truth validity it seeks. Further, scientists should not allow themselves to be coerced into doing any particular research or accepting a prescribed result.

2. **Come to voluntary agreements.** Scientists must collaborate in the process of doing science. Because force is excluded as a means of settling disputes, consensus must be reached through voluntary agreement of all parties. Dissent is permitted only when the dissent is also based on prescribed symbols and methods.

3. **Be honest.** Scientists must have the moral courage to face their failures. Further, they must regulate themselves in how well they follow prescribed methods to avoid tendering misleading results or fraudulent claims.

4. **Collaborate with your peers.** Science as an enterprise is above a given language, religion, culture, art, or historical perspective. It is above politics (or so it claims). This means that scientists must work with other scientists wherever they are in the world, regardless of local cultural considerations. This is the appeal to the largest group of people in principle, which serves to enhance the objectivity of scientific truth claims.

5. **Respect the opinions of other scientists.** Science requires collaborative effort and the cumulative work of many contributors. Hypotheses and results may be contested. As Popper pointed out, refutation of hypotheses is the order of the day for science. As a result, other scientists' opinions

need to be respected as long as they are based in scientific methods. Notice that a scientist need not respect another scientist as a person. But they do need to respect their scientific opinions if they are properly founded.

6. **Cooperate with other scientists.** As a key to scientific objectivity is the size of the population base that can accept a truth claim, it is wise to collaborate with as many other scientists as possible. Broad ascent for a hypothesis or result is part of how objectivity is established. A key scientific activity is to actually test another scientist's claims to see if the results can be replicated. This testing of each other's claims and results defines the cooperative nature of science. Moreover, because scientists never know where the next discovery might come from, it is prudent to collaborate widely and to understand what other scientists are doing.

7. **Demonstrate initiative and novelty.** Scientific method requires that a scientist develop a hypothesis and prove it (or not) with empirical tests. This means that as new areas of exploration are opened, scientists must seize opportunities for new discoveries and to predict novelty where they can.

8. **Refute based on evidence.** This precept sounds self-validating, but it is a requirement of all scientists. If scientists are to trust evidence and avoid fudging results or manufacturing evidence to support pet theories, all hypotheses and claims must be tested for refutability. Refutation is a central part of scientific activity, but it must be based on sound and accepted scientific evidence.

9. **Promote free inquiry and open collaboration.** It is not enough that scientists collaborate freely and openly; they must be seen to be doing so. The best way to ensure that science is not subjective is to promote inquiry that is free of cultural or political interference. Collaboration is one of the ways that scientists tune out subjectivity.

10. **Be public.** As mentioned above, part of the power of scientific objectivity is through formal and public articulation (publications, seminars, lecture tours, etc.). Private science is an oxymoron.

11. **Promote and invest in scientific processes.** For science to work, it needs to construct its own Framework for how a scientist thinks and

finds meaningful results. Hence, scientists need to invest in the building and maintenance of that Framework, and also invest in public interest in the scientific enterprise.

12. **Shun exclusivity.** Science achieves its objective standing as a public enterprise with honest cooperation, collaboration, and free public inquiry. To keep a discovery to yourself goes against the whole spirit of science. This precept is designed to keep scientists taking undue political, social, or commercial advantage from their discoveries. If all scientists kept their discoveries to themselves, science as an objective activity would be reduced to a speculative and subjective art form.

13. **Demonstrate scientific courage.** Demonstrating scientific courage is the scientific version of guardian fortitude, as well as commercial industriousness. When a scientist truly discovers something novel or controversial, and their evidence can meet the standards required of scientific methods, the scientist should have the courage to publish their findings (or theory) and accept the scientific community's cooperative and collaborative activities to sort out the truth value of the claim or discovery.

14. **Be competent and informed.** A scientist who does not keep up in their field of expertise will suffer from a failure of collaboration and public cooperation. This precept is a combination of how a scientist promotes free inquiry and collaboration and secures honesty. In general, a scientist who is well-informed and recognized as competent will find collaboration and respect easier to obtain from others.

15. **Seek novelty.** Because science is largely the discovery of novelty, scientists themselves must be open to what novelty is (allegedly) discovered. This does not mean that scientists must blindly accept all novel claims or that these claims should go untested, but scientists should not ignore or prejudge novel claims simply because they disagree with them. Rather, each scientist should seek novel discoveries to push the frontiers of knowledge forward.

From these precepts, it is evident that scientists *do* follow moral guidelines. However, any sense of social responsibility is missing. In its current form, science is socially responsible only in the sense that it improves our knowledge of the world, and so, in theory, betters the human condition.

Table 8.4: Scientific Moral Framework

SCIENTIFIC MORAL FRAMEWORK
Shun force
Come to voluntary agreements
Be honest
Collaborate with your peers
Respect the opinions of other scientists
Cooperate with other scientists
Demonstrate initiative and novelty
Refute based on evidence
Promote free inquiry and open collaboration
Be public
Promote and invest in scientific processes
Shun exclusivity
Demonstrate scientific courage
Be competent and informed
Seek novelty

Scientific moral precepts were formed within the context of Guardian and Commercial Frameworks. The scientific community is supposed to interact with and work with guardian and commercial interests. Because guardianship and commerce are not strictly scientific, science is a support Framework for both of these activities. Social responsibility is the purview of guardians and business leaders, not of scientists. This is, of course, the problem.

When we compare the scientific with Guardian and Commercial Frameworks, we can observe some interesting parallels and alignments.

Science draws many moral precepts from commerce. The difference is that science has a single product—knowledge. To promote knowledge for its own sake, scientists must push for objectivity and publicity and shun subjectivity and privacy. All precepts are designed to promote objective standing for the product of scientific activity.

Table 8.5: Comparison of Traditional Moral Frameworks and the Scientific Framework

GUARDIAN FRAMEWORK	COMMERCIAL FRAMEWORK	SCIENTIFIC FRAMEWORK
Shun trading	Shun force	Shun force
Exert prowess	Come to voluntary agreements	Come to voluntary agreements
Be obedient and disciplined	Be honest	Be honest
Adhere to tradition	Collaborate easily with strangers and aliens	Collaborate with your peers
Respect hierarchy	Respect contracts	Respect the opinions of other scientists
Be loyal	Compete	Cooperate with other scientists
Take vengeance	Use initiative and enterprise	Demonstrate initiative and novelty
Deceive for the sake of the task	Dissent for the sake of the task	Refute based on evidence
Make rich use of leisure	Promote comfort and convenience	Promote free inquiry and open collaboration
Be ostentatious	Be efficient	Be public
Dispense largesse	Invest for productive purposes	Promote and invest in scientific processes
Be exclusive	Be open to inventiveness and novelty	Shun exclusivity
Show fortitude	Be industrious	Demonstrate scientific courage
Be fatalistic	Be optimistic	Be competent and informed
Treasure honor	Be thrifty	Seek novelty

In this comparison, science challenges many of the guardian precepts. In particular, science cannot be effective in an environment where privacy, exclusivity, and prowess are the key values. In a sense, part of the appeal of science to move us beyond our current unsustainable and unviable policies is that science does appear to stand against guardian precepts. As stated above, the phrase "private science" is an oxymoron. If we value science above politics, surely science will help us out of our current difficulties!

Of course, because guardians pay for science with their largesse (and ostentatiously, if they are good guardians), they get to choose what science they will pay for, and how scientific results will get used. In Father Culture, science is at the mercy of guardian thinking.

However, science compares with democratic principles as well, as can be seen in Table 8.6.

Table 8.6: Democracy and Science

DEMOCRAT RULER FRAMEWORK	DEMOCRAT CITIZEN FRAMEWORK	SCIENTIFIC FRAMEWORK
Minimize the use the force	Fight the arbitrary use of force	Shun force
Obey the law	Promote those who best represent your interests	Come to voluntary agreements
Promote the rule of law	Fight corruption	Be honest
Collaborate with the community	Collaborate with your peers	Collaborate with your peers
Respect persons	Respect the rights of others	Respect the opinions of others
Cooperate with each other	Assemble peacefully	Cooperate
Demonstrate authority	Seek justice	Demonstrate initiative and novelty
Trust in the system	Dissent when you disagree	Refute based on evidence
Promote community well-being	Participate in the system	Promote free inquiry and open collaboration
Be tolerant	Personify	Be public
Promote the community's interests	Invest in democratic processes	Promote and invest in scientific processes
Be fair and impartial	Shun exclusivity	Shun exclusivity
Demonstrate moral courage	Promote the community's values	Demonstrate scientific courage
Be competent	Be informed	Be competent and informed
Be moral	Honor integrity	Seek novelty

Again, scientific precepts draw from other social precepts, but tailor them to the specific task of discovering new knowledge about our world.

The problem with the social accountability of science, then, centers on the fact that scientific precepts were formed within the Framework of Father Culture and were designed to work within that Framework. As a result, science works at the behest of those in power or authority with equal enthusiasm. While scientists follow many precepts that match citizen precepts (as these align most clearly with the efforts of science to let knowledge direct its course), they do so in the negative sense of being posited against corruption or power structures. At the end of the day, though, scientists go where the money is, whether the source is powerful or merely authoritative.

The problem can be restated in terms of thymotic values. How does science support and promote all our thymotic values? Remember, if it fails to do so, it is more like a mere ideology.

When we compare all our moral precepts, science depends on liberty and equality to work. Science cannot function in a society that places a greater importance on an economic or political agenda than these moral values. Further, science also includes tolerance as a value in the sense that competing linguistic, religious, or political views are irrelevant in favor of collaboration and respect for others. The problem is in the narrow scope of science. Respect for others means respect for other scientists, not other persons in a general communal sense. Further, science is specifically charged with promoting knowledge, not bettering humanity. The belief that knowledge production, in and of itself, betters the world is a naive belief, at best. This narrowness of focus means that science draws on thymotic values for legitimacy, but does not really promote them beyond its narrow agenda. To bring science to a more direct sense of social responsibility requires bringing science into the Ethical Framework. With this, it will be evident that how science works in this Framework is somewhat different from its current model.

Let's begin with a comparison of scientific and Ethical precepts, as seen in Table 8.7.

Table 8.7: Comparison of Scientific and Ethical Frameworks

SCIENTIFIC MORAL FRAMEWORK	ETHICAL FRAMEWORK
Shun force	Promote peace and harmony
Come to voluntary agreements	Come to voluntary agreements
Be honest	Be honest
Collaborate with your peers	Promote community
Respect the opinions of other scientists	Respect persons
Cooperate with other scientists	Promote personification
Demonstrate initiative and novelty	Seek natural justice
Refute based on evidence	Dissent for the sake of the public good
Promote free inquiry and open collaboration	Promote integrity
Be public	Promote unity
Promote and invest in scientific processes	Promote harmony and inclusiveness
Shun exclusivity	Invest in the global community
Demonstrate scientific courage	Demonstrate moral courage
Be competent and informed	Seek meaning and understanding
Seek novelty	Seek personal spiritual growth and fulfillment

The first six precepts are in agreement, although the focus of the Ethical view is not confined to just a scientific community. Notice that respecting opinions of others and cooperating are really the processes of respect and recognition. So far, science is in line with an Ethical approach. The main distinctions concern the scope of science as an enterprise. Although the Ethical Framework promotes the general community, science is largely directed at promoting its own scientific community. This presents science as a subculture in the global Framework, and this positioning determines much of the distinctions between the two Frameworks.

In the new Ethical Framework, demonstrating initiative and novelty is done in the context of what is naturally just. Recall that natural justice promotes a long-term moral appropriateness. In this sense, scientists are aware of which areas of study or results might introduce injustice into the community. Promoting free inquiry for science is seen to be part of the co-development web of the community. It presents the community with an expanding co-development web based on increasing diversity (specialization). This is how science contributes to social and community well-being. Notice that this is not knowledge for knowledge's sake, but knowledge in the context of a product that enhances community expansion in a measurable way. When the community invests in community via science, it expects a positive return. Science as part of the co-development web is largely funded and supported by the community (not just this or that authority or business interest). Scientific courage involves not only working on what benefits individual power elites, but also working on what benefits community well-being. Understanding how knowledge contributes to community well-being in the sense of the systemic effects of improved understanding is the key to meaningful scientific exploration. This becomes the scientists' version of seeking spiritual fulfillment through the community.

An Ethical science is a nonlinear science where systemic effects are regularly taken into account for all scientific activities. The actual value of any discovery is measured in terms of overall long-term systemic possibilities (or costs). While new knowledge will always present the possibility of abuse or harm, scientists are accountable for how they publicize and promote their discoveries.[89]

An Ethical society needs science to help to promote and sustain co-development webs. Indeed, some of these will be defined by science and facilitated by technology. Science is not in the service of an out of control guardian approach to knowledge, but is part of a structured program that directs our efforts toward viable and sustainable systems of behavior, and the knowledge needed to build and manage such systems.

For example, as new understandings evolve in the social, economic and political sciences, there will be opportunities to develop and deploy new social technologies that can enhance community well-being in new and exciting ways. With appropriate community oversight, science and

---

89 Literature abounds with stories of scientists committing atrocities to further science. Communities clearly understand the dangers of rogue science, and that scientists do not get to make these decisions alone. Part of the precept for collaboration is collaboration with the community.

scientific knowledge are one of the ways that we can be in control as a species, which stands in sharp contrast to the current out of control approach that guardians take with science.

One way of looking at this new perspective for science is to place science in an economic model. All energy transfers must be accounted for. Science helps to discover generalities that lead to differentiations, which lead to further generalities. Knowledge expands because of the co-development web between scientists and the political, economic, and social arms of the global community. This forms the context within which science is judged as responsible or not. Science develops and expands our knowledge only when scientific precepts are cast positively with Ethical precepts. Of course, scientists see themselves differently in an Ethical Framework. They understand that the current narrow-minded approach to discovery based on knowledge for its own sake misses the greater opportunities inherent in the larger co-development web with the community. In an Ethical science, personal value and place and the path for spiritual fulfillment is not abstract, with a vague notion of knowledge as a good as found in Father Culture, but is cast concretely in terms of recognition. Notice that recognition works both ways between scientists and between community members and is understood and appreciated as a source of objective validity.

United Nations

As a species, we only began taking stock of who and what we are in 1950. In 1953, the first global census determined how many people there were in the world. In the mid-20th century, we counted how many languages (over 5,000) and how many religions there were. Since that time, we have learned where our resources were mined, and where they were sold as products. Less than 50 years ago, we captured the earth in a single photographic image. The idea that we live on a single world was always known, but it was not made apparent to every mind until very recently. Ecology as a science has only existed for about 50 years, and it is still in its infancy. Only in the past 50 years have we begun to track global patterns of weather, disease, materials, and population. Only in the past 50 years have we gained any consciousness of the true scale of a global conflict, and how violent a species we are. The idea that soldiering is not an honorable profession and that war is hell is new. Even after the First World War and into the 1940s, many men and women signed up for military duty for the adventure of it. No one could really imagine what war would be like. The guardians had always kept the truth from the masses to ensure a steady supply of fodder for their battlefields. Most veterans were proud of their service, as all good servants are taught to be. They were taught that the sacrifice of their peers and their suffering would not be in vain. The defense of their only known way of life was more important than their comfort. They were heroes, one and all.

In 1948, the United Nations (UN) was formed as a global forum for diplomacy and peace. While the guardians crippled the Security Council with a rule of veto that could allow one guardian to frustrate the aspirations of the others, the UN has functioned in ways that add new strength to our species. The strength is not, however, in its peacekeeping abilities. Almost all the global knowledge we each have regarding how the world works from an administrative point of view comes from UN initiatives. These include a regular census, tracking on poverty, education, literacy, resource utilization, and food, and energy production. The UN has served very well as an agency to raise consciousness about who and what we are as a species. This work is a direct result of the global perspective that has been made public largely through its efforts.

While most guardians shun the UN unless it serves a specific purpose, and regard it as a failed institution, the UN succeeds in the areas that guardians do not imagine. For the first time, we can see guardians in their place. They are not, for example, world leaders in the sense that they are leading the world as a planet. They are each leaders of a small principality on planet Earth. Their thinking and their behavior is not global, but is very provincial. For example, the President of the United States of America rules over a specific area with a population of approximately 326.7 million people. This represents a small patch of planet Earth with about 4.6 % of the Earth's current population. The President is not being paid to look after the planet, only his/her small portion of it. This is similarly the case for all national leaders. So far, only the UN is tasked with whole-earth governance.

For communities where writing is only for the chosen few, written words spell power over those who cannot read. The knowledgeable and the literati become the elite of the community, and the chosen class to fill positions of power or authority. For those who seek to master others, clerics become the master's instrument for controlling the masses. With information and knowledge come power—not just authority—and this characteristic of literacy forms the ground of guardian societies.

However, the power of knowledge unleashed through education and science to a general public and through a sanctioned international institution also serves to undermine guardian values. Those who watch thousands die on a battlefield, or witness millions dying of starvation on their TV or handheld screens cannot ignore the world they support. Our economy is increasingly understood as a co-development web of companies across many nations. Because we do not account properly for this, we are subjected to recessions and depressions and general economic instability. We are subjected to increased taxes and public costs to offset the harm done by improper accounting procedures. We are subjected to a science that is directed and managed by political and economic elites who care only for themselves and who will lie, cheat, and manipulate on a mass scale to preserve their alleged advantage.

Against the propaganda, and against the overt and covert manipulations of a guardian-centric press, and against the self-serving policies of our guardian masters, an Ethical society is emerging. It is impossible to see the world as a whole and think in purely provincial terms. We are coming to understand that survival as a species is the result of co-development webs and proper accounting. The effects are systemic. While science has been slow in many areas to inform us of these issues, science has pointed us to an understanding that is beyond the traditional reductionist approach. A global understanding is beyond science because scientists continue to demonstrate that they are mired in Father Culture, and that they will not assume responsibility for what they discover. Yet, many scientists are beginning to emerge from under that Framework.

Global organizations such as the UN are the wellspring of this new understanding. While the UN is clearly mired in the politics of Father Culture, it is increasingly Ethical in its development of social capital. In this global context, knowledge is seen to be a major contributor to social capital, and science, here, has perceived value. Science measures toxic wastes, and the effects of population growth and pollution. Science provides the means to quantify unsustainability and has done so through groups such as the Club of Rome and other nongovernmental or economic groups. The key to shifting away from Father Culture is to focus on social capital, the one area that is of least concern to guardians and commerce. Social capital was ever-present in primitive communities, and was, in fact, what formed those communities.

Of course, social capital in this original sense did not magically disappear because it was inconvenient to masters. While guardians largely ignored it and sometimes actively suppressed it, it is still present in our global community values. Focus attention on the requirements of global social capital, and Father Culture is exposed in all its weakness. Before I bring all my ideas together into a plan of action, I have one last task. I need to directly address how these issues are currently being discussed under Father Culture. This will further expose the weakness of Father Culture thinking, and position the Ethical Framework as a basis for good governance.

Left Wing, Right Wing, and the Problem of Pertinence

The current dialogues within Father culture are positioned within Left Wing, Progressive versus Right Wing, Conservative points of view. From the perspective of putting ethics first, the whole context of the current Right Wing - Left Wing conversations don't make sense. The whole model is a quaint 20th Century way of thinking that we need to rise above.

We live in a complex, multi-dimensional nonlinear world. There are political, economic, religious, and cultural dimensions, to name a few. To reduce all of these to a one-dimensional Right Wing – Left Wing perspective is to reduce the inherent complexity of the world to an over simplification. There is much important information that is lost in this reduction.

To understand how information is lost by reducing three-dimensional things to a simple one-dimensional model, let's look at a very simple example—a top hat. Until you pop it into the third dimension, a top hat looks more like a plate. It is difficult to even know what it really is, let alone what its essential function might be. How can a plate be a hat? How would it stay on your head?

To focus the conversation on the plate might lead to non-sensical dialogs such as whether it is better to serve food on the left or the right side. The conversation would completely miss the operative questions such as, will the hat fit? Does it go with your wardrobe? These are questions you simply do not ask of plates.

To reduce three-dimensional nonlinear realities to one-dimensional simplicities is to do what Italo Gandolfi calls a *pertinence trick*.[90] This is when the focus on what is pertinent is intrinsically misleading. As we shall see, this is what characterizes the current debates. Let's "pop" these social models into the third dimension to see what happens.

To do this we need some overriding criteria that we can use that are neutral to political, social and economic thinking, but which also enable us to evaluate the success (or not) of any model being proposed. There are only two kinds of criteria that meet these requirements—scientific and ethical. As we are talking about social sciences, I will not critique the science. It should come as no surprise to the reader that I pick Ethics to evaluate the theories of the various social sciences.

When we do this, two things happen right away:

1. It is apparent that what we are really talking about pertains to the question of how we ought to govern ourselves. By moving into the third dimension, the whole conversation gains in comprehension and depth. The issues pertain to the principles of good governance. For example, it is an essential function of good governance that those in power and authority treat people properly. This is what is pertinent.

---

90 Gandolfi, Italo, *Logic Of Information*, p. 50.

2. If we take a proposed policy or practice from one of the social sciences and evaluate it against ethical criteria, it either passes or fails. Either way, who cares if it is Right Wing or Left Wing. It is the right way (or the wrong way) to treat people. The whole Right Wing – Left Wing controversy is exposed as largely irrelevant.

The principles of good governance are not a key priority or feature in the current one-dimensional debates. People propose policies and practices from both perspectives and never ask if it is the right way to treat people. They do not evaluate their positions against the criteria of good governance. They seem to assume that if the practice meets the criteria of their respective ideologies, it is the right way to proceed. This is an example of the pertinence trick. The approach inherently misleads the conversation away from the essential function of government—how should people best govern themselves—to some other lesser consideration that should be answerable to the criteria of good governance. Moreover, they do not actually evaluate their proposals against ethical criteria to see if they pass muster. The whole question of governance—good or bad—is assumed to be a matter of ideology, not a measure of quality or of success.

Ethics and Ideology are not the same things. Ethics is not even an ideology. We argue that until you get very clear about what constitutes the principles of good governance, and give these principles priority, you are misleading the dialog away from what is really pertinent.

What are the principles of good governance? We do not have a standard list, per se, but I argue that the principles of good governance follow directly from the precepts of Natural Ethics, but with a prescriptive imperative for those who would call themselves leaders. The idea is to actually deliver leadership:

1. Promote peace and harmony

2. Practice and keep voluntary agreements

3. Promote Honesty

4. Promote Community

5. Practice and encourage respect for persons

6. Encourage personification

7. Seek Natural justice

8. Dissent for the sake of the public good

9. Practice and promote Integrity

10. Support and promote World unity

11. Practice and promote Harmony and inclusiveness

12. Invest in the global community

13. Practice and promote moral character

14. Practice and promote meaning and understanding throughout the community

15. Practice and promote personal spiritual growth and fulfillment

There is a strong support for natural ethical principles (as indicated in the democrat, citizen, and Commercial Moral Frameworks). Add to this list the three kinds of ethics to guide how we implement good governance and we have a superb idea of what good governance means. There are proper working checks and balances to promote peace and harmony and to constrain abuses of power and authority with recourse for the victims of abuse. There should be both transparency and accountability out of respect for persons, and meaning and understanding. An Ethical approach supports the practice and the rule of law. Governments should honor their contracts, such as treaties and trade agreements. They should treat their citizens with proper dignity and respect, such as supporting fair working conditions, overseeing education and public health and safety. They should both demonstrate and encourage moral character and trustworthiness, as well as promoting positive overall consequences (minimizing harms), and practicing and promoting the four thymotic values.

With the precepts from the Ethical Framework as a guide to good governance, we contend that leaders would promote diversity with harmony, individuality with integrity, peace, and prosperity for all, and a proper respect for the environment on which we all depend.

Table 8.8: Principles of Good Governance

PRINCIPLES OF GOOD GOVERNANCE
Promote peace and harmony
Practice and keep voluntary agreements
Promote honesty
Promote community
Practice respect for persons
Encourage personification
Seek natural justice
Dissent for the sake of the public good
Practice and promote integrity
Promote world unity
Practice and promote harmony and inclusiveness
Invest in the global community
Practice and promote moral character
Practice and promote meaning and understanding throughout the community
Practice and promote personal spiritual growth and fulfillment

The one-dimensional model of social theory is a product of Father Culture thinking. It presents itself as more than just "the way we do things around here." In the context of the current political, social and economic debates, it has been objectified as "this is the way it is." Einstein said that we cannot solve the problems we created with the same thinking that created them. We need to think out of the box. The problem is that the box called Father Culture has been objectified as reality and entrenched with pertinence tricks. It would be helpful to shift our thinking to a new box, to envision what that kind of thinking would be like. I have outlined some of these features already. What I now need to do is pull this outline together to form a kind of game plan for how we can move forward.

CHAPTER 9
Toward an Ethical Society

I began this study of what an Ethical society would look like with a single objective: to move toward a peaceful and sustainable future for humanity. I suggested that we could measure progress toward this goal if we set proper objectives, and also suggested that we use the richness of cultural diversity as our yardstick. This immediately posed a problem. When we look around, we find an amazing richness of cultural diversity. Why, then, have we not produced viable and sustainable societies? We later learned that all societies must play power games, which were and are based on divide-and-conquer strategies. Our leaders promote themselves by going at each other while ruling the mob. Our leaders deliberately and willfully teach us to treat our differences as sources of antagonism and aggression—usually for ends designed to enrich themselves. If we are on the lucky team, we, too, might share in the rewards of these behaviors.

I next introduced the idea that all our civilizations to date have been religiocentric. I stated that we are at the end of such forms of civilization, and that we are embarking on a new civilization that is different in kind. The reason centered on culture lag, which is the result of disconnecting understanding from meaning and values. I argued in Chapter 1 that while science is moving us into the 21st century, our political and social institutions and values are still circa 1900. Historically, religion connected understanding with meaning through the metaphysical spirit world, through gods, or God. But, a religiocentric civilization constructs its own Framework to explain how the world works, so that the connection can be made between understanding and meaning. Science has replaced this Framework with a new scientific approach to understanding, and the new Framework has been developed independently of any connection with meaning or values. In the new model, understanding is connected with observation, not meaning, per se.

I also argued that part of the process toward a scientific understanding of the world included secularizing ethics. Liberty, equality, and even tolerance are not core moral values in any of the world's major religions. Ethical values are *different in kind* from traditional religious moral values. I maintain that in addition to the virtues, and a consideration of the consequences of our decisions and actions, life, liberty, equality, and tolerance are the foundational ethical values that we need to achieve our goal of a viable and sustainable future for humanity. In short, I have been arguing that if we shift our founding values from religiocentric ones to ethics, we can solve both of our problems. I argue that we need to put some quality thinking behind our actions and decisions, and that ethics provides the criteria we need to start this process. We can redirect our leaders to promote our differences as a positive good rather than as a source of antagonism and aggression, and we can reconnect understanding with how we find meaning in our lives. In these moves, we realize our humanity more completely.

I now have the complete perspective to explain these remarks. With the current understanding of how Frameworks develop and evolve through the symbolic forms of thought, language, myth, and art, and through intercommunal interaction, I can explain how religion developed to dominate our thinking in forming communities, and what we must now do to close the culture gap introduced by science.

Civilizations evolved through their respective periods of growth to their times of troubles. This was usually either a direct attack from a neighboring tribe, or some action that prevented the tribe from getting the resources it needed to survive. These resource requirements were a direct result of adopting an agrarian lifestyle. By adopting the ways of a power structure and conquering rival tribes, the civilization not only survived, but through recognition found its customs and values objectified in a new and exciting way. Cultural values, understood as "the way it is," were deemed universal. All rational and successful societies behaved this way. Religion was the centerpiece that consolidated the values of the community, so that individuals found meaning and place in the new order. Because their reality had been shattered, religion was particularly important for those who had been conquered. Under Father Culture, religion was perceived as the source of values and meaning and came to present the best way to control the masses and get them to find their servitude meaningful. Hence, the universal state was born.

Historically, Father Culture determined the criteria used to evaluate the success or failure of a given civilization. When the remnants of the Sinic (Chinese diaspora), or Christian, or Hellenic, or Syrian civilizations are examined from this perspective, it is not their property or their empires that are observed. It is the way they chose to recognize others. Humans, as a modern species, are living in the traditions of the universal Framework of each respective civilization. Each way of thinking is not just "this is how we do things around here," but has been objectified as "this is how it is." The Framework represents the social reality that each civilization constructed.

Father Culture began as a man-versus-nature activity. Through the Agricultural Revolution, followed by industry and information revolutions, man has conquered the natural world. However, man accomplished this through expansion—not in the natural sense of increasing differentiations to produce generalities that then produce further differentiations—but by curtailing diversity and geographically expanding. Father Culture is land-centric, which measures success in terms of the amount of territory a guardian controls. Through lock-up-the-resources mechanisms, combined with religiocentric values, guardians control the masses, and still keep us at each other's throats. Guardians maintain the objectivity of their worldview in this manner. In modern terms, we say that they own the forces of production (including their citizens).

When guardians succeeded in conquering the planet, further expansion was not possible. This process was completed by the 19th century. Humans are now making forays into space and under the oceans, but further land-based expansion is not really possible anymore. This leads to the problem of how to behave like a guardian in a world where Father Culture-type expansion is no longer possible. For most of the last century, guardians settled into balance-of-power games. These balances continue to shift and pull us further into a great abyss. We are now playing 19th-century balance-of-power games with 21st-century weapons of mass destruction.

To make matters worse, economic policies, which conform to the Father Culture dictate of expansion, have also run into a brick wall. There is very little capability to expand economies. All we can do is play endless balance-of-power games to dominate increasingly depleted resources. Under these pressures, we are actually increasing production to accelerate the depletion of the world's resources. Whole species have been extinguished, and many other natural resources are now declared to be on the verge of exhaustion as well. Our policies of creating waste are polluting our water and our soil and making it ever harder to sustain our methods of production. Science has declared that our current ways of doing things are unviable and unsustainable. In other words, the objective reality of how we do things around here is not sustainable. If we do not change how we do things, we are headed for possible extinction ourselves. This means we must change how we think about ourselves and our world.

That brings me to the main question of this book, which is: We know that our current methods of running the planet are unviable and unsustainable, but how is it that we are unable to shift gears and go in any other direction?

The answer lies in how we think. We cannot change gears because we are trapped in a Framework of thinking that perpetuates Father Culture. This Framework is so strong and has been with us for so long (all of recorded history) that it is very difficult to imagine any other way of thinking. To even suggest an alternative is to appear idealistic almost to the point of dreaming.

However, we can and do escape from oppressive Frameworks. The 19th-century historian W. Lecky described the rise and influence of rationalism or science in Europe from medieval to modern times.[91] Using my terms, he discussed the Framework for thinking in medieval times under the Catholic Church. Religious despotism encouraged a complete devotion to the afterlife without any regard for secular matters. Many of the horrors of the Inquisition and religious persecutions, such as burning

---

91 Lecky, W. E. H. (1955). *History Of The Rise And Influence Of The Spirit of Rationalism In Europe*. New York: George Braziller.

heretics at the stake, were completely consistent within the Framework for thought in that period of human history. Even the ideas of torture to elicit confessions were rational under the common belief system that had evolved.

Lecky pointed out that Europe rose out of this state of religious despotism and into the world of science through the gradual change in underlying values and attitudes that resulted from the rise of science. People did not simply wake up one morning and decide to behave logically and scientifically as a modern society. Lecky pointed to two underlying influences that brought about the change. The first was the increased skepticism about religious understanding of the world brought about by scientific discoveries. The second was the result of the great schism that broke Catholicism into many Christian sects. It became evident that if nation states were to be formed with a real sense of national identity, religious tolerance needed to become a necessary part of political and social harmony. Liberty was promoted along with tolerance as core social values. All major religions fought tooth and nail against these trends with all the weapons at their disposal. The penalty for knowledge and tolerance was torture and death by the most horrible means that could be devised. Yet science progressed, and as it did, more and more people simply came to disregard any theological arguments against liberty and tolerance. In short, knowledge undermined the theological Framework for understanding and increased the need for liberty and religious tolerance. Together, these brought about a change of attitude that treated theological arguments as generally and increasingly incredible, and to be ignored.

A similar situation exists today. The true state of our predicament is sinking in. More and more people are becoming aware that we must do something new. Doing more of the same will not work. The current situation does not allow for a slow and gradual change over hundreds of years. We are running out of time.

Will we all wake up one morning and behave rationally and logically, in an ecologically sustainable way? That clearly will not happen. But, the forces of change, forces similar to those described by Lecky, are driving us in that direction. As we learn more about how the world works, there is a growing skepticism that our current political and social institutions and methods of governance are viable and sustainable. We are being driven by a new global perspective that we are all in this together, which is driving a rising understanding that we need to embrace cultural tolerance as a key value. We are also coming to a common realization that science is not constrained by ethics the way political forces are, and that this needs to change. We are being driven to the realization that we must treat Father Culture arguments against change as increasingly incredible and should be ignored. We need to start ignoring those social, political and economic and spiritual leaders who want to keep us mired in more of the same old ways.

But we need to find some way to accelerate these kinds of changes. We need some mechanism to tip the balance toward an accelerated pace. By shifting the definitions of our foundational ethical values from a negative to a positive stance, we can tip that balance. With a subtle shift in the meaning of life, liberty, equality, and tolerance, we can redefine what constitutes good governance, embrace a global perspective toward others, and rein in science under the umbrella of ethical values and constraints. We can shift to a new Framework to define rational thought in a new way.

Are there any examples of these positive values contributing to viable and sustainable systems? Fortunately, the answer is yes. They are called ecosystems, and they are how the natural world really works. But to build a new Framework that can reconnect understanding with meaning, we need to gain a deep understanding of how Frameworks develop and evolve, and how we think within them.

I have discovered that all Frameworks are grounded in the symbolic forms that structure our thought processes. These, in turn, provide the basis for objective understanding and meaning. Father Culture dictates that personal meaning is to be found with the success of the community, and in particular at the expense of personal success. But I have discovered that personal meaning can also be found *through* the community if we select the right underlying values. The good news is that the underlying values are based on the recognition of persons, which goes to the core of who and what we are as a species. Thymotic values are universal because they are based on mental processes that are common to all humans as a species. When these values are brought to the fore, the opportunity to change the way we think presents itself.

Of course, all this assumes that we will give ethical values priority. In a broad general way, I am arguing against what I call the "duuhh" principle. Under the Framework of Father Culture and related thinking, our leaders have habitually given religious faith, political agendas, and economic and cultural initiatives priority over proper treatment of others. Under Father Culture, we chronically and persistently put ethics on the back burner whenever it is thought to be convenient or necessary to a particular objective or to reinforce a point of view. We then scratch our heads and wonder why the world is in such a sorry state. Well, duuhh!

We need to shift from the same old ways to putting quality thinking behind our actions and decisions. Ethics provides the criteria we could use to guide this change. This includes recognizing the four ethical (not religious) values to promote a viable and sustainable way of "doing things around here," and grant these values priority as foundational principles of conduct. Therefore, we would avoid more "duuhh."

Connecting Understanding with Meaning

We are in the grip of a culture lag between scientific understanding that is accelerating beyond control, and the institutions and values that are the source of meaning in our lives. The current Framework of Father Culture does not provide a basis for connecting understanding with meaning but is largely the source of this growing problem. How can we close this gap?

Start with a simple thought experiment. You are 90 or 100 years old, looking back over your life and asking the questions, "Did I have a good life? Was my life all that I wanted it to be? Did I find a true sense of meaning and purpose in my life?"

There are really two parts to these questions. The first refers to *what* you accomplished in your life. Did you become a doctor and help the sick? Did you become wealthy? Did you get to see and do all the things you wanted to do as you grew up? The second refers to *how* you lived your life. Did you remain or become the kind of person you hoped to become? Your parents were always working and were never there for you as a child. You swore you would not do that to your children. Were you a good parent who was always there for your children, or did you fall into the same pattern as your parents? You became wealthy, but did you end up sacrificing your family and friends, giving up what you valued most in the rush for material gain, or did you balance it all?

We have seen that the structure of society determines what our choices and opportunities are. A 7th-century Englishman is not going to aspire to become an astronaut or a scientist. These were not career options that were available at that time or place. On the other hand, they might aspire to be a great archer or servant to their lord. Conversely, a modern North American is not likely to aspire to become a great squire. We are each born into a particular culture at a particular time and place and must find meaning within the Framework of understanding that makes up the social reality we live in. Meaning in life mostly comes from the nature of the contribution that we each make to the well-being of the community or culture in which we live. This social reality defines what we can become and accomplish in life. But it also defines how we go about finding meaning, and this is the tragedy of Father Culture.

Guardians focus on controlling the masses. They employ a divide-and-conquer strategy to keep the masses in manageable groups. They create classes, divisions, castes, and so on as part of the hierarchy that supports guardianship. For example, this practice was a huge waste of human resources because, for most of human history, 50% of our population's knowledge and understanding was lost by repressing women. How many great scientists or doctors or spiritual leaders have been passed over because the individual was the wrong sex or was in the wrong class or was denied access to education or resources to develop their talents? There were exceptions, of course, but only exceptional people could break through the social barriers imposed by guardians.

The situation is not much improved in the modern world. How many great artists or engineers or scientists are a lost potential due to poverty, lack of education, or resources, or dependence on guardian traditions and social controls? While current ethical debates touch on such issues, it is not clear that these are ethical concerns as such.

By shifting the definitions of the foundational values of life, liberty, equality, and respect for the person to a positive footing, and bringing quality thinking to our actions and decisions, we can begin to correct these injustices and reconnect understanding with meaning in our lives. We judge the health of an ecosystem by the level of biodiversity that we find. The richer the biodiversity, the healthier and more robust the ecosystem. Conversely, a loss of richness in biodiversity points to an ailing ecosystem. The current loss of biodiversity leads scientists to predict at least one major ecological collapse within the next 50 years, if the trend is not stopped. For example, the rate of de-speciation is accelerating, soil and water depletion are of increasing concern, and resource depletion is threatening our ability to sustain our economic practices.

Natural ethics judges the moral credibility of societies by the level of cultural diversity they embrace as a positive value, and the way that they harmonize this diversity. The more cultural diversity we embrace, the more opportunities there will be for self-fulfillment in our lives. A patterned web of increasing diversity of opportunities based on the natural form of thymotic values promotes justice more often than not and reduces the injustice that denies so many people the opportunity for a meaningful life. It increases the ways that people can contribute to the well-being of the community and also enriches their sense of personal involvement and accomplishment. With increasing meaningfulness comes greater harmony. The combination results in greater overall robustness for the world's systems. Through natural ethics, we all benefit from positive contributions to the growing richness of the cultural and individual diversity within the social Framework.

Many people will aspire to and find meaning in improving knowledge, or through public service, or through emotional or spiritual guidance. As physical and emotional needs are met for more and more people, so, too, will there be increased opportunities to meet intellectual and spiritual needs. While some people will need a structured institutional form of personal growth and contribution, others will need less structure and will live outside of traditional institutional forms. All approaches will be recognized and embraced within the growing richness of cultural diversity that marks the success of the community. This is how we maintain harmony along with growing diversity.

The idea is that as science continues to push the frontiers of understanding forward, we will close the gap between how we understand the world and how we each find meaning in our life. Of course, understanding and meaning will continue to play off each other. As we close the culture lag and behave more responsibly toward ourselves and our environment, opportunities will open up to connect understanding with meaning in new and exciting ways. Rather than be subjected to a lag between the two, we might even find that the search for meaning will drive us into new and exciting ways of understanding ourselves and the world around us.

This speaks directly to the growing skepticism regarding the ability of our political and social institutions to lead us to a viable and sustainable future. Natural ethics under an Ethical Framework redefines what constitutes good governance. The goal is not to enhance power positioning at the expense of the community but to shift to create forms and institutions that promote cultural diversity and harmony. It humanizes us. How might this work in practice?

In the political arena, we currently read of efforts to unite the world. As mentioned previously, unity is defined as "many things taken together as one."[92] We are already a united world. The problem is not how to unite the world, but how to recognize the unity that is there. In other words, the question is not how to use political or economic force to expand to a global state. That is usually called conquering. Politicians need to shift the definition of good governance to capture the new sense of cultural diversity that is recognized and to create new policies and forms of government that embrace and promote cultural diversity and harmony. To do this, I am advocating that we move beyond the 19th-century balance-of-power games that are the current Father Culture approach to unite the world. Instead, we recognize the unity that is already there and measure success in terms of the richness of the cultural diversity and harmony that is present. The shift for thymotic values to a more naturalized form is the starting point and is the pivot upon which to construct a new Framework that can lead to a viable and sustainable future.

---

92 Fuller, *Synergetics.* Op cit.

What You Can Do?

How can we each contribute to this process? The first thing is to recognize that Father Culture is a failing Framework and begin to embrace all the criteria that promote virtues, beneficial consequences, and a principled approach to our decisions and actions. This includes the foundational ethical values of natural life, natural liberty, natural equality, and natural tolerance (respect for persons). In short, begin to evaluate the quality of our thinking using the criteria that ethics provides. We want to avoid any more "duuhhs." We need to begin to put ethics on the front burner in our decisions and actions. We also want to evaluate our leaders in terms of the new rules of good governance. I have tried to develop a set of moral rules that can tie directly to all ethical theories and principles to form a coherent ethical approach to decisions and actions.

Consider the tables comparing Democratic and Ethical Frameworks (Table 8.2). We can think of ethics as holding a person's character up to public scrutiny and evaluating their decisions and actions against a set of ethical or moral criteria. As a good citizen, you would combine these rules. For example, you would promote community through collaboration with your peers. You would respect the rights of others and promote community well-being by participating in the system and investing in democratic processes. You would demonstrate moral courage by promoting the community's values and honoring diversity and integrity.

More than this, you would judge community leaders against appropriate ethical and moral criteria. You would examine the quality of their decisions and actions to see if all criteria have been met. Remember the two rules. First, they must meet all ethical criteria relating to virtues, consequences, and principles to escape moral criticism. Second, they must promote all foundational ethical values in a positively balanced way.

In practice, this will look like the following: Is the leader acting with honesty, fairness, and integrity? Is there evidence that they have stopped to consider the consequences of their decisions? Have they selected a course of action that promotes overall benefits and mitigates potential harms? Have they identified the right principles of action? Should everyone in their situation behave the same way? Would they think they have a basis for complaint if others treated them the same way? Are they promoting the four thymotic values in a positively balanced way or are they cherry-picking? Are they subtly granting intrinsic priority to one value over the other or are they simply ignoring one of the values? Are liberty and equality being violated? Is the leader promoting intolerance (not respecting persons)? Do they promote law and order and collaborate with the community? Do they promote the community's best interests? Are they fair and impartial (as opposed to arbitrary)?

Commercial leaders can be evaluated as well. In addition to the same questions asked above, do they promote and invest in the public good? Are they honest, thrifty, efficient, and respectful of contracts? Do they invest in productive purposes?

Of course, if the answers are negative, this is more "duuhh," and you should not support their policies or products.

You are really looking for leaders who demonstrate quality thinking that promotes cultural and individual diversity and gives proper due to how people and our world ought to be treated. Political, economic, and religious leaders who promote cultural diversity and propose policies and actions that accord with our positive foundational values and the moral rules of the Ethical Framework should receive your support. You also need to recognize that ethics is an informal mechanism to achieve positive treatments. It only really works well when most of us participate. Building a stronger sense of a global community is, therefore, important. The cultural diversity inherent in the modern world should be recognized as a pillar in building a peaceful and sustainable future. Of course, because power elites will continue to have a vested interest in their local principality or commercial concern, they will most likely promote policies designed to maintain a divide-and-conquer approach to planetary management, which is more of the "duuhh" that we are trying to change.

The good news is that as more people participate in the new Framework, it will become easier to find meaning, and to connect that meaning with modern understanding. Thus begins an upward spiral toward a viable and sustainable future.

I presented my case with three arguments. The first outlined the case for what Frameworks are and how they are formed. I outlined the development of personal and community Frameworks and how a Framework objectifies behaviors. I showed how we get from "this is how we do things around here," to "this is the way it is." The first conclusion is that Frameworks are the virtual public structure of mind, as determined by language, myth, and art, and now science. Frameworks literally structure how we understand and find meaning in our world.

The second argument is that the current historical landscape is a world dominated by Father Culture, which continues to subvert ethical criteria and thymotic values. Father Culture manifests itself largely in politics and economics. It is the demonstrable Framework for poor-quality thinking, as ethics defines this. With an understanding of how Frameworks are built, and how Father Culture does not work, I contrasted our current economic theories with a natural economy as understood by science. This found that the energy accounting of our present commercial activities works to the detriment of social capital. More than this, though, ethics has historically been positioned negatively against the abuses of power structures. Ethics is largely an attempt to reintroduce thymotic values after the guardians subverted them in the original master–servant relation. I also argued that there was no real necessity to introduce master–servant relations in the Agricultural Revolution. That we did so is the historical legacy that must now be changed.

For the third argument, I presented the main ethical theories and positioned them as the criteria for quality thinking. Thymotic values have not been positively managed. The two rules of ethical criteria and values have not been properly identified and adhered to. I outlined the moral precepts that form the various social Frameworks that define political and commercial activities and saw that the Guardian and Commercial Frameworks do not follow my two rules. The Guardian Framework largely ignores virtues and consequences and attacks the foundational values. I explored democracy as an alternative, but although it is better than guardianship, it, too, was not clearly grounded in ethical criteria and the underlying values. To correct the problem, I proposed an alternative Ethical Framework based on scientific economic principles and firmly grounded ethical criteria and the underlying thymotic values. It is designed to follow the two rules. The Ethical Framework presents the first Framework that is firmly tied to fundamental values, which are themselves grounded in the principles that define who we are as a species.

To accomplish the shift from Father Culture to Ethics requires us to positively redefine the thymotic values of life, liberty, equality, and tolerance, as natural life, natural liberty, natural equality, and respect for the person. With a positive positing, I developed an Ethical Framework that could then be tied to democracy and commerce. I then humanized science and outlined the moral precepts of a Scientific Moral Framework. When the Democratic, and Scientific Frameworks are combined, an Ethical Framework emerges that shifts our thought processes to a new way of doing things. Under an Ethical Framework, we think in terms of co-development webs, differentiation, and political, and economic, and social systems that work with nature as a closed system rather than against nature, as with Father Culture. We act within the criteria of quality thinking and positive human values. The Ethical Framework provides clear principles defining good governance.

My argument is simple. The Framework called Father Culture is poorly thought, and yet still dominates our thinking. When you change the underlying values that determine how you think and set the rules to evaluate high-quality thinking, you have the potential to change everything. An Ethical society presents an example of how a new Framework might look. I do not suggest that the Ethical Framework as described is actually what will emerge. However, I do insist that by presenting an example of an alternative Framework for thinking, I stimulate the evolution of an emerging Framework that can lead us to a peaceful and sustainable future. We are entering a new civilization that is different in kind from any that we have known before. This is not a scientific civilization, but an Ethical civilization that begins to balance not power, but knowledge and fulfillment. This time, we cannot just allow things to happen; we must be self-conscious of what we are doing—and this is the difference. Guardian chaos keeps us out of control as a species. Guardianship is not the control mechanism that will lead to a peaceful and sustainable future. Guardianship is the cause of the problem, not the solution. We must each participate and take responsibility for who we want to be as a species. We are each responsible for the world our children and grandchildren will inherit. Each of us includes the current set of guardians. Because all humanity is at risk, we are all accountable. This shift answers the question from who is responsible and shifts the issue to how we will all be responsible.

Ethics First

In the first chapter, I observed that any view that does not account for all thymotic values is not an ethics. I also stated that any view that does not promote and support all the principles is a mere ideology.

This book was intended to show that by getting to the criteria for high-quality thinking and the underlying principles and values of our community, and by articulating these in a way that can contribute to the development and expansion of understanding, we could find a new path to survival as a species. The hope was that the shift in thought would not be so dramatic or extreme that a new Framework could not be envisioned.

The Framework called Father Culture, which seeks to maintain divide-and-conquer, master–servant, provincial residues of guardian precepts cannot expand to embrace the globe any more than it already has. The world is a closed system. What we are currently experiencing is Father Culture expanding within this closed system through further differentiations and parochial divisions. In a closed system, the problem is that such expansion is not viable and cannot sustain itself. This is why the current trend to Populism will not work. It is just more Duuhh. The fundamental violation of the first law of nature is exposed as a violation of the unity of the earth as a system. The Guardian Framework cannot predict or contain the systemic effects of its divide-and-conquer approach to raising political and economic capital. Those who think within the Framework of Father Culture simply do not have the rational tools to understand how their thinking processes undermine all long-term survival options. To them, Father Culture is the only viable survival option. But we now know that Father Culture is dying, and the masters will be the last to know, let alone admit their failure.

The new Framework is the global view that understands how to use knowledge, especially scientific knowledge, to enhance favorable systemic effects through a structured co-development web that encourages expansion within a closed system. This is a Framework that is clearly tied to ethical criteria and the underlying thymotic values and where all energy is accounted for in all development. Being self-conscious of how we develop and expand Frameworks is the first step to survival. Being self-aware of high-quality thinking and how science works, combined with a clear understanding of fundamental ethical criteria, is how we translate understanding into meaningful action. We saw the beginning of this with the new kind of science that is emerging—including social sciences that deliver a qualitatively different kind of understanding with a requirement for new institutions and social thinking.

I have followed this process through understanding science, symbolic forms, ethics, various competing moral Frameworks, and the nature of power structures—including the Sub-Framework patterns of behaviors that lead to adverse systemic impacts such as antagonism and aggression. I have shown how Father Culture is a power structure and outlined the moral precepts required of the guardians of the culture. I have also shown how ethics is positioned negatively to contain abuses of power and to try to break power by distributing it across manageable individuals. This led to the distinction between power and authority. The divide-and-conquer approach to thinking has reduced our comprehension to a set of mere ideologies that can compete within the Framework while not really challenging it. Contemporary discussions of right versus left, globalization, and corporatism are various ideologies that distract us from the more fundamental principles at stake.

To break the hold that guardians have on our thought processes, I have had to challenge the basic assumptions of Father Culture. I questioned ethics and found that the competing moral views within Father Culture failed to promote or support fundamental ethical criteria and the underlying thymotic values. Indeed, guardian precepts are actively opposed to ethics because such thinking would undermine a master's control over servants.

I exposed the idea of Frameworks of thought and looked at how these work to structure our thinking, our attitudes, and our understanding. This revealed how guardians find meaning in mastery and teach servants to find meaning in servitude, and also exposed how masters deny servants any other sense of meaning. This in turn led to how we are each reduced to separate individuals within a divided community, and how guardians keep us divided us from each other and from nature to better manage our servitude. I showed how this leads to the loss of self. Finally, I outlined how mastery is based on objectifying others and preventing active recognition of others as persons. In this way, we are trundled under the feet of our masters, kept in line, and kept fighting for their various and sundry causes.

There are two contesting trends within Father Culture. The first is the ongoing battle to keep the masses in their place. This includes a focus on political and economic capital, and how to mix these to benefit the elite. The second is the unleashing of science, which in theory produces knowledge to benefit all humans. The control of knowledge and science is a key strategy for mastery. This is a version of a problem raised at the beginning: Do we want to change, and how do we deal with those who don't and who resist change? There are fundamentally three reasons to resist change, but they are all based in fear. The first is that many people thrive under Father Culture, and fear losing their advantage. The second is an emotional attachment to the values and principles of Father Culture that dominates their thinking and provides their source of meaning. They are afraid they will not find meaning or a sense of place in the new order. The third is simple fear of the unknown. In short, they are either controllers or controlled within Father Culture. These people cannot see the whole system, and suffer system blindness from their relative place in their community. The best way to work to overcome such resistance is through active engagement. We need to develop ways and means to actively engage as many people as possible to help them to see the earth as a whole system—to overcome their system blindness. If we can engage enough people, we don't need to get everyone on the same page. If we get this right, it will be enough to engage a majority of people to overcome their system blindness. All of the strategies presented below are directed at this approach.

Against these strategies of economic globalization and the control of science, I have found that development of social capital is severely lacking. It is not clear within the Framework of Father Culture what social capital is. I have defined social capital as when the community is structured to promote positive natural values, such that each person can realize meaning in their life through the community (as opposed to *for* the community or *by* the community).

A shift of focus to social capital starts with a clear understanding of all ethical criteria and the underlying thymotic values, and how these translate into the moral precepts that promote community well-being. I called this the Ethical Framework.

The shift to an Ethical Framework outlines thought processes that embrace the world as a system, of all people unified through diversity. It posits ethics not as a negative fight against power, but as a positive valuing of community and individuality as distinctions within the community. This positive positing of the values of natural life, natural liberty, natural equality, and respect for the person shifts attention to the positive value of free recognition. It develops an association between understanding and meaning that results in a co-development web that expands various cultural Frameworks within the closed system of the earth. The expanded sense of meaning is really the spiritual growth of each individual through the community, rather than of the community as dictated by guardians.

Political and economic expansion is accomplished through increasing codependent development webs that facilitate expansion within a closed system. All materials and resources are transparent in all energy accounting. Economic and political capital is raised to promote social capital, measured as the overall well-being of the community at large (in this case the whole world), and by the increase in community and individual diversity enhancing the system's robustness. Science is nonlinear and participates in this measuring and development exercise. Technology is a major facilitator of co-development webs that unite individuals and groups in political, economic, social, or cultural activities.

I contend that under guardianship, humans as a species have always been out of control. We have operated in a haphazard, ad hoc, and opportunistic way that has led to some progress, but which has overall restricted our capabilities as a species. We have been so internally focused in our own respective provincial, cultural, and religious Frameworks that we have failed to notice that the world cannot support the infinite expansion of populations or guardian-based economies and politics. When we do think of the world as finite, our approach has been to think within Father Culture with this or that ideology and the reduced ethical values that such ideologies require. We think in terms of what least inconveniences guardians and their power structures.

If we are to think outside the box, as marketers currently express it, we must shift to a viable Framework of thinking that draws on all the principles and values at our disposal. These principles are not reducible to science nor are they to be judged by scientific standards. We must use our knowledge of all principles—be they physical, metaphysical, spiritual, or otherwise—to survive. A view that tries to identify all of our principles and values and that promotes and supports them all is called a philosophy. Anything less is mere ideology. Mere ideologies will not meet the requirements for a peaceful, sustainable world. The danger with mere ideologies is that they are all based on pertinence tricks and so fail to break our thinking out of the Framework of Father Culture.

We need to challenge the fundamental principles and values of the ideologies that support Father Culture and find the new Framework that can lead to a peaceful and sustainable future for humans and our world. This is based on Ethics, understood as quality thinking. It is a philosophy of individual and cultural understanding and meaning through the high-quality thinking that promotes virtue, beneficial consequences, and right principles. To follow up on Albert Schweitzer's second principle of civilization, this is how "man will conquer man." I contend that the outcome of such thinking leads to a new kind of civilization that is different in kind from all that has been developed up until this point in our history. Such a civilization is truly to tame power structures, and to use knowledge for the benefit of all people, and not just chosen elites. The time has come to stop doing more of the same, and to start doing something different as a species and not just as a collection of guardian-based principalities.

The beginnings of such a shift in larger geographic, political units such as the European Economic Community (EC), and with free-trade zones in other parts of the world is already emerging. The guardian concept of sovereignty to give themselves uncontested position and impunity is under attack. But these merely scratch the surface of what is required. To self-consciously take control of our planet and to construct a viable and sustainable civilization needs a deeper shift to universal values and an Ethical Framework for thinking. Humans have always behaved as "this is how we do things around here." We have objectified these behaviors as "this is the way it is." We can now understand that we chose to behave the way we did. We can undo our perceived reality of how things are and develop new ways of doing things. In time, these new ways will become objectified as "the way it is." Only this time, we can be self-consciously in control of what we determine to construct, and that, too, will be a different kind of civilization.

A Proposed Game Plan

What are some of the things we might do to really start us on our way? How can we promote quality thinking to develop an Ethical Framework or similar Framework?

First, we must begin to break out of the patterns of behaviors described above in the Oshry model.[93] If our social organizations cannot behave more as systems for the benefit of the whole, most of what follows will fail.

Oshry presents several strategies to break out of the patterns of our Sub-Frameworks, what we learned previously is called the dance of blind reflex. These are all predicated on a single observation from years of running his Power Lab simulations. Oshry observed that when people actually see the whole of the system they are in, the blinkers of the five kinds of system blindness start to fall away. They see how actions in their part of the system impact other parts of the system. They see how things got to be the way they are. They see how relationships are impacted in ways they did not understand before. They see how processes work, not just in their part of the world, but across the whole system. Seeing the larger

---

93 Oshry, B. (2007). *Seeing Systems: Unlocking The Mysteries Of Organizational Life.* Oakland, CA: Berrett-Koehler Publishers.

context and how the system behaves reduces the uncertainty people have about what they can do to positively work for the system. Rather than blindly and reflexively acting within their respective Sub-Frameworks, the dance of blind reflex comes to an end.

Oshry calls these moments *TOOTs*—Times Out of Time or seeing the whole. TOOTs depend on two conditions:

1. Telling the truth. People must be willing and able to describe their experiences truthfully, including their feelings, frustrations, and observations. TOOTs do not work in political organizations where secrecy is the norm; and,

2. People must be willing and able to listen to the experiences of others and accept them as valid. They must be willing to overcome their prejudices and stereotypes to see things as they are, and not as they would like them to be.

When TOOTs work, there are usually six outcomes:

1. **Illumination.** People are willing to move beyond their narrow perspectives to see the big picture.

2. **Empathy.** People begin to have more understanding and patience with each other.

3. **Depersonalization.** People start to see the context of others' actions, and so take these actions less personally.

4. **Revitalization.** Instead of simply reacting to others, people put more energy into the work of the system.

5. **Problem solving.** Problems are identified and dealt with, not from the Tops, but from the part of the system where they originate.

6. **Strategic planning.** As people gain understanding of others' worlds, they see how their own actions reduce cooperation and system coordination. They develop strategies to ease problems and promote cooperation and coordination.

Oshry offers several strategies pertaining to whether you are a Top, Middle, Bottom, or Customer. He summarizes these in his Magic Consultant's Card. In general, we need to create a system that is robust and looks after itself. For Tops, this means relinquishing control of the system. Tops tend to pull responsibility to themselves and away from others, so problems do not get solved where they are created. They fixate on protecting the system from turbulence. They assume responsibility to determine the system's fate. Bottoms hold others responsible for their fate and then fear their vulnerability. They never ask why they have tied their fate to these particular Tops. They remain dependent and must either adapt or revolutionize the system. Middles slide between the conflicting agendas and tend to focus on the needs of others at the expense of themselves. Tops need to create a system that is responsible for itself. Bottoms need to assume responsibility for their own contributions to the system's success or failure, and Middles need to use their unique position to coordinate cooperation and ensure that the left hand knows what the right hand is doing. These together define a robust system.

But this is not what the guardians have created. They assume responsibility for the system's direction and ability to be protected from turbulence. They protect the culture from change. Bottoms shun responsibility, and then hold the Tops completely responsible. They are the source of much of the turbulence from which the Tops are protecting the system. Middles are simply that, caught in the middle and ineffective at facilitating cooperation and coordination. The resulting culture is weak rather than robust and is easily assailed by turbulence; hence, the weakness of Father Culture.

We now have the criteria and values to evaluate the quality of proposed decisions, action, and strategies. Let's look at a possible strategic plan to see if it meets all requirements.

Strategic Planning in the Ethical Framework

To provide suggestions, I am going to borrow a tool that is often used in the commercial sectors of our planet to map out a strategy and produce results. It is called a strategy map. I will combine this with a technique called a results chain (borrowed from the Information Technology (IT) sector) to position several initiatives we might undertake to move the world forward down a more positive path. I assume in these suggested actions that the reader sees the system and has overcome the system blindness that otherwise keeps us mired in Father Culture.

I will start by articulating a vision and a mission for humanity:

Vision: To develop a robust system of planetary management that is responsible for itself. To live in peace and harmony with our environment and with each other as individuals, groups, and societies.

Mission: To pursue economic, political, cultural, and religious programs that promote diversity within the closed system of planet Earth for peace and sustainability of the human race, and that reconnect understanding with meaning for all peoples.

Finally, I will restate my objective for this study as an objective for humanity moving forward:

Peace and Sustainability Objective: To produce ethically aware and responsible citizens of Earth (to embrace an Ethical Framework). To ensure that quality thinking stands behind our actions and decisions.

I propose that there are two main problems—the problem of treating diversity as a source of antagonism and aggression, which is the direct result of power systems, and the disconnection of understanding from meaning. We will need at least two broad strategies to reach our objective—an increase-positive-cultural-diversity strategy, and a reconnect-understanding-with-meaning strategy.

Next, to produce a coherent strategic model, I will need to identify all relevant stakeholders in this strategy. For this I suggest that the main stakeholders are: (1) all the citizens of Earth—I call this the human perspective; (2) all people engaged in economic activities—I call this the economic perspective; (3) all politicians and people who manage our political institutions and bureaucracies—I call this the political perspective; and, (4) all those who are involved in religious and cultural activities around the planet—I call this the cultural/religious perspective.

Let's map out these two strategies and what we are looking for from all perspectives. The idea is to provide high-level overviews of how all stakeholders could participate in the two strategies. This, in turn, should lead to some suggestions for initiatives we might undertake to achieve positive results.

First, we will consider the "increase-positive-cultural-differentiations strategy." We begin with outlining the kinds of activities we associate with the Human Perspective in relation to our vision, mission, and the viability and sustainability objective.

For the increase-positive-cultural-differentiations strategy, we seek to work out the attributes of good governance. This breaks down into two further sub-strategies:

1. The development of the Ethical Framework.

2. A robust system of societies and cultures that actively promotes positively balanced individual and cultural diversity.

The first breaks down into two more activities:

a. Increase the quality of our thinking by embracing the criteria provided by ethics, including the underlying thymotic values that are the foundations of the Ethical Framework (the opposite of duuhh). We embrace the two rules of quality thinking. We need to meet all ethical criteria (virtues, consequences, and principles) and balance all thymotic values in a positive way (no cherry-picking).

b. Embrace the resulting moral precepts of the Ethical Framework as the guiding principles for being ethically aware and responsible human beings (i.e., good persons).

The second also breaks down into two activities:

a. That we should each contribute to the positive promotion of cultural and individual diversity (avoid treating our differences as a source of antagonism and aggression).

b. Promote and teach others how diversity is a positive benefit. This means that Tops, Middles, and Bottoms each accept their respective roles and responsibilities within the context of the whole system, such that coordination and cooperation are maintained in the face of change and turbulence.

When we examine the "reconnect-understanding-with-meanings strategy" from the human perspective and in relation to our vision, mission, and viability and sustainability objective, there are two key components of the strategy:

1. Promote positive intercommunal relations across the Earth— robust cooperation and coordination.

2. Embrace the transcultural values associated with our founding ethical values.

The first again breaks into two sub-strategies:

a. Processes that introduce new differentiations. These, in turn:

 + Promote new interaction opportunities that transcend myopic system perspectives (see the context of the whole); and

 + Promote new programs to engage people in positive differentiations.

b. Provisioning social mechanisms for feedback regarding possible new areas for meaningfulness. This suggests:

+ A focus on positively well-managed intercommunity relations (well-coordinated cooperative programs); and

+ Active cultural awareness and exchanges that encourage taking responsibility for our decisions and actions.

When we look at the two strategies side by side in relation to the vision, mission and objective, we produce the following strategy map:

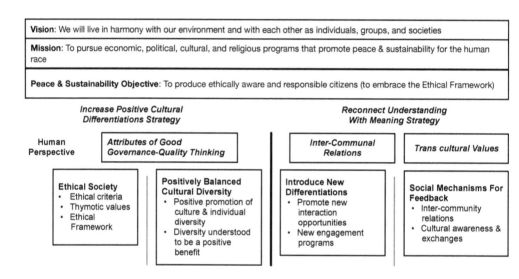

Figure 9.1: Strategy Map – The Human Perspective

The human perspective starts with qualifying good governance. This means we evaluate our leadership using ethical criteria, the four thymotic values, and the precepts of the Ethical Framework. The objective of this part of the strategy is to bring quality thinking to our leaders by imposing the quality measures we use to evaluate their success. We evaluate not only our leaders, but also the Bottoms and Middles. Is everyone in the system seeing the system as a whole and playing their part within it in a way that promotes the whole system, and not just their local and provincial interests? These acts of measuring success can begin the positive promotion of policies and practices toward individual and cultural diversity as a positive benefit. Diversity with harmony becomes a measure of the health of the planetary system and a criterion for evaluating our behaviors.

To begin integrating understanding and meaning from the human perspective, we must strengthen intercommunal actions. Part of the illumination and depersonalization that comes with seeing systems is a new perspective on our place within the whole. The knee-jerk reactions of the dance of blind reflex give way to empathy, and revitalization—working for the system rather than for ourselves. This encourages cooperation and coordination, which are realized with new interaction opportunities and new ways of engaging with each other. In accepting responsibility for the system, we each participate in initiatives that increase coordination activities. Each part of the world starts to care about and acts with sensitivity regarding impacts in other parts.

We treat ethics, thymotic values, and the precepts of the Ethical Framework as transcultural values. We use the measures for success as feedback mechanisms to improve intercommunity relations (increased cooperation), which in turn encourage more and greater cultural awareness and exchanges, and a general sympathy for the whole.

We now consider the two strategies from the economic perspective. Here, we are really looking for an *Earth productivity* strategy. This is the economic version of the attributes of good governance in the human perspective. There are two broad strategies from the economic perspective:

1. Establishing a realistic cost structure. This means:

   a. Aligning costs/prices with proper energy/resource utilization accounting;

   b. Improving the effectiveness and efficiencies of our production systems; and

   c. Improving our coordination and distribution systems.

2. More effective and efficient use of our resources:

   a. Better management of our resource capacities, such as waste reduction and conservation; and

   b. Coordinating human and knowledge capital (to be defined below) as the driver for these improved efficiencies.

In general, we are trying to solve five major problems in global economic terms. We need to raise the standards of living for all the citizens of Earth to bring all humans to the standard of living of modern Western societies. This means that we at least meet some minimum standards for the very poor. We need products and services that are affordable to all. Production processes need to be effective and efficient in their use of energy and resources and need to minimize waste. We need products and services that meet minimum quality and safety standards, and which are life-enhancing toward improving the quality of life for all peoples. We need effective and efficient coordination and distribution capabilities. It does little good to have effective production if we cannot get the products and services to those who need them. Again, this is of vital importance for necessities. We need adequate selection with many options and choices for consumers to meet the increasingly diverse needs a diversity-promoting strategy entails. Finally, our economic models need to ensure that products and services are functional and do not waste precious resources in frivolous ways.

In the reconnect-understandings-with-meanings strategy, the economic perspective is really about increasing opportunities for people to contribute to the economic potentials of all individuals and societies. It is about *economic stability* and growing economies within the closed system of intercommunal relations (rather than by geographic expansion). For example, we want to enhance economic participation in such a way that increasing diversification creates new codependency webs, which further create new differentiations, and so on. We are seeking to raise the standard of living for all peoples by creating opportunities to enhance the ways in which people might interconnect in how they provide and consume needed products and services.

Economic stability involves two key components:

1. Expand economic activities through the development of new differentiations and codependency webs; and

2. Enhance the codependency webs of global communal interactions. This can only be done if we improve the economic viability of all societies.

The second point is really about enhancing social values as measured in economic terms.

If we map out these strategies in relation to what we have already mapped out, we get the following:

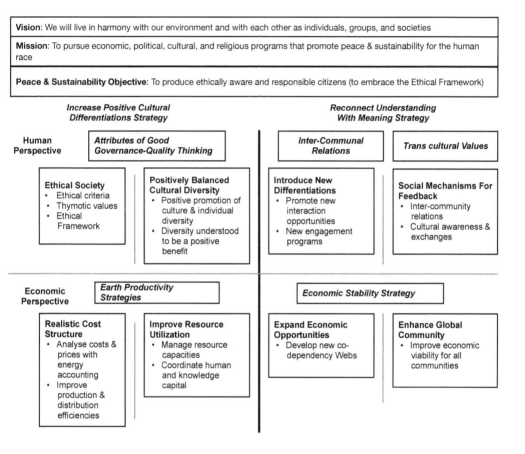

Vision: We will live in harmony with our environment and with each other as individuals, groups, and societies

Mission: To pursue economic, political, cultural, and religious programs that promote peace & sustainability for the human race

Peace & Sustainability Objective: To produce ethically aware and responsible citizens (to embrace the Ethical Framework)

Increase Positive Cultural Differentiations Strategy

Reconnect Understanding With Meaning Strategy

Human Perspective

Attributes of Good Governance-Quality Thinking

Inter-Communal Relations

Trans cultural Values

Ethical Society
- Ethical criteria
- Thymotic values
- Ethical Framework

Positively Balanced Cultural Diversity
- Positive promotion of culture & individual diversity
- Diversity understood to be a positive benefit

Introduce New Differentiations
- Promote new interaction opportunities
- New engagement programs

Social Mechanisms For Feedback
- Inter-community relations
- Cultural awareness & exchanges

Economic Perspective

Earth Productivity Strategies

Economic Stability Strategy

Realistic Cost Structure
- Analyse costs & prices with energy accounting
- Improve production & distribution efficiencies

Improve Resource Utilization
- Manage resource capacities
- Coordinate human and knowledge capital

Expand Economic Opportunities
- Develop new co-dependency Webs

Enhance Global Community
- Improve economic viability for all communities

Figure 9.2: Strategy Map – The Economic Perspective

This brings us to the political perspective. The political perspective really involves ways to integrate our various political systems into governance mechanisms that promote world order as a global system. Here, there are two components to the strategy. The first is how we develop and manage our political processes and institutions, and the second is what I call our citizen management processes.

1. Political Processes and Institutions. These are the processes and institutions that promote cultural diversity in a positively balanced and harmonious way. These activities give ethics priority (no more duuhh) and embed ethical criteria into our political accountability measures as the practices of good governance. For example, we always ask if the politician or institution promotes life and liberty and treats people equitably and fairly. Are our political leaders always respectful of others, regardless of cultural or other differences? Have they identified and are they acting on right principles (no basis for complaint if they were treated the same way)?

2. Citizen Management Processes. These are the processes and institutions that enhance citizen participation in political processes. The strategy promotes and distributes Top responsibility and asks Bottoms and Middles to accept more responsibility. The system becomes more robust and able to look after itself. Because democracy is the only political system we know of where we can overturn incompetent or tyrannical rulers by peaceful means, we are typically pointing to the various representational political systems, such as parliaments, assemblies, electoral systems, and democratic forums.

How we modify our political systems to embrace positive diversity will determine how difficult it will be to move toward these objectives. Without well-constructed and well-run political institutions with a real focus on ethics and with real accountabilities, without Tops relinquishing responsibilities to the system, no political leadership will move us toward our objective. How well our leaders develop and manage these kinds of institutions forms our basis for what constitutes effective political leadership. If we are going to take democracy seriously, we need to improve the ways in which all people can and do contribute to our political decisions—not just locally, but globally. For example, in the recent attempts at globalizing our economies, many protests led to violence and the destruction of property. Events such as these should signal that our political leaders have not provided effective mechanisms for people to participate in such processes in peaceful ways. If our leaders do not provision for adequate representation, they have no one but themselves to blame when those who oppose them seek less-than-peaceful means. If the Tops want to avoid the turbulence of revolutionizing Bottoms who want to accept more responsibility for the system, they must implement policies and practices that facilitate it. In the absence of proper representation, people have no other peaceful means of participating.

In the reconnecting-understandings-with-meanings strategy, we are really talking about social stability in the political perspective. From a values point of view, two political contributions increase diversification and create new codependency webs:

1. Innovate processes designed to promote codependency webs, such as opportunities to contribute, as well as infrastructure support to encourage engagement. Ethical principles and values promote a view that we want everyone to contribute to the whole community to their full potential. This is the basis of connecting understanding with meaning. This means we must provide the financial, educational, and health infrastructure to facilitate full and meaningful contributions; and,

2. Improve communities through superior regulatory and social processes. This involves active attention to public goods, such as the environment, health and safety, education, and positive intercommunity relations.

In this strategy, we seek ways for our political institutions to promote the kinds of community values and community relations that encourage people to find meaning in various ways. The strategy really encourages participation in and responsibility for the public good. Active support for systemic community benefits requires active and positive political capabilities that are supportive of such values and activities (Figure 9.3).

Finally, we arrive at the cultural/religious perspective. Here, we define the other capitals beyond political and economic. From this perspective, we are really talking about our capabilities, knowledge, and organizational capital. Social scientists call these social technologies, such as organizational structures (in contrast to physical technologies) to facilitate and promote cooperation and coordination. The modern business enterprise, parliamentary organizations, and nongovernmental organizations (NGOs) are examples of social technologies. Our values determine what roles we can play in our communities, outside of politics and economics. Teachers, clerics, artists, and so on, all provide the basis for human

Vision: We will live in harmony with our environment and with each other as individuals, groups, and societies

Mission: To pursue economic, political, cultural, and religious programs that promote peace & sustainability for the human race

Peace & Sustainability Objective: To produce ethically aware and responsible citizens (to embrace the Ethical Framework)

Increase Positive Cultural Differentiations Strategy

Reconnect Understanding With Meaning Strategy

Human Perspective

Attributes of Good Governance-Quality Thinking

Inter-Communal Relations

Trans cultural Value

Ethical Society
- Ethical criteria
- Thymotic values
- Ethical Framework

Positively Balanced Cultural Diversity
- Positive promotion of culture & individual diversity
- Diversity understood to be a positive benefit

Introduce New Differentiations
- Promote new interaction opportunities
- New engagement programs

Social Mechanisms F Feedback
- Inter-community relations
- Cultural awareness exchanges

Economic Perspective

Earth Productivity Strategies

Economic Stability Strategy

Realistic Cost Structure
- Analyse costs & prices with energy accounting
- Improve production & distribution efficiencies

Improve Resource Utilization
- Manage resource capacities
- Coordinate human and knowledge capital

Expand Economic Opportunities
- Develop new co-dependency Webs

Enhance Global Community
- Improve economic viability for all communities

Political Perspective

World Order Strategies

Social Stability Strategies

Political Processes & Institutions
- Political processes & institutions that promote cultural diversity in a positively balanced way
- Ethics priority
- Accountability

Citizen Management Processes
- Processes & institutions that enhance citizen participation
- Representational systems
  - Parliaments
  - Electoral systems
  - Forums

Innovation Processes
- Processes & institutions that promote co-dependency webs
- Opportunities to contribute
- Financial support
- Education support

Regulatory & social Processes
- Processes that improve communities
- Environment
- Health & safety
- Education
- Inter-community relations

Figure 9.3: Strategy Map – The Political Perspective

capabilities and skills. These, in turn, have some dependencies on our knowledge base, and these both are enabled or not within our organizational structure. We know that some organizations are more effective than others, so organizational capital can influence events. Organizational capital is measured in terms of leadership and community. We have the criteria for evaluating the quality of thinking of our leadership. We evaluate community based on how well each of the organization's parts sees the whole system and acts accordingly. This is the measure of how robust our global communities are, and how self-supporting they are. Leaders who fail to distribute responsibilities, or Bottoms who refuse to accept responsibility, all fail to see the whole and so keep the community mired in antagonistic and aggressive behaviors. Such communities continue to promote the mere sense of community rather than real community. We seek communities that promote an authentic person who finds their place through the community and not of or by the community. This is measured in part through the number and quality of codependency webs and the new diversities that are supported and encouraged. Remember that Tops who assume total responsibility for the system attempt to control the system through divide-and-conquer strategies that minimize the turbulence that increasing diversity would bring to the system. Change and new diversity opportunities are a direct measure of the health of the community as a systemic social organization.

In Chapter 6, I outlined how science works and its current future trends. As complexity and synergetics models become increasingly sophisticated, science will get much better at predicting real-world phenomena in the sense of systemic effects of scientific knowledge application. This will give scientists a better knowledge base with new tools to assume more responsibility for that knowledge being used in accordance with the precepts of a scientific moral Framework. This increase in knowledge capital will start to include responsible uses of scientific research and their potential applications. As social sciences converge with new understandings of social pattern dynamics, scientists will not just discover knowledge for knowledge's sake, but for humanity's sake, as well. As the economic and political systems evolve toward more productive and globally responsible systemic behaviors, these new social understandings will introduce new

Vision: We will live in harmony with our environment and with each other as individuals, groups, and societies
Mission: To pursue economic, political, cultural, and religious programs that promote peace & sustainability for the human race
Peace & Sustainability Objective: To produce ethically aware and responsible citizens (to embrace the Ethical Framework)

Increase Positive Cultural Differentiations Strategy

Reconnect Understanding With Meaning Strategy

Human Perspective

Attributes of Good Governance-Quality Thinking

Inter-Communal Relations

Trans cultural Values

Ethical Society
- Ethical criteria
- Thymotic values
- Ethical Framework

Positively Balanced Cultural Diversity
- Positive promotion of culture & individual diversity
- Diversity understood to be a positive benefit

Introduce New Differentiations
- Promote new interaction opportunities
- New engagement programs

Social Mechanisms For Feedback
- Inter-community relations
- Cultural awareness & exchanges

Economic Perspective

Earth Productivity Strategies

Economic Stability Strategy

Realistic Cost Structure
- Analyse costs & prices with energy accounting
- Improve production & distribution efficiencies

Improve Resource Utilization
- Manage resource capacities
- Coordinate human and knowledge capital

Expand Economic Opportunities
- Develop new co-dependency Webs

Enhance Global Community
- Improve economic viability for all communities

Political Perspective

World Order Strategies

Social Stability Strategies

Political Processes & Institutions
- Political processes & institutions that promote cultural diversity in a positively balanced way
- Ethics priority
- Accountability

Citizen Management Processes
- Processes & institutions that enhance citizen participation
- Representational systems
  - Parliaments
  - Electoral systems
  - Forums

Innovation Processes
- Processes & institutions that promote co-dependency webs
- Opportunities to contribute
- Financial support
- Education support

Regulatory & social Processes
- Processes that improve communities
  - Environment
  - Health & safety
  - Education
  - Inter-community relations

Cultural/Religious Perspective

Human Capital
- Capabilities
- Skills

Knowledge Capital
- Science
- Technology

Organizational Capital
- Leadership
- Community

Figure 9.4: Strategy Map – The Cultural/Religious Perspective

institutions and social methods. The current use of scientific knowledge to enhance guardian power will begin to dissipate in favor of overall enhancement for humanity. As Tops relinquish responsibility to the masses, and as the masses accept more responsibility and increase participation in global policies and directions, science can be harnessed to complete the man over man part of Schweitzer's rational formula for the success of civilization. Civilization can use this new kind of knowledge to enhance social technologies to promote greater cooperation and coordination, thus improving overall, beneficial systemic consequences of decisions and actions.

One of my main theses is that we need to grant priority to ethics over traditional religious and cultural values. This introduces a new factor in our presentation. I illustrate this by graying out the religious and cultural values that cut across our various capacities (Figure 9.5).

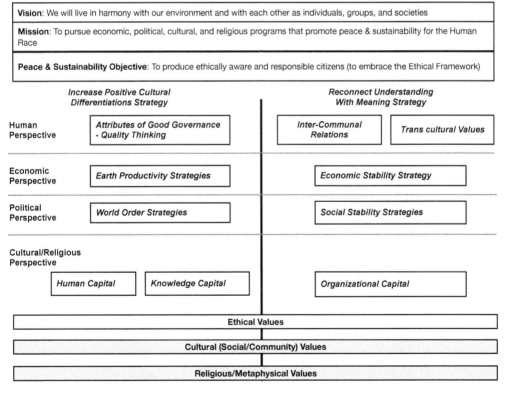

Figure 9.5: Strategy Map – Ethical Priority

With this overview we can see how all stakeholders contribute the main objective of a viable and sustainable future for humanity, and how the strategy works toward the vision and mission of the strategic exercise. We have some idea of what is needed, but how do we actually get there? What are some specific initiatives that we could undertake to realize our vision?

To present opportunities, we first need to examine our strategy in terms of specific step-by-step results. Any old initiatives or activities will not do. We need to find a starting point. We also need to visualize how the elements of the strategy hang together. What are the dependencies? What parts of the strategy could be done in parallel? Are there links that would be important if we were to undertake this strategy as a plan?

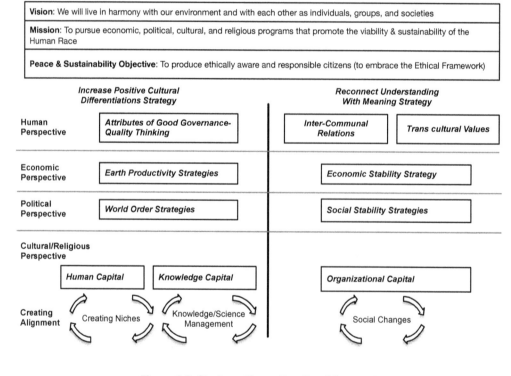

Figure 9.6: Strategy Map – Creating Alignment

The keys here are to ensure that we create alignment between the diversified niches we consider, the knowledge and science we will deploy, and the social changes that are reasonable to propose and work toward. To do this, I propose that we consider our targets as results to be obtained, and then work backward to determine what needs to happen to achieve those results.

Results Chain

The technique for sorting out these questions is called a *results chain*. The idea is to treat each element of our strategy map as a specific result we are trying to achieve, and then work out what we would need to do to get there. Results chains provide a powerful tool for visualizing what is needed. In Figure 9.2, we started with the components of the strategy map from each stakeholder. We now consider these to be results instead of strategic elements. The rounded boxes represent initiatives or activities that we could undertake to produce the sought-after results. The connectors point to the dependency relationships between initiatives and results. They also indicate horizontal relations between the two strategies that could be coordinated to activities running in parallel with each other. We read from the bottom to top to see the order of initiatives.

We start with the ethical criteria and thymotic values understood in their positive sense as natural life, natural liberty, natural equality, and respect for the person (natural tolerance). I suggest that we start with human capital—just taking stock of who we are as a species. We need a global inventory of our capabilities and skills. This starts to define who we are as a species, rather than who we are as Americans, or Chinese, or Christians, or Hindus, and so on. This work has begun, but it is far from complete. Although we track professionals, such as doctors and academics, we do not really have an inventory of the number of engineers, bankers, entrepreneurs, or other skilled labor in existence. While this might seem like a daunting task, it is important to know what we are capable of if we are to use all our human resources effectively.

Another inventory we need is an inventory of what we know both scientifically and technologically. R. Buckminster Fuller, who founded the World Game Laboratories, began this work in the mid-1970s. Under the direction of Medard Gable, the institute produced two volumes,

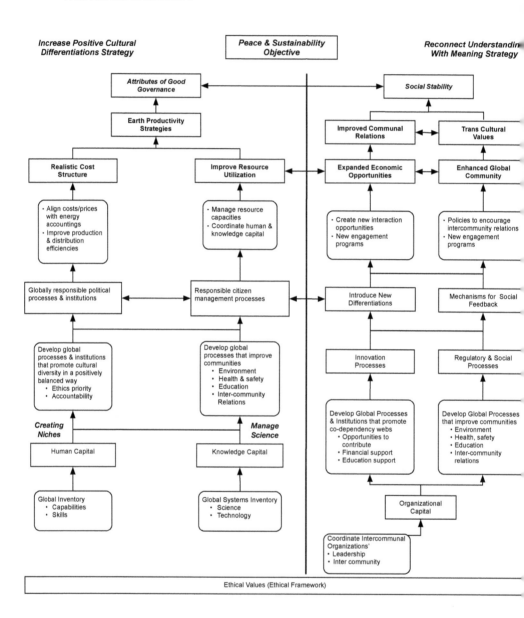

Figure 9.7: Strategy Map – Results Chain

Energy, Earth, and Everyone, and *Ho-Ping: Food for Everyone.* These works essentially provide a mid-1970s inventory of the science, technologies, and techniques for producing enough energy and food for all humans. Although this presents a great start, we have learned much since this effort, and these works need to be updated and made more available.

Next, we need an initiative to find ways to measure the effectiveness and efficiency of our social technologies to induce cooperation and coordination. We need to know what works and what does not in our organizations and communities to enhance the effectiveness of intercommunity relations and support. Whereas we know some of this for aid programs and many NGO efforts, we are not really very effective as a species at coordinating these efforts. We do not see all organizations as parts of a larger whole, because each operates as its own silo, without the benefits of interorganizational cooperation and coordination. For example, there are periodic interreligious meetings to work out ways and means of coordinating common values and reducing religious strife. However, these tend not to be coordinated with economic or political forums. It is as though each stakeholder perspective makes its own coordination efforts (which are more or less effective), but there is little cross-coordination across stakeholder perspectives. We think in parts without regard for the whole. We continue the behavior patterns that lead to antagonism and aggression. The result is that much falls through the cracks. If we can close these gaps and better coordinate all stakeholder perspectives, we will be much better organized overall to deal with the issues that seem to touch all stakeholder interests. I call this improved capability *organizational capital,* such that it is a goal to increase this kind of wealth.

With a more complete and accurate understanding of who we are, what we know, and how to organize ourselves, we are better positioned to produce more effective overall results toward our viability and sustainability objectives. These new understandings will directly impact our assessment of the political perspective and can lead to two new initiatives.

The first is to provide a basis for a more complete assessment of the policies and actions of our political leaders. Are they using our resources to the best advantage for all, or only to enrich themselves? How accountable are they for their actions and decisions? Do they think with quality, or are they just giving us more duuhh?

Some examples of a more positive approach would be to hold a world conference of all leaders—and not just representatives—but actual decision-makers. Part of what we need to do is change our language. There are no official world leaders. While there are a few diplomats who concern themselves with world issues, our national leaders are just that—leaders of small principalities who are being paid to think small in purely provincial terms. We also know that the best way to vilify an opponent is to keep them faceless and relatively anonymous—to deny them any identity that might be a positive value. The result is that although initial provincial leader conferences might not accomplish much, the symbolic value would be immense. Just having all provincial leaders actually meet and shake hands or sit in the same room means that the real decision-makers are meeting to discuss global issues and work toward agreeable solutions. As mentioned above, some adult supervision might be required for these conferences.

Another initiative could be to increase the number of people we pay to look after global interests. Consider that today, with a world population of approximately 7.6 billion people in 2018, we pay only a few thousand people (usually in the UN and affiliate organizations) at most to look after world interests. Even at that, the wealthiest nations in the world rarely pay their fees on time. We do not take caring for the world very seriously. We need to take steps to beef up our support for groups that look out for global interests and see that they are properly funded to do their work. A key criterion for the ethical evaluation of any provincial leader should be that they support such programs. Better still, do our provincial leaders actually defer to global interests because they see the whole system, or do they try to act as independents without regard to the consequences of their actions on other parts of the system?

A second political approach is to develop processes and institutions to enhance global citizen participation in the political process. These might include global assemblies such as the UN General Assembly, but with more participants than just provincial diplomats, global forums for plebiscites and referendums to all peoples, or other forums for people to have a voice in world affairs. Again, democracy is the only system we know of where we can remove corrupt, incompetent, or tyrannical rulers by peaceful means. This idea cuts two ways. First, we need to enhance democratic institutions for all peoples as a way to reduce much of the world's violence. Also, we need to ensure a proper democratic approach to global programs. Again, and at the risk of repeating myself, when the World Bank initiated its globalist program, there were many demonstrations that led to violence and much property damage. This should be perceived as a simple failure. The globalist organizations failed to provide adequate mechanisms for dissenting views, so they left dissenters no choice but to demonstrate and cause violence. In a very real sense, the World Bank and its globalizing supporters share the blame for the violence. We have known for approximately 5,000 years that when you deny people adequate mechanism for dissent, they tend to turn aggressive. You would think that the World Bank globalist supporters would know this by now and provide adequate and legitimate means for opposing views. Duuhh! While this does not excuse the violence, it does indicate the kinds of considerations we need to make when we propose large-scale global programs.

There are many NGOs that provide a wide range of services. Could we not use some of these groups to facilitate various forums for peaceful discussion of key issues? Of course, this need for coordination meshes precisely with the kind of increased organizational capital discussed above. The answer could be yes if we took the time to coordinate efforts between these organizations and other international bodies. There is much overlap and waste in uncoordinated organizations. If we cannot coordinate organizational behaviors, how will we ever promote cooperation? To promote organizational capital more completely, we need to develop global processes and relations to build cooperative and coordinating codependency webs across and between institutions. Politically, we need ways and means to provide more opportunities for people to contribute to global programs and the political support for these programs with adequate funding, education, and any other means.

This idea of developing codependency webs will be one of the most severely challenged initiatives. For example, recall that local/provincial interests won out over the proposal to create a global electrical energy grid. We missed a golden opportunity to develop a coordinating and cooperative codependency web of energy for all. Duuhh!

We really need to catch on to a simple reality. We are already an interconnected global system of systems in myriad ways, many of which already impose significant codependency relationships. I am proposing that we do this somewhat intelligently so that we improve the efficiency and effectiveness of our resource use. If we cannot get the politicians on board, the economic benefits will not follow.

A simple way to begin this process is to develop more effective and efficient processes that improve communities around the world. Again, today, we do this in a rather haphazard manner through charities and some NGOs. But well-coordinated group dynamics that increase organizational capital could focus on improving local environments, health and safety, or mechanisms to improve intercommunity relations. All of these require political support and political activity. We are wasting precious food and energy resources not only through poor use of technology, but also by localizing use where broader deployments would more effectively enhance the resource usage. Many communities reinvent the wheel to deliver basic services that have already been established elsewhere and could just be expanded to include a new community. The result is that competing stakeholder perspectives increase the ineffectiveness of proposed solutions and add waste to the system. Of course, these wastes are often seen as preferable in the context of local provincial interests, so it is important to identify systemic opportunities and hold political leaders accountable for their failure to act in the context of the whole.

Were we to move in these directions, the results would include more globally responsible leaders, more adequate and peaceful participation in our various political processes, and new innovations to increase code-pendency webs, thus creating more niches for contributions by members of communities that are healthy, educated, and working with other communities, rather than opposing them. These improvements would lead, in turn, to new differentiations, and improved social feedback mechanisms for peaceful participation in strategic programs.

This level of political support would induce some economic initiatives. First, with the increase in codependency webs, it will be much easier to begin to align costs with real energy accounting to encourage more efficient resource use and reduce waste. Improved cooperative community relations would also introduce opportunities to improve product and service distribution capabilities to make more products and services available to more people in more communities—with the result of a more realistic economic cost structure comes the economic incentive to manage our resources more effectively. Notice that this refers not only to natural resources, but also to human, knowledge, and organizational resources.

Improved economic accounting, combined with better-managed resources, would present opportunities for initiatives to create new intercommunal interactions, including offering more people the opportunity to participate economically. We want all people to contribute to our overall community to their full potential. Imagine what we can accomplish if all people were to contribute at that level. Science, art, community, religion, commerce, and politics would all benefit from such energy. This new energy would manifest itself as policies to encourage more participation, and more differentiation, including more effective use of the improved organizational capital we would have achieved. These initiatives would result in an enhanced global community with expanded economic opportunities for all (within the closed global economic system). It would make it easier for more people to see the system as a whole and work for the system.

Altogether, we would arrive at a state where we could begin to improve our earth productivity strategies continuously, based on improved intercommunal relations and transcultural values—quality thinking, leading to improved cooperation and coordination. Together, these would result in the attributes of good governance and social stability. The system would start becoming robust enough to look after itself.

These are where our two overall strategies meet toward the viability and sustainability objective. The adequate and effective use of our skills, knowledge and organizational capacities will increase positive cultural differentiations. When these are supported politically and economically, they will produce increasing systemic cooperating results that will reconnect understanding with meaning. Well-formed codependency webs create new differentiations, which lead to new codependency webs. With many more opportunities for social, political, economic, and spiritual participation come many more opportunities for people to find meaning in a modern scientific, global community.

The end result is not just that we meet our viability and sustainability objectives. The whole process effectively reinforces the Ethical Framework for how to think about ourselves and the world around us. We promote cultural diversity in a positive way, enriching the cultural diversity while increasing harmonization across the planet, and we reconnect scientific understanding with meaning in new and exciting ways. Embracing natural ethics as the foundation of our societies effectively grounds a new kind of civilization—a civilization that is different in kind from any that has gone before, and that presents a most promising future for all humanity.

The Ethical Society

In this book I have argued that the world is a mess—a mess of our own creation. We got into this mess through the historical accumulation of common ways of thinking and behaving. Our civilization has evolved globally in a completely arbitrary and ad hoc way. We are, and always have been out of control as a species.

We live in a time of the accumulated global systemic effects of these ways of thinking and behaving. Our religiocentric civilizations based on power structures that promote divisive, antagonistic, and aggressive have versus have-not systems keep us out of control and unable to affect the kinds of global systemic changes we need for a sustainable future.

But a new way of thinking is slowly developing. A global awareness is emerging. A new global civilization is emerging that is different in kind from the older religiocentered cultures. But true to human form, this new awareness is emerging in an arbitrary and ad hoc way. This condemns humanity to more of the same. As noted above, Einstein pointed out that we cannot solve problems with the same kind of thinking that created the problem in the first place. He also pointed out that doing the same thing over and over, and expecting a different result is a kind of insanity. More of the same is at best the wrong kind of thinking, and at worst a kind of insanity.

In traditional ethical thinking it is usual to contrast personal worldviews with collective worldviews. For example, Universalism (Deontological) ethics is about personal duties, and the kinds of ethical values that promote right decisions and actions. Likewise, Consequentialist ethics tries to direct personal actions to promote the greater good. The program for ethics is to get to a just society. This happens when we all embed ethical values and principles into our personal world views. The idea is that that if we each behave with proper ethical considerations, if we each are serious about our moral and social responsibilities, the community gets the overall benefits of collective personal right thinking. The collective world view is shaped by the accumulated effects of aligned personal worldviews. We get a just society.

I argue that this is backwards. This approach seriously and significantly underestimates the extent to which personal worldviews are structured and shaped by the collective worldview in which we, as individuals, live. The Frameworks of our various and sundry cultures (our various cultural worldviews) both shape and determine how we understand the world and find meaning in our lives. We cannot belong to a community and not be shaped by the collective worldview in which we live.

It turns out that as as species we are quite good at building what we might call single purpose societies, such as a militaristic (Sparta), Imperialistic (Rome and Great Britain), or Theocratic (Europe in the Middle ages, and Islamic State). These all work by designing a Framework based on the values that promote the desired purpose, and then building a grass roots movement of individual world views that are brought into alignment. But so far all these designer societies have been based on values that are purely parochial, with short term intentions. We have never tried this with values that are intended to be universal and long term.

With this in mind, I argue that the we must take at least some control over this new and emerging global world view if we are to truly change for the benefit of all. The idea is to see the whole world as a system (to overcome system blindness), but based on proper global universal values and understanding. Ethics, informed by science is the only mechanism we have to do this. Ethics and science are both global and universal in the sense that they are trans-cultural systems of thought that can guide personal behaviors and collective decisions and actions. But rather than wait for a supposed accumulation of personal worldview alignments, we take control at the other end. If we can create a kind of global, collective groupthink based on ethics and informed by science, this new collective worldview will structure and shape our respective personal worldviews. This is how we will get everyone on the same page.

It is time to take some control over our destiny as a species. It is time to behave as a species and not just a loose collection of out of control individuals and communities. It is time to hold our leaders accountable against the standard of quality thinking that ethics provides. It is time to see the world as a whole based on the kinds of values that move us beyond our traditional ways of thinking and behaving. It is time to put ethics on the front burner. It is time to create a world culture that promotes the values that will unleash full human potential.

APPENDIX A

The Process of Practical Ethical Thinking

Ethical theories are often treated as closed models with each type of ethical system presented as a fait au complete. But this fails to extend theoretical models into practical actions in the practical world.

It is usual in ethical considerations that when we find ourselves in a situation, call it situation X, our first question is, what I should do in this situation? Theorists then try to apply an ethical theory to that situation to determine what action "ought" to lead to an ethical result within the criteria specified by the theory.

All of this is based on a single assumption that we intend to do good deeds, however we define the word 'good'. This is what Kant called *good intentions*. If we do not have good intentions, why would we even ask about what we should do in any situation. All ethical acts depend on this, at least to some extent, so it would be useful to understand exactly what this might mean. The phrase 'good intentions' is a notoriously vague idea. How could we define this better? We could characterize the idea with what are called *indicator behaviors*.

Let's consider a non-moral example to illustrate this idea of indicator behaviors[94]. Another fuzzy idea would be the word *attitude*. Suppose you are my boss, and you say to me, "Carruthers I'll have to fire you. You have a bad attitude." What could you possibly mean?

I ask, "What in my behavior leads you to conclude that I have a bad attitude?" You respond, "You are often late for work. Your dress is

---

94 Take from Robert F. Mager, Goal Analysis Pages 15-22.

inappropriate for the office environment, and people complain that your work is late."

I can now respond, "So if I show up on time, properly dressed, and present my work on time, you will agree that I have improved my attitude?

You will have no choice but to agree, since that is how you defined your complaint. The point is, if you can do this for something as vague as attitude, we can do it for anything, including 'good intentions'.

So, what might be the indicator behaviors of good intentions? I propose a list something as follows:

1. Honesty (veracity)

2. Integrity

3. Genuine concern for the welfare of others,

4. Social responsibility

5. Accountability

It turns out that we already have an ethical discipline that defines these indicator behaviors – virtue ethics. Virtue ethics is grounded in the Greek idea of Eudaimonia – human flourishing. The idea is to build the kind of character that follows the virtues for a "well-lived life". While there is considerable variation in what should be on the list – what constitutes a virtue - there is a general consensus on the 5 items in my list. In practice we can add to this list as we go. The idea would be to garner consensus on a base list that is more extensive than mine, that we can use as a general guide to good intentions.

With this starting assumption, I propose that we move question 1, "What ought I to do in situation X?", to question number three. We can now develop a standardized process for getting to an ethical result.

Question number one is Kant's primary question, "how do we need to think to be able to correctly answer question number 3"?

Kant's ethical theory as presnted in the *Critique of Practical Reason* is based on two assumptions that arer the results of his *Critique of Pure Reason*:

1. All experience is phenomenal. As such, it is inherently subjective. Our primal subjectivity is a core condition of having experience. For example, we each experience the world from an absolute ontological perspective or point of view. No one can experience the world through my eyes or perspective except me. This inherent subjectivity exposes us to charges of solipsism in epistemology. But we don't believe in solipsism for a very good reason. We are able to transcend the subjectivity of personal experience to derive causal laws. A causes B causes C, regardless of individual or personal points of view or perspectives. This is how science works. It tunes out all subjective factors. If you present your hypothesis correctly (do the math correctly) and provide empirical observational results following accepted scientific empirical procedures, the result is scientific. It does not matter what language you speak, the color of your hair or skin, your race, sex, creed, religious belief, or sexual orientation. These are all irrelevant to the scientific proceedings. On the other hand, if you bring in any of these subjective factors the "science" is questionable.

2. We cannot escape the subjective conditions of experience, but we can and do transcend it. There must be a "transcendental logic" that enables us to do this. This is the point of Kant's whole program. In his *Critique of Pure Reason*. Kant thinks he has worked out how we accomplish this is with his categories of pure reason. This is how we get to true objective understanding. We transcend the conditions of experience by reasoning "categorically".

While it is unclear in Kant's discourse exactly how the categories enable such a transcendental outcome (Hegel didn't think they did – he thought the categories are just empty forms), it is clear that Kant considers this a prerequisite for proper reasoning, hence proper moral thinking. That is, correct moral thinking is scientific using the categories.

This is how Kant answers question number one. To correctly answer what I have called question number three (what should I do in situation X), it is imperative that we transcend the uniqueness of our subjective experiences. To do this it is imperative that we reason categorically, that is scientifically. This is the definition of the *categorical imperative*. We must tune out all subjective aspects of our experience. Language, race, color, sex, creed, religious belief, sexual orientation etc. are irrelevant to how we will correctly answer question number 3.

This sets the stage for how to think, but does not tell us what to think about, and that brings us to question number 2.

As with good scientific practice, we should observe the situation as completely as possible to garner the facts of the case. We make our observations and gather our facts as objectively as possible. We want to avoid missing relevant facts that might prejudice our choice of actions about what to do. We also want to gather facts in an unprejudiced way so we understand them objectively. We want to understand situation X as completely as possible. The intent would be a profound understanding of situation X. How would we characterize situation X? How did this situation arise? Who else is involved, or could be impacted in this situation? What are my choices of possible actions? It is this last consideration that allows us to move forward.[95]

Let's consider that we have applied good scientific observational skills to situation X, and we think we understand the situation well enough to consider possible actions. We determine that there are three possible course of action that could yield an ethical outcome. We could do action A, action B, or action C. How to decide which action to do?

The answer is to examine potential consequences in the light of normative criteria. These are based on what we called "good intentions". You desire to bring about a moral result. Mill and Bentham provided the answer for how to do this.

Mill and Bentham supposed that we must examine all available alternatives in situation X and select the action that maximizes positive good. We want to bring about the greatest good for the greatest number. We at least want to minimize potential harms. With this in mind, we can evaluate our options, A, B, and C, to determine as best we can, which course of

---

95 There are many multi-step forms available on the Internet to fill in these details such as the Ten Step Method of Decision-making by Jon Pekel and Doug Wallace or my Eleven Step variation found on my author Website (Ethical Society.ca).

action best meets our criteria. That is, which action appears to best meet our intention to do good. This is the ethical theory of Utilitarianism.

While how we define 'good', is not clear, we can continue to use indicator behaviors to clarify what we mean. Utilitarian ethics looks for potential benefits described in terms of utility or happiness, and using a kind of normative calculus advocates actions that bring about the greatest benefits to the greatest number. This seems to be a good description of what we might mean by the consequences of good intentions.

Let's say that we gather all the facts about situation X, and decide on action A as the correct thing to do. As good scientific thinkers (categorial reasoners), how can we verify or not that we have made the correct or best choice? First, we consider our choice of action A to be an hypothesis. Being good scientific reasoners, we need to validate our hypothesis. However, we are now in what we might call normative space rather than descriptive space, so we can't conduct experiments to validate or refute our hypothesis, so we need some other method.

To validate that we reasoned correctly – that we did tune out all subjective factors is akin to checking our math in descriptive science. We do this by assessing for any subjective factors. Would you have everyone, regardless of language, race, sex, color, creed, religious beliefs, and sexual orientation etc. do action A when in situation X? This is the first test that you are reasoning correctly to answer question 3.

We can then examine the actual consequences that obtained, and assess whether we did indeed achieve a greater good, or minimized harms. This provides an empirical validation of our well-reasoned hypothesis about action A.

We can now put this together as a structured process. Assuming good intentions, you apply categorical reasoning to gather all relevant facts regarding situation X. With objective understanding, you now have an idea of your options for potential action. By next examining the potential consequences of each potential action, measured against your good intentions to maximize good and prevent potential harms, you select your action. In this case you selected action A as best meeting the criteria of your good intentions. This action appears to maximize overall good with minimum harms.

We do action A as selected.

But the process does not end there. We can now do an empirical test of the results of our decision. By introducing consequences, we can now go into descriptive space and check to see if we did get the positive result we intended. Did our choice of action meet the criteria of our intended decision? This is an empirical test of the results of our deliberations and actions.

Overall, we must, being of virtuous character, first have good intentions. From here, we must reason objectively, and select the option that best aligns with our good intentions. We can then check both that we reasoned correctly and that we achieved the results we intended. If we failed, we can now examine why we failed.

Were we less than honest? Did we not understand situation X correctly? Were there potential consequences we didn't see? Did we fail to act with appropriate integrity? Was how we tried to get there that failed? And so on.

The point is, that this thinking is closed loop in the sense that it is based on our virtuous character, and desiring a moral outcome, which prompted us to ask the moral question to begin with. We have a methodology that includes correct reasoning, assessing potential courses of action, and criteria for choosing what to do and how to do it. We also have two methods for reviewing our behavior (right reasoning and examining consequences) that provide feedback on what worked and what didn't. All of this is a basis for continuous improvement towards better and better moral decision making. The process is, like science, self-correcting.

This also reinforces the opportunities to understand precedents. Both Rule Utilitarian and Rule Deontological ethics develop rules or moral guidelines for characterizing various similar situations. In such and such situations, following rule R1 tends to result in a consequent that meets the requirements of good intentions. While such rules are really guiding principles of behavior, they provide a basis for some consistency in ethical behaviors. Rules also simplify action selection. If we have an objective understanding of situation X, we can now ask if the rule applies. If so, we have a better understanding of likely consequences. In situations like

X, action A tends to result in consequence C1 – which more often han not, tends to be the ethical result we intended.

Of course, we cannot jump to rule behaviors in the absence of understanding that situation X does indeed qualify for the rule, or blindly enforce rules without having completed the requisite objective analysis. However, precedents do provide a minimum rule of thumb decision criteria to consider in step 2 of the ethical decision process.

With this approach, we move ethical reasoning from self-contained theories that we have difficulty applying, to a structured methodology that blends the best of the three major ethical theories in a practical way such that each compliments the others. The thinking process is closed loop that allows us to take corrective action, learn from our mistakes and build up a set of real-world precedents that can function as moral rules to guide our future decision process. When we publish these precedents, we establish a set of moral precepts for the community that everyone can follow.

APPENDIX B
Ethics in Modern Times

My approach to ethics is somewhat unorthodox when compared with current discussions. It is designed to combine the major ethical systems into a coherent model for thinking about ethics. In a sense, I am combining these three approaches in a rather idiosyncratic way. As a result, the presentation is less argumentative or structured than most ethical presentations. I am directing my ethical presentation toward the specific objective of enriching cultural diversity. Whereas this is not a unique objective, it presents an opportunity to direct ethical inquiries in a more specific rather than general direction.

A consequence of the specific direction of my approach is that I need to consider religious and cultural aspects of values and their relation to ethics. As mentioned in my introduction, ethical values have been secularized and may not be the same as theological or even traditional cultural values. How, then, can I tie my approach into more traditional theories and still meet my goals?

There are two contemporary approaches that illustrate the ethical trend I have presented. The first comes from Martha Nussbaum in her recent work *The Frontiers of Justice*. Nussbaum presents a new view of ethics tied to traditional deontological reasoning, particularly *social-contract* models, such as Rawls' *A Theory of Justice*. The second is an approach represented by Sissela Bok to explore values that we have in common across religious and cultural barriers that we could use as a foundation to develop common values for all humanity.

Nussbaum's model is called the Capabilities Theory of Ethics. This is the view that ethical values should be based on our capabilities rather than on more abstract principles. The idea is to tie human dignity to any concept of human rights. Her book, *The Frontiers of Justice*, presents a sustained argument for this approach. Nussbaum seeks to ground her theory in the social-contract ethics presented by Rawls. Rawls' position is to impose a "veil of ignorance" and then select the terms of a social contract that people would likely choose if they did not know what their position in that society would be. The idea is to assume that you might be the worst-off member of society. If that were the case, what moral rules would you buy into in any social contract?

Nussbaum correctly points out several missing elements in Rawls' presentation. This includes mental disability, temporary incapacity due to illness or injury, and responsibilities to animals and the environment. How should we structure a social contract to be ethically responsible for mentally disadvantaged members? What responsibilities do ethical people have in a social contract toward animals and the environment?

The capabilities model introduces the following 10 central human capabilities that would need to be included in any social contract:

1. *Life.* Being able to live to the end of human life of normal length; not dying prematurely, or before one's life is so reduced as not to be worth living.

2. *Bodily Health.* Being able to have good health, including reproductive health; to be adequately nourished; to have adequate shelter.

3. *Bodily Integrity.* Being able to move freely from place to place; to be secure against violent assault, including sexual assault and domestic violence; having opportunities for sexual satisfaction and for choice in matters of reproduction.

4. *Senses, Imagination, and Thought.* Being able to use the senses, to imagine, think, and reason—and to do these things in a truly human way, a way informed and cultivated by an adequate education, including, but by no means limited to literacy and basic mathematical and scientific training. Being able to use imagination

and thought in connection with experiencing and producing works and events of one's own choice, religious, literary, musical, and so forth. Being able to use one's mind in ways protected by guarantees of freedom of expression with respect to both political and artistic speech, and freedom of religious exercise. Being able to have pleasurable experiences and to avoid non-beneficial pain.

5. *Emotions.* Being able to have attachments to things and people outside ourselves; to love those who love and care for us, to grieve at their absence; in general, to love, to grieve, to experience longing, gratitude, and justified anger. Not having one's emotional development blighted by fear and anxiety. (Supporting this capability means supporting forms of human association that can be shown to be crucial in their development.)

6. *Practical Reason.* Being able to form a conception of the good and to engage in critical reflection about the planning of one's life. (This entails protection for the liberty of conscience and religious observance.)

7. *Affiliation.*

   a. Being able to live with and toward others, to recognize and show concern for other human beings, to engage in various forms of social interaction; to be able to imagine the situation of another. (Protecting this capability means protecting institutions that constitute and nourish such forms of affiliation, while also protecting the freedom of assembly and political speech.)

   b. Having the social bases of self-respect and non-humiliation; being able to be treated as a dignified being whose worth is equal to that of others. This entails provisions of non-discrimination on the basis of race, sex, sexual orientation, ethnicity, caste, religion, and/or national origin.

8. *Other Species.* Being able to live with concern for and in relation to animals, plants, and the world of nature.

9. *Play.* Being able to laugh, play, and enjoy recreational activities.

10. *Control over One's Environment.*

    a. *Political.* Being able to participate effectively in political choices that govern one's life; having the right of political participation, protections of free speech, and association.

    b. *Material.* Being able to hold property (both land and movable goods), and to have property rights on an equal basis with others; having the right to seek employment on an equal basis with others; having the freedom from unwarranted search and seizure. In work, being able to work as a human being, exercising practical reason and entering meaningful relationships of mutual recognition with other workers.

Nussbaum argues that with regard to each of these, if we imagine a life without the capability in question, would we find that life worthy of human dignity? She believes that such a list could gather broad cross-cultural agreement. She is, in effect, arguing that the capabilities approach is the key to such an agreement. No agreement would be possible if we could not link human rights with some idea of human dignity.

This brings us to Sissela Bok. Bok has undertaken extensive research on finding common cross-cultural values. She would, I think, agree with Nussbaum's directive of needing to link rights with dignity. However, Bok's approach is less theoretical and actually seeks to itemize values that appear to be in common.

While I commend both approaches, I have misgivings about the implementation of both views. My main objection to Bok's approach stems from the desire to find values we might already hold in common. My view is quite adamant. The issue is not about what values we may hold in common across cultures and religions, but what values we need for a peaceful and sustainable global community. Many of the values we hold in common would likely not suit such an objective and may even be counterproductive. Moreover, we are running out of time to sort all this out. We need to be clear about what values we need, and then we can look to see which ones we hold in common (if any) and figure out what we might do about the values that we do not hold in common.

Specifically, my objection arises from Bok's basing common values on

P. F. Strawson's minimal interpretation of morality—one that takes the recognition of certain virtues and obligations to be a "condition of the existence of a society": There are certain rules of conduct that any society must stress if it is to be viable. These include, "the abstract virtue of justice, some form of obligation to mutual aid, and mutual abstention from injury, and, in some degree, the virtue of honesty."[96]

Bok considers three categories of moral values relevant to a minimal approach:

1. The positive duties of mutual care and reciprocity;

2. The negative injunctions concerning violence, deceit, and betrayal; and,

3. The norms for certain rudimentary procedures and standards for what is just.

However, she finds that while there appears to be general agreement on these minimal standards, discussions invariably and quickly lead to other maximal values, and agreement starts to break down.

There is a good reason for this. P. F. Strawson's minimal interpretation is essentially correct, but it really pertains to the founding principles of a starting society. All members of a community need to embrace Bok's three categories for any community to get off the ground. The problem is that we are already a world society. We are not getting a global community off the ground; we are trying to get beyond such minimal values to the needed values to ensure survival for all. While we must certainly embrace such minimal values, they are clearly not sufficient to meet contemporary needs. As this is readily apparent, the discussion quickly moves to higher ground, and it is here that the disagreements arise.

Nussbaum's approach takes a higher ground, but her list is too long. If we can only get minimal agreement on minimal values, how are we ever going to get agreement on Nussbaum's list?

My main argument against Nussbaum is that while her approach is broad and certainly at a higher level than Bok's, she tries to ground the approach in a theory that is too narrow to meet her requirements.

---

96 Bok, S. (2002). *Common Values*. Columbia: University of Missouri Press. Page 16.

Nussbaum wants to embrace a virtues-based approach to supporting capabilities, but then shoehorns her model into a social-contract theory that was not designed to support virtues in the way she supposes. In much of the presentation, it is clear that a social contract would not necessarily embrace all of her capabilities. The base argument is that human dignity would form the basis of any social contract if people followed Rawls' "veil of ignorance" model and did not know where they would end up in society. The idea is that human dignity would attach to any rights that people would agree to. But the model overall assumes a traditional ethical perspective that seeks to constrain abuses of power. All the general capabilities listed above are worded in that context. However, a closer examination of these capabilities reveals that there is a positive approach that goes beyond these traditional methods.

I argue that my approach is much simpler and more direct. I argue for only four values that I consider as foundational. The rule is that we need all four values, and we must adopt rules, policies, and practices that promote all four values in as balanced a way as possible. Moreover, once we include the need for positive ethics, Nussbaum's capabilities list fits nicely into my four values. The problem is that Nussbaum does not really get the idea of any difference between a negative and positive positing of these values, and so she confuses the sense of each. By clarifying the difference, we gain a more complete sense of what Nussbaum intends, and how these capabilities, as links between rights and dignity, need to be nourished in the context of a viable and sustainable future. We did this in detail in Chapter 8, where I characterize ethics as negative in the sense that it is largely about constraining abuses of power.

With the objective to promote cultural and individual diversity, we must do more than just constrain abuses of power; we must positively encourage human dignity in our decisions, policies, and institutions. This is what I think Nussbaum is trying to get to. However, as a result of the confusion over positive and negative values, much needs to be sorted out.

1. *Life.* I argue that life is a thymotic value. Nussbaum's definition suits quite well in this context.

2. *Bodily Health.* Alludes to natural life, as defined in Chapter 8.

3. ***Other Species.*** This is a statement for an Ethical way of thinking.

4. ***Affiliation (7a).*** This is really *respect* for the person (tolerance), which is Kant's proscription that we treat others as ends in themselves and not as means. It is a nicely worded version of what I mean by respect for the person or *natural tolerance.*

The rest of Nussbaum's capabilities fall nicely into either liberty or equality.

5. **Liberty.**

   a. *Bodily Integrity.* The first part is a clear statement for liberty in the sense of constraining abuses of power. The second part regarding sexual satisfaction is really an example of *natural liberty.*

   b. *Emotions.* This capability is really a combination of liberty and natural liberty. Nussbaum is arguing that power that would hinder emotional attachment be constrained. But she is also arguing for a more positive approach to cultural and individual differences in emotional expression, and that these should be encouraged.

   c. *Practical Reason.* A straightforward definition of liberty.

   d. *Play.* Again, a clear statement for natural liberty.

   e. *Control over One's Environment (Political).* The first part about political participation is a straightforward statement in favor of liberty.

   f. *Control over One's Environment (Material).* The first part is a statement for liberty. If we assume my definition that we are each sovereign over our own mind and body, and we "own" these, then we are entitled to the fruits of our labors. This is where our property rights come from. Nussbaum restates the concept without the sovereignty language.

6. ***Equality.***

   a. *Senses, Imagination, and Thought.* This presents a well-defined addition to natural equality. It is the statement of a positive approach to promoting individual and cultural diversity.

b. *Affiliation (7b)*. A clear definition of equality, including the list of arbitrary treatments to be avoided by those in authority.

c. *Control over One's Environment (Material)*. The main content beyond the first statement really presents a definition of natural equality—institutions that encourage practical work, reason, and meaningful relationships.

If my analysis holds, my approach is simpler and clearer than Nussbaum's. I am presenting an approach to ethics that meets several conditions. First, it meets the requirement of the founding community Framework. If I am to promote an Ethics not tied to specific cultures or faiths, then we must select foundational values that are neutral to any specific culture or religion. My four thymotic values meet this requirement.

Second, if we are to reach the objective of a viable and sustainable future for humankind (and all life), my approach to ethics must be measurable against that objective. It is evident in this context that we need all our foundational values to promote a richness of cultural diversity.

Third, we must start with the values we need, not those that we can agree on. We might not agree to the right value set. Moreover, we cannot get too ambitious in our approach. While Nussbaum's capabilities are easily subsumed under my thymotic categories, they present too many possible places for disagreement and rejection. A shortened list is much easier to manage in practice.

Fourth, we need to be clear about the difference between traditional methods that negatively posit ethical values to constrain abuses of power, and those positive values that promote the richness of cultural diversity. The need to shift to a positive approach renders it difficult to tie my model to traditional ethical theories. It is really these aspects of Nussbaum's model that stand outside of traditional philosophies such as social-contract theories. In a real sense, traditional philosophies set the groundwork to secularize ethics in a modern context. Now that this is complete, we need to move to the positive positing, and that is where we break new ground.

Finally, we need to establish a rule about how these values work together. Nussbaum and Bok do not indicate how their proposed lists of values fit together. Do we need them all for ethics to work, or can we build up to a list as we go? Can we cherry-pick based on non-ethical criteria (such as other agendas)? How are we to balance any list of values against competing lists from various cultural and religious traditions? Traditional ethics does not answer these questions, per se, since it does not have a specific, measurable objective that it works toward in the positive sense that I am indicating. Rather, ethics is more generally about promoting right and good and reducing evil and harm. While I share this general objective, I think we need to be more precise about where we are going with any ethical theory to meet the requirements that we have a viable and sustainable future, and this is why I have not taken great pains to tie my approach too closely to traditional methods.

RESOURCES

Arendt, H. (2006). *Eichmann in Jerusalem: A Report On The Banality of Evil*. London: Penguin Classics.

Ball, P. (2012). *Why Society Is A Complex Matter: Meeting Twenty-first Century Challenges With A New Kind of Science*. New York: Springer.

Barnes, H. E. (1965). *Intellectual and Cultural History of the Western world, Vol 1: From Earliest Times Through the Middle Ages*. Mineola, NY: Dover Publications Inc.

Barnes, H. E. (1965). *Intellectual and Cultural History of the Western World, Vol 2: From the Renaissance Through the 18th Century*. Mineola, NY: Dover Publications Inc.

Barnes, H. E. (1965). *Intellectual and Cultural History of the Western World, Vol 3: From the 19th Century to the Present Day*. Mineola, NY: Dover Publications Inc.

Berger, P. L., & Luckmann, T. (1967). *The Social Construction Of Reality: A Treatise in the Sociology of Knowledge*. New York: Anchor Press.

Berkeley, Bishop (1710) *A Treatise Concerning the Principles of Human Knowledge*. Oxford: Cambridge University Press.

Bok, S. (2002). *Common Values*. Columbia: University of Missouri Press.

Cassirer, E. (1953). *The Philosophy of Symbolic Forms, Volume 1: Language*. New Haven, CT: Yale University Press.

Cassirer, E. (1953). *The Philosophy of Symbolic Forms : Volume 2: Mythical Thought*. New Haven, CT: Yale University Press.

Cassirer, E. (1965). *The Philosophy of Symbolic Forms : Volume 3: The Phenomenology of Knowledge.* New Haven, CT: Yale University Press.

Cassirer, E. (1998). *The Philosophy of Symbolic Forms : Volume 4: The Metaphysics of Symbolic Forms.* New Haven, CT: Yale University Press.

Castells, M. (2009). *The Rise of the Network Society. The Information Age: Economy, Society, and Culture, Volume I.* Hoboken, NJ: Wiley-Blackwell.

Castells, M. (2009). *The Power of Identity. The Information Age: Economy, Society, and Culture, Volume II.* Hoboken, NJ: Wiley-Blackwell.

Castells, M. (2010). *End of Millennium. The Information Age: Economy, Society, and Culture, Volume III.* Hoboken, NJ: Wiley-Blackwell.

Chomsky, N. (1998). *On Language: Chomsky's Classic Works Language and Responsibility and Reflections on Language.* New York: The New Press.

Commission on Global Governance. (1995). *Our Global Neighborhood: The Report of the Commission on Global Governance by the Commission on Global Governance.* New York: Oxford University Press.

De Kerckhove, D. (1998). *The Skin Of Culture: Investigating The New Electronic Reality.* London, UK: Kogan Page Ltd.

Descartes, R. (1999). *Discourse On Method, and, Meditations On First Philosophy.* Indianapolis: Hackett Pub Co Inc.

Descartes, R., De Spinoza, B., Leibniz, & Von Gottfried, W. (1960). *The Rationalists: Descartes: Discourse on Method & Meditations; Spinoza: Ethics; Leibniz: Monadology & Discourse On Metaphysics.* New York: Anchor.

Diamond, J. (1999). *Guns, Germs, and Steel.* New York: W. W. Norton & Company.

Diamond, J. (2011). *Collapse: How Societies Choose To Fail Or Succeed* (Rev. ed.). New York: Penguin Books.

Diamond, S. (1981). *In Search Of The Primitive.* Piscataway, NJ: Transaction Publishers.

Duttmann, A. G. (2000). *Between Cultures: Tensions In The Struggle For Recognition.* New York: Verso Books.

Esbjorn-Hargens, S. (2011). *Integral Ecology: Uniting Multiple Perspectives On The Natural World* (Reprint ed.). Toronto: Integral Books, Penguin Random House Canada.

Fetzer, J. H. (2005). *The Evolution Of Intelligence: Are Humans The Only Animals Eith Minds?* Chicago: Open Court.

Fine, A. (2009). *The Shaky Game: Einstein, Realism And The Quantum Theory.* Chicago: University of Chicago Press.

Fodor, J. A. *The Language Of Thought.* Cambridge, MA: Harvard University Press.

Frankl, V. E. (2006). *Man's Search For Meaning.* Boston: Beacon Press.

Fukuyama, F. (1995). *Trust* (Open market ed.). Toronto: Hamish Hamilton.

Fukuyama, F. (2012). *The Origins Of Political Order: From Prehuman Times To The French Revolution* (Reprint ed.). New York: Farrar, Straus and Giroux.

Fukuyama, F. (2014). *Political Order And Political Decay: From The Industrial Revolution To The Globalization Of Democracy.* New York: Farrar, Straus and Giroux.

Fukuyama, F. (2006). *The End Of History And The Last Man* (Reissue ed.). New York: Free Press.

Fuller, R. B. (1973). *Utopia Or Oblivion: The Prospects For Mankind.* New York: Viking Press.

Fuller, R. B. (1982). *Critical Path.* New York: St. Martin's Griffin.

Fuller, R. B. (1982). *Synergetics: Explorations In The Geometry Of Thinking.* New York: Macmillan Pub Co.

Fuller, R. B. (1983). *Synergetics2: Explorations In The Geometry Of Thinking.* New York: Macmillan Pub Co.

Gabel, M. (1975). *Energy, Earth, and Everyone: A Global Energy Strategy For Spaceship Earth.* New York: Doubleday.

Gabel, M. (1979). *Ho-Ping: Food For Everyone.* New York: Doubleday.

Gandolfi, Italo, *Logic Of Information*. Gandolfi *(April 14 2012)*. Amazon Digital Services LLC.

Gladwell, Malcolm (2007) *The Tipping Point:* Back Bay Books.

Goody, J. (1987). *The Logic Of Writing And The Organization Of Society.* Cambridge, UK: Cambridge University Press.

Gore, A. (2013). *The Future.* New York: Random House.

Hagen, S. (1995). *How The World Can Be The Way It Is: An Inquiry For The New Millennium Into Science, Philosophy, And Perception.* Wheaton, IL: Quest Books.

Haken, H. (2012). *Synergetics: An Introduction Nonequilibrium Phase Transitions And Self-Organization In Physics, Chemistry And Biology.* New York: Springer.

Halberstam, D. (2012). *The Next Century.* New York: Open Road Media.

Hallpike, C. R. & Prometheus Research Group. (2004). *Evolution Of Moral Understanding.* New Haven, CT: Prometheus Research Group.

Hawken, P. (2010). *The Ecology Of Commerce: A Declaration Of Sustainability.* New York: Harper Paperbacks.

Hegel, G. W. F. (1991). *The Encyclopedia Logic: Part 1 Of The Encyclopedia Of Philosophical Sciences With The Zusatze.* Indianapolis: Hackett Pub Co Inc.

Heisenberg, W. (2007). *Physics And Philosophy: The Revolution In Modern Science.* New York: Harper Perennial.

Hobbes, T. (2008). *Leviathan.* New York: Oxford Paperbacks.

Howard, M. (1984). *The Causes Of Wwars.* Cambridge, MA: Harvard University Press.

Hughes, J. D. (2009). *An Environmental History Of The World: Humankind's Changing Role In The Community Of Life.* Abingdon-on-Thames, UK: Routledge.

Hume, D. (1975). *A Treatise Of Human Nature.* Oxford: Oxford at the Clarendon Press.

Jacobs, J. (1994). *Systems Of Survival: A Dialogue On The Moral Foundations Of Commerce And Politics* (1st Vintage Books ed.). New York: Vintage.

Jacobs, J. (2001). *The Nature Of Economies*. Toronto: Vintage Canada.

Jacobs, J. (2005). *Dark Age Ahead*. Toronto: Vintage Canada.

Jensen, D. (2004). *The Culture Of Make Believe*. Hartford, VT: Chelsea Green Publishing.

Kant, I. (1999). *Critique Of Pure Reason*. Cambridge, UK: Cambridge University Press.

Keegan, J. (1994). *A History Of Warfare*. Toronto: Vintage Books Canada.

Kelsen, H. (2003). *Principles Of International Law*. Clark, NJ: The Lawbook Exchange, Ltd.

Kelsen, H. (2007). *General Theory Of Law And State*. Clark, NJ: The Lawbook Exchange, Ltd.

Kelsen, H. (2009). *Pure Theory Of Law*. Clark, NJ: The Lawbook Exchange, Ltd.

Kennedy, P. (2007). *Parliament Of Man*. Toronto: Harper Perennial Canada.

Langer, S. K. (1953). *Feeling And Form*. New York: Macmillan Pub Co.

Langer, S. K. (1957). *Philosophy In A New Key: A Study In The Symbolism Of Reason, Rite, And Art*. Cambridge, MA: Harvard University Press.

Langer, S. K. (1974). *Mind: An Essay On Human Feeling (3 volumes)*. Baltimore, MD: Johns Hopkins University Press.

Lecky, W. E. H. (1955). *History Of The Rise And Influence Of The Spirit Of Rationalism In Europe*. New York: George Braziller.

Leibniz, G. W. (2014). *The Monadology*. Oxford: Acheron Press.

Lin, Y., & Forrest, B. (2011). *Systemic Structure Behind Human Organizations: From Civilizations To Individuals*. New York: Springer.

Lofts, S. G. (2000). *Ernst Cassirer*. Albany, NY: State University of New York Press.

Mager, Robert F., *Goal Analysis, How to clarify your goals so you can actually achieve them.* Atlanta, GA, The Center For Effective Performance Inc.

Mill, J. S. (2011). *On Liberty.* Northampton, UK: White Crane Publishing.

Muller, H. J. (1961). *Freedom In The Ancient World.* New York: Harper & Brothers.

Muller, H. J. (1963). *Freedom In The Western World.* New York: Joanna Cotler Books.

Muller, H. J. (1966). *Freedom In The Modern World.* New York: Harper & Row.

Nussbaum, M. C. (2003). *Upheavals Of Thought: The Intelligence Of Emotions.* Cambridge, UK: Cambridge University Press.

Nussbaum, M. C. (2007). *Frontiers Of Justice: Disability, Nationality, Species Membership.* Cambridge, MA: Belknap Press.

Oshry, B. (2007). *Seeing Systems: Unlocking The Mysteries Of Organizational Life.* Oakland, CA: Berrett-Koehler Publishers.

Pagels, H. (2012). *The Cosmic Code.* Mineola, NY: Dover Publications Inc.

Pinker, S. (2007). *The Language Instinct: How The Mind Creates Language.* New York: HarperCollins Publishers Ltd.

Popper, K. (2002). *Conjectures And Refutations: The Growth Of Scientific knowledge.* Abingdon-on-Thames, UK: Routledge.

Popper, K. (2002). *The Logic Of Scientific Discovery.* Abingdon-on-Thames, UK: Routledge.

Popper, K. (2012). *The Open Society And Its Enemies.* Abingdon-on-Thames, UK: Routledge.

Quigley, C. (1979). *The Evolution Of Civilizations.* Carmel, IN: Liberty Fund Inc.

Quinn, D. (1995). *Ishmael: An Adventure Of The Mind And Spirit* (Reissue ed.). New York: Bantam.

Quinn, D. (1997). *The Story Of B* (Reissue ed.). New York: Bantam.

Quinn, D. (1998). *My Ishmael* (Reissue ed.). New York: Bantam.

Quinn, D. (2000). *Beyond Civilization: Humanity's Next Great Adventure.* New York: Broadway Books.

Robinson, Helier, *Renascent Rationalism,* Speedside Pub; 3rd edition (2000).

Sagoff, M. (2007). *The Economy Of The Earth: Philosophy, Law, And The Environment.* Cambridge, UK: Cambridge University Press.

Saul, J. R. (2006). *The Unconscious Civilization.* Toronto: House of Anansi Press.

Schmookler, A. B. (1995). *The Parable Of The Tribes.* Albany, NY: State University of New York Press.

Schweitzer, A. (1987). *The Philosophy Of Civilization.* Amherst, NY: Prometheus Books.

Smith, A. (2012). *Wealth Of Nations.* Ware, Hertfordshire, UK: Wordsworth Editions Ltd.

Spengler, O. (1991). *The Decline Of The West* (Abridged ed.). New York: Oxford University Press.

Spinoza, B. (2002). *Spinoza: Complete Works.* Indianapolis: Hackett Publishing Company, Inc.

Strawson, P. F. (1970). Social Morality and Individual Ideal. In G. Wallace and A. D. M Walker (Eds.), *The Definition Of Morality* (pp. x–y). London: Metheun.

Taylor, C. (1991). *The Malaise Of Modernity.* Toronto: House of Anansi Press.

Toynbee, A. J. (1987). *A Study Of History: Abridgement Of Volumes I–VI* (Reprint ed.). New York: Oxford University Press.

von Mises, Ludwig (1963) *Human Action,* New York, Yale University Press.

Ward, B. (1966). *Spaceship Earth.* New York: Columbia University Press.

Weatherford, J. (1995). *Savages And Civilization*. New York: Ballantine Books.

Webster, F. (2007). *Theories Of The Information Society*. Abingdon-on-Thames, UK: Routledge.

Wilson, E. O. (2014). *Consilience: The Unity Of Knowledge*. New York: Vintage.

Winner, L. (2010). *The Whale And The Reactor: A Search For Limits In An Age Of High Technology*. Chicago: University of Chicago Press.

Wolfram, S. (1987). *A New Kind Of Science*. Champaign, IL: Wolfram Media Inc.

World Commission on Environment and Development. (1987). *Our Common Future*. New York: Oxford Paperbacks.

Young, D. (1992). *Origins Of The Sacred*. New York: Harper Perennial.

ACKNOWLEDGEMENTS

I would like to express my special thanks of gratitude to the many people who helped with this project. I am grateful to Richard Holmes, *Professor Emeritus, University of Waterloo*, who read an early draft and focused my conclusions. I am also grateful to Arija Berzitis who edited an early draft and made many great suggestions.

I sincerely thank my test readers, especially Joshua and Donald Fowke who took the time to provide many valuable suggestions.

Kimberley Janssen provided artistic support for the graphics and cover design, as well as guiding the design process through production.

Nobody has been more supportive of this project than my wife Kathleen who provided guidance and encouragement.